KU-205-766

CENSORSHIP AND SEXUALITY IN BOMBAY CINEMA

LIVERPOOL JMU LIBRARY

3 1111 01454 4819

Monika Mehta

CENSORSHIP *and* SEXUALITY
in Bombay Cinema

UNIVERSITY OF TEXAS PRESS

Austin

COPYRIGHT © 2011 BY THE UNIVERSITY OF TEXAS PRESS
All rights reserved
Printed in the United States of America
First edition, 2011

Requests for permission to reproduce material from this work should be se
  Permissions
  University of Texas Press
  P.O. Box 7819
  Austin, TX 78713-7819
  utpress.utexas.edu/about/book-permissions

♾ The paper used in this book meets the minimum requirements of
ANSI/NISO Z39.48-1992 (R1997) (Permanence of Paper).

LIBRARY OF CONGRESS CATALOGING-IN-PUBLICATION DATA

Mehta, Monika, 1970–
  Censorship and sexuality in Bombay cinema / Monika Mehta. — 1st ed.
      p.   cm.
  Based on the author's thesis (doctoral)—University of Minnesota, 2001.
  Includes bibliographical references and index.
  ISBN 978-0-292-74759-3
  1. Motion pictures—Censorship—India—Bombay. 2. Motion pictures—I
  Bombay—History—20th century. 3. Sex in motion pictures. 4. Sex role in
  pictures. I. Title.
  PN1995.65.I4M44 2011
  303.3'76—dc23
                                        2011026895

First paperback printing, 2012

For Mummy, Daddy, Rajesh, and Sahana

I can't help but dream about a kind of criticism that would not try to judge, but to bring an oeuvre, a book, a sentence, an idea to life; it would light fires, watch the grass grow, listen to the wind and catch the sea-foam in the breeze and scatter it. It would multiply not judgments but signs of existence; it would summon them, drag them from their sleep. Perhaps it would invent them sometimes--all the better. All the better. Criticism that hands down sentences sends me to sleep. I'd like a criticism of scintillating leaps of imagination. It would not be sovereign or dressed in red. It would bear the lightning of possible storms.

—MICHEL FOUCAULT, *POLITICS, PHILOSOPHY, CULTURE: INTERVIEWS AND OTHER WRITINGS, 1977–1984*

CONTENTS

ACKNOWLEDGMENTS

A book, like a film, is a collaborative work; its credits roll includes institutions, teachers, colleagues, friends, and family. This is mine.

I am grateful to Jim Burr, Lynne Chapman, and their colleagues at the University of Texas Press for shepherding this manuscript through various stages. I am indebted to the two anonymous reviewers for their invaluable reports and their constructive criticism of my manuscript. At Binghamton and Ithaca, respectively, Brian Wall and Manolo Bevia devoted valuable time to help me generate illustrations. Martha Berry generously shared her articles on Raj Kapoor with me. Previous versions of Chapter 6 and Chapter 7 appeared in *Jouvert* and *Studies in South Asian Film and Media*, respectively. I thank both publications for giving me permission to publish revised versions of these articles. In addition, a portion of Chapter 8 appeared in *Cultural Dynamics*; I am grateful to Sage Publications for letting me reuse this material here.

During my graduate-school years at the University of Minnesota, the Harold Leonard Memorial Film Study Fellowship, the Harold Leonard Research Grant, the MacArthur Predissertation Grant, the MacArthur Dissertation Grant, and the University of Minnesota Doctoral Dissertation Fellowship enabled me to do research in India for this project. Later, the Chancellor's Postdoctoral Fellowship at the University of California at Berkeley, as well as the Dean's Research Leave from Binghamton University, assisted me in fleshing out the manuscript for this book. During my two years of fieldwork in India, many individuals at the Centre for the Study of Developing Societies, the Central Board of Film Certification, the Ministry of Information and Broadcasting, the National Film Archive, the Nehru Memorial Library, the Indian Institute of Mass Communication, and the Indian Law Institute helped facilitate my research by providing access to information and sharing their insights. This book would not have been possible without their generosity.

My teachers at the University of Minnesota provided an invigorating and safe intellectual environment for developing this project. I would like to express my gratitude to my Ph.D. advisor, John Mowitt. His painstaking attention to my arguments and lines of inquiry has helped me develop as a scholar and teacher. My committee members—Maria Damon, Lisa Disch, and Ravi Vasudevan—provided discerning and incisive comments as well as the space to challenge and question them. Furthermore, this manuscript is stronger because of the provocative questions and astute comments offered by colleagues and faculty members from different disciplines in the MacArthur Program at the University of Minnesota.

As a postdoctoral fellow at Berkeley, I was inspired by Linda Williams and Chris Berry, who broadened and deepened my knowledge of film theory. My colleagues and friends at the University of Texas at Austin provided a stimulating intellectual environment. Mia Carter, Akbar Hyder, Bob Jensen, Sharmila Rudrappa, Nancy Schiesari, Janet Staiger, Joe Straubhaar, Kamala Visweswaran, and Karin Wilkins generously shared commitments to politics, film, and food.

At Binghamton University, my interactions with colleagues and friends in a range of departments—English, Asian and Asian-American studies, cinema studies, comparative literature, philosophy, interpretation and culture, and women's studies—have further cultivated my scholarly and teaching interests. In particular, I have appreciated the keen questions and comments on drafts of this book by Donette Francis, Thomas Glave, Praseeda Gopinath, Joe Keith, Maneesha Lal, Dana Silberman, and Lisa Yun.

At varied times and places, the humor, affection, and intellects of friends have nudged me along and nourished this work. They have provided me deliciously long conversations, fierce and fearless discussions, and oodles of laughter; for that, I would especially like to thank A. Aneesh, Shaina Anand, Nilanjana Bhattacharyja, Monica Biradavolu, Erica Bornstein, Craig Borowiak, Sudipto Chatterjee, Preeti Chopra, Ruma Chopra, Laura Czarnecki, Kavita Datla, Elizabeth DeLoughrey, Deepali Dewan, Sara Dorow, Munis Faruqui, Angelica Fenner, Jonathan Gil Harris, Leila Harris, Jennifer Horne, Dale Hudson, Kajri Jain, Betty Joseph, Puneet Kohli, Premesh Lalu, Guang Lei, Humaira Mahi, Christine Marran, Madhavi Menon, Farina Mir, Rama Mantena, Kelly Maynard, Marissa Moorman, Poornima Paidipaty, Bahar Rumelili, Simona Sawhney, Scott Sherer, Suzie Soyring, Ashok Srinivasan, Uma Strobel, and Dongmei Wang.

I could not have completed my fieldwork in Bombay without Clare

Talwalker's help. Her hospitality, warmth, and chats over many cups of chai enabled me to wrap up my research there. Later she thoughtfully helped me evaluate and make sense of this information. Adam Sitze, whose brilliance is matched by his intellectual generosity, offered perceptive advice on initial drafts of this book. Latha Varadarajan and Shampa Biswas have been my cavalry, cheering me onward and providing insightful comments throughout.

Anupama Prabhala-Kapse's elegant thinking has honed my arguments. Our lengthy discussions on Hindi cinema, steeped in fandom and scholarship, have propelled my work. Lisa Patti has meticulously read numerous drafts of every chapter in this book. Her deft queries and observations reenergized both me and my manuscript. I am deeply indebted to her for helping me write a book that I like.

Nilgün Uygun has steadfastly provided me with intellectual and emotional security through graduate school and beyond. Her constant encouragement, dazzling acumen, and unswerving affection have been my lodestars, making it possible for me to come this far.

My partner, Rajesh Bhaskaran, has gone beyond his training in aerospace engineering and carefully read many drafts of this work. He has patiently listened to all my anxieties about writing, provided support for my flagging spirits, and shared the many labors of home (cleaning, cooking, taking out the garbage, and child care). It is his love and his confidence in my abilities that prodded me as I wrote. My daughter, Sahana, whole-heartedly embraced her inheritance, namely, a love of Hindi films, which proved to be a source of delight. I am immensely grateful to her child-care providers, Ubuntu Academy and Aspen Grove; their labor has been vital for the production of this book.

This project would not have been realized without the unconditional love of my parents, Usha Kiron Mehta and Vidya Sagar Mehta. While they may not have always understood what I was doing and may have strongly disagreed with my ideas at times, they have always offered their support. Most important, they have believed in me, even when I felt that I was faltering or stumbling.

Mummy, Daddy, and Rajesh have shouldered a bulk of work at home, giving me time to think and to write. Sahana's rightful demands for her mother's attention have ensured the timely completion of this work. The physical and emotional nourishment that they have unfailingly given has sustained this work. I dedicate this book to them all.

CENSORSHIP AND SEXUALITY IN BOMBAY CINEMA

1 Beginning

Beginning is basically an activity which ultimately implies return and repetition rather than simple linear accomplishment. . . . beginning and beginning again are historical. . . . beginning not only creates but is its own method because it has intention. . . . beginning is making or producing difference.   —EDWARD SAID, *Beginnings*

A critique is not a matter of saying that things are not right as they are. It is a matter of pointing out on what kinds of assumptions, what kinds of familiar, unchallenged, unconsidered modes of thought the practices we accept rest. . . . Practicing criticism is a matter of making facile gestures difficult.
    —MICHEL FOUCAULT, *Politics, Philosophy, Culture*

Producing an Object of Study

When I visited Delhi in the summer of 1993, the censorship controversy in which Subhash Ghai's film *Khalnayak* (The Villain) was enmeshed caught my eye. Newspapers, magazines, television shows, my family members, and neighbors were quite willing to comment on the deteriorating state of Hindi films. According to many, these films were full of vulgar lyrics, obscene dances, revealing costumes, and inane plots. Later, in 1995–1996 and 1997–1998, when I returned to do research on film censorship, meetings with officials revealed that the state, too, saw obscenity as a major problem, with satellite television viewed as the source. One of the officials noted that U.S. soap operas such as *Santa Barbara* and *The Bold and the Beautiful*, which had been brought to India by satellite television, propagated values that would undermine Indian society and culture. He also thought that the advent of satellite television had adversely affected commercial Indian films because producers had increased the amount of vulgarity in their works to compete with these shows. The official's comments pointed to a larger phenomenon, namely, the anxieties incited by the advent of liberalization in India. As new technologies and goods brought with them "Western culture," Indian citizens and the Indian state expressed concern that this culture would undermine Indian values; sexuality became a nodal point for articulating these anxieties. For this official and many others, censorship of sexuality was a key mechanism for enforcing and maintaining cultural boundaries.

My research on the topic of film censorship involving gender and heterosexuality[1] (particularly female heterosexuality) in Hindi cinema took me to many institutions, offices, and libraries in India, including the Ministry of Information and Broadcasting, the Nehru Memorial Library, the Indian Law Institute, the Indian Institute of Mass Communication, the National Film Archive of India, the Film and Television Institute of India, and the Central Board of Film Certification (CBFC). While graduate-school training had intellectually armed me with poststructuralist theory, which emphasizes the constructed, partial, and shifting nature of objects, the daunting task of chasing censorship at these varied sites often made me yearn for a fixed and readily available object of study. Whether it was deciphering legal or bureaucratic languages or conducting interviews, this fieldwork frequently required me to go beyond the comfort zone of my professional discipline, comparative literature.

I initially focused on collecting as much information as possible, and I constantly worried that I didn't have enough material, that the amount of information on various topics was uneven, or that the information simply did not make sense. As I learned more about film censorship, my major concerns turned to a different issue: how to weave a coherent narrative from all the information I had gleaned from film reports, personal interviews, direct observation of examining committees, legal cases, films, film magazines, newspapers, letters, and certification reports.[2] What troubled me specifically was that in the act of creating a narrative about censorship, I would have to edit, selecting some pieces of information and cutting others. The uncanny resemblance between the practices employed in the production of scholarship and the practices used in censoring films struck me.

One of the many questions I asked myself during the course of my fieldwork was which of the 27,000 feature films and thousands of short films in fifty-two different languages I would analyze. The initial cut was quick and easy. I decided to focus on commercial feature films in Hindi because of my familiarity with the language and Bombay cinema. The information that I was able to locate and to which I was able to gain access placed constraints on my choices. Time and length also exerted their force on my choices. I had a limited amount of time in which to complete my research, and I needed to write a "reasonable" number of pages to both complete the work in a timely fashion and to ensure its readability. My theoretical and historical interests in gender and heterosexuality and post-1970 India (from the time immediately before the Emergency to the initial years of economic liberalization, roughly 1970–1996) also reduced the number of films. I further narrowed my choices by formulating questions and selecting films that would engage with them. I was most interested in pursuing three issues: How was censorship practiced? How were gender and heterosexuality intertwined with discourses of censorship, tradition, and cinema? What were the productive effects of such intertwining? Eventually a handful of films became my entry points into these questions: *Gupt gyan* (1974; Secret knowledge), *Satyam shivam sundaram* (1978; Truth, God, Beauty), *Pati parmeshwar* (1989; A Husband Is Like God), *Khalnayak* (1993), and *Dilwale dulhania le jayenge* (1995; The brave-hearted will take away the bride).

In developing a theoretical framework to analyze these films, as well as other material I had collected, I extensively relied on Michel Foucault's works, specifically *Discipline and Punish: The Birth of the Prison* and the three volumes of his *History of Sexuality*, as well as several essays and interviews.[3] His insights enabled me to chart the complex relations among power, practice, and sexuality in producing censorship. In structuring my central questions, I drew on Foucault's astute observations in the article "Subject and Power,"[4] where he explains the difference between asking a question that begins with "how" and asking one that begins with "why" or "who." While the first method enables descriptions of practice(s), the second method leads one on a hunt for causes and subjects, respectively. Descriptions, I think, produce more complex versions of subjectivities, for they make visible overdetermined practices. For example, the practice of cutting is generally attributed to the state; in this model, *the censors are the ones who cut films*. But if we question this practice in the mode of *how* rather than *who*, we learn that cutting is not limited to or caused (only) by the state: directors and editors "cut" films for aesthetic and other reasons, audiences decide to patronize some films and not others, and scholars seek to narrow their studies, to name just a few relevant areas. A productive effect of this insight is an analytical rupture between subject and practice, which are intimately bound together in the notion that the *censors* are the (only) ones who *cut* films. This rupture enables us to see that the practice of cutting sediments the identities of the censors, directors, editors, audiences, and scholars; this practice, in turn, is attributed varied meanings, such as state authority, creative effort, entertainment, and scholarly work. What emerges is a field of relations between subjects and practices in which identities and meanings are blurred, leaking into one another rather than remaining fixed or rigid.

My study, which combines textual analysis, archival research, and qualitative fieldwork (personal interviews and direct observation of examining committees), makes possible such a dynamic vision of censorship. This interdisciplinary methodology does not aim at completeness. Rather, its purpose is to stretch the theoretical framework for viewing and understanding censorship. Scholarly accounts of film censorship analyze concerns pertaining to representation, film production, film reception, and state interventions largely in isolation from one another.[5] As Annette Kuhn's study on censorship incisively shows, such studies separate texts and contexts, reproducing an intellectual division of labor where textual analysis becomes the domain of film studies, research on industry and the state falls within the ambit of mass communication, and microlevel analyses of film production and reception take place in the fields of anthropology and sociology.[6] In contrast, my interdisciplinary methodology enables me to examine how central concepts of film studies, such as stardom, spectacle, genre, and sound, are employed and reconfigured within the compass of state censorship, thereby expanding the scope of their application and impact.

It will be helpful to situate my work in relation to film studies scholarship so as to elaborate on the contributions of this methodology. To do so, I will consider the articles in a recent issue of *The Velvet Light Trap* (2009) devoted to advancing our understanding of censorship and regulation in diverse international contexts. In conceptualizing this issue, the editors note that they "favored an incredibly diffuse notion of censorship and regulation." Therefore, they encouraged submissions that would chart innovative locations for studying these topics, thereby revealing the complex nature of censorship and regulation in the "current political and economic landscape of media production."[7]

These rich scholarly contributions offer new avenues for studying censorship by turning our attention to the roles played by technology (video, television, and Internet), sites of reception, national agendas, and alternative economies (piracy). Adopting a Foucauldian approach, Theresa

Cronin's "Media Effects and the Subjectification of Film Regulation" deftly demonstrates how the 1984 British Video Recordings Act, media effects scholarship, film reviews, and viewers' commentaries on web sites have sought to produce normative film spectatorship. Her examination of *Wolf Creek*'s (2005) reception reveals that despite professing problems with the film's slasher narrative, neither reviewers nor audiences called to cut or ban it. Rather, the debates on *Wolf Creek* sought to specify "how spectators should or should not respond."[8] In her absorbing essay "Exemplary Consumer-Citizens and Protective State Stewards: How Reformers Shaped Censorship Outcomes Regarding *The Untouchables*," Laura Cook Kenna, like Cronin, illustrates film reception's critical role in the study of censorship. Kenna shows how Italian Americans won "representational concessions" from the producers of the U.S. television show *The Untouchables* by presenting themselves as "exemplary consumer-citizens." In contrast, the officers from the Federal Bureau of Prisons were not able to leverage the rhetoric of public interest to bolster their case against the show.[9]

Both Nandana Bose's article "The Hindu Right and the Politics of Censorship: Three Case Studies of Policing Hindi Cinema, 1992–2002" and Tessa Dwyer and Ioana Uricaru's "Slashings and Subtitles: Romanian Media Piracy, Censorship, and Translation" rightly highlight the critical role national context plays in analyzing censorship. Bose draws our attention to an important political site for the study of censorship in India, namely, the relationship between the Hindu Right and the CBFC. She asserts that the Hindu Right did not simply seek to cut or ban objectionable content. Rather, it mobilized the mechanism of censorship to imagine a nation "predicated on a series of exclusions" that included the "Muslim, the sexual female subject, the poor, the rural, the lower caste and even the West."[10] Charting a course parallel to Bose's, Tessa Dwyer and Ioana Uricaru show how the Romanian state (during its communist avatar) employed censorship as a key mechanism for securing and defining its cultural and political borders. More specifically, they explain how Romanian state censorship regulated foreign films by mistranslating dialogues in subtitles; this practice produced a double spectatorship. The arrival of video posed a significant challenge to this state censorship, for it allowed viewers to watch pirated foreign films in the privacy of their homes; thus, technology assisted in circumventing the state's authority. Despite their poor quality, the pirated videos were viewed as "authentic" because they had not been subject to state censorship.[11]

Even as these articles pave fresh paths for the study of censorship and regulation, methodological oversights persist that limit our understanding of censorship. For example, these articles primarily rely on archival research and secondary scholarly sources; they do not include textual analysis or qualitative fieldwork. Consequently, they overlook the possibility of films themselves figuring as key participants in debates on censorship. For example, Cronin argues that the British Board of Film Classification (BBFC) and media-effects theorists presume that the spectator can only succumb to the seductive powers of the image. She rightly states that this assumption omits the possibility that the spectator might resist the image or adopt a more complicated stance vis-à-vis it. This argument could be buttressed by examining the spectatorial positions offered by *Wolf Creek* (2005) and engaging with theories of film spectatorship. Instead, the film text serves only as a mute site of debate.

Archival research in these articles generally highlights controversial media texts. For example, Bose invokes contentious films such as *Bombay* (1995), *Khalnayak* (1993), and *War and Peace* (2002) to make an argument about the Hindu Right's exclusionary national agenda. Thus, censorship emerges as a spectacular exercise of power affiliated with cutting and banning. Her argument neglects nondivisive texts such as *Dilwale dulhania le jayenge* (1995), which was certified by the CBFC and was crucial to (re) imagining the nation. Here, by paying attention to the mundane practice of certification, we see that censorship not only excludes but also *includes*.[12]

This point links to my final concern: that these articles cast censorship largely as a prohibition, albeit a productive one. Dwyer and Ioana point to practices of modification and excision pursued by Romanian state censors. Similarly, Bose considers only the deletions enforced or demanded by the Hindu Right. Kenna's analysis casts the Federal Communications Commission (FCC) as a police officer monitoring graphic violence. Cronin misses an opportunity to consider how the British Board of Film Classification uses certification to produce normative spectatorship. These works overlook the micropractices of the state or nongovernmental organizations. In doing so, they unwittingly offer a monolithic vision of these institutions, one that remains synonymous with prohibition. By expanding my methodological tools to include qualitative fieldwork, I was able to obtain an alternative vision of state censorship. More specifically, observing "examining committees" at the CBFC in Bombay,[13] I noted that the routine practices of certification and classification were as central to their operations as was the much-highlighted practice of cutting.

In *Discipline and Punish*, Foucault illustrates the importance of investigating such micropractices. Through painstaking attention to architectural details and movements of the body, he shows how disciplinary power permeates prisons, armies, and schools. By tracking this banal exercise of power at seemingly incongruous sites, Foucault is able to dismantle the fiction of the free, sovereign individual. His analysis invites us to direct our scholarly lenses to such practices so that we may generate material histories of both institutions and industries and place them in conversation with one another. Following Foucault, I craft the tale of censorship with an eye to the mobile practices of cutting, classifying, and certifying. I not only examine how these techniques are deployed at the site of state censorship, where I initially discovered them, but also track their application in the arenas of film production and reception.

A Tale of Excision and Prohibition

During my fieldwork a number of officials whom I interviewed advised me to read Aruna Vasudev's *Liberty and Licence in the Indian Cinema* (1978), a book they viewed as a valuable study and critique of film censorship in India. Several scholarly articles and book chapters on film censorship in India have appeared in the more than thirty years since its publication, but not until 2009, when Someswar Bhowmik's *Cinema and Censorship: The Politics of Control in India* came out, did another scholar offer a sustained engagement with the question of film censorship in India.[14] Vasudev's work has clearly enjoyed both a scholarly longevity and an institutional resonance. Despite its seminal status, however, and its impact in the corridors of state bureaucracy, this work has received little scholarly scrutiny. While later studies have drawn on the historical insights of Vasudev's work, they have neglected to examine its implicit theoretical framework (i.e., its construction of the state as a monolith and censorship as an act of prohibition) and its methodology—namely, its reliance on state archives, specifically government reports and parliamentary debates. In failing to interrogate this work, these studies have often reproduced the vision of censorship laid out by Vasudev.[15] In contrast to Vasudev, I complicate the concept of the state by analyzing its micropractices and decenter it by considering other loci of power—specifically, the sites of film production and reception; in addition, I argue that censorship is *productive*.

In the next few pages I closely examine Vasudev's work, which enables me both to critique her work and to outline my own theoretical framework. The publication of *Liberty and Licence in the Indian Cinema* coincided with two major political events, the end of the Emergency and the Janata Party's decisive victory in parliamentary elections. The Emergency, which lasted from 1975 until 1977, was known for its political excesses, including censorship of the media. Some familiarity with this event is crucial for understanding Vasudev's book, because it shapes her argument about censorship—just as, perhaps, the context of economic liberalization in India and the ensuing debates on sexuality mold my account of censorship.

In recounting the conditions and circumstances that produced the Emergency in 1975, Paul Brass focuses on Indira Gandhi's "distinctive strategy of rulership."[16] This style of leadership, Brass explains, was "highly personalized and centralized and . . . involved unprecedented assertions of executive power in the Indian political system." Gandhi's particular brand of leadership transformed the character of center-state governmental relations in the states controlled by her party, the Congress (R). For example, Gandhi removed every chief minister who had an independent base in a state and replaced each with chief ministers who, lacking an independent base, were completely loyal to her. In 1973–1974, food shortages and rising prices combined with local political grievances produced popular demonstrations and movements. The chief ministers appointed by Gandhi were unable to address these issues, for their lack of independent bases left them with little authority.

Furthermore, some members of Parliament in the Congress Party became increasingly discontented with Gandhi's economic policies. In March 1974 a new and ominous political development occurred as Jayaprakash Narayan took up the leadership of the Bihar agitation and offered to lead a countrywide movement against corruption—and against Gandhi's authoritarian rule. In the midst of these developments threatening Gandhi's authority, the Allahabad High Court found Gandhi's 1971 election invalid on grounds of corrupt practices. Soon after this ruling, forces opposed to Gandhi came together to plan a mass mobilization demanding her resignation.

Two weeks after the high court's ruling, on June 26, 1975, Gandhi acted to remove all threats to her leadership. All her principal opponents, including members of her own party, were arrested. Upon her demand, the president of India declared an Emergency under Article 352 of the Constitution. A twenty-point program was announced, emphasizing reforms for the poor and the landless. Parliament quickly passed new electoral laws superseding the laws under which Gandhi had been found guilty and her election voided. As the entire country came under Delhi's direct rule, Gandhi announced that the imposition of state-of-emergency strictures was simply a temporary measure to restore law and order.

Two infamous programs, the sterilization program and the beautification of Delhi, were instituted during this period "to improve" the conditions in the country. Under the sterilization program, for example, male government employees with more than three children were to be denied benefits such as government housing if they failed to undergo vasectomies. Some states were given quotas for the program. To meet their quotas, officials would often herd the poorer members of the populace—in particular men—and subject them to forced sterilizations.[17] The poor were also the targets of the "beautification of Delhi," which consisted of razing their residences so as to clear the city of its "slums." Both the slum residents and pavement dwellers were ordered to move and given new housing, usually miles from their places of work, making it difficult for them to find employment. Many of these demolitions and forced resettlements especially affected the Muslim communities.

During this period, state censorship prevented all forms of mass media from representing the government and its policies in a "negative" light. The state's exercise of censorship was a supreme act of control that sought to guarantee or prohibit certain meanings. However, this act produced unintended effects. Under these repressive conditions, underground magazines, fliers, and most of all rumors flourished, disseminating information against Gandhi's government. When Indira Gandhi eventually called elections in 1977, she lost, and the Janata Party, headed by Morarji Desai, assumed political leadership. Some argue that Indira Gandhi lost the elections because she was unaware of the extent of the public's discontent and anger against her government's policies. Despite the lack of open dissent in the mass media, the Indian public had been able to acquire information from other sources and, judging from the election results, seemed quite convinced about the undesirability of continuing with Congress rule.

Vasudev's *Liberty and Licence in the Indian Cinema* represents an important liberal-democratic attempt to intervene in Indian politics immediately following the Emergency. In her book Vasudev denounces the Emergency by drawing attention to the state's repressive powers. She characterizes the Emergency as an interruption in "an otherwise continuous pursuit of democratic freedoms since Independence in 1947" and concludes that "as such, it need not enter into the wider context of a general survey of control over the cinema."[18] The Emergency, in her opinion, was an aberration useful only insofar as "it illustrated graphically the total vulnerability of cinema to pressures from the central government and the distortions that can take place when decisions are based on individual, personal or narrow political considerations."[19] The "application of censorship," she emphasizes, "lost all semblance of rationale and logic. It was used as a stick to beat the industry with."[20] For Vasudev, the Emergency was simply a detour from the smooth course of independent India's democratic history, and the state's heavy-handed control of the media served simply to illustrate the dissolution of democratic rights during this period. By reducing the Emergency to an outlier on the bell curve of censorship practices throughout history, Vasudev trivializes this event and thereby sustains the myth of democracy that existed prior to and after the Emergency; in doing so, she loses the opportunity to interrogate the very democratic conditions and circumstances that produced the Emergency.

As a critique situated in a liberal-democratic framework, Vasudev's conception of the law and its operation is limited to the exercise of "government control." In her introduction, Vasudev lays out the issues that she explores in the work's subsequent pages, asking, "what are the reasons and need for its [censorship's] continuation, in what manner has it interfered with the liberty of the filmmaker and to what extent has it hampered the flowering of this huge cinematic output into a form of art[?]"[21] Drawing on official guidelines, government reports, parliamentary debates, and legal documents, she recounts laws created and administered by the colonial and postcolonial states as well as challenges to these laws by the film industry and the citizenry. Both the questions that drive her work and the sources for addressing these questions assume that censorship is a prohibition dictated by the state.

Vasudev denounces the practice of censorship during colonial rule, drawing attention to policies designed to justify and maintain that rule in India. As the discussion proceeds to postindependence India, Vasudev does not question the postcolonial state's decision to retain film censorship. She is critical of particular policies and practices of the postcolonial state, but she accepts that the institution of censorship is a political necessity in a complex democratic society. Censorship, in Vasudev's view, assists the democratic state in managing differences within the nation. In discussing the wide and varied viewership of popular Hindi films, Vasudev sympathizes with the censors, who must make sure that "nothing is portrayed which could offend religious, communal, or regional sensibilities."[22] She expresses concern about the effects of popular Hindi films on rural populations, claiming that "the glamourization and unrealistic portrayal of city life" distorts the outlook of villagers.[23] Moreover, such representation, she asserts, does "great harm to the vital and stated national goal of discouraging migration to the city."[24] She urges the state to develop a better cinema, one that is in concert with its policies for modernization and social welfare.

On the one hand, Vasudev repeatedly voices her disapproval of Bombay cinema's narratives; on the other hand, she notes that, at least in part, censorship causes the distorted character of these narratives. She explains that if the "sweeping" nature of the censorship guidelines were interpreted strictly, they "would result in almost all films being banned."[25] These "sweeping restrictions," she elaborates, have "driven producers to resort to indirect, unrealistic, suggestive modes of expression which are often vulgar and unaesthetic and convey the precise impression that the authorities hoped to eradicate."[26] In discussing the representations of sexuality in popular films, she acknowledges that "Indian producers did frequently film the female anatomy in a manner that was lewd and vulgar, and costumes were designed to heighten the effect."[27] At the same time, she concedes that these representations emerged in a climate where "the depiction of normal relationship between the sexes was denied," prompting producers to resort to other devices.[28] She concludes that "where honesty and frankness had to be replaced by suggestiveness, the result was bound to be either puerile, or offensive."[29] Vasudev's discussion begs the question as to what constitutes an honest and frank representation of sexuality. According to her argument, such a representation would reflect reality, the "real" social order. The "real" assumes a status of self-evident truth—and censorship stands in the way of representing this truth.

At the end of her work, Vasudev proposes a balance between freedom and restriction—in a word, reform. She urges the government to make an effort to understand the cinema and to harness its potential for the purposes of development. Furthermore, she insists that the state recognize that popular films are not simply entertaining but in fact "carry information on values, behaviours and social mores, from which people will learn."[30] Censorship, she contends, needs to regulate the kind of information that these films impart. In particular, she refers to films that belittle women's education or offer a "glamourized and unrealistic portrayal of the city." While she advises the state to police narratives produced by Bombay cinema,[31] she recommends a more liberal interpretation of the censorship code for art films and applauds the central government's decisions to certify controversial films such as *Garam hawa* (1973; Hot Winds) and *Samskara* (1970; The Sacrament).[32] She concludes by commending the exercise of censorship in India and by encouraging efforts toward better relations between the state and the cinema—and better censorship.

Later in her career, Vasudev sought to promote better cinema as the founder and editor of *Cinemaya*, a journal devoted to examining art cinema in Asia. She became the president of the Network for the Promotion of Asian Cinema, organizing film festivals in India. She also served as a member of the Film Appellate Tribunal, an advisory committee that examined films that had been refused certification by the examining and revising committees. In fact, she was one of the three members who supported the ban on *Pati parmeshwar* 1989)—which I analyze in Chapter 6—because she believed that the film promoted women's servility. In supporting this ban, she sought to make a progressive political intervention.

(Re)framing Censorship

Annette Kuhn's perspicacious book *Cinema, Censorship and Sexuality* radically reimagines the field of censorship and helps us spot the oversights in Vasudev's work. Kuhn's work focuses on the emergence of film censorship in Britain and investigates "institutions and practices involved in the constitution of cinema as a public sphere of regulation."[33] Through a meticulous analysis of specific case studies, Kuhn shows how acts of censorship categorized and defined both films and audiences in Britain, all the while shoring up a bourgeois morality. Employing a Foucauldian approach, she argues that by focusing on the state and its apparatus, many scholarly works (including Vasudev's) assume censorship to be the duty of the censors specifically and the domain of the state more generally. My analysis of *Liberty and Licence* shows that in localizing power in the state and its apparatus, Vasudev could describe power only in terms of repression and prohibition. Such a description suggests a limited understanding of power. To assume that power "only prohibits or represses," Kuhn aptly writes, "is to forget that power also has productive effects."[34] Moreover, she reminds us, works on censorship that concentrate on the state overlook other sites where power operates.[35] In doing so, such studies assume that power is a privilege of the state or the particular institutions earmarked to administer censorship guidelines.

Following Foucault, Kuhn argues for a model of power as diffuse, one made possible by analyzing specific case histories; she rejects analyses that examine only macrolevel polices of institutions, which simply reassert the dominant position of institutions by placing them at the heart of accounts on censorship. Kuhn's framework thus rescues films from a subordinate position in scholarship on censorship and relocates them at the center of her case histories. Whereas films appear in Vasudev's work largely as "cuts," for Vasudev either identifies particular films that were cut or notes the parts that were cut, in Kuhn's case histories they transform into active participants in discussions on censorship. These case histories both demonstrate that the field of censorship is multivocal and complicate the place of the state and other regulatory institutions in the study of censorship.

Thus, censorship emerges as a dynamic activity. Taking my cues from Foucault and Kuhn, I seek to show that power is a relation and not a possession by placing state censorship in dialogue with film production and reception. Moreover, like Kuhn, I advocate a case-study approach since it makes visible both ties and ruptures among different players in the history of censorship.

My account, however, diverges from Kuhn's in certain methodological and theoretical aspects. Even as Kuhn interrogates the prohibition model of censorship, her focus on spectacular aspects of censorship (i.e., cutting and controversy) ties her to this model's penchant for constructing censorship as an act of "excision" or "cutting-out."[36] Thus, censorship remains a prohibition, but one that has "*productive effects.*" The manner whereby Kuhn deploys Foucault's insights has had an enduring legacy in film studies; for example, Theresa Cronin's previously mentioned article illustrates the resilience of this method. In contrast, my work foregrounds banal aspects of censorship—namely, certification and classification—and seeks to cast cutting as quotidian. Unlike Kuhn, who primarily relies on textual analysis and archival research, I augment these methodological tools with qualitative fieldwork. By watching examining committees at work, I recognized the significance of classification and certification as well as the ubiquitous nature of cutting. My observations compelled me to mobilize a Foucauldian term underdeveloped in film studies, namely, *micropractices.*

The insights that I gained via qualitative fieldwork affected my archival research and selection of films. Kuhn's archival research highlights explicit and divisive discussions on sexuality through its focus on sex-hygiene films. While I share Kuhn's interest in examining spectacular forms of sexuality, my eclectic selection of films expands the scope of both censorship and sexuality by investigating normative and less visible representations, such as the (re)production of kinship relations and tradition and the self-sacrificial woman. Paralleling Kuhn's work, my analysis of *Khalnayak*'s provocative song "Choli ke kya peeche kya hai?" (What is behind the blouse?) illustrates that a censored text can become marketable precisely because the act of censorship is known. Unlike Kuhn, however, I also demonstrate, through my examination of the figure of the self-sacrificial woman in *Pati parmeshwar*, that censorship does not always produce desire or profits. Finally, Kuhn's work suggests that both the range and impact of debates on censorship were limited to Britain as nation. In contrast, my postcolonial account, which is indebted to Vasudev's historical research, demonstrates that the *location* for discussions on censorship, its development as an institution, and its effects extended to the colonies of the British Empire and shaped postcolonial states. Metropole and colony were mutually though not equally constitutive.

In summary, Vasudev's work provides a macrolevel view of censorship, focusing on parliamentary debates over state regulation, but neglects its microlevel operations. Kuhn offers us a more detailed account of censorship by examining specific cases, but she does not examine how organizations such as the licensing authorities or the BBFC performed their work. In both cases, the everyday work of institutions of censorship remains unclear and limited to prohibition. In contrast, my theoretical framework, which is forged in dialogue with Foucault and attends to micropractices—namely, *cutting, classifying, and certifying*—reconceptualizes censorship. My examination of the CBFC and of the legal documents, correspondence, and reports of examining committees, revising committees, the Film Appellate Tribunal, and the Ministry of Information and Broadcasting shows that the practices of cutting, classifying, and certifying are central to the workings of state censorship. As I demonstrate through my film analyses, these techniques do not belong solely to the state but also surface in the domains of film production and reception. Thus, I argue that state censorship, production, and reception share one characteristic: *selection*.

In India, producers bring their films to the CBFC, where an examining committee views them and, if deemed necessary, demands certain cuts be made. My investigations into *Gupt gyan* and *Pati parmeshwar* show that in demanding cuts, state censorship seeks to legislate not only decency but also taste. The examining committee then certifies the film according to categories such as "U" (unrestricted exhibition), "UA" (exhibition restricted to those twelve and above), "A" (exhibition restricted to adults), and "S" (exhibition restricted to specialists); it also has the authority to refuse certification. In the chapters devoted to *Satyam shivam sundaram* and *Dilwale dulhania le jayenge*, I show how processes of certification regulate not just morality but also a film's potential markets. The committee also classifies films according to categories such as "short film" (which includes newsreels, educational films, documentaries, children's films, scientific films, trailers, advertisements, and feature films) and "long film" (which includes features, children's features, and documentaries). In the case of feature films, it also assigns a "thematic classification" ("social," "historical," "biographical," "mythological," "devotional," "legendary," "horror," "fantasy," "action/thriller," "crime," "satire," "comedy," "spoof," and "adventure").[37] In the chapters on *Gupt gyan* and *Dilwale dulhania le jayenge*, I demonstrate how genre classification becomes pivotal in a film's evaluation and its certifications (or decertifications). In the case of *Gupt gyan*, the censors' inability to classify the film led to the production of a new category—the previously mentioned S certificate. My work expands the discussions on genre by drawing attention to ways in which the state deploys and generates genre classification.[38] Cutting, classifying, and certifying constitute the mechanisms through which films are marked and a proper audience is designated for them.

If the examining committee cannot reach consensus or the producer refuses its decision, the film is referred to a revising committee, which performs a similar exercise. If a decision is not reached at this level, it is passed on to the Film Appellate Tribunal; from there it can go to the head of the Ministry of Information and Broadcasting and finally to the judiciary. I describe the extreme case to underscore that the practice of censorship is divided and hierarchical. This diffusion of power enables the system to function and allows spaces for intervention—and corruption.

But cuts emerge from sources other than censors, too, which further underscores the diffuse nature of power. Editing is central to the process of filmmaking; the first cuts are those made by directors and film editors. The examining and revising committees, the film critics, and the audience have their say at later points. Cutting thus does not occur in a linear, uncomplicated fashion. Moreover, it is not driven simply by creative impulses. The so-called director's cut is often hailed as a creative endeavor, an *intact* masterpiece, but my work shows that directors base many of their editorial decisions on considerations of finances, distributors, exhibitors, censors, critics, and audiences, to name a few factors. At various stages of film production, they make choices about the story, cast, music, film or sound editing, and so on for reasons other than aesthetic ones. In addition, because Indian filmmakers are well aware of the state's censorship guidelines and practices, these guidelines and practices inform film production all along. Indian directors and producers often push these guidelines by inserting more sex scenes (hoping that some will be passed), bribing committee members, using powerful allies to bolster their case, and finding alternative ways to represent sexuality: the drenched heroine, the almost-kiss, and the "cabaret dance." The final product, the film that audiences and film critics see, then, results from a series of complex creative and regulatory selections. If state censorship seeks to guarantee a certain reading through the act of excision, then filmmakers similarly attempt to frame our vision through the technology of the camera, film editing, and the insertion of an intermission, as well as ancillary elements such as trailers, soundtracks, and promotional documentaries showing behind-the-scene footage and interviews.

Once a Hindi film is exhibited or even before, at the release of the soundtrack, critics and audiences voice their opinions about it; this commentary adds to the way a film is understood. My analyses of *Satyam shivam sundaram* and *Khalnayak*, where calls to eliminate scenes emerged at the site of reception rather than within government, demonstrate that the viewers who watch these films are not passive consumers. Considering that 85 percent of commercial films in India flop, 10 percent recover their costs, and only 5 percent earn profits, audiences, who decide which films to watch and, as my analysis of *Dilwale dulhania le jayenge* shows, even which portions to watch, exert considerable influence on content. In fact, the film financiers and producers use public choice as an important index for financing and making new films. This large cast involved in discussions on cinema generates a verbose commentary on both the manner in which films portray social customs and mores and the role of cinema in society. My theoretical framework enables an analysis of these multivocal debates and varied selections.

Debating and (Re)viewing Sexuality

Sexuality has been a key site for disputes on film censorship in India; Vasudev, among others, has argued that censorship suppresses sexuality. These disputes include, above all else, debates concerning whether representations of sexuality will harm, deprave, or corrupt children or those "whose minds are open to such immoral influences"; whether the representation of sexuality is consonant with or contrary to Indian tradition; whether "double standards" for judging Indian films and foreign films maintain Indian values, preserve colonial puritanism, or reinforce a patriarchal status quo; and whether this national prudishness in any way affects the state's (and a portion of the public's) much desired goal—to be modern and democratic.[39] These discussions and, more generally, the practices of state censorship frame cinema as a national object and therefore demand a continued investigation into the concept of "national cinema."[40]

The representation of sexuality as part of or opposed to "Indian tradition" occupies a central place in debates on film censorship. A well-known journalist and a former member of an examining committee, Kobita Sarkar, contends that the prohibition on such representations is a residue of a puritanical colonialism. She wonders, what led Indians to "import British values and impose them on [their] audiences, whose approach and out-look are so radically different? Where nudity in real life is a commonplace in our villages, or among the poor, why do we have this strange puritanical reaction (which is today being discarded in the West itself)?"[41] In addition to pointing to "nudity in real life," Sarkar also gestures toward the culture's tradition of erotic sculpture and painting, demanding, "why is nudity or at least partial undress, which is perfectly consonant with our culture . . . , dealt with so harshly?"[42] The thrust of Sarkar's argument reveals how a dispute on the representation of sexuality connects to a larger concern about defining Indian culture. Firoze Rangoonwalla, a prominent film critic, offers a response to Sarkar's rhetorical question: "Using the parallel of statues to claim censor freedom is also false. The statues are seen in their historical milieu and perspective by a select minority which goes on costly touristic visits. But the screen can bring the erotica, in blazing color, to every town and village."[43] Rangoonwalla's explanation presupposes a division between a "select minority" and the unruly masses, a split that reinforces class inequity. What kind of erotica did Rangoonwalla fear would be available to all? In Bombay commercial cinema, scenes that have been identified as sexual, incited debate, or been excised from a film have generally shown kissing, scantily clad female bodies, close-up shots of female breasts and thighs, and female nudity. It is the female body that has been marked as the sexual body and the body that must bear the burden of Indian tradition. Conversely, until the late 1980s, the male body had not been sexualized via the media. While male nudity has never been sanctioned, recent displays of bare, well-toned male chests or scantily clad men have not been fodder for debate.

A cursory glance at another charged censorship issue, violence, reveals the gendered nature of censorship debates. In discussions on violence in Bombay commercial cinema, no one questions whether it is part of Indian tradition, and no one seeks to use Mohandas Gandhi's arguments concerning the tradition of nonviolence in India to combat the rise of representations of violence. The fact that concerns about representations of violence are not framed in the context of Indian tradition raises a set of interesting issues: How is violence defined? Which body is associated with violence? In commercial films, scenes are identified as violent if they contain fighting, shooting, blood, and gore. Generally, such scenes are performed by male heroes and villains; their struggles determine the fate of the heroine, the family, and the nation. In patriarchal discourse, male bodies occupy the status of subjects. These bodies are not the object or the site of debate on tradition. In discussions on violence, neither *tradition* nor *national identity* rears its head; both, however, are central to debates on sexuality.

The ubiquitous charge of "double standards" that the film industry, journalists, and the public level at the CBFC refers to the different standards used to censor Indian and foreign films (read as "Western" films); more "explicit" sex scenes are allowed in the latter.[44] The CBFC and the policy makers explain this practice by referring to the different cultural traditions of the West and of India: different traditions demand different standards of judgment. For example, in an interview in a popular film magazine, *Star and Style*, a former minister of information and broadcasting, K. K. Shah, notes:

> There is no double standard in the Censor Board. Those who speak
> of it forget that film is a product of a certain socio-cultural setting
> and it has to be judged in this context. Certain practices, mores and
> manners prevail in certain societies, which may be frowned upon
> by members of other societies with "holier than thou" attitudes and
> denounced as immoral, etc. But here lies the rub—it is not so much
> what is shown but how it is shown that is of vital importance. Obvi-
> ously some representations are improper and are very likely to arouse
> passions and aggressive tendencies which cannot be encouraged.
> Indians, by and large, are less given to excessive expression of feelings
> of lust for example. This is a matter of training and what is considered
> acceptable in good society—that's all. There is therefore no reason
> why Indian films should be encouraged to inculcate wrong notions
> about our ways or accelerate tendencies which we regard as harmful.[45]

According to Shah, then, Western audiences can routinely absorb an amount of cinematically represented lust that could have an adverse effect on Indian audiences, who are not used to such an "excessive expression" of it. This explanation ostensibly claims that in employing varied standards to judge films, censors simply bring a cultural and social sensitivity to dissimilar contexts of production and reception. The explanation demonstrates that cultural difference is central to the construction of Indian national identity; this identity is forged partly in relation to the West.

An anonymous writer disagrees with Shah's explanation:

> If censorship is to be enforced on sound democratic lines and for
> the good of the masses, the censors cannot pick and choose produc-
> ers and artists for the use of their official yard-stick. Thus, under the

same adopted code, adapted to suit the convenience of the members, different adaptations are followed. One code is applied in censoring foreign movies, the second code for Raj Kapoor films (lenient censoring, example *Jis Desh Main Ganga Behti Hai* [The Country in which the Ganges flows]) and the third for the other Indian movies.[46]

This writer draws attention to the fact that censors not only distinguish between foreign films and Indian films but also use different criteria to judge films made by well-known producers and directors and those made by lesser-known ones. Apparently, works from respected filmmakers, such as Raj Kapoor, receive treatment different from that accorded to works by filmmakers who are less well known or well established. The censors thus seem to attend not just to sociocultural setting but also to a director's social status, thus creating a hierarchy in which sexual scenes in films by respected and powerful directors were characterized as aesthetically pleasing but similar scenes in other films were denounced as vulgar and obscene. In short, such practices reveal that the censors' assessment of a director's symbolic capital (to use Pierre Bourdieu's concept) is crucial in making aesthetic and moral judgments about a film.

Whereas the writer who points to the censors' use of multiple standards demands that films be treated equally, Chidananda Das Gupta, a noted maker of "art" films and a film critic, argues that "the attempt to apply the same standards to all films irrespective of their integrity, moral and artistic value has turned film censorship in India into a farce of measurements."[47] He elaborates:

> Whether it is overtly admitted or not, some element of quality judgment is inevitable in intelligent censorship. Unless the principle is admitted that the need and the justification of frankness in a film is in the honesty and integrity of a film and not on the boundaries of what is physically shown, it is useless even to discuss the reform of censorship. Liberalization without this understanding would only mean a greater amount of "exploitation" and sensationalism in commercial cinema; stringent regulation will prevent the honest artistic film of controversy or love from being made.[48]

In calling for "intelligent censorship"—basically, a system where art films would be judged more liberally—Das Gupta reproduces a hierarchical division between art and commercial cinema in which the former is imbued with honesty and integrity and the latter is characterized as exploitative and sensationalist. Interestingly, many of the censors share the views presented by Das Gupta, producing an odd alliance between the censors and the supporters of art or progressive films.[49]

Much of the "double standards" debate has focused on these issues. Kobita Sarkar points to an often overlooked arena in the practice of double standards:

> While on the subject of double standards, isn't it strange that no one has objected to the double standards of behaviour in judging a "hero" and "heroine" over the same misdeed in the Indian cinema? The heroine of *Bhumika* [Foundation] who wanted to lead her own life gets an "A" [exhibition restricted to adults] certificate for doing the same things that many a film hero has done. He not only gets a "U" [unrestricted exhibition] certificate, but a lot of applause as well for a similar outlook![50]

In gesturing to the different standards used to judge the actions of heroes and heroines, Sarkar broadens the debate on censorship by inviting us to consider how the practice of censorship is gendered. Her comments also suggest that the practice of gendered standards is not limited to the censors. Rather, the audiences also employ such standards. Furthermore, her remarks reveal the pivotal role of certification in generating such gendered evaluations.

Determining whether the practice of censorship is democratic constitutes another contentious issue central to these debates. Arguing that this practice is undemocratic, Boyd explains that the prerelease censorship of films fetters filmmakers' imaginations and that there is little "opportunity for public appraisal and criticism of a system of prior restraint because it operates behind a veil of informality and partial concealment. Hence, the policies and procedures of licensing authorities do not as frequently come to public attention and the reasons for such official action are less likely to be known and criticised."[51] Unlike books or artworks, films are subject to censorship before they enter the public domain. This regulation is undertaken by the examining committees, which include select members of the public, generally middle-class and well-educated individuals. This practice not only regulates what viewers see but, more important, screens its own operations. Those defending censorship claim that it guards public morals and point out that the decisions of the examining committee are subject to appeal. To bolster their claims, they point to other states that also use various methods to regulate cinema to protect their citizens. Censorship becomes a practice that constitutes the state and its relations with its citizens. In tracking these discourses, we can see how female sexuality is fundamentally tied to notions of being Indian.[52] Furthermore, censorship is central to clarifying conceptions of the state, democracy, and liberalism. Finally, it is crucial for the (re)production of the state. After all, the state makes its case for intervening precisely by constructing the film spectator as a vulnerable child or a member of a lower class or group that is inclined toward prurience. Moreover, such classifications assist the state in managing potentially unruly cinema audiences.

To analyze and interrogate these discourses, I draw on Michel Foucault's work on the history of Western sexuality.[53] Historically, Foucault tells us, there have been two great procedures for producing the "truth of sex."[54] He describes "societies—and they are numerous: China, Japan, India, Rome and the Arabo-Moslem societies—which endowed themselves with an *ars erotica*" whereby "truth is drawn from pleasure itself."[55] Unlike these societies, he claims, Western societies "practice a *scientia sexualis*" and over the centuries have developed procedures "for telling the truth of sex which are geared to a form of knowledge-power."[56] In distinguishing between the two approaches, he overlooks two significant issues crucial for understanding the development of sexuality in India. First and foremost, in placing India among societies "which endowed themselves with an *ars erotica*," Foucault draws on precolonial sources and fails to account for the effects of the colonial encounter. Second, in examining precolonial texts such as the *Kamasutra*, Foucault does not analyze the social relations that informed the production and reception of this text in precolonial India. An examination of these relations reveals that far from being an emancipatory text, the *Kamasutra* was shaped by and reproduced unequal gender relations.[57] Although Foucault suggests the story of repression is primarily a Western one, this narrative appears in debates on sexuality in India as well. For this reason, I find Foucault's insight that repression should be read afresh as an incitement to discourse useful in illuminating debates on film censorship of sexuality in India.

Until the mid-1980s in India, few works focused on the role of the mass media in the social organization of sexuality.[58] Hindi cinema, a major force in Indian mass media, has been pivotal in the social organization of sexuality within and increasingly, in the era of liberalization, beyond the territorial borders of the Indian nation-state. For the most part, feminists and activists have engaged with questions of gender and on-screen sexuality by undertaking campaigns to remove vulgar billboards, protesting against sexist representations of women, making claims linking on-screen gender violence to real-life violence against women, or lamenting that images on-screen do not adequately represent reality.[59] More innovative scholarship demonstrates how the narratives of Bombay cinema produce and disavow female desire and agency; how they depend upon dichotomies such as heroine/vamp and wife/courtesan; how the coordinates of stardom, gender, and culture are pivotal to film narratives and industrial hiring practices; and how the practice of censorship reveals informal pacts between the Indian state, the Bombay film industry, and indigenous patriarchy—pacts made at the expense of female subjectivity. I agree with John and Nair in their assertion that "'sexuality' must connote a way of addressing sexual relations, their spheres of legitimacy and illegitimacy, through the institutions and practices, as well as the discourses and forms of representation, that have long been producing, framing, distributing and controlling the subject of 'sex.'"[60]

In the subsequent pages I draw on and seek to extend these debates. To do so, I situate the story of censorship in a broad social field and trace the intriguing ways that the heated debates on sexuality in Bombay cinema actually *produce* the very forms of sexuality they claim to regulate. Specifically, I show the counterintuitive ways in which cinematic representations of the female body work to engender India's national identity. The debates on sexuality in newspapers and film magazines betray the fact that film is not simply entertaining but indeed central to constructing everyday sexual practices. Questions that inform my analysis of film censorship of sexuality include the following: What images are identified as sexual and incite debate? How do the censors attempt to regulate sexuality? What scenes or acts are characterized as "obscene" or "vulgar"? Which representations of sexuality are easily certified? Are challenges to these regulations interventions, or are they about the fetishization of sexuality? How do practices of cutting, certifying, and classifying at sites of state censorship, film production, and film reception differentially structure and define female heterosexuality?

Sneak Preview

In this chapter, I have outlined the contours of the debates on film censorship of sexuality and provided an analytic framework for situating those debates. The next chapter turns to the history of film censorship, focusing on the representation of sexuality, and provides a macrolevel view as well as a critique of the postcolonial state. This enables me to offer a counterhistory via my ethnographic encounters as well as the specific case studies in the later chapters. In Chapter 3 I use fieldwork anecdotes to present an account of the microprocesses of censorship. I borrow Arendt's notion of the art of storytelling and Foucault's strategic use of description as means for creating effects. My intentions here are twofold: first, to foreground routine, arbitrary, unstitched, and intentional practices in the process of censorship; second, to disturb a disciplinary mode of constructing and presenting an argument. The techniques of storytelling and description enable me to gesture toward uncanny resemblances among censorship, scholarship, and film production. In drawing attention to a set of formal and formulaic actions shared by this trio, I show that power is neither distant nor extraordinary.

In the next five chapters I focus on a specific period, 1973 to 1996, analyzing *Gupt gyan, Satyam shivam sundaram, Pati parmeshwar, Khalnayak,* and *Dilwale dulhania le jayenge.* In examining these films, I seek to question conventional understandings of both censorship and sexuality. Released in the 1970s, both *Gupt gyan* and *Satyam shivam sundaram* stretched the representation of sexuality on Indian screens. *Gupt gyan* confounded officials as well as examining and revising committees by using elements from the documentary and feature film genres to craft a narrative about the importance of sex education. Its innovative topic rendered *Gupt gyan* subject to bureaucratic shunting. Its not-so-powerful director-producer, B. K. Adarsh, drew on the support of more influential figures to navigate the rough waters of state censorship. After much wrangling and numerous cuts, the film was released in 1974 and met with success at the box office. Soon afterward Indira Gandhi's government declared a state of emergency, and *Gupt gyan,* among other films, was banned. It was rereleased only after the Janata Party gained control of the government, promising freedom of speech. Ironically, under the Janata Party's reign, *Gupt gyan* underwent cuts more severe than those demanded in its first review, revealing that the newly ensconced party shared its predecessor's concerns about the effects of cinema and sought to regulate them via censorship.

Unlike Adarsh's film, the famed Raj Kapoor's *Satyam shivam sundaram* smoothly sailed through the Central Board of Film Censors. However, it encountered brickbats at the site of reception because Kapoor had tampered with audience expectations about Zeenat Aman's and Lata Mangeshkar's status as "visual" and "aural" stars. While both *Gupt gyan* and *Satyam shivam sundaram* incited debate because of their explicit representation of sexuality, *Pati parmeshwar* faced a ban a much less controversial depiction of a self-sacrificial wife. It shuttled through courts for two years for glorifying woman's servility and was finally released to a damp reception in 1989. The censors' objections to *Pati parmeshwar* appeared odd because for decades film-examining committees had consistently passed such representations and focused on censoring sexually suggestive images such as close-ups of bosoms, thighs, and gyrating hips. The debates on *Pati parmeshwar* reveal the contested visions of tradition and modernity that shaped the state and the construction of the "Indian woman."

My analysis of *Khalnayak* returns to the themes of sexuality, stardom, and sound that inform my examination of *Satyam shivam sundaram* and relocates them in the context of economic liberalization. I track the nearly censored song "Choli ke peeche kya hai?" as it moved through the CBFC, public reception, legal petition, the music industry, and filmic narrative and demonstrate how each sought to contain female sexuality by framing it as a part of Indian tradition, as immoral Western influence, or as a commodity. The case against *Khalnayak* reveals the importance of the music industry and technologies such as audiotape cassettes and cable and satellite television in shaping the practice of censorship.

Finally, I turn to *Dilwale dulhania le jayenge*, which like *Khalnayak* emerged in the context of economic liberalization. Unlike *Khalnayak*, however, it does not traffic in "vulgar" or "obscene" lyrics or images. Rather, it portrays a happy union of sanitized and sumptuous tradition with modern consumerism. In examining *Dilwale dulhania le jayenge*, I seek to broaden and challenge a conventional understanding of censorship, namely, one that associates the practice of censorship with cutting or banning. I highlight a ubiquitous but much less debated aspect of censorship—*certification*—by analyzing a film that was approvingly characterized by its examining committee as a "family love story" and granted a U certificate, enabling all audiences to see it. These film analyses enable me to highlight both the formal and informal exercises of power by the state, film industry, and audiences; I show how context, technology, and concepts of stardom, spectacle, sound, and genre shape negotiations among the state, film industry, and audiences. I conclude with brief analyses of *Censor* (2001) and *My Name Is Khan* (2010) through which I show the continued relevance of my theoretical framework and suggest new avenues for research.

On a final note, I wish to underscore the unpredictable and asymmetrical nature of my filmography, which generates productive juxtapositions, allowing me to chart the diverse locations, strategies, and subjects of censorship. While thematic or historical classifications such as "sex-education films," "art films," "controversial films," or "films from the Emergency" would have yielded a more narrow view of both censorship and sexuality, the broad rubrics underlying my choices—gender and heterosexuality—enabled me to investigate censorship and sexuality from frank, clinical representations of sexuality (e.g., warts on genitalia in *Gupt gyan*) to sublime marriage (e.g., wedding celebrations in *Dilwale dulhania le jayenge*).

2

Revisiting the History
of Film Censorship

History serves to show how that-which-is has not always been; i.e.,
that the things which seem most evident to us are always formed
in the confluence of encounters and chances, during the course of a
precarious and fragile history. —MICHEL FOUCAULT,
FOUCAULT: POLITICS, PHILOSOPHY, CULTURE

This chapter presents a historical overview of film censorship in India from its emergence in 1917 to the recent draft of
the Cinematograph Bill 2010, focusing largely on gender and
heterosexuality. Given that more than thirty years have passed
since the 1978 publication of Vasudev's *Liberty and Licence in the*
Indian Cinema, this account serves as a supplement, filling a historical gap.[1] Unlike Vasudev's work, in which censorship assumes
an instrumental and functional garb, this chapter shows that the
legal-juridical apparatus of censorship has considered and relied
on assumptions about the role of cinema (entertainment vs. education) and audiences (e.g., children, adolescents, or immature
natives). These assumptions have played vital roles in formulating laws and policies on censorship. As I indicated in Chapter 1,
Vasudev primarily uses state archives to construct this history.
Expanding the archive of censorship, I include letters written
by readers of the popular film magazine *Filmfare.* This enlarged
archive enables us to see that this history was not made only at
state institutions by government officials. Rather, a larger public
was invested and involved in shaping it.

Three underlying areas of concern should be kept in mind as I
chart my postcolonial account of this history. First, colonial and

neocolonial forces have been central to constituting cinema as a public sphere of regulation in India, just as they have been crucial to the formation of the Indian nation and state. Thus, this account aligns itself with scholarship that insists on locating and investigating the development of cinema, the nation, and the state within global scenarios.[2] Second, and related to the first issue, concerns about cinema in Britain were exported to its colonies and expanded to include the "natives." Kuhn's and Cronin's studies show that within Britain as nation, discussions on film censorship imagined the film spectator as a vulnerable child, an immature adolescent, or a prurient, uneducated lower-class adult.[3] Such characterizations enabled the state and other regulatory institutions and organizations to intervene in the development of British cinema. In the colonies, while anxieties about the effects of cinema on children and adolescents continued to be voiced, the native spectator was conflated with these viewers and similarly deemed puerile and volatile. Such categorization helped construct the colonial state as a mature parental figure and justified its rule over the Indian subcontinent. The postcolonial Indian state adopted a similar view of its citizens, showing continuity in colonial and postcolonial practices. Although the colonial legacy has clearly shaped contemporary state censorship in India, even new rules and policies (e.g., the recent effort to transform certification practices in India by introducing "twelve and older" and "fifteen and older" certificates similar to the ones used in the United Kingdom) show the influence of global forces.

Third, the export of censorship rules and practices from the United Kingdom to India invites reflection on distinctions between state censorship, nongovernmental evaluations, and "voluntary" censorship (e.g., the MPAA in the United States) that are crucial to a discourse of development and assist in differentiating between mature and developing democracies. In the United States, filmmakers choose to submit to the MPAA's classification process, and they sometimes edit films with a view to achieving a certain rating (or reedit a film to get a rating different from one initially received). In Britain, a nongovernmental organization—namely, the British Board of Film Censors (the name later changed to the British Board of Film Classification, presumably to reflect a more benign exercise of power)—eventually gained authority to examine and evaluate any films to be exhibited in Britain. Both before and after independence from British rule, however, censorship in India remained within the state's ambit. Attention to identity (e.g., state censorship vs. nongovernmental regulation) suggests that the application of state power was and is more formidable. However, an analysis of practices—the use of similar rules as well as techniques of cutting, classifying, and certifying—discloses astonishing parallels between state censorship and regulation via nongovernmental organizations.

British Colonialism and Censorship

In India, the concept of film censorship was first introduced by colonial administrators.[4] Introducing the first Cinematograph Bill in the Legislative Council on September 5, 1917, Sir William Vincent said:

> Most other civilized countries have found it necessary to revise and supplement the existing law for the control of spectacular entertainment with special reference to this form of exhibition. Two points are to be considered: (a) Safety of the audience and (b) Prevention of objectionable films being exhibited. It is obviously necessary to guard against the exhibition of indecent and improper films, or those which wound religious or racial feeling.[5]

Ostensibly, the colonial state instituted censorship to guard the morals of the natives and to prevent them from sinking into depravity, religious bigotry, or ethnic strife. Like other institutions and legal constraints, censorship contributed to the formation of the colonial state and helped to justify its rule. For these reasons, despite the objections of the Indian members of the Legislative Council on grounds of liberty, the colonial state passed the first Cinematograph Act in 1918.[6]

The Cinematograph Act of 1918 dealt with two matters, the licensing of cinema houses and the certification of films as suitable for public exhibition. Regarding the latter issue, the act stipulated that no film could be exhibited unless the proper authority had deemed it suitable for public viewing. Two years later, in 1920, censor boards were instituted in Bombay, Calcutta, Madras, and Rangoon to examine and certify films; subsequently, in 1927, another censor board was established in Lahore. Certifying authorities initially worked without specific guidelines for evaluating films. Later, the Bombay and Calcutta boards used the guidelines of the British Board of Film Censors to draw up a list of suggestions, called the General Principles of Film Censorship, for guiding the inspectors of films, tailoring India to a British cut; the other boards did the same. The diverse locations of these boards generated variation in evaluations.[7] As I discuss later, the postcolonial state (unsuccessfully) attempted to produce more uniform results by shifting the administration of censorship from the level of individual states to the center.

Throughout the 1920s Britons in both England and India mounted strong protests against screening Hollywood films in India. According to Poonam Arora and Prem Chowdhry, individuals and citizens primarily demanded tighter control and stricter censorship because they were concerned about the way these films represented whites. In particular, Arora notes, they worried about sexualized representations of white women that constructed these women as sexually available. Such representations, they feared, would undermine England's moral authority—and harm white women, for brown men might molest them after viewing portrayals of this sort. Significantly, these protesters saw a need for censorship not because of the film's content per se but because of its potential spectators—specifically, the *volatile, male native spectators*.[8]

Ann Stoler's insights on race and desire in colonial Southeast Asia illuminate such anxieties. By representing native men as sexually excessive, colonial discourse constructed them as degenerate and uncivilized while shoring up a bourgeois, European male identity associated with civility, self-discipline, and sexual restraint.[9] This identity was central to maintaining the legitimacy of colonial rule. In her analysis of the 1927 Quota Act, Priya Jaikumar points out that the protests reveal the colonial state to have been beset by not only racial anxieties but also political and economic ones. The British were concerned about the mushrooming North American film industry and its impact on British cinema and the empire. In 1926, for example, of the 897 films screened in India, approximately 80 percent were North American, 10 percent were British, and 10 percent were Indian. The British wanted to reduce the exhibition of North American films and replace them with British films.[10] The act granted state protection not only to British films but also to those made elsewhere in the empire; the act imagined empire as a space where all empire films—British, Australian, and Indian, among others—would circulate with ease.[11] Jaikumar notes that the anticolonial picketing of British films such as *The Drum* in India, as well as doubts about the welcome that Indian films would receive in Britain, indicates the problems with such a fantasy. She insightfully points out that discussions about cinema's (especially Hollywood's) potentially detrimental effects on the natives were not simply a disguise for the real economic interests of the imperial state. Rather, they enabled the discussion of economic policies. In suggesting that Hollywood films were harmful and that British films might offer better representations, the colonial state was putting forth the possibility of quota ostensibly for other than economic reasons—namely, it wanted not simply to help the British film industry but also to protect the natives.[12]

To address these concerns, the colonial authorities formed the Indian Cinematograph Inquiry Committee in 1927 and charged it with examining and reporting on all aspects of film distribution, production, exhibition, and censorship. Headed by a prominent Indian lawyer, T. Rangachariar,[13] the committee comprised British and Indian members from white-collar professions. In the course of interviewing witnesses who included distributors, exhibitors, producers, and colonial administrators, among others, the Rangachariar committee made a noteworthy discovery. A majority of witnesses vociferously asserted that "the cinema was a demoralizing influence, but when examined had to admit that they very seldom visited cinemas for the reason that they believed them harmful . . . [and] inartistic."[14]

Considering that many of these witnesses rarely went to watch films and some had never even been to the theater, their passionate denouncements appear to be ill-founded. Indeed, these responses were not based on empirical proof. Rather, the evidence for these sentiments lay in another register, namely, the psychic one. Their denunciations underscored the fact that the very idea of cinema evoked much anxiety. The agitated statements of the British Social Hygiene Delegation are revealing in this regard: "In every province that we visited the evil influence of the cinema was cited by educationists and representative citizens as one of the major factors in lowering the standard of sex conduct and thereby tending to increase the dissemination of disease."[15] These statements, like the later media effects theory, assume that spectators cannot resist the seductive powers of the image. Not only did the Rangachariar committee find the delegation's statements to be "doubtful," but "it appear[ed] obvious to them that they [were] made without adequate enquiry and partly at least as a result of a pre-existing obsession."[16]

Another point that recurred in the interviews concerned the effect of Western films on Indian morals and European interests. The National Council of Women in Burma argued that the exhibition of Western films would be harmful because the "East" and the "West" had different standards and values:

The majority of films shown are actually those shown in Western countries but the general standard is lower here because a smaller proportion of really good films are imported. Owing to the different standards of behaviour many films which would be harmless in the West are definitely pernicious here. . . . It is . . . necessary to ban the numerous pictures in which sex is treated with vulgarity and physical side of it overemphasized.[17]

The postcolonial state would later adopt a similar formulation in justify-ing differing standards for evaluating Indian versus foreign (i.e., West-ern) films. The Rangachariar committee did not disagree entirely with the National Council of Women on the question of cultural difference; how-ever, it argued that the Western films in question wrought little harm since most Indian audiences did not understand, did not like, and did not go to see "social films" that contained sex scenes:

> The type of play that the ordinary Indian audience does not under-stand and does not like is the more subtle social drama, especially what is known as the sex drama. It is exactly this kind of the film that is alleged to depreciate Western life in the eyes of the Indian. We witnessed several such films being exhibited to nearly empty houses with hardly an Indian present perhaps except the educated Indian who can see them in their true perspective as dramas not necessarily true to life, and that they do no harm worthy of notice to European interests.[18]

In her article "The Crowd outside the Lettered City: Imagining the Mass Audience in 1920s India," Manishita Dass points out that the committee's questionnaire and its oral interviews were steeped in class rhetoric (as the previous quotation shows), constructing a hierarchy of spectators whose class defined the extent to which they would be able to comprehend films and to resist the seductive invitations of the screen.[19] Dass astutely notes that the committee's work reveals that the colonial state as well as the national elite did not imagine the nation as a "fraternal, . . . horizontal" community," à la Benedict Anderson. Rather, their vision was far more hierarchal.[20] Extending Dass's argument, I contend that practices of cen-sorship—certifying, classifying, and cutting—were crucial to (re)produc-ing this tiered vision.

While the committee felt that the "ordinary Indian audience" was safe from harm and the "educated Indian immune" to "social films," their pos-sible effect on adolescents continued to trouble the group: "Suggestive impropriety in dress, conduct, and love-making should be somewhat more jealously discountenanced[;] we say this not because such scenes harm European interests or Indian morals in particular, but because they have a tendency to corrupt the morals of adolescents of all communities."[21] After national independence, postcolonial officials and the citizenry affirmed the committee's views on the matter. By imagining the film spectator as an undeveloped adolescent, both the colonial and the postcolonial states paved the path for their own paternal interventions. These views, along with the ones on cultural difference between East and West, became a staple of discussions on censorship. At this juncture, a discussion about the practices of censorship—namely, cutting and certifying—began to emerge. While the committee supported regulating cinematic sexuality by demanding that scenes deemed offensive be removed, it did not approve of certifying films as suitable for adults only. The committee noted that children's moral development was not to be regulated via state certification. Rather, parents or guardians of children needed to "protect them and keep them from harmful entertainment."[22]

A more pernicious source of harm, the committee felt, was the production and distribution of pornographic films. On the one hand, the committee was completely "satisfied that censorship [had] prevented and [would] prevent the public exhibition of such films," adding, "it is not the function of censorship to deal with private exhibitions."[23] On the other hand, it worried that individuals might view this as a loophole: "[If] private [i.e., noncommercial] exhibitions are to be exempt from control, the conditions will be need to be carefully defined; otherwise, exhibitions which are in effect public may masquerade under the guise of private and necessary control be avoided."[24] The committee's cautionary and ambivalent views indicate the difficulty of negotiating and drawing the boundaries between the private and the public, boundaries that are important in the production of the cinema—and in the production of the state.[25]

In its 1928 report, the committee noted that it had found no justifiable complaints of excessive leniency. It maintained that the overwhelming majority of the films exhibited in no way tended to demoralize the Indian public or bring Western civilization into contempt. Although the Rangachariar committee's recommendations were not implemented by the colonial state, and the provincial boards continued to follow the earlier guidelines, the report was productive in other ways. As Jaikumar notes, it constituted a challenge to a colonial state that wanted to mobilize racial and moral anxieties about North American films in order to implement a quota for empire films.[26] This report also constituted an official forum for both gathering knowledge and designating the terms for debating censorship. Moreover, it helped set the parameters for future discussions on censorship, which often involved reiterations, in both substance and style, of the issues identified by the committee: the cinema's detrimental effects on children and the criminally inclined; its representation of nation, tradition, and culture; and its role in the formation of a democratic and modern nation-state.

The Postcolonial State and Censorship

After India's independence in 1947, the national government, while against censorship in art and literature, viewed the very medium of cinema in a different light and felt it necessary to retain film censorship.[27] The postcolonial state expressed grave concerns over the cinema's effects on public morals:

> The motion picture wields a very strong influence on the people. True, the majority of people come to see the pictures just for entertainment, little realising that what they see on the screen is going to have an influence on their tastes and on their outlook on life. This influence is more pronounced on adolescent minds. The students and youths who go to see movies are very much influenced by them.[28]

In fact, the postcolonial state adopted not only the institution of colonial censorship but also its concerns and anxieties, for it imagined (and still imagines) spectators of films primarily as "students and adolescents." Postindependence reports sponsored by various government bodies, such as the *Report of the Film Enquiry Committee* (1951), the *Report of the Film Enquiry Committee on Film Censorship* (1969), and the *Report of the Working Group on National Film Policy* (1980), justify censorship on the grounds that it is necessary for public protection—and as the statement just quoted shows, they envisioned this public largely as adolescent. Interestingly, they all contain references to other nation-states, such as Denmark, Britain, the United States, and the Soviet Union, emphasizing that all nation-states have some form of censorship. This revealing observation suggests that censorship assists in the production of a state. A state does not exist outside its activities. Rather, it arises out of such micropolitical processes. In short, it is an effect of such processes. It lacks fixity and so must reproduce itself. It is through its mimicry that it produces in its citizens the recognition that *this body is like a state.*[29]

After independence the Indian government amended the Cinematograph Act of 1918. The Cinematograph Act of 1949 (first amendment) created two categories of censorship certificates: "A" for films restricted to adults and "U" for unrestricted exhibition. The films in the A category were increasingly defined by the amount of sex and violence they contained. This distinction marked children as innocent, vulnerable, and susceptible; conversely, adults, except for those who were "criminally inclined," were characterized as experienced, strong, and therefore less susceptible. Thus, the practice of certification defined both films and potential audiences. Interestingly, the 1927 report had urged that films not be certified for adults only because such a certification would arouse prurient interest; spectators would actually attempt to gain entry for this very reason. Therefore, the official restriction would not serve its purpose. The report indicates that prohibition produces desire. It is precisely because we are excited by the prohibition that its transgression becomes a more regulated "freedom."

In addition to introducing film certification, the Cinematograph Act of 1949 (second amendment) made a provision for setting up a central censorship board to replace the provincial boards. In 1951 the Ministry of Information and Broadcasting formed the Central Board of Film Censors, thus restructuring the system set up under the Cinematographic Act of 1918, which had operated through regional censor boards. In 1952 the government-appointed Film Enquiry Committee, under the chairmanship of S. K. Patil, submitted its report suggesting measures to help film develop into an effective instrument for promoting national culture and education, and offering healthy entertainment. The committee proposed a wholesale reorganization of censorship largely by creating institutions that would help guide the producers. The report was left to gather dust by the Indian government, whose interest in the recommendations far outstripped its zeal in their implementation.

In 1952 a consolidated statue called the Cinematograph Act of 1952 was enacted, superseding all previous legislation on the subject. This act gave the central government authority to constitute a censorship board and to appoint full-time regional or assistant regional officers at the various regional centers of the film industry as well as to appoint members of advisory panels at these centers. The principles of censorship were set out in this act:

> (a) A film shall not be certified for public exhibition if, in the opinion of the authority competent to grant the certificate, the film or any part of it, is against the interest of the security of the state, friendly relations with foreign states, public order, decency or morality, or involves defamation or contempt of court or is likely to incite the commission of any offense, and (b) Subject to the provisions contained in sub-section (1), the Central Government may issue such directions as it may think fit in sanctioning films for public exhibition. A provision was made for an appeal to the Central Government

against a decision of the Board (a) refusing to a grant a certificate, (b) granting only a certificate for exhibition to adults and; (c) directing the applicant to cut or delete portions of the film.[30]

Clearly, the cinema needed to be regulated because its capacities posed a threat to state authority and legitimacy. While the state prohibited certain representations, it also created a space for voicing objections. By creating such a space, the state sought to define the grounds for appeal and to demonstrate that it was willing to negotiate with the film industry and the citizenry. On the one hand, the state retained its authority, since protest could take place only on the terms and in the spaces designated appropriate by the postcolonial state; on the other hand, this gesture contributed to the state's democratic ethos since it *allowed* and *regulated* protest.

A debate held in the Rajya Sabha (the Indian Parliament's upper house) on December 10, 1954, reflects the state's grave concern over the effects films might have on the morals of a public unable to resist the influence of such "undesirable films": "This House is of the opinion that moral standards in the country are affected to a considerable extent as a result of the exhibition of undesirable films and recommends to the government to take such steps as are necessary either by legislation or otherwise, to prohibit the exhibition of such films, whether foreign or Indian."[31] Parliament's concerns about the public's moral well-being and its subsequent demands for greater control and surveillance were shared by some viewers. For example, in 1954, 13,000 women of Delhi presented a petition to the prime minister asking him to curb the evil influence of films, for, they said, movies were making their children play hooky, acquire precocious sex habits, indulge in other vices, and so on. Such petitions confirmed the state's vision about the films' potential spectators—*they were like children*—as well as their possible detrimental effects. Responding to this petition, Prime Minister Nehru stated, "Films have an essential part to play in the modern world. At the same time it is true that any powerful medium like motion pictures has a good effect and a bad effect. We have to take care therefore that we emphasize the good aspect of it."[32]

The Rajya Sabha debate, the petition by the Delhi women, and Nehru's subsequent response to the petition contribute to a powerful discourse that links cinema to the development of moral character. Whereas debates concerning cinema had a strong moral flavor, discussions about other industries and technologies were not articulated specifically in *moral* terms. As previously mentioned, cinema, unlike other industries, had not been granted status as "legitimate." By casting cinema as morally suspect, the state assumed the role of the nation's moral guardian—and the petition from the women in Delhi affirmed this role. While cinema became the venue for moral dramas, morality all but disappeared from discussions about industries that would make India a "modern" and "developed" nation; it seemed that their moral status did not require any contestation.[33]

Others challenged or supported views that constructed film as the sole producer of impropriety and immorality. In the course of her presidential address at the annual conference of the Bombay Presidency Women's Council in March 1952, Lilavati Munshi argued:

> As a member of the Central Board of Film Censors, I feel that something has to be done to prevent the unhealthy influences which are in evidence in some of the films produced locally or imported from outside. Films are the greatest weapon which can make or mar the future generation. Drink, crime, sex and brutality, if presented in an attractive form, will influence the subconscious mind of the younger generation and make children with their formative minds, lose more values.[34]

Munshi's statement reinforces the Delhi women's concerns, raised in their petition, about the cinema's effects on children. It confirms the vision of the film spectator as a susceptible child who requires protection, which in turn implies that the practices and policies of censorship must prevent this "child" from viewing objectionable or harmful content. For Munshi, the problem lay with the films rather than with the other institutions and practices that were also crucial in forming "young" minds. Therefore, she contended that the exhibition of "unhealthy films" that aroused "the baser instincts of man" needed to be curtailed.[35]

Opponents of censorship also denounced any attempt to incite the "baser" instincts of human beings, but they demanded the right to present "reality" as well. In 1954 the *Journal of the Bengal Motion Picture Association* chastised the censor boards for their obsession with sexuality:

> Censorship in India is fast becoming a censorship of the female anatomy with the emphasis currently on vogue in cutting the "emphasized bosom" of heroines in some of our pictures. We deplore any attempt on the part of anyone to exploit the lower emotions of man, but we cannot agree that the female anatomy should be tampered with to please the neo-realist eye that is the Indian censor.[36]

According to this writer, it is the state's practice of cutting that tampers with the "female anatomy." As I note in Chapter 1, however, such an argument presumes films to be whole, complete objects before they arrive at the censor board. In fact, the practice of cutting is central to the process of filmmaking. This practice, in turn, is informed by codes of realism that are themselves normative. These codes draw on perception, which itself is cut up, organized, and assembled to construct "reality."[37]

Again, film censorship has traditionally been associated with destruction—cutting—and film production, with creation. Such characterizations have generated specific roles for those involved in the theater of censorship. Whereas directors have been identified as creators of films, censors have been maligned as destroyers, as "cutters." This vision divides and limits the space of politics and aesthetics, for it assigns to the censors the task of political prohibition and to the directors the task of aesthetic production. The point here involves the *kind* of relation forged between identity and practice; this relation confines an identity to a particular practice and a practice to a singular identity, i.e., the censors are the ones who cut films, and the only ones who cut films are the censors. This relation between identity and practice is central to the constitution and articulation of a discourse on censorship; it produces limits and boundaries within which such a discourse functions.

Filmfare's Forum on Censorship

In its March 4, 1955, issue, the popular film magazine *Filmfare*[38] announced a forum on film censorship. The editors randomly selected and reproduced cuts imposed on films after the central censorship board had been set up, in 1951, and the new censorship rules came into force; they invited readers to "give their own views on a controversial subject."[39] The public responded to this call and sent forth their opinions. How do we make sense of this event—a film magazine soliciting and publishing "public opinion" on film censorship? Although *Filmfare* would later transform into a gossipy magazine under the editorship of Khalid Mohamed, its editorials indicate that in the 1950s it saw itself as a forum for improving the film industry and protecting it from the state's arbitrariness in matters of financial exactions and censorship. *Filmfare* wanted to institute a regime of excellence and professionalism in the industry. The *Filmfare* awards; competitions to target new actors; articles on the technical dimensions of the trade by award-winning editors, directors, and sound engineers, among others—all these things constituted efforts by *Filmfare* to establish excellence and professionalism. For the magazine's editors, state censorship warranted discussion because it exercised an often arbitrary and whimsical power over the industry and even questioned its legitimacy.[40]

To put the matter in Althusserian terms, the forum interpellates would-be participants as readers of *Filmfare*. A quick perusal of the letters, from both male and female readers, reveals that the writers resided in different parts of India, espoused varied religious beliefs, and belonged to distinct ethnic communities, which suggests that *Filmfare's* readership was wide and varied and thus representative of public opinion in India.[41] What were this group's thoughts on film censorship? Jal Jehangir, a reader from Bombay, wrote:

> Much has been said in *Filmfare* on the "official" and the "industry" viewpoints. But what about the viewpoint of the audience? As a father of grown up and little children, I venture to put forth some observations. The newsreel and documentaries enable my children to follow events in the country and thus widen their knowledge. Cartoons and feature films help to train their power of observation, memory and their critical faculties. Regarding "crime" and "Western" film, I have never found the sympathies of my children on the wrong side. Young people can differentiate between good and bad. Screen romances similarly make scarcely any impression on the young, and if boys and girls sometimes adopt mannerisms, a little family teasing soon puts an end to that! There is one remarkable fact in our censoring of films. There are numerous movies which our censors have seen and not certified for public exhibition. Have these banned pictures, seen only by the censors, transformed them into criminal or led them to commit excesses? Obviously not. Then how can these very films be presumed by the censors to have that effect: "This film will harm my neighbour, but not me because I am a superior being." What strikes one as being necessary is a common sense view by the censors of their function, and less of the holier-than-thou attitude.[42]

In contrast to many, Jehangir's letter asserts that children, the imagined spectators of discourse of censorship, are robust rather than vulnerable and thereby interrogates practices of censorship. His letter also points to vital issues at stake in the debate on film censorship: What kinds of spectator are imagined by the discourse of censorship? How does the cinema affect the public? Is cinema educational or simply entertaining? Should parents or the state decide what children should watch? Are the censors effective representatives of public opinion? These questions reemerge in other letters, sedimenting this debate. Anant Kumar Suri, a reader from Punjab, chided the government for magnifying the cinema's effect on the public:

> The cinema theatre is neither a school nor a temple. People visit it after a day's hard work for amusement and the primary aim of the motion picture is to entertain and amuse. Freedom of expression here should be as unrestricted as it is in the case of newspapers, literature, painting, music and the other arts: The citizen's character is formed at home and in school, not at the cinema. Indeed, one forgets a film the moment one comes home from the theatre. . . . The film industry must not be blamed for producing pictures which cater to the tastes of the public and the censor should not be a killjoy.[43]

While Jehangir believed that the cinema was socially valuable and taught useful skills, Suri thought that it was simply an amusing distraction. Many espoused Suri's view, but only a few shared Jehangir's opinion of the cinema.[44]

Like Suri, the state characterized film as simply entertaining. Even as the state adamantly maintained that commercial cinema lacked any instructional value (apparently, instructional value was to be found only in state-sponsored documentaries and newsreels), it continued to insist that the medium required regulation and adopted the role of a moral guardian. How did the "public" respond to the state's assumption of this role? Angered by the state's concerns about public morals, Mr. Majumdar and S. Mukerjea from Allahabad, echoing Jehangir's sentiments, sarcastically inquired about the censors' moral health: "The censors proclaim that they cut 'offending' scenes and dialogue lines which would have a degrading effect on the community. They themselves belong to the community and the rest of us are naturally curious to know what effect the deleted portions had on the morals of the censors."[45] Many wondered how the censors remained immune while the public was vulnerable, constantly under the threat of infection. Such queries questioned the construction of film spectators as defenseless. As did Jehangir's, the letter just quoted points to the fact that in the act of fighting immorality, the censors exposed themselves to this contagion. In order for the censors to be inoculated against this contagion, they had to be injected with a strain of the contagion, suggesting that immorality is a part of state practice.[46]

While some readers protested the practice of distinguishing between the censors and the citizens, others called for reform. They argued that current film censorship guidelines limited both freedom of speech and expression, rights that were enshrined in the Constitution of India. Supporting the film industry, Mrs. Leelabai Gambhue from Adilabad argued:

> The film industry is a democratic body run by the people for the people. If censorship means control of the industry[,] such control should be in the hands of the people. The film industry should be allowed to develop without hindrance from the Government. The industry is asked to deliver the goods under conditions which are far from being conducive to the best results. More liberal censorship, accompanied by lighter taxation, would be the best method of promoting the industry's development.[47]

Gambhue advocated self-regulation by the industry rather than state censorship, suggesting that this approach is more democratic and would better advance the industry's growth. Like Gambhue, Kadani Venkatao Rao from Hyderabad questioned the institution of state censorship:

> The censor cuts published in "Filmfare" are completely unjustified. Love and crime are part of life. We see them every day and, if the cinema film depicts them, it is because all art forms mirror life. There are many erotic passages in our ancient literature, but nobody condemns them for being such. The censors contend that films should not criticise the Government or its policy, while the Constitution of the country guarantees freedom of speech and expression to the citizen. When the press itself is free, is there any justification for the censors to deny filmmakers freedom of expression on the screen?[48]

Rao contended that films simply represent life, and if such representations are allowed in literature and newspapers, then cinema should be granted the same rights. Given that the censored portions of films were published in the *Government of India Gazette*, which was available to the public, the state's stance appeared all the more ludicrous. Commenting on the state's practice, H. Suryanarayana from Bangalore wrote: "It is amusing to note that the censor deletions are published in detail in the *Government of India Gazette*. The purpose of censoring is to guard the public from the offending passages in the film. Will not the morals of the public be affected by reading those excerpts?"[49] What assumptions undergird this discriminatory policy? Presumably, audiences who read the *Government of India Gazette* would be educated—and able to read. While as a government publication the *India Gazette* is available to all, it is not necessarily accessible. Anyone familiar with the convoluted machinations of Indian bureaucracy would shirk from seeking out this document. The ability to read, in this case, cannot be separated from a desire to read or from literacy.

This might appear to be simply another instance that demonstrates the state's class bias, yet a nagging question compels me to continue with this inquiry: why is film subjected to prerelease censorship in India, whereas literature, art, and newspapers are entitled to freedom of expression? Successive governments have provided a ready answer: since the cinema possesses greater circulation and influence than do other forms expression, it requires stricter regulation. This visual medium, in the words of Supreme Court Judge M. Hidayatullah, has an "instant appeal" because of "its versatility, realism (often surrealism), and its co-ordination of the visual and aural senses. The motion picture is able to stir up emotions more deeply than any other product of art."[50] The danger of cinema lies in its uncomfortable proximity to reality, its appeal to the senses, and its capacity to rouse emotions.

According to this argument, cinema's fatal flaw is that it neither requires nor promotes cognitive activity, whereas other forms of expression demand thought and interpretation. In other words, while thought and interpretation mediate and perhaps even mitigate the effects of other forms of expression, there is no such mediator between the cinema and its audiences. To presume that cinema's relation with audiences is direct and instantaneous is to forget that visual literacy is acquired. This process is neither natural nor given: one learns how to see. For example, audiences who watch Hindi films slowly become aware of the ingredients required for creating a *masala* movie: the three-hour length, the "intermission," stock characters, melodrama, slapstick comedy, all-too-familiar stories, and songs and dances, to name a few elements. The audiences use this knowledge in *reading* films.

Unfortunately, cinema's relation to thought and to literacy is constantly undermined by arguments such as the one espoused by G. N. Bhattacharya from the University of Allahabad:

> The censors in all countries prevent the exhibition of films harmful to the public and since illiteracy is still widespread in India, we need strict censorship. Most of our film producers exploit the human

weaknesses of the masses. They are concerned only to extract money from them at the box-office, and it is the censor's duty to prevent this type of exploitation. All films that corrupt should be banned. The censors, however, should be more liberal in the case of Western films, because such films are shown to educated audiences.[51]

Bhattacharya's conservative and hackneyed argument, which follows colonial logic in striking ways, informs us that India requires "strict censorship" because widespread illiteracy there makes the masses vulnerable to exploitation. In his letter, film spectators are predominantly the illiterate and therefore infantile "masses." Such a situation demands that the censors become the moral guardians of the nation, protecting the public from the venal film industry. While the illiterate masses need the censors' benevolent protection, the educated audiences can take care of themselves. As literate beings, the educated can understand commercial and "Western" films using tools learned in schools and universities; more important, such tools prevent them from being manipulated, exploited, or influenced by the cinema.[52] Bhattacharya's argument reeks of class bias and reinforces a logic that fails to take account of visual literacy. The opinions presented in these letters give a sense of the relations in which film censorship is enmeshed. Terms such as "democracy," "morality," "tradition," "freedom of expression," "state authority," and "the rights of the film industry and the public" cluster around film censorship; they reemerge in later debates, carrying historical traces.

The Khosla Report and the Kiss

In 1969 concern about increasing sex and violence in films prompted the government to set up a committee to inquire into the existing procedures for certifying films for public exhibition and other, related matters. The committee, a *Filmfare* correspondent stated, made many recommendations concerning the principles of censorship, but the debate on the report focused solely on the representation of sexuality:

The popular interest in either opposing or supporting the kiss and nudity has, by a strange coincidence, clouded other serious recommendations of the committee. It has objected to the length of films, for instance. The indiscriminate use of song-and-dance has rightly come in for severe criticism. Other recommendations: Appointment of a powerful new board of censors, the censor office should be located outside the film-producing cities; the Chairman of the Censor Board should be of the rank of a High Court Judge. But the most important recommendation is listed last in the summary placed in Parliament. It says that should all measures to improve the standard of Indian films fail and should producers continue to put profits above social responsibilities then certain social controls could be imposed on the industry.[53]

With regard to sexuality, the committee advised the censors that if "in telling the story it is logical, relevant or necessary to depict a passionate kiss or a nude human figure, there should be no question of excluding the shot, provided the theme is handled with delicacy and feeling, aiming at aesthetic expression and avoiding all suggestion of prurience or lasciviousness."[54] In fact, during an address to the Rotarians, G. D. Khosla, the committee's chair, asserted: "Our present attitude towards sex, which frowned on nudity and kissing in films, was not grounded in tradition. . . . ancient Indian temple sculpture featured carved human figures in various sexual postures."[55] A flurry of articles and interviews that sought to (re)define Indian tradition followed this report. Whereas the proponents of censorship contended that representations of sexuality such as kissing and "exotic love scenes" were "un-Indian," its opponents argued that such scenes were a part of the Indian tradition.[56]

In the months following the publication of the Khosla report, *Filmfare* was flooded with letters on the representation of sexuality in cinema. P. I. John from Bombay wrote:

> I am surprised at the controversy in and outside Parliament about kissing in Indian films. The people who oppose it contend that it is against our culture. Those who live in cities like Bombay have only to look into the taxis, back seats of public buses and corner benches of public parks. The censors permit shots of lips drawing closer and then a shot of two birds kissing. I think we have outgrown that stage of hypocrisy.[57]

Demonstrating that kissing was a part of Indian culture, John pointed to the prolific amount of kissing in a variety of public places. Was the argument about the existence of kissing or its representation? If it was the former, then John's evidence undoubtedly testifies to the existence of kissing. But the debate concerned not the existence of kissing but its on-screen representation, which raised questions about conduct and definitions of public and private. Sexuality was marked as private, so that the public display of it was deemed improper and indecorous.

Such displays, Mrs. Vijaya Subramaniam from New Delhi asserted, simply imitated Western practices:

> Already there is so much aping of the west in music, moods and morals, thanks to "desi" films. And east is no more east, at least here in India, if one were to believe the films. It is the height of absurdity to cite the example of Khajuraho and other temple art. These sculptures are not viewed by millions as films would be. And then sculpture is a different form of art and cannot be compared to films loaded with sexy scenes. Viewers are drawn to Khajuraho by its artistic merit and historic value rather than by its erotic content. Or do we hope to net foreign audiences by this move: Is lack of kissing at the crucial moment the sole reason why Indian films flop at international festivals? To the Indian cinegoers "muhabbat" [love] has come to mean bear hugging between two buxom persons. There need be no doubt about the story justifying kissing scenes: in fact there will be no justification for any story that does not revolve round and round kissing orgies! The thing will be done to death and Vatsayana put to shame if producers have their way. What is to be done when cinegoers get tired of this apparently new phenomenon? Then nudism will have to be brought in with the help of some new committee! The West, whom we are so eager to copy in its vulgar aspects, has reached a point of no return. Kissing and stark nakednesses have become kid stuff. The "act" is the "thing" now. Is this our goal too?[58]

According to Subramaniam, Hindi cinema endangered Indian culture by imitating and promoting vulgar Western mores and practices. Occupying a prominent role in these debates, the "West" emerged as a central figure in relation to which Indian identity would be forged. "The West," Subramaniam declared, was spiraling into depravity, and by eagerly following in its footsteps, India would do the same, sacrificing its identity in the process. Instead of imitating vulgar aspects of the "West," Subramaniam bemoans, why couldn't India emulate its more worthy traits, such as Western filmmakers' "craze for perfection, technical excellence, eye for detail and quest for fresh subject?"[59]

Interestingly, according to Subramaniam, the West was not totally irredeemable; it possessed valuable attributes from which Indians could learn and through which they could better themselves. In matters concerning sexual conduct, however, India was morally superior and needed to maintain this superiority.[60] The important point here is that the difference between the West and India was not the existence of sexuality but how it was performed. For example, Subramaniam found it utterly absurd to compare the Khajuraho temples to obscene displays of sexuality on the screen. The defining characteristic of the sculptures was not their "erotic content." Rather, they were objects of art, rich in religious and historical value and worthy of pilgrimage. Conversely, commercial films were cheap entertainment, filled with "sex scenes," easily available anywhere to anyone. Subramaniam's statement suggests that the Khajuraho temples merited a place in the domain of national culture, whereas the commercial film industry was a national embarrassment and an eyesore. Such characterizations paralleled the state's own position on cinema. In fact, the state's foray into cinema through the production of documentaries and newsreels and, later, state-sponsored art cinema were attempts to develop a better national cinema.

Unlike Subramaniam, Dikes Mills from Poona wondered why the moral guardians were discriminating against kissing when many other aspects of the West could be found in the narratives of Hindi films:

> The most widely discussed topic in film circles and also among cinegoers is a four letter word—the kiss! . . . Already our films have borrowed everything else from the West: necking scenes, champagne in Paris (followed by an inebriated act), cabarets, imitating James Bond (smudged carbon copy), the seductive girls, and of course, fashion (ranging from Dior to Irene Sharaff) low-cut dresses, plunging necklines. Then why discriminate only against the kiss?[61]

It does seem odd that furor over "the kiss" eclipsed other erotic practices, including scenes where Helen, an Anglo-Indian actress who played a vamp in many commercial Hindi films, performed cabaret dances in low-cut dresses. Why would kissing produce such a virulent reaction? A brief statement in *Filmfare* suggests an answer:

> Recommendations of the Khosla Committee as published in newspapers have been generally welcomed by the South Indian film industry. However, the clause allowing "kissing" and "nudity" is sharply reacted to by many leading artists and others in the industry. The Tamil screen matinee idol, M. G. Ramachandran said he could not even dream of such a development as kissing in Tamil films since he

felt it was wholly against Tamil culture and tradition. It was his considered opinion that this sort of display on the screen would lead to a debasement of the image of Indian womanhood. By the very nature and power of the film medium, this would have grave consequences on Indian life and culture. And as for nudity his reaction was even more violent.[62]

Like Subramaniam, the Tamil superstar M. G. Ramachandran contended that kissing and nudity imperiled Indian "culture and tradition." He astutely voiced comments consonant with his screen image as an abstemious hero. In fact, many of the romantic sequences in his films were conjured by moonstruck female characters. For Ramachandran to have stated otherwise would have imperiled this carefully nurtured persona.[63] According to Ramachandran, "culture and tradition" were inextricably linked to "the image of Indian womanhood." Not only were women viewed as representatives of Indian tradition and culture, but their bodies were overtly and overly marked as sexual bodies.[64]

Within the film industry, the most vocal opponents of nudity and kissing were Hindi film actresses. In response to their opposition, A. K. Singhal from Ahmedabad wrote:

It is surprising to note that some prominent film actresses came out with the puritanical statement that with the introduction of kissing, no self-respecting woman would like to take to acting. They don't mind overstepping the bounds in London, Paris and New York, but once back in India they want to present themselves as the embodiment of ideal Indian womanhood. When our Asha Parekhs and Meena Kumaris can act in scenes which involve passionate embraces and allow themselves to be kissed all over except for the lips, why do they suddenly turn shy when it comes to kissing?[65]

In an industry where women's sexual mores have always been under suspicion, the actresses' stance is not that surprising. Initially identified as "loose," the women who first entered the film industry in India consisted of Anglo-Indians, prostitutes, dancers, and vaudeville performers. This label of "looseness" derived from their class status and racial background. Moreover, it reflected deep-seated cultural practices and attitudes regarding women. Traditionally, women from middle- and upper-middle-class Muslim and Hindu families were kept behind a screen, hidden from the gaze of strangers. This partition is known by the Urdu word *purdah*, which means "screen" or "veil." Purdah was a sign of modesty and honor; modest and respectable women remained behind the screen. But the word *purdah* refers to the cinematic screen as well, so that these cultural attitudes were translated into the world of film: only "loose women" moved to the front of the screen and allowed strangers (especially men) to look at them. Thus censorship, which "veils" the kiss, is productive of the screen of gender and the gender of the screen.

In the 1930s Devika Rani, an upper-class Brahmin woman, was hailed for breaking these taboos and easing the path for upper- and middle-class women to enter the industry. Even now, however, when actresses from upper-middle- and middle-class families are quite prominent, these mores continue to govern the fate of their careers; they remain sexually suspect. Film magazines are filled with gossip about the private lives of both actors and actresses but appear to be particularly concerned with the marital status of actresses. If an actress gets married or contemplates getting married, film magazines herald the end of her career. As a married woman, an actress cannot romance with screen heroes; such acting would be deemed disrespectful and dishonorable. Moreover, her primary duty is supposed to be to her husband and his family rather than to her career. Actresses do continue to act after marriage, but their roles diminish considerably in both number and romantic content.[66]

While public discourse on cinema constructed actresses as sexual suspects, Hindi films exacerbated the situation by typecasting actresses as either the "good" or the "bad" woman. Audiences strongly identified film stars with their roles; therefore, "real-life" statements contrary to the roles they played could damage their image. When Singhal sarcastically remarks that these actresses could "overstep the bounds" in Western cities but wanted to "present themselves as the embodiment of ideal Indian womanhood" once back in their own country, he unwittingly points to the cultural boundaries that supposedly divide India from the West.[67] The fact that these actresses adopt the role of ideal Indian womanhood at home and perhaps a less than ideal role abroad does not signify hypocrisy. Rather, it sadly testifies to their limited roles both at home and abroad.

In addition to noting hypocrisy in their conduct at home and abroad, Singhal also takes offense at the fact that these actresses accept scenes with abundant kissing everywhere but on the lips. Singhal's grammatical structure allows women limited sexual agency: they "allow themselves to be kissed"; they do not themselves kiss. Why are lips considered to be a sacred and forbidden domain? In fact, Bombay cinema is littered with scenes that enact the "sacred and forbidden" nature of this particular sexual act: the shy heroine turning away as the camera's gaze and the hero's lips draw closer to hers, followed by a quick cut to flowers or birds kissing each other. Such dramatization constructs the kiss as private and hidden—and as that which is unrealized.

Tales of film censorship tell us that this situation did not always exist: kissing and nudity were represented in Indian films in preindependence India. In fact, one writer informs us that

> before 1947, the British passed a film after determining whether it was anti-British or not. The semi-nude dances, the kisses were all there. After 1947, the deshi government started spoon-feeding the public on their conception of morality. Any exposure to nudity, any conception of sex or other facts of life was thought of as a corrupting factor.[68]

While reading the certification board's reports from the 1920s and the 1930s at the National Film Archive of India, I found several references to scenes of kissing and nudity. The examining committees often asked the producers to shorten a prolonged kiss or nude scene or to remove excessive scenes of passion. The committees did not ban kissing or nude scenes; rather, they modified them. They were concerned not about the existence of kissing or nude scenes but about the amount of sexuality represented on-screen. In the certification board's reports from the late 1930s and the 1940s, references to scenes of kissing and nudity disappeared. Emerging in their stead is an increasing and fervent obsession with anticolonial and pronationalist sentiments. It is easy to understand why the colonial state was more worried about the rising nationalist fervor, both in real life and in representations, than about depictions of sexuality. The disappearance of scenes containing kissing and nudity, however, is more difficult to understand.[69]

As it was centralizing censorship in 1951, India's postindependence government gathered and combined censorship guidelines from different regional offices. While most of the guidelines contained rules restricting the representation of sexuality, only the Bombay office had a guideline restricting kissing in particular. The new guidelines produced by the postindependence government reiterated that sexuality needed to be restricted, but they did not define sexuality or list forbidden sexual acts; they say nothing about the need to censor the kiss in particular. How did the kiss become a representation of sexuality that would be censored? Madhava Prasad interprets this prohibition as a way to differentiate India from the West, to assert India's cultural difference and shore up its national identity. He also reads this prohibition as a site of informal negotiation between the postcolonial state and indigenous patriarchy. The kiss marks a space of privacy and nuclear family, so that its public display poses a threat to the indigenous patriarchy, which normally polices sexuality and subjecthood in structures such as the joint family.[70]

Given Prasad's argument, how does one explain the reappearance of the kiss in commercial Hindi cinema following economic liberalization, especially when the Indian family and culture were seemingly imperiled? I propose that the transformation of the on-screen family coupled with the emergence of the multiplex and a liberalization of censorship enabled this reappearance. Most scholarship on the postliberalization resurgence of "family films" contends that the family assists in dealing with the onslaught of liberalization. While Sangita Gopal does not deny this function of the family, she perceptively points out that the family supports rather than restricts desires; in short, the family, along with the state, is liberalized.[71] In addition, single-screen exhibition prevailed in the period central to Prasad's analysis, and family audiences dominated these theaters. Members of the film industry assumed that on-screen kissing would alienate these audiences, but the postliberalization rise of multiplexes and introduction of simultaneous screenings abroad have drawn new audiences—youth, professionals, couples, and diasporic audiences. Unlike the family audiences envisioned by the film industry, these new audiences, it is presumed, are drawn to rather than disaffected by such "realistic" representations of sexuality. To allay concerns and retain its old audiences, the Bombay film industry has also been attempting to reconcile on-screen kissing with the "family entertainer."[72] In addition to demographic shifts at the site of exhibition, changes have occurred in the practices of state censorship, too. Previously, a kissing scene might have been chopped or the film might have been granted an A certificate, limiting its potential audience. As liberalization has proceeded, films containing lip-locks, especially ones made by respected production houses and directors, have generally received UA certificates.

The media continues to give ample coverage to the kiss: showering attention on kisses by prominent stars; dubbing the actor Emraan Hashmi a "serial kisser," since he seems to kiss in every film he's in; publicizing the seventeen kisses in *Khwaish* (2003; Desire); noting that the fastidious Aamir Khan agrees to only two kisses per film; and circulating the rote statement by (mainly) actresses and actors that they will kiss only if a scene requires it. I suggest that this coverage of the kiss is a respectful nod to the feudal family, even as the industry, practices of censorship, and many Indian families themselves move away from it.

The K. A. Abbas Case

While the Khosla report suggested administrative reforms and changes in censorship with respect to kissing and nudity, N. N. Satchitanand noted that it kept silent on subjects such as "administrative corruption, political craft, [and] judicial inefficiency" and lamented these lacunae:

> Those are burning problems in contemporary India, but unfortu-
> nately, the most far-reaching medium is forbidden to tackle them.
> When the Press can write so freely about them, why should the
> Cinema be barred from exposing them? In fact there are many film
> makers and writers who want to boldly tackle these subjects and
> if they are allowed to, the Indian cinema, especially in the Hindi
> medium can acquire strength and quality and purpose. Otherwise
> it will remain just an adolescent peepshow with the advent of liberal
> censorship. Why for example, does K. A. Abbas' film, "A Tale of Four
> Cities," remain banned? Is it because it dares to show the prevalence
> of prostitution in Indian cities? Is reality then to be shunned by the
> Indian cinema because it shocks, or reveals the carelessness of the
> authorities and the Government? Where then is the much vaunted
> Freedom of expression which we are supposed to enjoy? It is a pity
> the Khosla Commission did not tackle these restrictions in as bold
> and forthright a manner as it did those on sex.[73]

Soon after the release of the report, K. A. Abbas, a filmmaker and a member of the Khosla committee, challenged for the first time the legal standing of censorship in India's Supreme Court. He objected to the censorship code and prior restraint on films. The examining committee had given Abbas an A certificate for his short documentary film *A Tale of Four Cities*, but he refused to accept its decision.

After presenting his case to a series of committees that rejected his petition, Abbas finally took his case to the Supreme Court, which ruled in his favor and granted the film a U certificate without the cuts previously ordered. While ruling in Abbas's favor, however, the Supreme Court also affirmed the necessity of film censorship. Supreme Court Judge M. Hidayatullah's decision, quoted previously, sets out the argument:

The treatment of motion pictures must be different from that of other forms of art expression. This arises from the instant appeal of the motion picture, its versatility, realism (often surrealism), and its co-ordination of the visual and aural senses. The motion picture is able to stir up emotions more deeply than any other product of art. Its effect particularly on children and adolescents is very great since their immaturity makes them more willingly suspend their disbelief than mature men and women. Therefore, classification of films into two categories of "U" films and "A" films is a reasonable classification.[74]

The judgment stated that film should be regulated because it affects audiences more strongly than do other media; specifically, films can harm the development of children and adolescents. It thus relied on and reproduced the dominant practice of conceiving film spectators as vulnerable and susceptible "children and adolescents." Once more, the state transforms into a surrogate parent who protects the youth from harm.

The court did not see prior restraint or censorship guidelines as problematic; rather, it viewed the lack of distinction between "artistic and inartistic presentations" as the central defect:

[The] real flaw in the scheme is the total absence of any direction which would tend to preserve art and promote it. The artistic appeal or presentation of an episode robs it of its vulgarity and harm and this appears to be completely forgotten. Artistic as well as inartistic presentations are treated alike and also what may be socially good and useful and what may not.[75]

In the court's view, then, the Abbas case highlighted the need for nuanced judgment that could distinguish between the "artistic" and the "inartistic." To further explain this point, the court cited *Ranjit D. Udeshi vs. State of Maharashtra*:

It has held the test of obscenity to adopt in India is that obscenity without a preponderating social purpose or profit cannot have the constitutional protection of free speech and expression, and obscenity is treating sex in a manner appealing to the carnal side of human nature or having that tendency. The obscene matter in a book must be considered by itself and separately to find out whether it is so gross and its obscenity so decided that it is likely to deprave and corrupt those whose minds are open to influences of this sort and into whose hands the book is likely to fall. In this connection the interests of our contemporary society and particularly the influence of the book on it must not be overlooked.[76]

The judgment in *Ranjit D. Udeshi vs. State of Maharashtra* was based on sections 292, 293, and 294 of the Indian Penal Code, which regulates obscenity in India and is a remnant of its colonial legacy. By citing this case as well as section 292 of the code, the court sought to clarify the distinction between works of "art" (not obscene) and inartistic presentations. According to the judgment in *Ranjit D. Udeshi v. State of Maharashtra*, classification as "art" exempts a work from the charge of obscenity; conversely, a work characterized as inartistic is suspect of obscenity. This judgment contended that works of "art" are socially redeeming because they do not aim to arouse sexual desires, whereas the inartistic lack any redeeming value and simply seek to arouse "baser" desires. This definition reveals that the representation of sexuality formed the sole criterion for determining obscenity. And the court was charged with determining who this material affected and how it affected them.

Censorship during and after the Emergency

An account of censorship in India would be incomplete without referring to the events that transpired during the nineteen months of the Emergency (discussed in Chapter 1). Members of the film industry and media often describe this as a period of utter chaos when the central government arbitrarily censored works and forbade printing or exhibiting anything that challenged the state's authority. During this period, Indira Gandhi's government contended that these sanctions were necessary to reestablish discipline and order. The public, however, understood that the sanctions were imposed so that Gandhi could retain power. When she eventually called elections in 1977, she lost, and the Janata Party, headed by Morarji Desai, came to power.

The Janata Party promoted itself as committed to democracy and freedom of speech. In this spirit, it reviewed the situation regarding film censorship and acknowledged the need to develop fresh guidelines to encourage the growth of good films.[77] However, there was no substantive change in the government's approach toward vulgarity, obscenity, depictions of lasciviousness or violence, and the like.[78] Moreover, members of the film industry soon discovered that the Janata government matched Indira Gandhi's in its concern about on-screen representations of the state and challenges to its authority.[79] The Emergency was a repressive assertion of state power, but to view it as an anomalous event that interrupted the normal course of "democracy" would be to miss an important lesson about the nature of power. The continuity between the practices of Indira Gandhi's Congress Party and the those of the Janata Party with regard to state censorship reveals that the exercise of power did not disappear in a democratic society.

In 1980 Indira Gandhi's Congress Party returned to power, and the Working Group on National Film Policy, which had been set up in 1979 by the previous Janata government, submitted its report.[80] The group forcefully voiced its disapproval of government intervention, criticizing the "revisional powers" (power to overrule) of the central government, which enabled it to meddle in the affairs of the CBFC. In addition, the group spoke out against the oft-deployed practice of political patronage in selecting members of the CBFC. For the most part, this report made recommendations with respect to the production, distribution, and exhibition of art films, which it urged the government to support.[81] The group also reviewed the extant system of certification and suggested the inclusion of two new certificates, namely, UA and Q. The UA certificate would be an intermediary between the U and A certificates; the Q certificate, which would qualify the others, would mark a film as a "quality" product. Unlike the UA certificate, the Q certificate was never put into operation, though it was revived in 1998 in the Bharatiya Janata Party's cultural manifesto. While Nandana Bose points to the Q certificate's pertinence to the Bharatiya Janata Party's Hindu Right agenda, historical research indicates that recommendations for the certificate emerged first in the Khosla report, then in the working group's recommendations, and subsequently in the Bharatiya Janata Party's manifesto.[82] The certificate's history indicates that progressive, center, and right-wing forces all have been invested in deploying certification to define and produce "quality" cinema.

In 1983 the rules governing the certification of films for public exhibition were amended again. The new amendment renamed the Central Board of Film Censors as the Central Board of Film Certification, which indicated that the board was to function in a "positive" rather than "negative" fashion. It also introduced two more classifications: UA for unrestricted but subject to parent's permission for children younger than twelve and S for public exhibition restricted to "members of any profession or any class of persons having regard to the nature, content and theme of the film"—in short, *specialists*. These new classifications produced further divisions in the population, thereby creating new subjects, namely, the *adolescent* and the *specialist*.

I argue that these categories were instituted to manage the effects of new genres that emerged in the 1970s, the teen romance and sex-educa-tion films.[83] The UA classification, which targets the adolescent, can be seen as a technique for producing knowledge about the adolescent; such knowledge has the potential to circumscribe the representation of sexual-ity. The S classification allowed specialists such as physicians and medical students to view, say, anatomy films as a part of their professional develop-ment—and prevented the "masses," who might be titillated by such films, from having access to them. These new classifications increased the regu-latory powers of the state and enabled it to manage its population.

Technology and Economic Liberalization

In the 1980s both the state and the commercial film industry encoun-tered threats in the form of new media: cable and video. Whereas the state wondered how to regulate these new media, the film industry sought ways to lure audiences to theaters. Many viewers found that it was cheaper to rent a video and a VCR than to buy theater tickets. In addition, viewers had access to pirated videos of new or prohibited films. Cable television[84] also increased access to films and other programs. In any neighborhood, viewers could easily ask their local cable service to screen films or pro-grams of their choice. The fact that these new media circumvented state authority and in the process gave the public access to unregulated material provoked the anxieties of the state. What was at stake was the exercise of control over mediating technologies—and the nation. The state sought to expand its control over these technologies and the nation by passing new laws that policed video piracy and required video certification.[85] Further-more, the dip in the film industry's profits also affected state revenue. With fewer viewers attending theaters, the state lost a portion of the entertain-ment tax on film tickets, which tended to be exorbitant.

During the 1990s audiences returned to theaters to see megaproduc-tions such as *Hum aapke hain koun?* (1994; What is my relation to you?) and *Dilwale dulhania le jayenge* (1995), which raked in profits, but new media continued to be a problem for the state and the film industry. With the advent of liberalization, the state and the film industry encountered a powerful adversary in the form of satellite television. Since satellite televi-sion was not subject to state censorship, it provided viewers easy access to films and programs prohibited by the state. Because satellite television easily breached state authority, state censorship appeared to be pointless. The film industry added to the state's troubles by pressing for more liberal censorship guidelines with respect to sex and violence so that it could compete with satellite television. With the state, the film industry, and the citizenry all anxious about these changes, the 1990s saw vigorous debate about the relevant issues: How could the state reestablish its authority? How could the film industry compete with new forms of entertainment? How would the quantity and quality of available entertainment change the social fabric? How could India protect its culture and traditions from the onslaught of Western culture and values represented in the films, sitcoms, and soap operas shown via satellite television?

In 1991 and again in 1994, the government sought to bolster its authority by asserting that various complaints regarding objectionable scenes and songs compelled it to revise and reissue its censorship guidelines. The government issued a list of objectionable material and asked the Central Board of Film Certification to ensure that

> human sensibilities are not offended by vulgarity, obscenity or
> depravity; such dual meaning words which obviously cater to baser
> instincts are not allowed; scenes degrading or denigrating women
> in any manner are not presented; scenes involving sexual violence
> against women like attempt to rape, rape or any form of molestation,
> or scenes of a similar nature are avoided, and if any such incident is
> germane to the theme, they shall be reduced to the minimum and no
> details are shown.[86]

This list suggests the following notions: sex is base, and (hetero)sexual exposure denigrates women; a form of sexual exposure, the representation of rape or sexual violence is a problem because it dishonors women; and not only are female bodies overly and overtly marked as sexual bodies, but these bodies are also required to maintain an "honorable" status. For the most part, however, the focus on sexualized representations of women has overlooked other images that might be denigrating, such as representations of the good, self-sacrificing wife, the long-suffering mother, or the dutiful daughter. During my fieldwork in Bombay, I asked Shakti Samanta, then the CBFC chairperson, if the board had ever considered censoring such images because they too promote sexist stereotyping and consequently are denigrating to women. He immediately retorted, "Why would we censor those images? There are no protests against them." Samanta's riposte was factually incorrect; there had been protests against these and related themes.[87] The postcolonial state's failure to take account of such images cannot be understood as a simple oversight, for it had enabled the (re)formation of patriarchal alliances in the Indian nation-state, especially during the advent of economic liberalization, when the Indian family was assumed to be under threat.

In the 1990s bawdy commercial film songs (which I discuss in greater depth in Chapter 7, on *Khalnayak*), as well as Shekhar Kapur's *Bandit Queen* (1994), Deepa Mehta's *Fire* (1996) and Mira Nair's *Kama Sutra* (1996), were the focus of incendiary debates on censorship because they disrupted structures of heternormativity and gender central to conventional under-standings of the Indian family and Indian film history. The three films brought explicit sexuality to Indian screens, showcasing detailed lesbian and heterosexual lovemaking scenes.[88] Similarly, Deepa Mehta's *Water* (2005), which focuses on the lives of widows in Varansi, encountered pro-tests by members of the Hindu Right during its production in 2000. In April 2003 the CBFC refused to certify Sridhar Rangayan's *Gulabi aaina* (The pink mirror), which focuses on transsexuals, calling it "full of vulgar-ity and obscenity."[89] These films were spectacularized via national, interna-tional, and scholarly debates.[90] Drawing on Annette Kuhn's insights, I sug-gest these films became marketable and earned accolades in part because of their status as forbidden objects; this status was produced by the widely discussed and circulated knowledge that the films had been censored; the labels "banned" and "censored" became advertising gimmicks to entice global and local audiences. Thus, censorship often fuels desire, resulting in an increase in revenue (both material and symbolic) for filmmakers and film industries. These advertising gimmicks also shape perceptions of nation-states; those permitting exhibition take on a democratic sheen, while those prohibiting screenings are deemed repressive.[91]

As I mentioned in Chapter 1, this book focuses on 1970–1996. The cases of *Water* and *Gulabi aaina* illustrate that sexuality continued to play a central role in debates on censorship during the twenty-first century's first decade. Moreover, the following discussion of the XA certification points to my theoretical framework's relevance for studying contempo-rary censorship debates. In 2002 Vijay Anand, a well-known filmmaker and the chair of the CBFC, proposed a comprehensive review of the 1952 Cinematograph Act. Anand made a number of suggestions that included granting the CBFC fiscal autonomy and selecting members for its advi-sory panels on professional rather than political considerations. His most provocative plan, however, received maximum media coverage, namely, the introduction of an XA certificate that would legalize screening of "soft-core" pornographic films in select cinemas. Anand advocated fol-lowing the rating systems used in the United States and Britain because he believed that, unlike prohibition, certification would *reduce* desire. In addition—though Anand did not state this—certifying such films would allow the government to share in their lucrative profits via high taxation.[92] Moreover, these profits would be legal, unlike the *haftas* (bribes) exhibitors and distributors paid local police officers to screen such films. Anand's proposal angered the Ministry of Information and Broadcasting, which barred the CBFC from discussing such proposals internally. Later, Anand resigned and was replaced by a Bharatiya Janata Party politician, Arvind Trivedi, who espoused conservative views. In an interview Trivedi unequivocally stated, "I am completely against such a proposal [XA certification]. It is against our culture and does not reflect nicely on our society. . . . I would hate this kind of cinema."[93] Trivedi served as an interim chair and was soon replaced by an industry stalwart, Anupam Kher.[94] Kher was himself sacked by the United Progressive Alliance when it came to power in 2004 and initiated a "detoxification" campaign. These shifts in the CBFC leadership, all reflecting the political agendas of changing governments, disclose the board's relatively weak position within the state hierarchy. Moreover, they reveal a lack of consensus within the state about censorship, cinema, and sexuality.

Whereas Anand recommended more liberal reforms in his comprehensive review, T. Subbarami Reddy submitted an amendment to the Rajya Sabha in 2002 that called for strengthening the restrictions against "excess sex, vulgarity, and violence," which he said were "corroding the morals and values of the people and thereby, creating negative impact on the minds of the people, especially the youth."[95] This amendment sought to change not only the guidelines but also the structure of the boards. It noted that women had limited representation on the board and that their representation needed to be increased so that they could police films "which depict women in an indecent manner."[96]

The first decade of the twenty-first century also witnessed disputes on important political documentaries including *Jang aur aman* (2001; War and Peace) and *Final Solution* (2004), which deal with violence, gender, and religion.[97] To curtail the circulation of such films, the Hindu Right sought to expand the realm of censorship in 2005 by demanding certification of Indian films shown at film festivals. As a rejoinder, three hundred filmmakers organized the "Campaign against Censorship" and later formed an organization called "Films for Freedom."[98] In 2006 the Congress Party–led government formulated a law that ostensibly allowed both domestic and foreign films to be exhibited without certificates; however, a cursory look at this regulation demonstrates that both nonstate and state authorities regulate the screening of films at festivals.[99]

I close this chapter by considering the Ministry of Information and Broadcasting's newly proposed Draft Cinematograph Bill of 2010. The draft opens with the statement that "processes of certification of films" need to be updated in order to keep up with "the changed times and also to make it an effective tool to combat piracy."[100] The architects of the bill invited comments from the "general public/stakeholders" by April 15, 2010.[101] The tenor of this note underscores India's status as a liberal democracy that values its citizens' opinions. A quick perusal of the contents, however, reveals that despite the ministry's expressed desire to craft a bill in step with the twenty-first century, the document for the most part remains entrenched in the twentieth century, continuing to bear traces of the nation's colonial legacy. Like the Cinematograph Act of 1952, the draft bill paves the way for government intervention by constructing potential viewers as vulnerable and immature audiences who cannot resist the visual and aural pleasures of the screen. Nonetheless, it introduces some noteworthy changes. First, in an effort to extend the state's technological reach, the draft provides a more detailed explanation of the term *cinematograph*: "'Cinematograph' means any apparatus, product or device, analogue or digital or any other technology, used for representation of moving pictures or series of pictures."[102] Its new definition for *exhibition*, however, is fairly broad. For example, there is no attempt to distinguish between public and private or for-profit and nonprofit exhibitions: "Exhibition means display of cinematograph film or making available a cinematograph film to persons not directly connected with the production, distribution, promotion and certification of that film."[103] The sweeping nature of this definition appears to grant the state authority to regulate all forms of exhibition and distribution. Its breath, however, raises questions about the possibility of administering such a policy.

The next two changes are directed at the structure of the CBFC. The draft proposes that women should constitute "at least one-third" of its members and the advisory panels.[104] While one might think this is a nod to "affirmative action," the previously mentioned 2002 amendment suggests that more is at stake in choosing women rather than members of other less-advantaged groups. Similar to Vijay Anand's proposal, the draft notes that the appointed chairperson, members of the board, and advisory panels must possess either experience or professional credentials or be deemed esteemed public figures.[105] These administrators would be *experts*, not mere political appointees. This shift would provide state censorship with cultural capital that in turn would assist in legitimizing its operations.

The final set of changes pertains to certification. The 1952 Cinematograph Act stipulated that certificates be valid for ten years, after which they had to be renewed. Ostensibly this rule enabled censorship practices to adapt to changes and to reflect contemporary mores. The 2010 draft has no stipulations regarding the period of validity. Whereas the earlier act required all promotional material to display the certificate prominently but mandated no penalties for violators, the new version adds a penalty for flouting this requirement. This disciplinary mechanism seeks to reinforce the state's categorization and reading of the films. Furthermore, following the British Board of Film Classification, the draft introduces two new certification categories, twelve and older and fifteen and older, to replace the UA certificate. The earlier UA certificate invited parents to evaluate whether a film was appropriate for their children; the new categories make no such attempt. Media reports suggest these categories emerged from discussions with filmmakers who believe that the earlier certification system put a dent into their profits by reducing their audiences. These new categories reveal how certification tailors films' potential markets (I discuss this further in Chapters 5 and 8). They also illustrate that the practices of Indian state censorship are forged not in isolation but in continuous dialogue with other nation-states. Moreover, they show that Britain still plays a vital role in shaping practices in postcolonial India. Finally, the most interesting aspect of the draft bill is its effort to link certification and copyright to control piracy: "if the applicant for the certificate in Section 6 is the producer, as defined in Section 2 (uu) of The Copyright Act, 1957, then the certificate granted to him under this section shall be deemed to be evidence of copyright owned by him respect of the cinematograph film."[106] Film-processing labs are advised that they will be penalized for circulating unauthorized negatives or copies of films. According to the statement, labs should give a negative or a copy of a film only to the applicant for the certificate—that is, the copyright holder.

The subsequent chapters do not offer detailed investigations of contemporary films and policies, but my model of inquiry, which attends to practices of cutting, certifying, and classifying, is pertinent for analyzing them. The current Cinematograph Act is about to be replaced, making it all the more important not only to consider the state form at a macrolevel but also to investigate its micropractices. Having mapped the broad contours of debates on censorship in this chapter, I will be able to offer counterhistories in the next chapter and the subsequent case studies.

3 | Close-Up
The Central Board of Film Certification

It was a dark and stormy night. Do you smile at this introduction?
Allow me to submit for your consideration the saying that tales
with unoriginal beginnings are those most likely later to surprise.
—MOHSIN HAMID, *MOTH SMOKE*

As I noted in Chapter 1, the material that I gathered during the course of my fieldwork was uneven and incomplete; it was also quite banal, which compounded my anxiety and made me quite nervous about the future writing process. I learned that the topic of film censorship was not as sensational as I had imagined. During interviews, my questions about film censorship in India generally brought forth a spate of generic answers from many officials. They included a brief history of Indian cinema beginning with Dada Phalke and proceeding to other luminaries, as well as an account of important events, government reports, and major players in the history of censorship. These officials also urged me to read Aruna Vasudev's *Liberty and Licence*, which I examine in Chapter 1. Vasudev's work covered much of the terrain that they treaded in our conversations, indicating how a narrative of censorship had been both standardized and institutionalized.

Much later, as I expressed my frustration about the "unsuccessful" interviews in conversations with friends and colleagues, I realized that my search for interesting reflections had blinded me to the importance of the banal. In *Eichmann in Jerusalem* Hannah Arendt offers a thoughtful and provocative conceptualization of banality. She demonstrates that the Holocaust was an effect of power that was produced by "normal" human beings following routines, procedures, and habits. Arendt's insights enabled me to think critically about the normal, the daily, and the routine in the context of film censorship in India and to situate both my "successful" and "unsuccessful" encounters as part and parcel of banal processes.[1] Whereas Foucault's work led me to focus on the specific practices of state censorship, reading Arendt compelled me to reflect on their routine nature. During my fieldwork, though, I was happy and relieved when I was able to conduct interviews that offered new information and to learn about the workings of the Central Board of Film Certification (CBFC).

I had been warned beforehand that I was unlikely to obtain permission to view the CBFC's records because of the convoluted nature of Indian bureaucracy in general and the secretive disposition of the CBFC in particular. My eventual access to the records and my opportunity to interview officials and examining committee members, as well as the serendipitous chance to view films with the "censors," were mediated by formal and informal means. Official letters from the University of Minnesota and the National Film Archives of India testifying to my academic credentials paved my way, as did the images of me as a "fellow career woman," "daughter," or "child" among the various civil servants, officials, and examining committee members with whom I interacted. The privileges accorded to me were also a result of the generosity of officials who wished to remain anonymous.

The Central Board of Certification at Work

The CBFC is a branch of India's Ministry of Information and Broadcasting. The chairperson and members of this board are appointed by the central government (the chair usually for three years and the members typically for two). The roughly twelve to twenty-five board members generally consist of prominent judges, journalists, politicians, and members of the film industry. For the most part, board members do not participate in the daily work of viewing and certifying films, though sometimes they are called to advise on difficult cases. The chairperson generally serves as spokesperson, addressing queries and concerns about censorship from the public, journalists, and members of the industry. The work of viewing and certifying films is carried out by advisory panels—examining committees and revising committees—located at the regional centers. First, an examining committee offers its appraisal of a film. If the producer is unhappy with the decision, he or she can appeal the decision, sending the film to a revising committee for further evaluation. A producer who is still not satisfied can request the Film Appellate Tribunal, located in Delhi, to review the film. After the tribunal rules, the producer has the option of appealing to the head of the Ministry of Information and Broadcasting or taking legal action. As I noted in Chapter 1, this multitiered system not only points to the diffuse nature of power but also buttresses the democratic ethos of the Indian state. In short, it seeks to construct censorship as a democratic process.

The CBFC bureau in Bombay, where I observed examining committees at work, is one of nine film certification offices; the others are located in Bangalore, Calcutta, Cuttack, Delhi, Guawahati, Hyderabad, Madras, and Trivandrum.[2] Bombay's is the "main" office in the bureaucratic hierarchy and the most recognized. Its stature is due in part to its location in the heart of the prominent Hindi film industry, which dominates other regional film industries in terms of reach; this reach, in turn, is due in part to the fact that Hindi, one of India's official languages, is compulsory in central government schools and employed in central government offices. As I outline in Chapter 2, the institution of censorship was centralized after independence, and guidelines used by different offices were merged and recrafted into a single document for application throughout India. The new configuration constituted an attempt to produce a standardized culture through the uniform application of censorship guidelines.[3]

The use of multiple branches enables the division of immense labor. In 1995, for example, the CBFC issued certificates to 3,532 works, 2,204 on film and 1,328 on video.[4] It also enables offices to recruit members who know not only the languages of the films they will be evaluating but also the specific film cultures of the productions. Nonetheless, despite the attempt to use the uniform application of the CBFC's twenty-eight censorship guidelines to produce a standardized national culture, differences among regional offices persist, as does concern about these variations. Both officials and directors told me that producers often went to Hyderabad and Madras to obtain film certificates because these offices were more lenient with respect to representations of sex and violence. At one point I accompanied an official to watch Ram Gopal Verma's *Daud* (1997);[5] the official had heard that the Hyderabad office had passed racy scenes and wanted to inspect the film. This drew my attention to three points: the presence of the multiple branches enabled producers to evade strict state censorship; the varied film cultures and audiences disrupted the state's attempts to produce a homogeneous culture; and state censors did not simply police films but also informally regulated their own practices.

The CBFC's Bombay office has about 100 members drawn from the public, including housewives, doctors, journalists, teachers, civil servants, and members of the film industry, among others; mostly, the members were chosen from the middle class. This membership nods to the ethos of a democratic state in not being restricted to bureaucrats, and it blurs the boundaries between state and civil society by inviting public participation in an ostensibly state enterprise; nevertheless, it also demonstrates the continuing importance of class. The membership, in a word, reflects the "ideal" citizen of the Indian nation.

Officials and examining committee officials whom I had interviewed said that there were two ways of becoming a member, either filing an application or being the beneficiary of political patronage. Their comments revealed how the informal exercise of power helped shape the membership of an ostensibly formal institution. During the course of my fieldwork, I had the opportunity to ask members of *Die Hard*'s examining committee how they had been selected, how they viewed their role in this process, and what they thought of censorship. They generally responded that they had applied for the position and thought that they had been selected because they were representative of the larger public. They believed that censorship was necessary for the protection of children, lower classes, and Indian moral values and for the "proper" representation of Indian culture; for the most part, they viewed their participation as an act of public service. While the members listed these laudable reasons for their participation, the presiding officer provided me with the more mundane ones. Although most members repudiated Hindi films, the officer noted that they preferred attending and examining those films and remarked that the benefits of viewing a Hindi film included the prestige associated with attending the first showing of a film and the charm of being paid by the state, albeit only 100 rupees, to watch a Hindi film.[6]

During the course of my fieldwork, there was some discussion among the members about the entry of lower-class, "uncouth members." These new members had supposedly been appointed because they had assisted particular government officials in their election campaigns. The older members lamented that censorship would become lenient and less rigorous, with a greater number of erotic and violent scenes being allowed in certified films. They were also concerned that these new members would damage the respectable image of the certification board. Their discussion confirmed the importance of class in the makeup of the CBFC membership.

An examining committee formed to evaluate a "long film" (e.g., a feature film or documentary) comprises four to five members, including the regional officer; two of these members must be women. In the case of a

LIVERPOOL JOHN MOORES UNIVERSITY
LEARNING SERVICES

"short film," only one member and the regional officer are required to be present, and one of the two must be a woman. One might well wonder, however, why the rules accord "equitable" representation only to women and not to, say, Muslims or lower castes.[7] The answer lies in the way the inclusion of women addresses the two-pronged concern of modernity and tradition. It emphasizes the postcolonial state's commitment to gender equality and buttresses its democratic ethos. In the language of film distribution, women are generally clubbed with the family; both constitute crucial film markets and are imagined as audiences who are likely to reject obscene and excessively violent films. This vision of film distribution likely informs the selection of women on examining committees, for the state presumes that women will police the boundaries of sex and violence, in effect standing in for the family. In her humorous and thoughtful first-hand account of serving on examining committees, Kobita Sarkar notes that, unlike the male members, the female members were more troubled by representations of violence than of sexuality.[8] Sarkar's comments partly challenge the view, common among both film distributors and the state, that places women (or at least "good" middle-class women) and sexuality in opposition to each other.

Examining committees are formed after an application form filed by film producers or their staff members is approved. Generally, all film producers or their staff must submit an application[9] with a prescribed fee to one of the regional centers.[10] In the case of domestic films, the production location—the place where the film title is registered or the production office is located—determines which office will evaluate the film. Some producers creatively respond to the form's question about place of production to secure an evaluation at a more lenient regional office.[11] Three additional points regarding this form are noteworthy. First, in five places the application directs the producer to address questions related to language and dubbing, revealing a concern with both sound and national and regional identities. The concern with sound is further demonstrated by a rule in the Cinematograph Act of 1952, which requires the producer to submit "complete films" including the background score and sound effects.[12] Second, the application requires the producer to indicate both the type of film being submitted—"newsreel/documentary/scientific/educational/ feature/advertisement film"—and the desired type of certificate. Both pieces of information shape the evaluation of the film. The latter also shows how state censorship shapes filmmaking, since a film producer who desires, for example, a U certificate is likely to know the elements that would jeopardize receiving this certificate (see appendix A). Third, the form solicits details about any advice concerning censorship that the producer might have received. This question creates an *official* space for exerting *informal* power. As I will show, this power served to smoothen *Gupt gyan*'s journey through the CBFC.

Out of a pool of roughly one hundred persons, four or five members are chosen to form a unique examining committee to evaluate each film, after which a date is set for viewing. For security purposes, the committee members, excluding the regional officer, are given information about the film only on arriving at the designated theater. This rule was instituted to prevent any breach of confidentiality by members who might find it difficult to resist bribes; the rule, however, assumes that a regional officer is able to resist such temptations. Information about these viewings is easily available to film producers, who generally know how to circumvent official rules via informal means. When the committee members gather at the theater, they are told the title of the film they will be viewing and are given forms on which they will later write their individual assessments. The form suggests that they "study the guidelines issued by the Government" before viewing the film.[13] During the course of my viewings with the committee members, I did not see anyone who reviewed these guidelines before a screening.

After screening the film, the members discuss it and fill out individual reports. Officials told me that the forms used by the examining and revising committees have been modified over the years. These modifications have either been prompted by feedback from the board to the Ministry of Information and Broadcasting or initiated by the ministry itself. The form I saw during my fieldwork was used by both the examining and revising committees; the revising committees, however, also had access to the relevant examining committees' reports.

The form proceeds as follows:

[1.] I certify that I have carefully examined the above film with reference to the guidelines.

[2.] I recommend refusal of certificate to the film or I recommend the grant of the following certificate to the film: "U"/"UA"/"A"/"S," With excisions or/and modifications, Without excisions or/and modifications.

[3.] In the case of grant of "S" certificate, please specify the class or group of persons which should constitute the specialised audiences.

[4.] Reasons for refusal of certificate or grant of UA/A/S certificate.

[5.] Details of excisions/modifications [provide the reel number], clear and specific description of excisions or modifications [and] reasons with specific reference to guidelines.

[6.] Thematic classification (only in the case of feature films).

[7.] Any other remarks (including justification for permitting certain visuals and/or words which *prima facie* appear to be objectionable.

[8.] I certify that there would be no infraction of the guidelines if the film is granted a certificate as recommended above. I also certify that the film has been judged in its entirety from the point of view of its overall impact; the film has been examined in the light of the period depicted in the film and the contemporary standards of the country and the people to which the film relates; and that the film does not deprave the morality of the people. I certify that while recommending the film for unrestricted public exhibition I have satisfied that the film is suitable for family viewing, including children.[14]

A close look reveals that as it gleans a member's assessment of the film, the form operates to produce a subject, namely, an ideal committee member. This person presumably watches the film carefully and attends to the guidelines, to the context of the film's production and reception, to "family values," and to social mores when assessing it; hence, both family and country are produced as ideals. The form is designed not only to standardize the assessment process but also to produce committee members who share the same ethos. (This effort to produce "ideal members" is similarly visible in the workshops organized in 1996 by the CBFC, where the "Chairman/Regional Officers requested the members to apply the guidelines strictly and uniformly so as to curb the depiction of sex and violence in . . . film[s].")[15] The forms are then compiled to generate the examining committee's report, which includes the summary of the film, the committee's discussion on it, the precise excisions or modifications required (if any), the committee's thematic classification of the film, and the committee's decision about the film's certification. Both the individual forms and the committee's report are part of routine bureaucratic procedure, one that, I later learned, is carried out quite mechanically.

Observing Examining Committees

Several important points emerged from my observations of these committees: (1) Albeit formal institutions, the committees included noticeable informality in their everyday evaluation of films and in the practice of accepting bribes.[16] (2) Committee members examined films casually rather than vigilantly. (3) Both the forms and the members' everyday practices revealed the routine nature of state censorship. (4) The committee meetings were often shaped by habitual hierarchies; in evaluating films, members would defer to the regional officer. (5) The assessments were molded both by context and by categories such as Indian versus foreign and explicit versus implicit content. (6) Last but by no means least, archival research alone cannot provide an adequate account of censorship in India; for example, conversations within examining committees are not transcribed, which, as I later show, allows officials to deploy rules strategically to obtain a desired outcome.

Unlike the subjects assumed in the previously discussed form, the examining committee members with whom I interacted were less than "ideal"; they watched films casually, not vigilantly. They did, however, share the moral and social concerns expressed in the form. At the first viewing, I settled myself into a soft seat in the corner of the presiding officer's office so that I could unobtrusively view both the film and the committee members. The committee members strolled into the office, making small talk while waiting for tea and biscuits to show up. After most of them had arrived, the officer told them they would be viewing Balu Mahendra's *Sadma* (1983; Shock). This film recounts the story of a young woman who receives a head injury in an automobile accident. She loses her memory and begins to behave like a six-year-old child. Leaving the hospital unattended, she ends up in a brothel but is rescued by a young man who takes her to his home in the mountains. Meanwhile, her parents and the police are looking for her, and just as she is cured, they come to take her back to Bombay. She thus regains her memory of her old life but forgets her time in the mountains and the young man who helped her. This Hindi-remake of Mahendra's successful Tamil film *Moondram Pirai* had been given an A certificate because it contained some sexually explicit dialogues and scenes. The committee members were charged with ensuring that it had been edited to make it appropriate for a U audience because it was to be exhibited on Doordarshan, a state-sponsored television channel that shows only U-rated films. The lights were dimmed, and the committee members adjusted their seats so that they could watch the video recording of the film on the television set. Soon after the film began, the fourth member arrived and made his apologies. Ten minutes after his entrance, the tea and biscuits arrived. The members munched on the biscuits, took periodic bathroom breaks, and made occasional notes. Secretaries briefly interrupted when they needed the presiding officer to sign papers or to answer an official call. What struck me most was the casual and informal atmosphere in the office and the fact that the film was not paused when any of these interruptions took place.

When the film ended, the officer invited the members to voice their opinions. The members noted which sexually explicit scenes and dialogues they thought needed to be cut; a few differences arose among them, all quite amicably resolved. In a matter of minutes, the process was over. The producer's assistant was invited into the office and informed of the decision, which he easily accepted. I felt somewhat cheated by the routine nature of the process and the nonchalant attitude of the members. I had expected the committee to be vigilant rather than distracted viewers. Furthermore, I had looked forward to a lively discussion, not this anticlimatic affair.

My next viewing proved to be relatively more exciting. The venue was a baroque and intimate space tucked away among the offices of the Liberty Theatre. Sitting on well-cushioned red-velvet seats with attached reading lights, we viewed a Hollywood-made Bruce Willis action drama, *Die Hard: With a Vengeance* (1995). In this sequel to *Die Hard*, Bruce Willis returns as Detective John McClane. McClane is now separated from his wife and has been suspended from the New York Police Department, but he is called to active duty because a man named Simon has set bombs all over New York City and is challenging McClane to find them before they detonate. McClane, of course, does find the bombs, catches the bad guys, and (perhaps) reunites with his wife. Its violence and explicit language gave the film an R rating in the United States, restricting it to viewers eighteen and older. While the members were not necessarily cognizant of this, the regional officer would have been acquainted with the application form and thus would have been aware of the U.S. rating.

Members of the film industry, journalists, and audiences often argue that censors are more lenient when assessing foreign films. Officials regularly ascribe this difference to differing cultural and moral standards, underscoring the role of cinema in constituting national identity. In the case of *Die Hard*, the members discussed only the representation of violence while deciding which certificate to issue. In contrast, in two later viewings of Hindi films, where they debated a rape scene and a comic murder-for-hire sequence, the discussions on violence were much more concerned about the local context and reception. With *Die Hard*, the members were less apprehensive about the visual enactment of violence than about its aural avatar, i.e., the use of abusive language.

During *Die Hard*'s screening, the members as usual jotted notes, went to the lavatory, and answered cell-phone calls. Theater employees bringing drinks and sandwiches to our seats provided more welcome interruptions. When the film ended, some members expressed concern about the use of words such as *fuck* and *shit* and felt that it made the film inappropriate for teenagers. The members debated what rating to give the film—UA or A, because of the violence in it—but the differences were easily ironed out; the committee eventually gave the film an A certificate. During the first viewing I described, I had noted that the members tended to concur with the presiding officer, even copying the responses on the official's form; events at the second viewing suggested that this tendency was a habit rather than a happenstance. The habit was *partially* surprising because this particular officer was not an autocratic bureaucrat but in fact encouraged members to express their views. I then remembered that the members were habituated to interacting with officials in a subservient capacity of the "Yes, Madam," "No, Sir" variety. Habit disciplined this discussion.

After the examining committee had decided on the appropriate certification and cuts, the presiding officer turned to me and suggested that I interview the members about the process of censorship. I did this by invoking an example. The excessive violence in Rahul Rawail's *Anjaam* (1994; Consequence) had provoked a heated public debate.[17] This Hindi film recounts the story of a spoiled wealthy man who falls in love with an air hostess. She does not reciprocate his feelings, however, and eventually marries an airline pilot. The jilted lover is unable to accept this fact and continues to pursue her, murdering many of her family members in the process. At the end of the film, she gets revenge by killing him. Many viewers had walked out of the theaters while watching this film because they had been disgusted by the violence. Focusing on the gruesome and gory scenes, though, the debaters had ignored other sites of violence. During the course of the film, the heroine urges her husband to stop working for the man who is pursuing her; she asserts that she will resume working so that he can quit. As soon as she finishes her sentence, her husband slaps her. Neither the examining committee that certified the film nor the majority of the public found this scene to be violent. Pointing to it, I asked the members how they identified violent scenes. While the majority of them agreed that the scene was violent, they also stated that it was not graphic.

Disagreeing with the majority, one member asserted that the scene was not violent because it took place within the space of marriage, where the husband was simply asserting his right. Quickly and furiously voicing their dissent, the other members challenged the notion that marriage exculpates violence. Two points warrant comment here. First, the members did not find the scene to be unusual; it was a violent but still regular feature of a Hindi film. Second, although some of them found the scene to be objectionable, they did not think that it was "violent enough" to be cut. Regardless of this second claim, the censorship guidelines include other clearly relevant criteria, such as the decree that the final release contain no "scenes degrading or denigrating women in any manner."[18] My point is not to enter into a debate concerning whether the scene should have been cut but to highlight how the object of censorship is identified and, in this case, to show how patriarchal norms inform such processes.

The case of Indra Kumar's *Ishq* (1997; Love) further illustrates how committee members apply official rules differently. This Hindi film tells the story of two wealthy fathers who go to great lengths to prevent their children from marrying lower-class partners. At the end of the film, the fathers realize the error of their ways and allow the lovers to get married. After viewing *Ishq*, the members as usual discussed how they should certify the film and what cuts should be made. Members strongly disapproved of a long rape scene in which one of the heroines is kidnapped by goons hired by her lover's father. They thought the scene was titillating and degrading to women. In fact, the presiding officer noted that by focusing on the victims instead of the rapists, rape scenes in general and this one in particular eroticize the act of rape. All the members agreed that the scene needed modification. When the director and producers entered to receive the committee's verdict, they were told the scene needed to be cut because it was vulgar and obscene (the film ultimately received a UA rating contingent on cuts being made). In making this demand, the committee cited Rule 2 (vii) of the censorship guidelines, which urges members to ensure that "human sensibilities are not offended by vulgarity, obscenity or depravity."[19] I found the characterization peculiar considering that a few minutes earlier they had described the scene as objectionable because it eroticized rape and consequently degraded women.

The committee could have invoked one of at least three official rules:

2 (ix) scenes degrading or denigrating women in any manner are not presented;

(x) scenes involving sexual violence against women like attempt to rape, rape or any form of molestation, or scenes of a similar nature are avoided, and if any such incident is germane to the theme, they shall be reduced to the minimum and no details are shown;

(xi) scenes showing sexual perversions shall be avoided and if such matters are germane to the theme, they shall be reduced to the minimum and no details are shown.[20]

Why did the committee members cite rule 2 (vii) rather than these other ones? The context of economic liberalization, in which the terms *obscenity* and *vulgarity* were regularly employed to discuss sexual representations, might have influenced their decision. Alternatively, perhaps they chose it because the producers and the director could have contested the rule concerning women's representation by arguing that the rapist is punished in the end, so that the scene does not depict women's degradation but instead demonstrates that justice prevails against villainy. To evade the other two rules, producers could argue that the scenes were "germane to the theme."

The rule invoked, that "human sensibilities are not [to be] offended by vulgarity, obscenity or depravity," has an extensive institutional history in both the cinema and the judicial systems. Sections 292, 293, and 294 of the Indian Penal Code (IPC), along with sections 3 and 4 of the Indecent Representation of Women (Prohibition) Act, regulate obscenity in India. Cases and judgments (e.g., *K. A. Abbas v. The Union of India* and *Ranjit Udeshi v. Maharashtra*) draw on these legal provisions and build a legal edifice, generating a hegemonic discourse on obscenity. First and foremost, this discourse constructs subjects who are likely to be corrupted by reading or viewing "obscene" materials.[21] Unlike censorship as understood through my theoretical model, censorship is cast here as a mechanism for policing these subjects. Second, this discourse assumes an objective criterion whereby obscenity can be assessed. Third, it establishes a simple causal relation between the material and the viewers, as if obscenity could be hypodermically injected into a collective and infect it. Last, it purports to protect viewers from moral decay by adjudicating on obscenity. This arrangement enables the law to exercise authority by constituting an objective criterion for obscenity and then assessing materials with regard to this criterion. The examining committee's decision to cut the scene in *Ishq* on grounds of obscenity becomes more textured when it is situated in institutional history and practice. The invocation of objectivity and that of causality are both powerful techniques, and an alliance forged between the two establishes a powerful defense for the examining committee. This particular instance illustrates a more general phenomenon, namely, the strategic deployment of rules by examining committees to anticipate and pre-empt counterarguments by producers. For me, this incident also underscored the immense value of direct observation, because such discussions are not transcribed and thus remain absent from archival documents. In effect, it pointed to the limits of archival research. It is, however, a dialogue between direct observation and archival research that allows for this assessment; had I not enjoyed access to the committee's reports, I could not have come to this conclusion.

For me, direct observation also revealed the importance of context in the evaluation of films, as the following account of viewing David Dhawan's comedy *Deewana mastana* (1997; Crazy lover) reveals.[22] This Hindi remake of *What About Bob?* (1991) tells the story of a successful psychiatrist, Neha, who is courted by two men. One suitor, Raja, claims that he has businesses in the United States; the other, her patient Bunnu, is terrified of fire, heights, and water. The story becomes hilariously complicated when both suitors discover they are rivals. Initially they try to out-do each other, and later each tries to kill the other. The saga reaches a climax when Neha asks both to accompany her to the registrar's office, where she marries her fiancé. The examining committee focused on the scene where Bunnu tries to hire a killer to murder Raja, leaving him the sole contender for Neha's affections. This slapstick scene was reminiscent of other comic sequences in Hindi films; however, the presiding officer wanted the members to examine the scene in the light of a recent spate of killings in Bombay. In August 1997 Gulshan Kumar, the head of Tips, a major cassette company, was gunned down by members of the underworld[23] in broad daylight because he refused to turn over 10 million rupees (around $277,712). Soon thereafter, major stars, directors, and producers were threatened by gangsters who wanted to extort money and silence. They were also interrogated by the police, who wanted information about Nadeem Saifee, a famous music director—and the main suspect in the murder of Gulshan Kumar—concerning a June 12 gathering at Dawood Ibrahim's[24] residence in Dubai. These events led industry figures to cancel celebrations and show-biz parties in an effort to dim ostentatious displays of wealth; moreover, the beleaguered stars and film personalities generally went about with one or two security guards in tow. When I was at the CBFC in the summer and fall of 1997, producers and directors generally came to the office flanked by security guards. The committee's decision in this case reveals the importance of a contingent political context to the process of censorship. A scene that otherwise would have passed without a thought was both noticed and cut because the members feared that it would fuel existing fires.

Cutting, Classifying, and Certifying

During the course of my fieldwork, I had the opportunity to view cut scenes both at the CBFC and at the National Film Archive. The fragments at the National Film Archive were housed in a cramped room of the Film and Television Institute; they were uncataloged and arbitrarily spliced together. For example, scenes cut from a 1970 Hindi film would be next to those from a 1975 Tamil film, which means that anyone viewing them is jumping among different film industries, narratives, and times and places. It was difficult to identify the source film, much less to speculate why the scene or snippet had been excised. Therefore, unlike Salvatore in *Cinema Paradiso*, my viewings were surreal as opposed to euphoric. More contemporary material was housed at the CBFC; these fragments were easier to identify because they were labeled and I had recently watched the source films. As I viewed them, I was often struck by the uncanny resemblance between censors' excisions and the cuts that a film editor might make for any number of reasons—say, to shorten a film or improve continuity. At other times the offensive content clearly indicated state censorship, as in a deleted shot from *Darmiyaan* (1997) that shows a knife drawing close to young boy's penis in order to transform him into a eunuch. During the course of my research, some individuals at the CBFC suggested destroying the film fragments because the board was running out of space to house them. While the motive for doing away with the cuts was practical, not political, such acts do have unintended political consequences.

While cutting has been a much discussed function of the censors, I came to realize during the course of my interactions with the examining committees that classification and certification were also crucial functions. This insight was pivotal for formulating the theoretical framework that I discuss in Chapter 1 and for undertaking film analyses presented in Chapters 4 through 8. As I note in Chapter 1, examining and revising committee reports classify films according to length, type, and theme. The first question that comes to mind is why the report would lay out this complex system of classification, which appears more appropriate for a film industry report than for a government document. The result provides a marvelous archive for members of the film industry and scholars interested in tracking the shifting fortunes of genres, but why would the CBFC, a government institution, be interested in such classification? My later archival research revealed that an evaluation of a film often rested on its "thematic classification" and that new genres could hinder examining committees' abilities to properly assess and certify a film. As I show in my analyses of *Gupt gyan*, *Pati parmeshwar*, and *Dilwale dulhania le jayenge*, classification by genre has been and is mobilized to advance a moral vision of the nation and the state.

In addition to classification, certification is a critical task of the CBFC. In 1995 alone, the CBFC certified 795 feature films, and 503 of them received U certificates.[25] The certificate issued by the CBFC is valid for ten years. Although the state cites shifting social mores to justify expiration dates, it neglects to mention changing governments can and do affect certification. After the certificate is issued, any alterations to the film must be reported to the CBFC before the film may be exhibited. This certificate becomes an integral part of the film text, for every screening begins with the film certificate, both indicating the state's approval and framing a reading of the film. The film's rating appears in large bold letters at the top of the certificate. Below this, the film's title, number of reels, and the signature of the chairperson appear. A small triangle at the certificate's right-hand corner indicates that cuts have been instituted. In 1996 the certificates began including names of examining committee members, but the small lettering made them difficult to read. This veneer of transparency is also visible in the CBFC web site, which was created in 2001; it discloses both CBFC rating and any cuts made at the board's request. This transparency shows how the language of economic liberalization has slipped into state practices. Between 2006 and early 2010, either by neglect or design—or some combination of both—the CBFC web site was not functional. My web searches during this period yielded the following only: "Sorry, 'www. cbfcindia.tn.nic.in' does not exist or is not available." On April 30, 2010, a new version of the web site was launched, and at the time of writing, it remains operational.

Through the certification process, examining committees match films or film content to appropriate audiences; certification produces a film's potential market. Consider, for example, Mira Nair's film *Kama Sutra: A Tale of Love* (1996), which shuttled in and out of courtrooms and the CBFC for a while. Set in sixteenth-century India, the film centers on two girls, Maya and Tara. Though Maya is a lowly servant and Tara, a noble princess, the two are raised together as children. But Tara is raised as nobility, while Maya, her servant, is always reminded of her subordinate position. Deploying her physical charms, Maya exacts revenge on Tara by seducing her husband on her wedding day and thereby beginning a destructive struggle for power. Nair's status as a diasporic Indian director, the film's explicit sexual content, and the fact that the film's narrative and setting were "Indian" combined to generate controversy. I was struck by the fact that no such debate had taken place during the discussion of *Die Hard*, which is also a foreign film, the difference pointing to the CBFC's and, more generally, the Indian state's investment in the way "India" is represented as well as in the centrality of sexuality (rather than violence) in defining "Indian culture."

After much debate and discussion about *Kama Sutra*'s sexual content, the director and the CBFC reached an agreement, but shortly afterward problems arose because Nair wanted to dub the English-language film into "vernacular languages."[26] The CBFC firmly stated that if Nair dubbed the film in the vernacular languages, more scenes would have to be cut, because the audiences who would view these films lacked "proper" education, making them more inclined to imbibe and spew vulgarity. The class pretensions and presumptions undergirding this decision can be easily articulated. First, to be educated is to count among the English-speaking, upper-middle- and middle-class population in India. In addition, members of the upper and middle classes possess appropriate class traits, such as taste and distinction. Finally, these traits enable them to see erotic films such as *Kama Sutra* in their "proper" light.

In a conversation with an official at the Central Board of Film Certification, I remarked that the examining committees' project of demanding cuts to objectionable scenes before issuing certificates and sanctioning "unobjectionable" ones raised the issue of the grounds on which the CBFC decided what is unobjectionable—that is, certifiable. The official appreciated the formulation but objected to the word *sanction* because it attributed more power to the boards than this person thought they exercised. Elaborating on the CBFC's limited powers, the official stated that the boards did not create policies but only applied the given rules. Moreover, while the CBFC in Bombay and the regional offices issued certificates, they did not have the political or administrative authority to enforce their decisions. This was the task of the local state police, who, many Hindi films depict, often arrive late at the scene of the crime. The police have also been willing to overlook the relatively small transgression of certification violation, at least for a price.[27] Hence, interpolations of material previously excised under the terms of certification or never viewed by the committees (generally clips from porn films) have been regularly inserted in films, especially ones exhibited in small towns and cities. These additions point to exhibition as a crucial site for analyzing censorship; later, in Chapter 8, I note arbitrary deletions from *Dilwale dulhania le jayenge* when it was screened at the Plaza Theatre in New Delhi. The official whom I interviewed felt that theaters' failure to check for underage viewers further undermined the value of the state certificate, a comment that underscored the key role of exhibition. Last, the official stated that the certificates could be forged or simply recycled (the name of the original film could be erased and a new name written in its place). All these comments pointed to the fact that the censorship process involved not only the central bureaucracy and a select public but also the local government and the police. These observations were important because they revealed that censorship as a practice was constituted by and constitutive of various institutions. They decisively challenge Aruna Vasudev's claims in *Liberty and Licence in the Indian Cinema*.

Conversations with film directors and officials provided more information about the circumvention of censorship. The film industry, they said, has negotiated with or evaded state authority though various "illegal" activities, such as bribing state officials, making two sets of negatives instead of one,[28] exhibiting fake certificates, screening objectionable scenes in small towns and rundown theaters, and passing copies of uncertified films or films that contain "objectionable" scenes through customs for exhibition abroad. Moreover, officials at the CBFC revealed that producers and directors would offer them gifts ranging from cassette tapes to fruits in gold bowls, ostensibly as tokens of their respect or appreciation. Those with whom I spoke all said they would promptly return the gifts, but they named a few of their colleagues who had accepted them.

I witnessed an altercation in which the issue of bribery was raised among the committee members. In the midst of an ugly argument at a screening I attended, a disgruntled committee member indignantly remarked that the honorarium for examining movies was so low that members were forced to accept bribes from producers and directors. The challenge was obvious: either the state increased the honorarium, or the member would have to accept the small "tokens" that came his way. Prohibition, then, is instrumental in increasing the economic productivity of an informal sector that ironically is located at the heart of the state. An institution that is supposed to be guarding public morals is actually instrumental in producing corruption and prurience.

Apart from using bribery, the industry employed other strategies in dealing with the CBFC. For example, the directors might attempt to circumvent state authority via the "excessive shooting strategy," a gambit that requires ample raw stock. Consider this simple example: the director shoots an extra close-up of the heroine in a bikini but in a later scene (one the director wants) presents her in a one-piece swimsuit. The committee members, comparing the two and finding the latter to be less offensive, ask the producer to cut the first scene and leave the second one; thus, they feel satisfied that they have done their "duty." The producer is happy because the desired scene was left intact—and if by chance the members pass the first scene, that's just icing on the cake. Another oft-used industry tactic is to argue that the scene or incident is germane to the narrative or the character; for example, a cabaret dancer must "necessarily" wear skimpy clothes and dance suggestively, for such attire and practices are constitutive of the character. Finally, as was noted earlier, producers sometimes file their applications at a more lenient regional office, say, Hyderabad or Madras. As these strategies demonstrate, the film industry has devised means for resisting the state.[29]

The Importance of Banality

During the course of my research, I not only asked questions but also answered them. The people who regulated my access to research materials, the people whom I interviewed, and the people whom I observed were curious about my background and reserach: Where was I from? *Ah, so you're from Delhi.* Where was I studying? *Oh, you're studying in America. We also know x, y, z who is in America.* What was I studying? *Com-parative what? Achha,[30] comparative literature.* What did I compare? *So, you're studying Indian films. Why would Americans be interested in that?*[31] Of all the questions I was asked, the most troubling was, "Are you for or against censorship?" The question disturbed me because it demanded that I take a position on a predetermined object—and that the position I took, at some level, would define who I was. I feared that if I took a position opposed to my questioner's, I would jeopardize my access to research materials and potential interviewees, and so I did not answer the question, at least not directly. I explained that I was focusing on the *process* of censorship and not on positions vis-à-vis the matter. Nonetheless, the compelling nature of the question remained with me. I disagreed with its formulation—and its promises of easy political alliances, in which one could locate "us" and "them," the good guys and the bad guys. The promises were seductive, however, and I was drawn to them. They reminded me of the familiar and comfortable moral landscape of commercial Hindi films, where the heroes and the villains are easily identifiable.

I quickly discovered during my fieldwork that members of the Bombay film industry were not the only ones who employed formulas. What most struck and irritated me was the tedious similarity of the accounts of censorship, whether oral or written. My most memorable event was turning pages of certification reports ranging from the 1960s to the 1990s and finding that sex and violence dominated the cuts demanded in each decade. Moreover, not only were similar cuts required, but the language used to describe them was the same. Film censorship, then, was as formulaic as the films it censored. We know that formulas and repetition are essential to the narration of ideologies. They work to construct that which is familiar, recognizable, and legible—in short, that which makes sense. At the end of my fieldwork, I discovered what was both simple and amazing: formulas, routines, procedures, and habits produce powerful effects.

Thus, as I examine *Gupt gyan, Satyam shivam sundaram, Pati parmeshwar, Khalnayak*, and *Dilwale dulhania le jayenge* in the upcoming chapters, my task will be to disturb formulaic understandings of censorship, sexuality, and tradition. These films have been produced in postcolonial India, specifically during the period between 1974 and 1995. The present of these films includes events such as the Emergency, the rise of parallel cinema, the Shah Bano case, the Roop Kanwar immolation, the growth of the music industry, and liberalization, all of which informed their production and consumption. However, this present is not a simple present, walled in by a past on the one side and a future on the other. The present isn't the present because, to begin with, the *past* is not *past*; it continues to shape the reception of these films and conversations about cinema in India. The future is another question altogether.

4

The First Sex-Education Film

A Classification Conundrum

Characterized as the "first sex education film," *Gupt gyan* (1974; Secret knowledge) confounded committees at the body then known as the Central Board of Film Censors, as well as officials at the Ministry of Information and Broadcasting, on two related counts. First, as a "hotchpotch of a documentary and a featurised story,"[1] it eluded generic classification. Second, by partly adopting a documentary approach, it smuggled in sex via diagrams of male and female organs, animated scenes of reproduction, and still shots showing symptoms of venereal diseases, as well as lectures and discussions on sexuality and family planning. While that era's censorship guidelines included rules for regulating representations of surgical operations and venereal diseases and the inclusion of explicit diagrams,[2] the reports and the correspondence on *Gupt gyan* reveal that neither the committee members nor the officials had been asked to adjudicate such representations. With respect to sexuality, their habitual dealings would have involved reducing or cutting salacious dialogues, close-ups of breasts or thighs, and erotically charged song-and-dance sequences from Hindi commercial cinema. For the most part, their practices both rested on and reinforced the assumption that sex is situated in the realms of morality and entertainment. *Gupt gyan*, however, even as it invoked the familiar sexual landscape of Hindi cinema through its "featurised story," medicalized sex by placing it in a techno-scientific context. While the committee members and officials may have imagined themselves as moral guardians, they clearly did not see themselves as *medical experts*, leaving them ill-equipped to deal with this new form of representation.

To better understand the stakes in this matter, it is useful to turn to scholarship on nationalism in India. Most work on this topic has focused on relations among the figure of the Indian woman, tradition, and sexuality.[3] While this scholarship has yielded valuable insights, it has, as Sanjay Srivastava notes, neglected discussions of nationalism where sex is not situated in an inner sanctum, shielded from the "onslaught of modernity."[4] Rather, sex is linked to the project of modernizing India. How are these visions articulated within the postcolonial state of India? Partha Chatterjee argues that the nationalists believed they needed to resolve "the woman question" if they were to win their struggle against the colonizers. In the public arena, the nationalists wanted to demonstrate to the British that they were as modern as their colonizers. Within their private sanctums, however, they wanted to preserve their superior, spiritual culture.[5] Chatterjee explains the powerful dichotomy of the spiritual and the material that framed nationalist discourse:

> Now apply the inner/outer distinction to the matter of concrete day to day living and you get a separation of the social space into *ghar* and *bahir*; the home and the world. The world is the external, the domain of the material; the home represents our inner spiritual self, our true identity. The world is a treacherous terrain of the pursuit of the material interests, where practical considerations reign supreme. It is also typically the domain of the male. The home in its essence must remain unaffected by the profane activities of the material world—and woman is its representation. And so we get an identification of social roles by gender to correspond with the separation of the social space into *ghar* and *bahir*.[6]

The indigenous male elite believed the British had been able to colonize India because of their superior material techniques. Consequently, they wanted to cultivate these skills to match the British in the public arena. Within the space of the home, however, they wanted to preserve Indian tradition. They allocated this task to the women, making them the guardians of Indian tradition. While acknowledging British supremacy in the public arena, they wished to maintain their own privileged position in the private sphere. Consequently, the gestures they made to women in the outer world were limited and did not challenge inequalities in the inner world. Extending Chatterjee's argument, I suggest that the framework of *ghar*/inner versus *bahir*/outer was as crucial to the nascent postcolonial nation-state as it was to the nineteenth-century nationalists. Cast as a "developing" nation within the international stage, the newly independent India continued to occupy a secondary status in the world. Thus, we can see how the concept of *ghar*/inner assisted in articulating tradition, womanhood, and sexuality as sites of cultural difference where the postcolonial nation-state reigned supreme, whereas *bahir*/outer served as the stage on which the postcolonial state could address pressing concerns of development, central to which was the reduction of the population.[7]

This division appears in the structure of the Indian postcolonial state. On the one hand, the Central Board of Film Censors was working to screen sex; on the other, the Ministry of Health was *publicly* pursuing the task of decreasing India's population, enlisting various forms of media to support its efforts, as family-planning scholarship in postindependence India reveals. At the Ministry of Health, sex was not *gupt* (secret) but rather *gyan* (knowledge)—*gyan* that was essential to India's development. *Gupt gyan* brought to movie screens these two related efforts of the postcolonial state, which had thus far been kept in separate domains. My main task in this chapter is to examine how *Gupt gyan* stages this dichotomy and to analyze the subsequent concerns and queries that appear in examining and revising committee reports, as well as in official correspondence.

To begin this, I offer a brief summary of *Gupt gyan*. In my subsequent analysis I will develop several plot points to examine topics such as ambiguity of genre, the medicalization of sex, melodrama versus realism, and *darsan* (roughly, "seeing").[8] *Gupt gyan* recounts the story of Dinesh, who discovers that both his classmate Kanchan and his own mother are infected with syphilis. Upon his mother's death, he vows to study sexology to help his fellow citizens. Dinesh is assisted in this task by a childless patron, Bhargava, as well as by Dinesh's devoted servant, Radhia. In college Dinesh concentrates on his studies, rejecting his classmate Chanchal's sexual advances. After completing his education in India, Dinesh, with Bhargava's help, goes to the United States for further study. Before leaving, Dinesh requests that Bhargava and his wife, Tara, employ Radhia as a servant. After his father dies, he returns to India and opens a hospital. Dinesh's newly acquired medical expertise and Radhia's prayers help Bhargava and his wife, Tara, conceive a much desired child.

Jealous of Dinesh's successful practice, Dr. Sarkar and his fellow charlatan doctors conspire with the scorned Chanchal to implicate Dinesh in a rape case. While Dinesh is in police custody, Tara goes into labor. Upon Bhargava's appeal, the police release Dinesh briefly to supervise the delivery of Tara's son. Later, in a judicial hearing about the rape charge, Chanchal recants her charge, and Dinesh is set free. Unhappy that the charges against Dinesh have been dismissed, Dr. Sarkar, the leader of the quack doctors, hires a hit man to kill him. Dinesh survives this attempt, but Radhia is shot in the arm. As a dejected Radhia lies in the hospital, lamenting that she will no longer be able to serve Dinesh, he proposes to her; the film ends with their marriage.

Gupt gyan had neither a stellar cast nor a well-established production team. B. K. Adarsh, its producer, director, and writer, was better known as the publisher of *Trade Guide*, which provided information about film earnings. Prior to *Gupt gyan*, Adarsh had made a number of films under his family banner, alternately titled Adarsh Arts or Adarsh Lok. A family production house that used novice or relatively lesser-known actors, Adarsh Arts produced mainly small-budget, "B-grade" Hindi films, including *Mano na mano* (1955), *Teerth yatra* (1958), *Fashionable Wife* (1959), *Ramu dada* (1961), *Durga puja* (1962), *Harishchandra taramati* (1963), *Spy in Rome* (1968), *Balak* (1969), and *Putlibai* (1972). Adarsh's filmography indicates his experience with varied genres, for it comprises social, spiritual, action, suspense, devotional, and mythological films. It also shows that he multitasked, often working as a producer, writer, or director in many of his films. As the publisher of *Trade Guide* and a filmmaker, Adarsh would have been familiar with the more powerful members of the Bombay film industry, but he clearly was not part of the industry's A list. His lack of status has two consequences important to my argument. First, since Adarsh was not an A-list figure, he may have been able to explore topics that the stalwarts of the industry were unlikely to examine in their works. Second, Adarsh's background partly helps explain his need to get testimonials from his colleagues, medical experts, and politicians to support his film.

Significantly, *Gupt gyan's* production team included both members of the film industry and medical experts. Dr. B. N. Purandare, a gynecologist, and Dr. Dhurandhar, an eminent physician, "performed technical scenes in the film"; Dr. Niranjan Patel, a "Germany returned" specialist, served as the film's medical adviser.[9] The involvement of experts at the level of production lent authenticity to the film and helped Adarsh forge *Gupt gyan's* identity as a legitimate sex-education film. In addition, Nitin Sethi, the Film Finance Corporation's general manager, appeared in the film, which must have assisted in navigating the rough waters of state censorship.

The "real" actors in the film included Adarsh's wife, Jaymala Adarsh, who performs the role of Radhia. She acted mainly in their family productions and also served as an executive producer for some of their films. The protagonist, Dinesh, is played by Bharat Kapoor, who had just entered the film industry; in fact, *Gupt gyan* and *Nafrat* were his first releases.

Following the success of *Gupt gyan*, Kapoor played a similar role in *Kaam shastra* (1975; The study of pleasure). The other cast members included Sarita, Manhar Desai, Kishore Bhatt, and Kader Khan, all of whom generally performed supporting roles in films. Khan, who has a cameo in *Gupt gyan* as a lecturer, is a well-known writer and actor. Print sources provide little information on the other members of the cast.[10] Even though *Gupt gyan* had a small budget and lacked crucial Hindi film ingredients, including big stars, song-and-dance sequences, and picturesque locations, it managed to be a hit at the box office; in trade circles it was even compared to Raj Kapoor's *Bobby* (1973), an immensely successful big-budget commercial film.[11]

Gupt gyan was released during a period when both the nation and the Bombay film industry were undergoing dramatic changes. Scholars have underscored citizens' general disaffection with the government in the 1970s, pointing to peasant and urban strikes.[12] Within the Hindi film industry, as Madhava Prasad has documented, this period saw the emergence of middle and parallel cinemas, as well as the rise of Amitabh Bachchan, who epitomized the "angry young man."[13] The two major successes of 1973, the year that *Gupt gyan* was certified, included Prakash Mehra's *Zanjeer* and Raj Kapoor's *Bobby*. *Zanjeer* marked the beginning of Bachchan's meteoric rise, and *Bobby* scorched the screen with its representation of teen sexuality. *Gupt gyan*'s hero, however, is neither the aggressive protagonist of *Zanjeer* nor the young romantic hero of *Bobby*. Rather, Dinesh resembles what Sanjay Srivastava calls the "Five-Year Plan (FYP) hero" of 1950s and 1960s Hindi cinema. The Indian state's much publicized "Five-Year Plans" followed the Soviet model and proposed to put India on the road to development. The "FYP hero" was thus a "modern male improver" who possessed both "technological aptitude" and "scientific knowledge. . . . [He] was typically portrayed as an engineer (building roads or dams), a doctor, a scientist or a bureaucrat."[14] This heroic figure was aligned with the Nehruvian vision of the Indian state, which emphasized the importance of science and industrialization for national development.

Unlike other FYP heroes, who follow more conventional careers, such as building dams or curing tuberculosis, Dinesh pursues sexology. In choosing this unusual path, Dinesh—and *Gupt gyan*—encroached on territory that had been the sole domain of the Indian state's Films Division, entering an arena where sex was indexed to India's development. At the behest of the postcolonial Ministry of Health, the Films Division produced shorts on family planning, vigorously spreading information about practices such as "the rhythm method," vasectomy, tubectomy, the use of condoms and intrauterine devices (IUDs), child spacing, and delaying marriage, all with a view toward controlling the population and promoting economic welfare. In the Five-Year Plan (1969–1974) preceding *Gupt gyan*'s release, the state, which was confounded by its inability to effectively regulate the rising population, made family planning a "programme of the highest priority"; it produced "an average of 80 films per year" on the subject.[15]

While *Gupt gyan* explicitly expressed its alliance with the state's family-planning efforts through the activities of its "FYP hero," its canvas was considerably greater than those of the state-sponsored films. In addition to representing reproduction and birth control, it provided information on venereal diseases, menstruation, and problems related to intercourse, among other things.[16] *Gupt gyan* drew on two regimes of representation, staging different modes of sexuality. First, it used conventions largely associated with family-planning films produced by Films Division. These conventions included a background of state-produced music that drew on elements of Indian classical and folk music (henceforth I will refer to this as Films Division music), a pedagogical address, and little-known actors. Second, it employed the repertoire of commercial films, including songs, melodrama, action, romance, and stereotypical characterizations——hero/villain and virgin/vamp. How, then, do these two regimes of sexuality relate to each other in *Gupt gyan*? What kind of sexual speech did *Gupt gyan* urge? How did it draw the boundaries of sexuality? How did it engage with the question of tradition?

The Booklet: Producing a Reading of *Gupt gyan*

Aware that *Gupt gyan* would incite debate, B. K. Adarsh employed various strategies for meeting challenges even before he submitted the film to an examining committee. He produced a booklet that identified the subject of the film as sex education and affirmed the film's status as predominantly educational; to shape the censorship board's assessment of *Gupt gyan*, Adarsh submitted this booklet along with the film. The film, Adarsh contended, "had nothing to do with the *Kama Sutra* or *Kokshastra* or any techniques of sexual intercourse" and did not contain "a single frame . . . suggestive of obscenity or exciter of baser instincts."[17] While Adarsh attempted to underscore the film's medical vision by distancing *Gupt gyan* from ancient Indian texts that focus on sexual technique and sexual pleasure, a character in it, Mr. Vyas, invokes them to demonstrate the "openness" of sex in ancient India.

Contrasting *Gupt gyan* with the ubiquitous fare of commercial cinema, Adarsh noted:

> It is evident that "GUPT GYAN" may be a feature film literally, but *in essence, it is a documentary*. It is never a formula film. It has no melodrama, no music, no songs, no violence, no thrills, no comic, no love-spots, not an iota of routine ingredients. On the contrary, the contents are full of class-room lectures, demonstrations, operation theatres, conferences, seminars and sessions of questions and answers.[18] [emphasis added]

While *Gupt gyan* was not entirely a "formula film," it did employ many of Hindi cinema's "routine ingredients." Adarsh's disavowal of these elements in his address to the examining and, later, revising committees seeks to secure a reading of *Gupt gyan* as an educational film. In producing this reading, Adarsh invoked a dichotomy between documentary and commercial films that was central to the state's understanding of cinema. The state claimed that—unlike commercial cinema, which merely entertained the masses—short documentaries produced by its Films Division strove to inform and educate the citizens of India. Aligning his project with state initiatives, Adarsh suggested that in providing information on "Venereal Diseases, Birth Control methods, sexual abnormalities and their root causes, [and] common and everyday problems of adolescents," *Gupt gyan* sought to "unveil the ignorance and impart true knowledge to the layman"—and in effect, supported the state's pedagogical objectives.[19]

The film's good intentions were affirmed by a series of letters and notes from members of Parliament, medical experts, professors, judges, lawyers, professors, social workers, and other established professionals who expressed appreciation for its content, saying that the film provided much needed information on sex. Besides including these letters of support in the booklet, Adarsh also provided the "Certificate of Approval," granted by the All India Film Producers' Council.[20] Shakti Samanta, the CBFC's chairman when I was conducting my fieldwork and a former member of the All India Film Producers' Council, recalled that Adarsh had requested the council to view the film and to speak to the censor board on his behalf. The council screened the film and recommended an A certificate subject to cuts. Subsequently, Samanta informally spoke with the then-chairman of the board, Virendra Vyas, and conveyed the council's views on the film. Presumably the film appeared before the examining committee after Adarsh had made the council's recommended modifications.

The path taken by this film suggests that a film need not follow a simple trajectory, beginning its journey with an examining committee. In showing the film to well-established people in "private" screenings and gathering letters of appreciation, Adarsh sought to circumvent official authority via informal channels of power. In this informal exercise of power, techniques normally associated with the censors—namely, classification, certification, and cutting—were deployed by prominent viewers to produce a reading that supported Adarsh's interpretation, namely, that *Gupt gyan* is a sex-education film. Again, regulation is not solely the domain of the censors. As this instance demonstrates, a film's production and interpretation are molded by other parties, too, and education and status, as indices of a class system, possess their own quotient of force in that regard. S. E. Hassnain, a member of *Gupt gyan*'s revising committee, interrogated this practice of private screenings, inquiring, "Does not it attempt to influence the verdict of the censors? Is it not illegal? Such tendencies should be discouraged and privileges of censors strictly maintained."[21] Clearly, Hassnain sought not only to guard the censors' "privileges" but also to uphold the authority of the state in these matters and to maintain a division between the formal and the informal.

Educating Spectators, Producing a Pedagogical Vision

The prominent "unofficial" viewers of *Gupt gyan* resurface in the opening credits of the film under the rubric "acknowledgments." In *publicly* thanking his patrons, Adarsh was also able to garner *publicity* for the film, for the names of these eminent patrons endow it with respectability. This respectability is further secured by the film's dedication to "persons who have suffered due to a lack of sex education" and by continued gestures to literariness, which was also invoked earlier in the booklet. In the opening scenes, against a soundtrack of Films Division music, the camera slowly pans across books entitled *Physical Chemistry, Grammar and Composition, Secretarial Practice, Elements of Zoology, Elements of Physics, Commerce,* and finally, *Sex Education and Family Planning.*[22] The camera stops at the last book and the first page is turned, revealing "Adarsh Arts" as the author/director[23] of this book/film. This scene seeks to establish *Gupt gyan*'s pedagogical character by suggesting that it is like *a textbook.* What is the significance of employing a literary medium to construct an analogy? Traditionally, cinema in India has had to struggle for respectability, whereas books have largely been viewed as sacred; in common understanding, books are what impart knowledge and educate. Adarsh draws on this common understanding to suggest that as do books, *Gupt gyan* will convey knowledge and teach the masses.

In *Gupt gyan*, as in the U.S. sex-hygiene films analyzed by Annette Kuhn and Eric Schaefer, "education is at the axis of character function" as each character "functions to either receive, promote, stifle, or create the need for education about sex and reproductive health."[24] Schaefer notes that unlike what Kuhn calls the "psychologically rounded individuals" of conventional Hollywood narratives, characters in sex-hygiene films "operated as representatives of certain moral positions."[25] But whereas Hollywood looms large in the sex-hygiene films both Kuhn and Schaefer discuss, *Gupt gyan* is produced in a space dominated by Hindi commercial cinema. Archetypal characters are a staple of this cinema; I turn now to the way *Gupt gyan* employs this standard ingredient to recount its tale.

At the beginning of the narrative, we are introduced to Kanchan, Dinesh's unfortunate college classmate. Kanchan is light skinned, has blond hair, wears a short dress—and bears an uncanny resemblance to Helen, the legendary vamp of Hindi cinema. Through her confession, we realize that Kanchan is not a sexually aggressive vamp but an innocent victim who contracted syphilis because her greedy mother pimped her. Social circumstances force Kanchan to remain silent, so that the disease spreads. Thus, the film's pedagogic drive transforms the transgressive figure of the vamp into a victim of sexual disease. In case the viewer and Dinesh are not completely moved by Kanchan's plight, the narrative provides the figure of Dinesh's mother, who contracts syphilis from her debauched husband. In both a personal address to Dinesh and a more general direct address to the audience, the mother's doctor explains that her disease has reached an advanced stage because she did not seek help in a timely fashion. Both Kanchan's confession and his mother's death cement Dinesh's decision to go to medical school. When Dinesh approaches his father to obtain his blessings (and possibly monetary assistance) in pursuing this goal, he is rebuffed. Toward the end of the film, the father is punished for his sexual philandering and becomes bed-ridden with syphilis himself. At his deathbed, he apologizes for his errors and leaves Dinesh his estate.

Undaunted by this initial obstacle, Dinesh attempts to get a loan for his education. He fails but fortuitously meets Bhargava at the money lender's office. Impressed by Dinesh, Bhargava decides to become his patron. At college Dinesh encounters Chanchal, the Westernized "bad" girl who entices men and steers her college mates who suffer from sexual ailments to a charlatan, Dr. Sarkar. At the film's end, she is struck with cervical cancer, a punishment for her many sins, which include attempting to frame

Dinesh for rape. A forgiving Dinesh promises to assist in curing her. Unlike Hindi commercial films, in which characters such as Chanchal or Kanchan would most likely have been killed or, in some cases, reformed, *Gupt gyan*'s pedagogic drive generates other fates for these characters— namely, medical treatment.

Contrasting to Chanchal, who tries to lead Dinesh astray and harm his practice, Radhia, Dinesh's dedicated servant, offers him her jewelry to help fund his education. She cooks and cleans for him so that he can concentrate on his studies. When he opens his practice, she dutifully accompanies him on his medical rounds. While the film distances itself from the voyeuristic activities of Chanchal, it embraces *darsanic* vision and authority (another staple of Hindi cinema), which are figured through Radhia's actions. Radhia's devotion to Dinesh suggests that he is a "godlike" figure. During the period when Radhia works for Bhargava and Tara, she prays to God, asking him to fulfill her mistress's wish for a baby. In this case, our vision is first organized via the experience of *darsan*, which is then fulfilled by Dinesh's medical expertise. The film's investment in aligning science and religion can also be witnessed in Dinesh's interaction with Meena, a female patient who visits the hospital to find a remedy for her period, which will arrive during an important religious ceremony. Dinesh resolves her problem by prescribing pills to delay her period. *Gupt gyan* portrays science not as posing a threat to religion but rather as collaborating with and even facilitating it. To this end, one could also read Dinesh and Radhia's marriage as the wedding of science and religion—and of pedagogic and darsanic vision.

Serving as a counterpoint to Dinesh, the villainous Dr. Sarkar inhabits neither the world of legitimate science nor that of religion. He prescribes fake medicines, gives false advice, overcharges his patients, and most important, lacks a proper medical degree. As noted earlier, he also leads the attempt to frame Dinesh for rape—and later, to murder him. Eventually Dr. Sarkar's practice is shut down by the police, who ask him to produce a legitimate medical degree. The characters in *Gupt gyan* establish an ignorant and corrupt world that requires reform through the intervention of sex education, an education that works in concert with divine authority.

How do Dinesh and, by extension, the viewers acquire "proper knowledge" about sex? Within the filmic narrative, information about sexuality is exchanged in five major sites: the auditorium, classroom, seminar room, lecture hall, and hospital. Hindi cinema's melodramatic and sensuous song-and-dance sequences, I suggest, are replaced by these realist sites, de-eroticizing sex and enabling its medicalization. Thus, mise-en-scène is crucial for constructing *Gupt gyan* as a sex-education film. Dinesh initially learns about sexology at a college lecture sponsored by the All India Students Association. In an auditorium, Vyas, a student leader from Baroda, delivers a speech arguing that sex education should be made compulsory, given its importance for daily life. Narrating a standard account of the history of sexuality in India, he explains that in ancient India, sex was "open," citing saints, the Vedas, and Vatsayana (the author of the *Kamasutra*), as well as the Konark and Khajuraho temples. Vyas contends, however, that in modern India sex has been hidden, and thus the people can acquire knowledge of it only through informal sources such as footpath literature[26] or juvenile conversations. According to Vyas, this culture of repression and informal education has associated sexuality with feelings of guilt and shame. He exhorts his audience to learn more about the topic to improve their lives. Foucault reminds us that the incitement to learn about sexuality does not necessarily herald liberation or freedom. Rather, knowledge of sexuality constitutes a condition of possibility for power to discipline us.[27]

In his speech, Vyas emphasizes the value of *formal* sex education. When Dinesh initially tries to enter medical college, he is asked for a "donation." The narrative suggests that he manages to secure this "donation" and enroll in Bhatia Medical College with the help of his patron, Bhargava. Both these informal activities, "donation" and patronage, are central to Dinesh's entry into a formal institution. Moreover, they parallel the informal practices Adarsh employed to secure certification for *Gupt gyan*. Both instances reveal how the informal works in tandem with the formal—and often occupies a crucial role in the functioning of formal institutions such as colleges or state censorship.

On his first day at college, Dinesh is waylaid by more advanced students who jokingly predict his failure at becoming a doctor. Issuing a quick riposte, Dinesh continues to make his way to the classroom. He next encounters Chanchal, who attempts to entice him with romantic poetry; however, he does not succumb to her charms—and her effort to lure him into the landscape of Hindi cinema. At this juncture, a commercial Hindi film would almost certainly have inserted a song. Instead, we, along with Dinesh, are led into a large lecture hall where Dinesh's sex education begins. One by one, various professors instruct a rapt student audience on the topics of reproductive organs, venereal diseases, pregnancy, and birth control. In the lectures medical terms are given in English, Latin, and a Sanskritized Hindi, lending legitimacy to these topics. The lecture on reproductive organs begins with color diagrams of male and female genitalia, and later the instructor provides an account of heterosexual intercourse, making a point to note that the length of the penis does not matter to intercourse. He also underscores that the main purpose of intercourse and these organs is reproduction. A later lecture on pregnancy includes animated male and female figures embracing, and a voice-over tracks conception from the sperm's journey into the Fallopian tubes to birth. Thus, while medical science assists in dismissing misconceptions about male sexuality, it simultaneously regenerates a conservative discourse about sexual intercourse, aligning it with reproduction.

Another lecture presents types of venereal diseases, including syphilis, gonorrhea, chancroid, granuloma inguinale, and lymphogranuloma venereum (LGV). Showing diagrams of syphilis, the instructor stresses that it can harm and even kill fetuses. Gonorrhea, he warns, travels from prostitutes to men. As circuits of medicine are joined to circuits of morality, the confluence yields the familiar argument wherein women who are sexually active outside marriage are constructed as contagious. Interestingly, the fictional segment appears to challenge this line of thought by constructing Kanchan as a victim and characterizing Dinesh's dissolute father as a vector of disease. At the end of this lecture, the students and the viewers are shown close-up photographs of a vagina, a penis, faces, and upper portions of male bodies infected with venereal diseases. Thus the camera becomes an instrument of medicine allowing us intimate access to bodies in order to display how sex can hurt us. The last lecture, a nod to the government's family-planning program, focuses on birth control. Reciting the government's position, the instructor states that family planning is necessary for controlling the population. He discusses various methods for birth control: condoms, spermicidal creams, diaphragms, IUDs (their insertion shown via a model),[28] and surgical sterilization (vasectomy and tubectomy). (Later in the film, Dinesh inserts an IUD, the Lippes loop, for free since it assists the government's efforts in family planning.) Last, information about abortion is covered in this segment. The instructor criticizes botched abortions that are performed by untrained persons. The camera thus constructs a pedagogic vision by using the space of the classroom; medical terminology; still photographs; expert instructors; medical instruments, such as the vacuum machine used in suction-aspiration abortions; and a soundtrack of Films Division music, which evokes the aural landscape of Films Division shorts. As in the ancient India that Vyas invokes, sex is once more open, but this "openness" is now indebted to medical authority, which sanctions the viewing of hitherto illicit material.[29]

After completing his studies in India, with the help of Bhargava, Dinesh goes to the United States for further study. In a seminar room, a diasporic Indian addresses a small group of international students. Like Vyas, the diasporic Indian professor underscores the need to speak openly about sex. He advocates using "psychosomatic treatment" for sexual "ills" such as frigidity, homosexuality, "lesbianism," and impotence. Armed with a foreign education that increased his knowledge and a foreign degree that increases his value, Dinesh returns to India. He is invited to give a lecture on sexology at the Indian Cultural Society, in a venue that recalls the auditorium where Dinesh heard his first speech on sex education.

In a sequence comprising fifty-seven shots, the camera cuts back and forth between Dinesh seated on the stage with two other colleagues and the middle- and upper-middle-class Indian men and women seated in the audience. Unlike other stages, this is a space not for entertainment but for education. It is clear that the hall in the diegetic space mirrors the theater in which audiences watch the film, inviting them to view the screen as a site of education. The process of education begins for both the on-screen and off-screen audiences as Dinesh requests the on-screen audience to ask questions about sexuality. The diegetic audience asks Dinesh the following sixteen questions:

Why are venereal diseases increasing in India?
What is frigidity?
What is nymphomania?
Should women breastfeed their children?
Is masturbation harmful?
How does one ensure a happy and satisfactory sexual life?
What specific techniques should one employ to better one's sexual
    life?
What is an orgasm?
What is the function of female breasts?
How does one deal with a tight vaginal opening?
What is menstruation?
How do men become impotent?
Are homosexuality, "lesbianism," and incest permissible forms of
    sexual activity?
Should men be worried about the size of their penis?
What is the correct frequency of sexual intercourse?
How does one have sexual intercourse? [my translations]

The question and answer session, which transpires at the level of plot, is mimicked by a Socratic mode of editing designed to suture us and develop a pedagogic vision.

While Dinesh refuses to answer questions relating to sexual technique, he is happy to share his medical knowledge. This public refusal at the level of narrative underlines Dinesh's—and by extension *Gupt gyan*'s—commitment to pedagogy rather than performance. When a member of the audience asks Dinesh to define frigidity and its causes, he confidently replies that women become frigid because of traumatic events that occurred in their childhood and haunt them as adults, thus destroying their capacity for sexual pleasure; consequently, they make life hell for their husbands. Such an answer draws on and confirms the notion, common in popular psychology, that identifies frigidity as a woman's problem. The causes for such behavior are located in a traumatic past, overlooking problems in the present. Another member of the audience inquires how one could ensure a happy and satisfactory sexual life. Dinesh explains that women are sexually passive by nature, and men should arouse them by foreplay, making them ready for intercourse. This response reconstructs an old and familiar patriarchal dichotomy in which men are sexual actors and women are passive recipients. Dinesh further reveals his conservative views when he replies to a query about the validity of homosexuality, "lesbianism," and incest. He quickly brands these practices as unethical and immoral, urging everyone to protest against them. Thus, the film's "openness" about sex is accompanied by a conservative sexual logic. In relaying knowledge, then, *Gupt gyan* sought not only to enlighten its viewers but also to discipline them, contributing to unequal gender and sexual relations.[30]

The final site for producing the film's pedagogic vision and authorizing medical science is the hospital Dinesh builds to treat patients suffering from sexual illnesses. The sequences in the hospital, with its white-coated doctors, are juxtaposed to Dr. Sarkar's counterfeit clinic, producing the hospital as a legitimate site for dispensing treatment. At the hospital, Dinesh resolves his patients' various problems, such as premature ejaculation and painful or untimely menses, and implements birth control with sage advice and inexpensive medicine. In contrast, Dr. Sarkar, dressed in garish attire, first frightens his patients with medical mumbo-jumbo and then fleeces them. Music is central in establishing the authentic versus fraudulent medical sites. Songs from popular commercial films such as *Bobby* (1973) and *Aradhana* (1969) accompany Dr. Sarkar's nefarious activities in his clinic. Thus, Dr. Sarkar and his clinic are affiliated with the fantasy world of Hindi cinema, invoked by the romantic and sensuous song sequences of *Aradhana* and *Bobby*. In contrast, Films Division music supplements the activities in the hospital and, earlier, the instruction at the Bhatia Medical College. Through the villainy of Dr. Sarkar and his cohort, however, Chanchal disrupts the space of the hospital as the site of legitimate medical authority by seeking to frame Dinesh as a rapist.[31] In making the charge of rape, Chanchal positions us as voyeurs seeking to undermine Dinesh's authority and the status of the hospital, but she is punished for this transgression by Dinesh's declaration that she has cervical cancer. The results of his medical examination reposition us and the site of the hospital within a legitimate techno-scientific space.

Because of Chanchal's accusation, Dinesh is taken into police custody. When medical complications arise with Tara's delivery, the attending doctors tell Bhargava that only Dinesh is qualified to solve this knotty problem. Medical authority receives a further boost as Bhargava rushes to the police department armed with a sheaf of letters from these prominent physicians stating that only Dinesh can safely deliver his child. Receptive to this request, the police allow Dinesh to go to the hospital. Dressed in a blue surgical uniform, Dinesh enters the operation theater and begins his treatment by reminding Tara how much she and her husband have desired a child. He subsequently shows her posters of plump male babies, ending with a ubiquitous poster of the god Krishna as a child. At this point, loudspeakers are brought close to Tara's ears, and Radhia lights a set of firecrackers near another set of speakers. In the ensuing cacophony, we are shown a close-up shot of a vagina as a child is being pulled out. Thus far, the film has studiously avoided aligning medicalized sex with melodrama (the dominant mode employed in Hindi cinema), preferring a realist mode associated with the Films Division's documentary approach for narrativizing medicine. In the film's denouement, however, the fictional drive overtakes the documentary approach for the purpose of generating a climax. The operation theater transforms into a spectacular space in which Dinesh uses his medical acumen to save the day, becoming an "FYP hero." This melodramatic visualization of the "psychosomatic treatment" and childbirth endangered the film's credibility and status as a sex-education film, as responses by the Ministry of Information and Broadcasting and the film's examining committees reveal. For the ministry, this sequence raised doubts about the film's veracity. Examining committees in 1973 and 1978 asked Adarsh to delete the close-up shots of the vagina in this sequence, keeping only those that were absolutely necessary. Clearly, the committees suspected that this footage might be titillating and not simply instructive.

Official Screenings, Reports, and Decisions

Gupt gyan, the film and its booklet, first appeared before an examining committee on August 8, 1973. After considering both the film and the booklet, two members of the committee recommended an A certificate contingent on the director's making certain cuts, but three members—the majority in this case—felt that the film was not suitable for public exhibition. A Mrs. Wahi, who was opposed to passing the film, noted that

> though the film is educative to a certain extent, it is too technical and hence not meant for the layman. She felt that the operations shown in the film in close-ups are gruesome and the visuals of persons suffering from venereal diseases, particularly the live shots of male and female organs, are loathsome and unsuitable for public exhibition. Over and above, there are some suggestive dialogues.[32]

Additional Regional Officer Amar Varma, who was chairing the committee, concurred with Wahi's opinion and added that the film in its present form violated many censorship guidelines.[33] Three other members of the committee had reservations about the "authenticity" of the information presented in the film and suggested that it be "referred to a Panel of Doctors to find out (1) whether the statements made in the film are true according to medical science and (2) whether it is likely to impart the knowledge and serve the purpose which it claims to do."[34] The members' comments suggest that a concern about the film's veracity was coupled with the worry that it was too authentic. The committee's apprehensions about the film sprang in part from its groundbreaking nature and from the extent to which its content lay beyond their expertise, so that they felt a need to invite doctors to judge the film. The members also felt that because sex education was in "a very preliminary stage" in India, it was "doubtful how the general public would react to it if the film in its present form [were] exhibited."[35] Furthermore, while the film imagines a middle- and upper-middle-class audience, the committee members might have worried that the film's audience would in fact be more diverse. Thus, the terms "layman" and "general public" could be read in opposition to specialists or experts, but they could also euphemistically refer to the lower classes. Because of the "complicated nature of the film" and the "difference of opinion," Varma referred the film to a revising committee.[36]

On September 1, 1973, the revising committee, headed by the chairman of the Central Board of Film Censors, and a panel of physicians engaged by the committee "to verify the authenticity of the contents" met to examine the film. After viewing it, the medical panel noted that "the film on the whole was not unauthentic as such, but it had certain flaws. Four doctors were of the opinion that the film would be suitable for exhibition to adults provided certain scenes showing the sex organs are cut out. Two others were of the opinion that the film was not suitable for public exhibition."[37] While the physicians seemed more or less comfortable with the film's content, they, like the members of the examining committee, expressed concern about the film's public exhibition. After considering the experts' opinions, three members of the revising committee felt that the film was "of educational value to adult audiences" and recommended it be given a clear A (PE [for "Predominantly Educational"]) certificate (I discuss the PE classification later in this chapter). But five members— the majority—suggested that the film "could be granted an 'A' ('PE') certificate" only if the director made cuts.[38] The cuts recommended included reducing the scenes showing Seth (Dinesh's father) molesting a stenographer and Radhia and generally deleting "the close-ups of surgical operations showing the male and female organs wherever they appear as [well as] the delivery of the child."[39] In supporting the minority's decision, the board's chair, Virendra Vyas, contended that the film was "meant mainly for educating the spectators on the subject of sex, about which" he added, the Indian population was "generally ill-informed," and that any deletions "would take away the educative impact of the film."[40] Vyas's support is indicated in a letter that Adarsh wrote, once more demonstrating how the board of censors functioned in part through informal relations. In the light of differences among the committee members, Vyas referred the film to the central government.[41]

The Ministry of Information and Broadcasting, however, did not share Vyas's opinion of the film:

The film is a far from happy mixture of scanty scientific knowledge and vague generalisations about certain aspects of sex education. There is a story of sorts, though many of the scenes are not only irrelevant but also offensive. Information is conveyed through long lectures and demonstrative models and diagrams before a group of medical students. In short, the film is a hotchpotch of a documentary and a featurised story.[42]

In its response, the ministry expressed its concern in terms of genre, or more specifically, genre confusion: *Gupt gyan* is an unsavory hybrid of documentary and feature film. Furthermore, it noted that the film "makes sex ugly rather than making it simply normal and natural."[43] Making editorial interventions that did not pertain directly to its task, the ministry recommended several ameliorative modifications, among them redoing illustrations and diagrams to tone down the "strong garish colours" used in the film and thus "keep the message . . . low key."[44] The ministry's unexpected comments with respect to *Gupt gyan*'s aesthetics inhabit the realm of taste. Through its recommendations for improving the film's look, the ministry assumed the role of a codirector and sought to legislate taste. It also suggested deleting detailed close-ups of genitalia and removing titillating scenes that, it said, served no educative purpose:

> There was a feeling that certain sequences in the story[—]for instance, the advances made by the Seth towards his lady stenographer and the near assault on Radhia, the main in her quarters[—] were inserted mainly to titillate and not serve any educational purpose. The climax was also contrived with unrealistic scenes of the so-called psychosomatic medication. Evidently, the film has not been produced in consultations with competent professional advice on the subject.[45]

Like the examining committee, the ministry also expressed a concern about the film's veracity and recommended getting clearance from medical experts, which implies that ministry officials either neglected the physicians' report attached to the file or were not wholly satisfied by its conclusions. Despite its coterie of misgivings regarding the film's aesthetics, medical content, and titillating sequences, the Ministry of Information and Broadcasting decided that the film could be granted an A certificate if certain cuts were made. The ministry referred the film back to the board of censors, ordering the formation of another examining committee that would review the film and recommend specific deletions.

On November 17, 1973, another examining committee met and implemented the directives of the Ministry of Information and Broadcasting. It gave *Gupt gyan* an A certificate on the condition that the director make eleven cuts, which largely involved reducing or cutting technical sequences and those deemed titillating or obscene.[46] The practice of reducing a sequence was intended to minimize the scene's impact. While I was doing my fieldwork, I noted that this practice often seemed to have a negligible impact on the scene. For example, removing a few gyrations from a song-and-dance sequence did not reduce its erotic charge. Reduction could disrupt a film's continuity, generating a gap between shots or a mismatch between the sound and image tracks. Worse, as in the case of *Gupt gyan*, it could change the meaning of the sequence. For example, Adarsh Arts was asked to remove the following underlined words from a dialogue involving the representation of the state: "Aaj family planning par karodon rupaya karch ho raha hai. Doctoron ki poori army lagi hui hai, parivar niyojan ke peeche, *lekin safalta nahin mil saki*" (Today the government is spending millions on family planning. An army of doctors is supporting these efforts, *however, their efforts have not been successful so far*). The original dialogue implicitly criticizes the state, whereas the edited version lauds its efforts.

With respect to sequences involving vasectomy, tubectomy, abortion, and cesarean sections, however, the examining committee required complete deletions. These directives underscore the overlapping work of cutting. To begin with, surgical incision is crucial to all these medical procedures, which seek to intervene in reproduction, and again, the Ministry of Health vigorously advocated vasectomy and tubectomy as population control. Within the context of the film, moreover, these incisions make a lascivious reading impossible. The surgical incision also literalizes the internal/external dichotomy by giving us access to what is inside. In placing the agenda of development (i.e., *bahir* [outer]) inside (i.e., *ghar*, which is the locus of morality, tradition, and culture), *Gupt gyan* disconcerted officials, who became anxious both about their ability to evaluate the film and about the eventual audiences for these graphic and "gruesome" scenes and who consequently demanded that these scenes be deleted. The cuts, in turn, generate gaps in film continuity, drawing our attention to the process of arranging a film through editing. First, all this should again remind us that state censorship is not the only locus of excision. The varied processes of cutting just mentioned play a crucial role in regulating and producing meaning. Second, this conjuncture reveals that Indian state censorship's concerns about representation did not always overlap with policies elsewhere (e.g., in the Ministry of Health) and demonstrates the difficulty of negotiating the state's twin concerns of *ghar* and *bahir*.

After receiving the committee's decision, Adarsh wrote a letter to the chairman of the censorship board appealing against three of the required cuts. On considering Adarsh's request, the board decided to modify two demands for cuts pertaining to IUD insertion and abortions via either the vacuum sucker or cesarean section and to sustain a demand for one concerning a suggestive dialogue.[47] Soon thereafter, the board received another appeal from Adarsh asking whether it had considered granting *Gupt gyan* a PE certificate.[48] While an A certificate might have slotted

Gupt gyan as a "titillating film," the additional PE classification would have modified this and reasserted its status as a sex-education film. In addition, the PE certificate could exempt the censorship examination fee and customs duty; later, it could also be used to request tax-exempt status for the film. This certificate would therefore have enabled a reading of the film as "educational," and this reading could be crucial to accruing financial benefits. Aware of these potential benefits, Adarsh bolstered his case by sending the following to the Central Board of Film Censors: letters from prominent persons who had commended the presentation of sex education in *Gupt gyan*; the previously mentioned booklet containing "opinions of top doctors, MPs, Ministers, educationists etc. declaring the film as nothing but educational";[49] and "some new paper-cuttings and 'letters to the Editor' published in various newspapers" supporting his case. Once more, Adarsh drew on informal resources to influence the decisions of the committee members. He also indicated in the attached letter that medical personnel had been involved at the level of film production and had guaranteed the work's veracity. Vyas forwarded Adarsh's appeal to the Ministry of Information and Broadcasting, which reconsidered its earlier stance and asked Vyas to form a committee of medical experts who would assess the film's "suitability for classification as Predominantly Educational."[50] After viewing the film, the medical experts concluded that the film

> contained a few inaccuracies from the medical point of view. But, on the whole, it had educational values as it vividly gave reliable and useful information for the lay public regarding sex. In their opinion, the film was bound to be of immense educational value not only to non-medical students but also to students who were seeking a medical career. They agreed that the film had a little exaggeration but such an approach was inescapable from the commercial point of view. In their opinion, the film as a whole succeeded in its attempt to impart informal sex education to the lay audience.[51]

Dismissing the examining committee's concern about the film's audience, they sympathetically suggested the film would "impart *informal* sex education to the lay audience." While the medical experts supported Adarsh, they also seemed to reassert their expertise by indicating that film's audience would obtain an informal education, reserving medical school as the site for formal learning. Significantly, Dr. B. N. Purandare, who had been involved with the production of *Gupt gyan* and had even acted in the film, was a part of this committee. There is a high probability that he influenced

the committee's unanimous decision to classify it as "Predominantly Educational," another instance showing the role of informal protocols in state
censorship.[52]

Decertifying *Gupt gyan*

Gupt Gyan was exhibited in theaters for almost thirty months, earn-
ing a healthy profit for its producer; in fact, as I noted earlier, industry
professionals referred to it as a small *Bobby*, gesturing to the 1973 blockbuster. While Adarsh had sought to distance *Gupt gyan* from the likes of
Bobby even as he helped himself to its chartbuster songs, commercial success clubbed the two together. Soon after the Hindi film opened, Adarsh
released versions of it dubbed in Tamil (*Vazhkai ragasyam* [1974]), Telugu
(*Gupt gyanamu* [1974]), and Malayalam (*Dhampathya ragshyam* [1975])
to reach a wider audience—and to increase his bank balance. *Gupt gyan's*
lucrative run did not pass unnoticed in the world of commercial cinema,
where hits are quickly cloned. Watching *Gupt gyan's* fiscal success, producers churned out three similar films: the previously mentioned *Kaam
shastra*, *Gupt shastra* (1975; The Study of Secrets), and *Stree purush* (1975;
Man and Woman). *Kaam shastra* focused on venereal diseases, *Gupt shastra* explored sexual techniques, and *Stree purush* engaged the problem of
male impotence and its resolution. The subsequent films appeared to blur
the boundaries between education and sex—and to deploy the genre classification of "sex-education film" to enter more transgressive and illicit
domains.

    Gupt gyan and its progeny (both dubbed versions and imitators) saw
their profitable runs cut short by the Emergency, for the central government at first suspended their certificates and later banned all these films
outright. A letter to Adarsh written May 29, 1976, informed him that *Gupt
gyan* would be decertified because it "contravene[d] propositions related to
'decency or morality'" contained in the Cinematograph Act. Whereas the
processes of certifying *Gupt gyan* had tempered the role of public morality and the censors by introducing concerns related to the film's medical
content, the act of decertifying it reinscribed morality's primacy and the
censors' power. Curiously, even though Vyas had been a staunch advocate
of the film, he was part of a working group in Bombay that "proposed not
to allow any such films in future."[53] Official correspondence suggests that
Gupt gyan had managed to elude censorship in part because it eluded genre
classification; perhaps its decertification resulted from guilt by association
with the later, more salacious "sex-education" films taken as a genre.

Could there have been other reasons for decertifying this group of films apart from their supposed violation of "decency or morality"? An article in the July 1977 issue of *Picture Post* suggests that the bans were politically motivated. H. N. Jagwani, the producer of *Kaam shastra*, alleged that he had "been victimised[,] as Mr. Shukla wanted the banning of pictures of other producers of educational films[,] particularly Bohra and B. K. Adarsh[,] as they had actively campaigned against him in the Lok Sabha poll."[54] It is possible that Shukla used powers allocated to him during the Emergency to settle personal and political grievances. One can also speculate that Indira Gandhi's Congress Party might have feared that these sex-education films would incite discussion on its heinous family-planning policies during the Emergency, namely, the forced sterilizations performed mostly on the poorer segments of the Indian population.[55] It is well known that Indira Gandhi's government, and its leadership, was anxious about its public image and sought to control "negative" representations. Like the colonial administration during its last years in India, when it excised any cinematic representation that hinted at or gestured toward nationalism, Indira Gandhi's government prohibited any portrayal that might threaten its rule.

When the Janata Party won the elections in 1977, it promised to reinstitute democracy and freedom. Seeking to capitalize on this supposedly more benevolent political climate, the producers of *Gupt gyan* petitioned the Supreme Court for recertification and were referred to a new examining committee. Its report makes this examining committee appear taciturn compared to its earlier, more loquacious counterparts. The report simply notes that *Gupt gyan*, "a sex education film which also contains some elements of a story and some crudely made drama," was screened for the committee; subsequently, the committee was informed of the film's bureaucratic history. The report does not any offer any insight into the possible discussion among the committee members. It says merely that the "members came to the conclusion that the film was suitable for public exhibition restricted to 'adults,'" provided that fifteen cuts were made. The four additional cuts focused on shots of venereal diseases, IUD insertion, tubectomy, and a vagina during the birth sequence.[56] The process of recertifying *Gupt gyan* shows that the difference between the Janata and Congress governments lay in the respective methods adopted for regulating cinema. Whereas the Congress government had banned many films during the Emergency, the Janata government, professing a more "liberal" attitude, largely regulated cinema by cutting, classifying, and certifying films—banning only a few films outright. As this exercise of power demonstrates, the Janata Party fully equaled the Congress Party in its commitment to the regulation of cinematic representations.

Aggrieved by the examining committee's decision, Adarsh petitioned against these cuts, requesting that a revising committee examine the film. In a letter written to the chairman of the central censorship board, he argued that the cuts diminished the film's "educational value" and violated his "democratic right of free expression."[57] In particular, he contended that the sequence containing live shots of genitals infected with venereal diseases—a sequence that the committee wanted him to delete—was "meant to shock the people so as to reform them and [to] act as an eye-opener for the entire audience, thereby forming a crux of the film's educational value":

> In fact, the audience when the film was exhibited . . . had applauded and appreciated this truthful and authentic representation, because the layman could not imagine that V.D. could be such a horrible disease. It is a fact that consequent to this sequence in our film, clientele in the red light districts of Bombay and elsewhere drastically dropped. Flesh peddling shops remained empty for a long time.[58]

The officials who examined *Gupt gyan* in 1973 invoked the category of authenticity both to question the film's veracity and to suggest that it was "too real" and thereby unsuitable for public exhibition. Adarsh deploys this category to argue against further cuts, claiming that they would dilute the film's reformist agenda. Unlike titillating scenes, Adarsh argued, these shocking images showed the "layman" how sex could hurt *him*—and consequently, decrease *his* visits to prostitutes (the imagined the carriers of venereal diseases). Adarsh also protested the deletion of the childbirth sequence because it would jeopardize the fictional narrative, leaving the story "incomplete" and annulling the "hero's ultimate effort," when Dinesh demonstrates his skills as a sexologist by assisting in a difficult delivery. He argued, "[w]hat is shown is *the reality of life, the creation, the birth, God's biggest miracle, the essence of sex*, which is certainly by all normal standards neither obscene nor even indecent."[59] Despite his earlier disavowal of the film's fictional elements, the twin arguments Adarsh makes reveal the film's (and his) investments in genre conventions of "documentary and featurised story." For the most part, the revising committee was not moved by Adarsh's petition and chose to retain all the demands for cuts, declaring that the scenes were "repulsive and . . . likely to offend human sensibilities."[60] It modified only the demand for the cut pertaining to the birth of the child, stating that only the shots that did not show close-ups of the vagina could be retained. It granted *Gupt gyan* an A certificate provided that the cuts were made.

Gupt gyan and other sex-education films significantly influenced the process of state censorship, as is attested by the emergence of new classifications in 1981: UA (exhibition subject to parental permission for children below twelve) and S (exhibition restricted to "members of any profession or any class of person having regard to the nature, content and theme of the film"; in short, *specialists*). These classifications reveal how state censorship was compelled to generate new policies to monitor new films and genres. While the former designation was designed to address and manage the emergence of teen sexuality on screen, as represented by films such as *Bobby*, the latter was aimed at films such as *Gupt gyan*, where the question of expertise was central to discussions about public exhibition. Unlike the PE certificate, which defined a film as educational but did not restrict its audience, the S certificate restricted access to films so designated.[61]

Coda I

I was not able to access *Gupt gyan*'s exhibition history. I presumed that, like the U.S. sex-hygiene films Eric Schafer discusses, *Gupt gyan* was screened at second-rate theaters or in morning shows, which showed pornographic films. This assumption was confirmed by my brief glimpses of tattered posters of *Gupt gyan* near a grimy theater I passed on my bus rides to the CBFC office. Only recently, while discussing *Gupt gyan* with colleagues, did I learn that they had seen the film in "respectable" theaters— and that they had wanted to see the film for its instructive content.

Coda II

I bought a copy of *Gupt gyan* in Delhi's Palika Bazaar, an underground shopping mall offering both legal and illegal products. The availability of the videocassette and more recently a VCD that I purchased via the Internet shows that the film continues to generate both interest and income. My conversations with various shopkeepers in Palika Bazaar indicated that they did not display *Gupt gyan* on their shelves. As a "sex" film, it was generally kept under the counter, in drawers, or in backrooms with pornographic or erotic films. Despite or perhaps even because of Adarsh's efforts, some viewers still read *Gupt gyan* as an illicit and titillating film rather than as an instructive documentary.

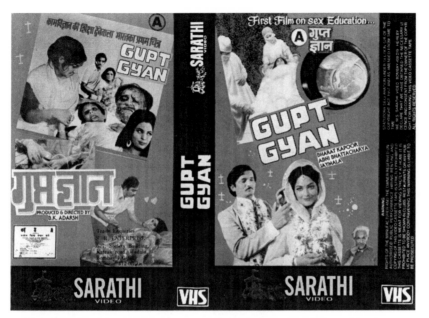

The VHS copy of *Gupt gyan* prominently features the A rating granted by the CBFC as well as a miniature version of the Indian state's certificate in the lower-left corner.

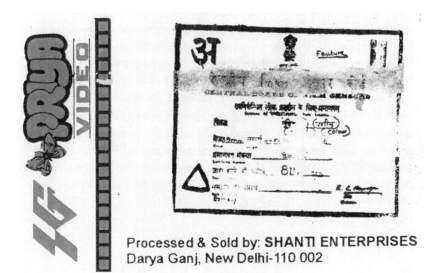

Processed & Sold by: SHANTI ENTERPRISES
Darya Ganj, New Delhi-110 002

The label on the Sarathi VHS video of *Gupt gyan* with a smudged U rating.

Gupt gyan continues to circulate in a VCD version; this one contains a much less readable state-issued certificate.

The cover of the Sarathi Video release of *Gupt gyan* that I purchased from in the bazaar displays the A rating in bold, along with a miniature version of the official state certificate. In contrast, a label on the videocassette shows a smudged U official certificate. While this difference could simply be the result of a casual mistake, it does demonstrate that certificates can be creatively generated at the site of distribution. The videocassette cover also declares the video to be "the exact copy of the original censored celluloid film." Since I did not have access to the bits of film cut from *Gupt gyan*, I could not determine whether the video was a copy of the 1973 or 1978 version. During the 1970s and early 1980s, video was not subject to regulation; rules policing videos were made in 1984 as more Indians began to watch films on videocassette. The Cinematograph Act rules suggest that the regional officer, with prior approval from the chairperson, can issue a certificate for a video version of a certified theatrical film without subjecting it to reexamination as long as the applicant is requesting the same certificate and has confirmed that no one has tampered with the original.[62] This official procedure creates both the space for the informal exertion of power and the possibility of inserting new or deleted scenes. Given this, it is possible that the VHS and VCD incarnations of *Gupt gyan* escaped the excisions required in 1978.

5 Satyam shivam sundaram
(Im)proper Suturing of Sound, Scar, and Stardom

Both B. K. Adarsh's *Gupt gyan* and Raj Kapoor's *Satyam shivam sundaram* (Truth, God, Beauty) extended the representation of sexuality on-screen. While *Gupt gyan* inaugurated a new genre, the sex-education film, *Satyam shivam sundaram* saturated the screen with sexuality ranging from kissing (which was rarely represented);[1] revealing clothing, such as low-cut *cholis* (blouses) or gauzy saris (preferably white and wet); phallic symbols, such as the *Shiv linga*, pillars, and bananas; coy looks; Peeping Toms; coital dance movements; and sexual propositions. Most importantly in this sexual cornucopia, spectators were granted the rare sight of young females as desiring subjects. The film's heroine, Rupa (played by Zeenat Aman), wraps her body around the *Shiv linga* as she washes it; she shoots come-hither glances at the idol of Krishna; she leans back dreamily against a temple pillar, eyes half-smiling and mouth parted in postcoital pleasure; she admiringly and desirously gazes at the hero Rajiv (Shashi Kapoor) as he bathes, and unable to control her desire, she moves closer to caress his back; and she accepts the role of mistress to enjoy sexual pleasures she is denied in her marriage. In addition, the film makes visible the desires of the other young village girls as they longingly look at Rajiv, attempt to entice him, and in one case even suggest a brief dalliance in the fields.

The staging of sexuality in *Satyam shivam sundaram* was clearly inimical to the project of *Gupt gyan*, which sought to foreground a pedagogical address and produce a medicalized vision of sex. These two divergent representations of sexuality met differing receptions within the state bureaucracy and at the box office. On March 22, 1978, approximately two months before recertifying *Gupt gyan*, the Bombay board of censors passed Raj Kapoor's *Satyam shivam sundaram* with a clear A certificate. In other words, the board issued the certificate without demanding any cuts but restricted the film's exhibition to persons eighteen and older. Whereas *Gupt gyan* received an A certificate only after making an arduous trek through state bureaucracy and being edited significantly, *Satyam shivam sundaram*'s journey went much more smoothly; this is especially noteworthy given the politically turbulent times, namely, the Emergency and the shift in governments. Despite its difficult passage through state bureaucracy, however, *Gupt gyan* enjoyed a great deal of success at the box office, while *Satyam shivam sundaram* performed below average there. Ironically, *Satyam shivam sundaram*'s overhyped publicity produced disparaging reviews, vitriolic letters to the editor, marches protesting the amount of exposed female flesh, and three court cases alleging that the film was obscene, with only a minority defending this creation of the renowned Raj Kapoor. Instead of celebrating the viewing of an "uncut" and "intact" film—an auteurist dream—the public demanded excisions.

Unlike the circumstances surrounding *Gupt gyan*, where calls to modify the film came from the state, in the case of *Satyam shivam sundaram* they emerged at the point of reception, with the public decrying the film and charging the Central Board of Censors with negligence, a failure to perform its duty, *a failure to cut*. The history of *Satyam shivam sundaram* thus illustrates my contention that an examination of censorship cannot focus simply on the state or state archives but must turn to other sites as well, namely, reception and production. In the following pages, I argue that the extratextual mechanism of stardom mediates relations among state censorship, reception, and production. Raj Kapoor's stardom enabled *Satyam shivam sundaram*'s smooth journey through the Central Board of Film Censors. However, Kapoor's play with the "visual" and "aural" star personas of the actress Zeenat Aman and the playback singer Lata Mangeshkar produced adverse reactions from audiences.[2] By mobilizing, joining, and undercutting Aman's and Mangeshkar's established images as sex symbol and virginal voice, respectively, Kapoor toyed with viewers' expectations and pleasures, thereby evoking violent responses at the site of reception.

I begin with a brief plot summary of *Satyam shivam sundaram*. I will subsequently show how stardom as refracted through the pivotal themes of scar and sound pressures this narrative. *Satyam shivam sundaram* recounts the story of Rupa (loosely translated as "beautiful"), a village girl who possesses a melodious voice and a scarred face. In a flashback, we are told Rupa's unfortunate tale. On the night of Rupa's birth, her mother dies, leaving the girl to be raised by a poor and resentful father. As a child she is pelted with abuses from her father and other villagers, who blame her for her mother's death. The only affection she receives comes from a toy seller. One day, as she and the toy seller are preparing *puris* (bread) to celebrate her birthday, she accidentally steps on a makeshift stove. The bubbling oil flies out of the frying pan and scorches her face. After seeing her scarred flesh, her father bemoans his ill luck, wondering how he will ever be able to marry her off. As Rupa grows older, his fears appear to be confirmed. Despite his pleas, no one wants to marry his daughter.

Meanwhile, a young engineer, Rajiv, arrives in the village to assist with a dam project. He hears Rupa sing the song "Satyam, shivam, sundaram" and falls in love with her at *first sound*. Despite frequent meetings, he does not see her face, for both the camera and her veil combine to hinder his view. He assumes that her face must be as beautiful as her voice. After he marries her, Rajiv lifts her veil and sees the horrendous scars. Disgusted and distraught, he storms out and begins searching for the "real" Rupa, who possesses a beautiful voice and a flawless face. Realizing that Rajiv thinks she is an imposter, the sad and hurt Rupa dons her veil and continues to meet with him in the guise of his lover. The situation becomes complicated when Rupa becomes pregnant, and Rajiv accuses her of infidelity. Despite Rupa's protests that she is carrying his child, Rajiv refuses to believe her. She leaves his home, leveling against him a curse that he will never see his lover again. Soon afterward, heavy rains engulf the village as nature seemingly manifests Rupa's fury. Threatened by flood, the villagers quickly try to cross the bridge—and Rajiv searches for his lover.

During his search, Rajiv hears a voice singing and discovers that his wife *is* his lover; he admits his mistake and asks for her forgiveness. Shortly thereafter, the dam that Rajiv has helped build bursts, and the bridge collapses. The volatile river engulfs the villagers and their belongings. Only Rupa and Rajiv manage to survive the flood, doing so by holding on to a temple's spire. The film concludes with Rajiv's recognition of Rupa's inner beauty, presenting an idyllic Hindi film ending.

Certifying *Satyam shivam sundaram*

There is little information in print available on B. K. Adarsh; in contrast, the innumerable magazine articles on Raj Kapoor's personal life and work, biographies, bio-pics, and scholarly analyses of his films attest to Kapoor's stardom.[3] Kapoor was a well-known and respected director, actor, and producer both in India and abroad; in contrast to Adarsh's multitasking, which is read as a sign of frugal filmmaking, Kapoor's adoption of various hats marked him as a complete "showman." An integral part of the famous Kapoor clan,[4] an institution in the Bombay film industry, Kapoor began his career as a clapper boy and went on to build R. K. Studios into a major force. His films gained much appreciation abroad, particularly in the former Soviet Union, the Middle East, and Africa. The fifteenth film produced under the R. K. Studios' banner, *Satyam shivam sundaram* followed Kapoor's blockbuster *Bobby* (1973). Kapoor's stature clearly had an impact on *Satyam shivam sundaram*'s viewing at the Central Board of Film Censors, as was made clear by K. L. Khandpur, then the board's chairman: "Though the film has erotic elements, they have been done aesthetically and gracefully. Some say that we have been too liberal but I would say that we have been fair to the film-maker."[5] The board's reading of *Satyam shivam sundaram*'s depiction of sexuality as aesthetic and graceful rather than vulgar and obscene hinged on Kapoor's stature and stardom. Thus, the *A certificate with no cuts* handed to Kapoor was

Until relatively recently *Satyam shivam sundaram* was a part of Yash Raj Films' "Forever Classic" DVD collection. Note that the British Board of Film Classification PG rating is imprinted thrice on this 2004 DVD cover.

in deference to this stardom, a fact later referenced by the film's reviewers and audiences.

What does an A certificate signify and how does it impact a film's viewing? As was noted before, A certificates are given to films with politically sensitive, sexually explicit, or extremely violent content. Ostensibly so as to protect children, films given this rating can be exhibited only to those eighteen and older, so that this certificate reduces the film's audiences and its potential markets. Thus, the process of certification and, by extension, state censorship serves as a gatekeeper not only of public morality but also of the market. Functioning much as genre does, this certificate also guides audience readings and shapes their expectations of a film. According to common understandings generated by distributors, exhibitors, and reviewers, family audiences, which form the bulk of the viewing market, do not patronize A films. For example, the noted journalist Khalid Mohamed attributes *Satyam shivam sundaram*'s box-office failure in part to the A certificate, conjecturing that it would have "kept a sizable chunk of the women and family audiences away."[6] The links between an A certificate, the film's timely distribution and exhibition, and its commercial success are effectively summarized in the following remarks:

> It is believed that a producer or financer will lose 30 percent of business straightaway if his film is given an "A" certificate as opposed to a "U"; moreover distributors may ditch him, publicity building may prove a waste and his reputation for collecting finance in the future may be endangered. Many will agree to the cuts, or reshoot sequences, rather than invoke disagreement with the censors which may involve a one-year wait.[7]

For the most part, producers and directors try to ensure that they get a U certificate (which places no restrictions on a film's public exhibition) either by limiting sex and violence in their films or by accepting the cuts demanded by the examining committees.

Kapoor emphasizes both the financial and creative stakes involved in acquiring an A certificate: "I expected censor trouble. I had two options before me. I could either accept an A certificate or make several cuts which would have destroyed the soul of the film. I called my distributors and placed the option before them. They voted for an A certificate, and that was that."[8] What did Kapoor have in mind when he spoke of cuts that would destroy the "film's soul"? Given a general understanding of the workings of state censorship, these cuts would have been largely directed at the body (e.g., reduction or deletion of scenes showing exposed parts of the heroine's body and the removal of scenes where the two leads kiss). Thus, *the body is "the soul of the film."* This radical formulation reverses a traditional hierarchy within popular Hindi cinema, one in which sound/voice (the playback singer), not image/body (actor/actress), is characterized as the film's soul.

Kapoor's comments also reveal an attachment to the idea of an uncut film. This auteurist vision of "the film's soul," as Kapoor's remarks demonstrate, was subject to distributor demands and commercial considerations. In the same interview, Kapoor states that he did "reshoot the film a little," not to accommodate the censors, but in response to the comments of a "few respected friends" who had viewed it. Bunny Reuben, Kapoor's biographer and the publicist for *Satyam shivam sundaram*, provides more information on these informal viewings:

> The film was officially completed and previewed in October 1977 to a select audience of about a hundred close friends, associates and distributors. Raj had planted writers V.P. Sathe and Jainendra Jain to talk to everybody after the preview and keep a detailed record of their reactions. The most surprising response came from Laxmikant and Pyarelal [the film's music directors]. The latter was raving over what he saw, while the former expressed his dissatisfaction, and insisted that some basic alterations were needed. On the basis of these, Raj re-edited a second version and held a second preview. After the second set of reactions from the second preview were studied and digested, Raj decided that some reshooting was necessary. He finished it and got ready with the final version and previewed it again, this time for a tight group of associates. Now, assured that they were satisfied, Raj Kapoor entered the final phase . . . , the negative cutting and background music phase.[9]

These previews bear an uncanny resemblance to the meetings of the examining and revising committees. While Kapoor distinguishes the demands of the censors from his friends' comments on grounds of creative control, both processes involved an exercise of power. Considering that the "respected friends" included associates (directors, producers, actors, film journalists, and possibly even government officials) as well as distributors, Kapoor's creative desires would have been subject to aesthetic, political, and market considerations. After the debacle of *Mera naam Joker* in 1970, distributors apparently were more wary of Kapoor's productions. In fact, a hurt Kapoor notes that they demanded to view *Bobby* before bidding on that film.[10] Although his fame generated interest in his work, Kapoor was a waning star; he no longer played the hero, and his films were far removed from the *masala* cinema of the 1970s. By his own admission, Kapoor was a "dinosaur," uneasy with the dominant trend of multistar action films.[11] Thus, he would have needed to take into account a distributor's comments because they would affect the film's purchase and its price on the market. The practice of cutting, or more precisely editing, is thus a task executed at the behest not solely of the censors but also of powerful close associates.

The informal screenings of *Gupt gyan* served to bolster Adarsh's argument that it was an educational film; Kapoor invoked his previews of *Satyam shivam sundaram* to argue that he had produced a moral tale, not an erotic spectacle: "I have conducted quiet surveys among those who have seen the film. And the common impression is that beyond the second reel you forget that she is Zeenat Aman. You get into spirit. . . . You get involved in the message I am conveying, you go beyond the titties, curves and the navel."[12] How did Kapoor propose to ensure that his audience would forget they were watching Zeenat Aman and "get involved in the [film's] message?" Centrally, he enabled reading this film as a moral tale with a "message" by using Rupa's disfigured visage to interrupt the reading of Aman as sex symbol. These "quiet surveys" also provided Kapoor with some assurance that the censors would be receptive to this reading.[13] To guarantee that they would, Kapoor submitted a completed film, perhaps hoping that that the censors would return an uncut, complete film. In an interview, he notes that earlier he submitted films for inspection "before the insertion of background music so that music could be used as the gentle merger to cover up the hacked-off portions." But in *Satyam shivam sundaram*, Kapoor changed this practice, noting that "the music forms an integral part of the interpretation of the scenes, which may be seen in a different light without the music."[14] Notice two points. First, as discussed in Chapter 3, the guidelines for submitting a film for certification require producers to submit a "complete" film—one that includes the background score. That Kapoor was able to decide when he wanted to turn in a finished product testifies both to the flexibility of such rules and to his repute. Second, Kapoor's sensitivity to sound's pivotal role in shaping the reading of the images in *Satyam shivam sundaram* is further demonstrated by his decision to use devotional songs rendered in Mangeshkar's rarified voice.

Kapoor's anxiety, reflected in his decision to submit a complete film, might have been related to the shift in government when the Congress

Party lost to the Janata. Since Kapoor was known to be on good terms with the Congress Party, a film journalist suggested that he might need to "reshoot the film to accommodate" the changes in administration. Kapoor denied that he had received any guarantees from V. C. Shukla, the minister of information and broadcasting during the Congress Party's reign, whom he had shown a few reels,[15] but an interview with the eminent journalist Khuswant Singh suggests otherwise. Singh was also given the privilege of viewing these sexually charged reels, and he warned the director, "You will never get this past the censors"; Kapoor replied, "Shukla has seen it. . . . He liked what he saw."[16] As did incidents in the case of *Gupt gyan*, Singh and Kapoor's exchange demonstrates how informal networks lie at the heart of the workings of the state. Moreover, Kapoor's comments draw attention to Shukla's voyeuristic inclinations, suggesting that the twin pull of Kapoor's stardom and Aman's physical assets (a crucial feature of her stardom) contributed to Shukla's support of the film. These inclinations are visualized in *Satyam shivam sundaram* as Rajiv, a civil engineer working for the government, looks through a camera to record information about the water level behind the dam. When Rupa crosses the camera's line of vision, his attention quickly moves from the dam, which epitomized the Nehruvian discourse of development, and begins to voice measurements not of water levels but of Rupa's waist, breasts, and hips. Ironically, it is through their positions as state representatives, as surveyors, that Shukla and Rajiv are able to indulge in voyeurism. More generally, Kapoor's association with both Shukla and Singh indicates that the film industry's informal alliances with the state and the news media rest in part on a shared voyeurism.

Publicizing the Body

As soon as Kapoor announced that he would be making *Satyam shivam sundaram*, film magazines began running articles speculating as to who would get the coveted roles of Rupa and Rajiv. Ending months of conjecture, Kapoor officially announced that the role of heroine would go to Zeenat Aman. Apparently, his first two choices, Hema Malini and Dimple Kapadia, had declined because of the revealing scenes in the film and a recent marriage, respectively. Kapoor is reputed to have debated long about casting the hero, considering many options and finally choosing his younger brother, Shashi Kapoor, a well-known star. While all this speculation bears witness to Kapoor's stardom—an RK film would generate interest in the film industry and make good copy for the reading public—Bunny Reuben's biography of Kapoor suggests that both Kapoor and Reuben, the film's publicist, generously cooperated with the media to secure this visibility.

This cooperation is apparent in the previews that I cited earlier, as well as in Kapoor's decision to invite "organized groups of journalists to visit . . . the shooting at Raj Bagh."[17] The publicity machinery for *Satyam shivam sundaram* went into overdrive, with numerous articles about activities at Raj Bagh and erotic publicity stills surfacing in magazines and newspapers. A primary focus of these articles—and the publicity machinery—was the film's female lead, Zeenat Aman. With speculation running rampant, many wanted to know how Aman—a former model known less for her acting skills than for her highly sexualized body—could have bagged this role. According to Reuben, "Zeenat Aman, one day, got herself made up like a tribal, suitably deglamorised, and with her generous bosom popping out from both above and beneath the abbreviated *choli*, walked dramatically into Raj Kapoor's cottage and got the role."[18] Kapoor made no attempts to deny this apocryphal story, clearly enjoying the idea of being courted by a well-known beauty. The gossip mill remembered Raj Kapoor's (and the Bombay film industry's) fondness for large breasts, with a rumor circulating that Kapoor had declared, "[g]ive me a woman with boobs and I'll make an actress out of her."[19] Aman's behavior, the gossip mill contended, was only to be expected, for Zeenat was a forward and Westernized woman whose parents were divorced, who had lived in Southern California, and who had been involved in a number of romantic relationships. The off-screen gossip about Aman was sutured to her on-screen persona. Some members of the press declared that she had gotten "the screen woman away from her preoccupation with 'mangalsutras' and 'sindoor'"[20] and inaugurated the era of the "the new urban Indian woman."[21] Others claimed that Aman's most outstanding achievement was erasing the traditional Hindi cinematic boundary "between the heroine and the vamp."[22] According to most, Aman was not the traditional Hindi film heroine because she was willing to strip for the camera and to portray characters who smoked and drank.

Consider the issues in this discussion about Aman: whether an actress was willing to strip, whether she played the heroine or the vamp, whether she was married or not, whether she deployed her physical assets to obtain roles, and whether she acted in "traditional" or "Westernized" roles. As these questions reveal, a discourse on sexuality came to govern the way in which decisions about actresses were framed, and sexuality per se was "materialized" through women's bodies. A cursory look at these discussions demonstrates that the decision over the male hero was not subject to the same discourse. The burdens of sexuality (woman as sexual being) and morality (woman as responsible for regulating sexuality, i.e., herself) were placed squarely on the female body.

While the bulk of *Satyam shivam sundaram*'s advertising and press coverage was devoted to Aman's curves (publicity stills and hoardings—painted billboards—showed Aman in either low-cut *cholis* or a white-sequined bra with a matching short skirt), some attention was paid to the familial environment of RK Studios, in which Aman's acting abilities were being developed and molded. In both cases, the discourse of sexuality continued to frame the discussions; the focus simply moved from titillation and vulgarity to kinship. Thus, Kapoor transformed from a lecherous old man into "a patient father-figure," and Aman, from an uninhibited and aggressive star into a "hard-working daughter." Aman nostalgically recalled *Satyam shivam sundaram* as the "greatest celluloid experience of [her] life": "It took almost two years to shoot the film. Much of it was picturised on his [Raj Kapoor's] farm. We were like a family there. All of us stayed in his house—and we'd dine together, discuss the day's work, see his old films in the night, do everything together."[23] Commenting on Aman's presence and work in *Satyam shivam sundaram*, Kapoor noted:

> At the outset Zeenat's appearance in a film titled SSS would strike one as paradoxical. I took a big risk in casting her as an *Adivasi* [tribal woman], but the gamble has paid off. She has done a perfect job of her role. Look at the hurdle she'd had to overcome. She thinks in English, and it comes out foreign when speaks Hindi. But she has the will to learn. I corrected her diction, [her] expression[,] and she was quick to check her mistakes.[24]

Given the unofficial tagline of *Satyam shivam sundaram*—"an ugly girl with a beautiful voice"—it is significant that "diction" is central to Kapoor's project of transforming Aman's on-screen (and by extension off-screen) persona. In most of Aman's previous performances, the focus had been on reproducing her as a sex symbol; as such, her dialogues were limited, and when she was called on to speak, her Western diction confirmed her status as sex symbol. While Aman had been successful in blurring the boundaries between the heroine and the vamp, she was contained by a new dichotomy, the division between sex symbol and actress. Thus, by altering her diction and giving her a meaty role in which she could display her skills in delivering dialogue, Kapoor stove both to convert Aman into an actress (a goal Aman herself sought) and to reinforce his status as a skilled director.

After the wedding Rajiv lifts Rupa's veil and encounters the gruesome scar. From *Satyam shivam sundaram.*

By changing her diction, Kapoor also sought to align her voice and her persona with Mangeshkar's "[very] Indian, very proper" image.[25]

Kapoor's bid to change Aman's image is visible in the opening credits of the film, which read "Presenting Zeenat Aman," a credit line generally reserved for newcomers and not accorded to seasoned stars such as Aman, who had been working in the industry for nearly seven years. Echoing Kapoor, Aman characterized him as a "taskmaster" who "would not compromise on anything": "My association with him helped me to a great extent in developing and improving myself as an actress."[26] Kapoor's carefully engineered publicity mobilized Aman largely as sex symbol, that is, as *body*, and with less certitude promised the prospect of re-presenting her as an actress; presumably, it was as an actress that she would convey the film's soul, its "message." In a characteristically frank manner, Kapoor explained this decision: "In Indian cinema, subtlety is a big gamble. So, this time I'm not repeating old mistakes [i.e., the debacle of *Mera naam Joker*, a film with a message]. I've put a lot of body into Satyam. For those who miss the soul, there's something else worth seeing."[27] As I have noted earlier, closer to the film's release, Kapoor asserted more often that he had made a film with a "message" and that after the first two reels audiences would forget that they were watching Zeenat Aman. How did Kapoor hope to accomplish this feat? He rested this willful amnesia on both sound and the scar.

In the film, the camera introduces us to Aman by showing a close-up of her beautiful, partly covered face and providing a generous view of her untrammeled breasts in a thin, white sari. The camera moves leisurely to her smooth, silky back as two village men discuss her marital status. Initially, the technology of the camera (re)produces Aman's star status as sex symbol, thereby affirming our voyeuristic pleasures. But when one of the men caustically exclaims, "Who would marry such an unlucky girl? Just look at her face!" Rupa/Aman angrily turns around to face her detractor. The camera zooms in on her scar, a lingering residue of her childhood injury, an *improper suture* whose stitching is rendered glaringly visible so that it interrupts the flow of smooth skin and splits Rupa/Aman's face. The village men drop their eyes, and spectators are invited to do the same as the scar arrests their voyeuristic gaze. Later, in the film's most opulent song sequence, "Chanchal, Sheetal, Nirmal, Komal" Rupa imagines herself sans scar romancing with Rajiv. When Rajiv leans to kiss her, the gruesome scar resurfaces. Rajiv turns away in horror and the dream sequence ends abruptly. This sequence foreshadows Rajiv's response when he lifts Rupa's veil on their wedding night. Kapoor invokes the transgressive pleasures offered by erotic song-and-dance sequences and appears to further gratify spectators by inserting a kiss, a rare sight in Hindi cinema at this juncture; however, these pleasures wither at the appearance of the scar. Like a conventional spectator, Rajiv is initially enticed by the sumptuous spectacle and then covers his horror-struck eyes as this "fantasmatic body"[28] morphs into a disfigured body covered by a lurid purple-hued scar, a monstrous figure that appears more appropriate for a B-grade horror film than for an erotic song-and-dance sequence.

Through this unsubtle scar, Kapoor takes spectators below the body's surface to its skeletal innards so that they can acquire the film's "message": an appreciation for inner beauty as opposed to outer looks. Along with imparting this mundane moral lesson, *Satyam shivam sundaram* teaches a more important lesson about the way Hindi cinema both constitutes and solicits our pleasures through the process of splitting and stitching body/soul, heroine/vamp, tradition/modernity, and image/voice, among other things.

Sewing Body to Voice

If part of the burden of conveying the film's "message," was shouldered by the scar, the other rested on Mangeshkar's voice. In sharp contrast to Aman, Mangeshkar was represented in the media as an ascetic, moral figure; she was characterized as a simple woman who chose to remain unmarried so she could care for her family, an image expressed by, among others, Partha Chatterjee: "Perhaps, an early exposure to the duplicity and moral degradation within the film industry made her turn away from worldliness and seek emotional sustenance in a less troubled private world. The result of this experience was startling: her singing has an innocence and naiveté that was completely at odds with the trying world in which she had lived."[29] The taint of the film industry clearly does not sully Mangeshkar, who bolstered this image by donning white saris and refusing to sing "vulgar" songs. Magazines did not gossip about her affairs or the fabulous wealth that she had amassed. During the thirty years of her reign, from the 1950s to the 1980s (if not till the present, for her voice has become the model at which others aim), Mangeshkar served as the "ideal norm of aural femininity."[30] Srivastava attributes this unmatched success to the fact that Mangeshkar's voice allayed national anxieties about the representations of women in public spaces, cavorting in parks and on streets with heroes (who were after all strangers with whom neither the characters nor the actresses playing them had any kinship or socially sanctioned relations): "How does nationalism deal with the publicness of woman[?] . . . the threatening sexuality presented by the amblings of women in public spaces was thinned out by . . . Lata's voice."[31] Her voice functioned as an aural harness, reining in the amorous desires of the heroines for whom she sang. It also served to veil the "dubious" reputations of these actresses. Consider Nargis, for example, the actress for whom Mangeshkar sang in RK productions during the 1950s. The daughter of a Hindu doctor and a Muslim *tawaif* (courtesan), Nargis played the heroine in Kapoor's films; in real life, however, she was his mistress. Mangeshkar's voice conferred innocence and respectability to characters played by Nargis and by extension to Nargis herself. Michel Chion's insightful, albeit brief, observations about the much under-theorized concept of playback singing alert us to the power wielded by Mangeshkar:

> In playback there is someone before us whose entire effort is to attach his face and body to the voice we hear. We are witnessing a performance whose risks and failures become inscribed on the film. . . . Playback marshals the image in the effort to embody. . . . In playback, the body confesses to being the puppet brought to life by the voice.[32]

Thus, Mangeshkar's voice, which was prerecorded and played during filming, asserted dominance over the image, compelling the body to move according to the voice's dictates.

According to his biographers, Kapoor was besotted with Mangeshkar's voice, relying on it from the 1950s onward to modulate the sexual accent in his cinema.[33] In *Satyam shivam sundaram* Kapoor deploys Mangeshkar's aural stardom to temper the erotic charge of the film in general and of Aman in particular. Breaking with the convention of releasing an album containing all of a film's songs, Kapoor released only three songs from *Satyam shivam sundaram* before the film's public exhibition—significantly, three devotional songs.[34] By coupling Mangeshkar's voice with devotional songs, Kapoor gestured to the ubiquitous association of Lata with Meera, Krishna's pure and most ardent devotee. Thus, the songs both served as a marketing device and affirmed Kapoor's assertion that the film is a moral tale, a story with a message. As I noted earlier, Kapoor was sensitive to music's role in shaping *Satyam shivam sundaram*'s reading. Given this, he would have been cognizant that the double dose of divinity—devotional songs rendered in Mangeshkar's voice—would be crucial for *Satyam shivam sundaram*'s safe passage through the censorship process.

If through sound Kapoor invoked Mangeshkar's aural stardom, then through the scar and the strategic deployment of Aman's body he unshrouded, dismantled, and challenged its reign. As invisible voice, Mangeshkar might have performed the arduous task of reining in and retailoring Aman's star persona. However, Kapoor's publicity made this task insurmountable by suggesting that the story of *Satyam shivam sundaram* was inspired by Mangeshkar herself, thereby embodying the voice and making Mangeshkar visible. According to Kapoor's biographers, as well as *Satyam shivam sundaram*'s publicity, Kapoor envisioned the film's story in the 1950s as *Soorat aur seerat* (Face and Soul) and had wanted to cast Mangeshkar as the film's heroine.[35] Approximately twenty years later, he returned to this story, describing it in interviews during the film's production as the tale of an ugly girl with a beautiful voice. This description understandably did not sit well with Mangeshkar, who saw it as a pointed reference to her pockmarked face, a residue of childhood smallpox (Rupa, too, acquires her scar as a young girl). Her biographer Bharatan writes:

Lata's accent had all along been on her voice, never on her visage. She saw no call, therefore[,] for Raj Kapoor to have brought the issue of her visage, plain as it was, into the SSS theme. Raj's ugly-beauty talk would have hurt any woman. It hurt Lata all the more, seeing the hue it assumed on zingy Zeenat. Not one recording with Lata for SSS after this went on schedule. There was cancellation after cancellation. . . . Never had before Raj Kapoor been made to feel so small as he felt during the SSS song taping. For the first time in his musical life, Raj found that he was not in tune with the Mangeshkar.[36]

Indeed, the combination of Zeenat and Lata repulsed Bharatan:

> Inane, naïve, stupid—that is how Zeenat Aman finally looked in SSS in spite of Lata singing at her best for her. . . . How could you possibly reconcile Lata's *Yashomati maiya se bole Nandlala* [a devotional song in the film] with Zeenie baby. . . . If Lata's voice was the aurally arresting fantasy, Zeenat Aman was the revoltingly revealing reality to the one in whose vocal image the theme was supposedly cast.[37]

In the film, the first rendition of "Yashomati maiya se bole Nandlala" (Mother Yashoda tells Nandlala) is picturized[38] in a temple on a young Rupa played by Padmini Kolhapure (who coincidentally happened to be Mangeshkar's niece). When her father begins to cough and is unable to sing, Rupa takes over and completes the song so that a wealthy boy's birthday ceremony will not be interrupted. The young Rupa's innocence dovetails with Mangeskhar's voice. Moreover, with the extratextual knowledge that Kolhapure is Mangeshkar's niece, this innocence assumes a genealogical force, for image and voice are aligned genetically and not simply with the assistance of mundane technology. Kapoor irreverently situates the song's second rendition, the one that evokes Bharatan's ire, at a waterfall, the site of many erotic sequences in popular Hindi cinema. In this sequence, Rupa (now played by Aman) dances in a wet low-cut *choli* and half-sari, throwing provocative glances at Rajiv. Thus, through gesture and dress (and assisted by the technology of the camera), Aman's body flagrantly counters Mangeshkar's voice instead of meekly bending to it and thereby infuses sexual desire into the song. This desire was antithetical to Mangeshkar's image, inviting both Bharatan's and Mangeshkar's rage.

Apparently, Mangeshkar was agreeable to having Hema Malini,[39] a more "respectable" actress, play the role of Rupa but was shocked to learn that the "dare-and-bare" Aman had been cast. Mangeshkar appeared to have detested the "Zeenatising" of *Satyam shivam sundaram*, which "went against [her] musical grain."[40] This "Zeenatising" transformed the film into a "fusion of vision and passion" rather than of "emotion and vision."[41] Such a fusion had no place for Mangeshkar, who saw her task as bringing emotion to Kapoor's cinema. Mangeshkar's virulent reaction to this project foreshadowed the response of viewers; in effect, she becomes the model resisting viewer.

To examine Mangeshkar's response, I return to the themes of sound and scar. Given the film's publicity, it is impossible not to read the scar as a visual metonym for Mangeshkar and the physical manifestation of her voice. This visualization exposes two related industry scandals. First, it reveals the hidden workings of technology whereby the secret marriage between sound and image takes place and discloses the source of sound.[42] Second, by divulging the source of sound, it draws attention to the longevity of female playback singers' careers compared to those of female actresses. While Hindi film viewers know that film songs are performed by playback singers, they willfully suppress this knowledge to experience the pleasures of the "fantasmatic body," an exquisite voice matched with a beautiful body. In the film, when Rajiv asks Rupa to lift her veil, she refuses to comply. He inquires whether she's simply being shy. Rupa sadly replies, "A girl veil's is lifted only once in her life [i.e., on her wedding night], and that day will never occur in my life." Rupa's statement literalizes the trope of marriage, which governs scholarship on sound and image. Rajiv's blasphemous desire to see the face behind the voice drives him to ask for Rupa's hand without seeing her face. Rupa's efforts to stop this wedding are analogous to Mangeshkar's attempts to delay the film by canceling her recordings. But Rupa cannot prevent her unveiling in marriage just as Mangeshkar could not prevent hers in the film's public exhibition.

Kapoor masterfully uses the terms of a social contract to overturn a film industry pact, for on the fateful wedding night, Rajiv unveils Rupa and to his shock encounters the scar. Unlike the conventional suture, which conceals the operations of technology, this improper suture or scar is conspicuous, revealing the stitching of Mangeshkar's voice to Rupa/Aman's body and rendering the source of sound visible. Like a conventional spectator, the repulsed Rajiv disavows the scarred Rupa because he desires a fantasmatic body and does not wish to see how this body is put together. Much as it does in Hollywood, visual stardom in Hindi cinema, particularly for women, hinges on the body, as both the publicity and the public reception of *Satyam shivam sundaram* attest; aural stardom has escaped this fate. While visual stardom, especially for actresses, has a short shelf life, aural stardom, which has not been similarly visible, under scrutiny or subject to the gaze, has persisted much longer. Mangeshkar, for example, sang for a range of actresses from the 1950s to the mid-1980s.[43] Through the scar, however, Kapoor discloses this normative industrial practice. In effect, he shows that Rajiv/Shashi Kapoor was romancing and was being romanced by both the alluring Rupa/Aman and the pockmarked spinster Rupa/Mangeshkar. Mangeshkar appears to have understood that the power she wielded depended on "invisibility," on being behind the screen rather than in front of it, leading her to place her "accent on voice" rather than "visage." *Satyam shivam sundaram* would have undercut this power and tainted her reputation by associating her voice with Aman's body. Thus, Mangeshkar forcefully opposed this project. In doing so, she distanced herself from the failure of both the film and its music, which would otherwise have been a blemish on her career. In disavowing this project, Mangeshkar laid the blame on the overprojection of Aman's "obscene" body, anticipating the responses of *Satyam shivam sundaram*'s audiences.

"Wishful Cutting"

On June 9, 1978, *Satyam shivam sundaram* was released in major cities all over India. From the outset, majority of the audiences and reviewers responded negatively to the film.[44] A number of viewers claimed "they felt cheated and in many theatres the management were on the horns of a dilemma as the ticket-holders became restive, some *knifing through the chairs*" (emphasis added).[45] This ferocious and destructive reaction literalizes my contention that cutting is not the prerogative solely of censors. The film was exhibited widely; in Bombay alone, it was shown in twenty-five theaters during the first week. Attendance at suburban Bombay cinemas appears to have dropped dramatically after the first day's matinee as word got around that the film was a "bore," that the story was "absurd," and that it was "nothing but Zeenat Aman's body and she [looked] repulsive." A few stray voices repeated the slogans on the film's posters, calling the film "very artistic," saying that Aman looked "sensational," and characterizing the work as "a picture showing love sublime,"[46] but the overall dearth of appreciative voices was underscored by the removal of many "house full" signs after the first week of the film's exhibition. The film and its heroine's overexposure had the unexpected effect of alienating audiences. Resorting to a safe cliché, industry professionals commented that the film was not a commercial bonanza, like Kapoor's *Bobby*, but also not a total disaster, like his *Mera naam Joker*.

Letters to editors as well as newspaper and magazine articles state diverse reasons for disliking the film. Some audiences were repulsed by the way Kapoor had haphazardly stitched together various religious traditions and the depiction of the desiring female body within the space of the temple:

One section of the audience felt that it was repugnant, if not revolting[,] to see a half-clad girl, Zeenat Aman, clinging to the Shiv Linga. In many parts of the country, no devotee is allowed inside the sanctum sanctorum where the deity is installed, let alone touching [*sic*] it. Even in areas where devotees are allowed inside, the women are totally barred from touching the Shiv Linga. As for the Shiv Linga itself, even in the Vedas and subsequent writings, there are all sorts of interpretations with the result the origin of the Linga is shrouded in mystery and confusion. Many female filmgoers were sore at this sequence in the picture. Another said that no temple whose deity is Lord Krishna could have the idol of Shiv or the Shiv Linga. Also in some parts of India, Radha is not considered a goddess, and a few temples have Krishna and Radha installed as the deities, although this is seen, in certain parts of the North.[47]

Others found the story to be implausible, wondering how a civil engineer could fall in love and marry a girl without seeing her face.[48] Clearly, the character of Rajiv did not fit the image of the "FYP hero" as the exemplar of scientific vision and rationalism. Unlike *Gupt gyan*'s Dinesh, Rajiv is not a modern savior; in fact, he is too distracted by his emotional woes to save the village from the floods. His atavistic fear of ugliness and subsequent maltreatment of Rupa is no different from the villagers' superstitious characterization of Rupa as *abhagan* (unlucky).

Where some viewers objected to distorted portrayals of tradition and modernity, others declared that they felt "cheated" by the film's title, as well as by "the *bhajans* [devotional songs] and temple atmosphere in the picture," which had led them to believe that they would be watching "a mythological movie."[49] Thus, the film failed to meet their genre-based expectations. Perhaps these viewers assumed that they would be watching an upgraded version of the successful low-brow mythological *Jai santoshi maa* (1975; In Praise of the Mother Goddess), not an unsavory combination of *Jai santoshi maa* and the soft-core porn blockbuster *Avalude raavukkal* (1978; Her Nights). Another derogatory review invokes genre in its criticism of *Satyam shivam sundaram*, dismissing it as a "cheap exploitation film":

Suitably bare and bra-less, now gyrating her hips in provocative coital rhythms, now hugging a lingam in what must surely pass as the most blatant piece of phallus worship in the whole history of Indian cinema (It is also the only visual equivalent of masturbation fantasy I have seen in films), now bathing, Diana like, in the waterfalls so that the sex millions are able to satisfy their languorous longings. . . . I have yet to see a film, Indian or Western[,] where the womenfolk hungrily eye a man so unabashedly. They are the greedy brides of Dracula eager to suck the life juice out of the hero. One of them tries to drag him into the safe covers of wheat field for a quick tumble.[50]

This reviewer, Gautam Kundu, describes the film's voyeuristic pleasures in detail even as he condemns and distances himself from them. His rancor is directed not simply at the display of sexuality but more specifically at the desiring female bodies; it is their sexual appetites that he finds monstrous.

Significantly, then, even as the technology of the camera, the editing processes, and the abbreviated, sheer costumes in *Satyam shivam sundaram* constructed female characters as sexual objects, the film also offered these characters opportunities to assume the atypical role of sexual subjects. For example, the film initially offers a familiar sequence where Rajiv peers through the bushes to watch Rupa bathe under a waterfall, but later, as Rajiv bathes under the same waterfall, Rupa longingly stares at him. Thus, the film both undercuts the conventional visual hierarchy where only men look and women are looked at and interrupts the pleasure-in-looking associated with this hierarchy. This instance poses yet another challenge to Mulvey's much debated concept of the male gaze, a concept to which I return in the chapter on *Khalnayak*.

The clamorous objections to *Satyam shivam sundaram*'s "vulgar" content, focusing on Aman's revealing costumes, camera shots displaying her body, and her lack of inhibition (which was linked to a lack of acting skills), assumed a greater force. For example, the following letters to the editor appeared in *Star Style* and *Filmfare*:

Zeenat, unfortunately, proves anything but an actress (or to be specific, just a seductress). She has spoiled quite a few scenes (like the Bhor Bhaye number which looks only vulgar). Affected in her speech, she has yet to shed her Westernised looks. . . . Raj's direction has come down to its lowest ebb. He had failed miserably to extract a reasonably good performance out of Zeenat.[51]

Raj Kapoor's *Satyam shivam Sundaram* is an utter disappointment. It has neither art nor story nor any merit except an unconcealed attempt to pander to the sex-starved box-office audience of India. From one scene to another Zeenat Aman has obligingly modeled but not acted. Zeenat has shown how uninhibited and emancipated she is. It is the nearest to a blue film which the censors have passed.

Raj Kapoor has crossed all limits in filming "S.S.S." He has also made fools of us; I don't think anybody in his right frame of mind can appreciate this movie. Raj has stripped Zeenat in the name of God, and beauty and soul.

[W]hy blame the censor authorities if they do not see anything bad in S.S.S.? Raj Kapoor himself truthfully declared that people will see the film again and again at least for Zeenat Aman's breasts, if not for anything else. Still our holy censors do not even believe Raj Kapoor.[52]

In his letter, Ramraj Deshmukh, a particularly vigilant viewer, mimicked the language of the censor board and with an uncanny bureaucratic precision listed the cuts that should have been made to *Satyam shivam sundaram*:

Our censors have been extra kind and nice to Mr. Raj Kapoor in giving him an A certificate for his unaesthetic erotica, "Satyam shivam Sundaram." Thereby they have also given him a clean chit to show all the unclean things he wanted to show. Had the film come from somebody else and through the usual censoring, the whole situation would have changed. So let me indulge in some wishful thinking about what the censor report in the government gazette should have been like. You may call it my wishful cutting of R. K's opus.

DELETE the shot where Roopa in the mid-long view in the temple bends down and a part of her bosom is exposed.

REDUCE considerably the close-ups of Roopa singing near the lingam in the temple where she seems to wash, kiss and lick the stone structure.

REDUCE by half Roopa's shower-bath under the water-fall where different parts of her body are exposed.

DELETE the lip-to-lip kissing of the lovers, in the dream sequence which has an overall crude effect and is an example of bad aesthetic sense.

DELETE the kissing scene of Roopa and Rajeev in the field as it is too conspicuously shown and does not form an integral part of the story (or whatever of it was to be found in the film).

REDUCE the scene of five scantily clad village girls in the fair making passes at the hero and speaking dialogue to attract him.

DELETE the scene of married Roopa taking off her dress up to the waist in the bedroom when her bosom is seen in profile.

REDUCE the scene of lovemaking between Roopa and Rajeev sleeping near the hills and making a public nuisance of themselves.

After all of these cuts have been carried out, the film can be given an A certificate.[53]

As these letters demonstrate, the viewers felt that the censors had been swayed by Kapoor's celebrity status and neglected their duty; in the name of public morality, the audience assumed the mantle of the censors, demanding cuts. While some people objected to the titillating content on grounds of obscenity, others voiced concern about the "indecent" representation of women in cinema.[54] As the suggested cuts just quoted reveal, in both cases the burden of sexuality was placed largely on the female body. The reactions foreground the public's investment in the project of state censorship. Again, censorship is not simply the work of or the domain of the state but also a key site at which the public exercises its power.

The vociferous nature of the objections to *Satyam shivam sundaram* on grounds of obscene and vulgar content appears puzzling given the fact that sex-education films, soft-core pornography, and adult-themed films dealing with questions of sexual desire had a wide circulation at this time. Perhaps the disappointment and anger the film provoked were related to Raj Kapoor's status as an A-list director. While the public might have accepted films engaging with such topics from unknown or small-time directors, they resoundingly rejected such fare from Kapoor because it did not match their nostalgic vision of the "showman" who had established his reputation on more lofty themes of nationalism, socialism, and patriotism.

More centrally, though, the objections to *Satyam shivam sundaram*'s ostensibly vulgar content reflected viewers' desires to contain anxieties evoked by its unruly suturing, which dislodged and shifted characters and stars from their "proper" places. In doing so, the film highlights the central role that splitting played in Hindi cinema's resolution of the "woman question." To elaborate on this, I turn to the film's unusual staging of a theme ubiquitous in Hindi cinema, the division between the wife and the mistress. After their marriage, Rajiv refuses to acknowledge Rupa as his wife. Despite all the evidence at his disposal, he denies that she is the "real" Rupa whose voice ignited his love. His desire for a fantasmatic body generates this disavowal, which in turn produces the split between the wife and mistress. It is through Rupa's dress, her movement from her marital home to the waterfall, and Rajiv's responses to her different avatars that the camera foregrounds this division. Rupa as wife is modestly attired in a long *kameez* (a long top) and *ghagra* (skirt); most important, her scar remains visible to both the spectators and Rajiv (although Rajiv violently closes windows and doors on Rupa and her scar numerous times). In one scene Rupa hurries home from a rendezvous with Rajiv and applies a *bindi* (a cosmetic dot) and *sindoor* (red powder), which are marks of a married woman; thus, her impersonation draws attention to the constructed nature of this split. The camera often lingers on married Rupa's forlorn figure, portraying her largely as a pitiable, suffering body bearing her wayward husband's abuse. Conversely, as a mistress, Rupa wears a low-cut *choli*, concealing her scar with a black shawl; in this garb, she is showered by Rajiv's love and attention. The camera moves salaciously over Rupa's body and in the process (re)produces Aman's status as sex symbol. While the technology of the camera enables the spectator's illicit voyeurism, the knowledge that Rupa is Rajiv's legitimate spouse complicates the response. Furthermore, Rupa as mistress is not a home breaker. Rather, she recognizes the wife's plight, that is, her own unfortunate circumstances. In the song "Woh aurat hai, mein mehbooba" ("She is a woman, I'm only your lover"), rendered in Mangeshkar's poignant voice, she urges Rajiv to return to his proper place: to his wife and thus *to herself*.

Rupa's movement from wife to mistress recalls Aman's famed industry intervention, namely, blurring the boundary between heroine and vamp by having the former adopt the latter's dress, gestures, and desires. This extratextual knowledge invites spectators to think about the pivotal role the heroine/vamp dyad has played in developing Hindi film narratives and shaping the careers of actresses in the Bombay film industry. By going outside the home and donning the guise of a mistress, Rupa is able to partly satisfy her emotional and sexual desires. While this movement is sexually liberating and fulfilling for Rupa, it also testifies to the pain of masquerade, of splitting. A fellow villager uncovers this impersonation and asks Rupa why she is pretending to be Rajiv's mistress. In an agonized voice, Rupa answers, "It is only by begging that I can obtain and enjoy the rights that I deserved to get as a wife." Thus Rupa enjoys the pleasures of her wedding night not in her marital home but in a darkened cave close to the waterfall. Irritated by this dislocation, the critical reader Deshmukh, quoted previously, grumbles about Rajiv and Rupa's "public" display of affection. By situating marital sex at the waterfall, the film places this secret act under public view. In doing so, it draws attention to the significance of sexual pleasure, particularly for married women.

Kapoor also stages the punishment women endure when they defy social conventions to fulfill their desires. While the privileged spectator knows that Rupa is meeting her husband (a relation sanctioned by social convention and tradition), Rajiv believes that she has committed adultery when he discovers that she is pregnant. Forgetting his own transgression, he turns into an ugly patriarch and publicly humiliates her before the entire village before casting her out. Eventually Rajiv recognizes Rupa as his wife and his lover; the two are restitched, and the scar is relegated to a secondary position in favor of a flawless soul.

The Surveillance of State Censorship

The objections from various groups were vociferous enough that when a group of officials from the Central Board of Film Censors met with L. K. Advani, the new minister of information and broadcasting, *Satyam shivam sundaram* was screened for him. Apparently Advani supported the panel's decision.[55] One could view this show of support as a way to assert the ministry's unity on the issue. Despite this affirmation, the strong objections prompted the chairman of the censorship board, K. L. Khandpur (formerly the chief producer of the Films Division), to conduct an "informal survey" by handing out postcards at theaters in Bombay, Madras, and Calcutta where the film was being screened and encouraging viewers to return the short questionnaire printed on them. According to the findings, it appeared that at least the viewers in Bombay and Calcutta agreed with the board's decision to grant the film an A certificate without any cuts, but no clear consensus on the CBFC's evaluation of *Satyam shivam sundaram* emerged:

The results of the random survey as disclosed by the censor chief, Mr. K. L. Khandpur, at a meeting arranged by the Film Journalists Society on Nov. 18, are as follows: 52% of opinions in Bombay, 53% in Calcutta and 28% in Madras stated that the censors were right in giving a clear "A" certificate. 11% in Bombay, 13% in Calcutta and 12% in Madras said the grant of "A" certificate was all right but some scenes should have been deleted. 8% in Bombay, 9% in Calcutta and 17% in Madras said that the "A" certificate was wrong and that the film should have been given a "U" certificate with some deletions. 21% in Bombay, 9% in Calcutta and 31% in Madras were of the opinion that the "A" certificate was wrong and that the film should have been given a "U" certificate without any deletions. 8% of the subjects in Bombay, 16% in Calcutta and 12% in Madras opined that the film should have been refused a certificate. The overall result of the survey was as follows: 44% agreed that censors were right in giving a clear "A" certificate, 12% said that "A" certificate with deletions would have been right, another 12% percent said that the film should have been given a "U" certificate with some deletions, 21% said that a clear "U" certificate would have been right and 11% said that the film should have been banned.[56]

How do we make sense of this survey? Most obviously it was a tactic deployed to save the tarnished reputation of the censorship board; it was an attempt by state officials to address the objections of the public, demonstrating that power is a negotiated relation, albeit an uneven one. It sought to produce not just public opinion but also the state as a body that "listened" to its citizenry—in short, to show that the state was *democratic*. By gathering and compiling public opinion, the state sought to manage the views of its populace and to highlight statistics that would favor its decision. After presenting the results of the survey, Khandpur stated that a team of social scientists would conduct another survey in Bombay, Delhi, Madras, and some semiurban areas to determine the extent of permissiveness the general public was willing to accept on the screen, and that these results would be taken into consideration while forming new censorship guidelines. However, he made it clear that the board was not committed to accepting all the suggestions made in the survey report, confirming that the exercise of authority is uneven.[57]

Curious Effects: State Censorship Benefits the Film Industry

In addition to public protests, three separate court cases were lodged against the film in Jammu, Delhi, and Madhya Pradesh. In Jammu in August 1978, an advocate filed a case against Raj Kapoor, Zeenat Aman, and the film's distributor, charging them with depicting obscenity on the screen.[58] That same month, in Delhi, R. C. Gupta registered a complaint against Raj Kapoor "under sections 292/293 read with section 34 of the Penal Code for alleged punitive prurience, moral depravity, and shocking erosion of public decency of the film Satyam shivam Sundaram."[59] There is no further information available on the case filed in Kashmir. The one filed in Delhi was considered by the Supreme Court (under special leave) because of a technicality. Kapoor had sought to stop the proceedings in Delhi but did not produce the appropriate documents, and so his plea was dismissed. He then turned to the Supreme Court for assistance, citing the state-issued certificate as his primary defense. The Supreme Court judges expressed their disapproval with the Delhi High Court for dismissing the case on a technicality and asked it to reevaluate the case. They conceded that a "certificate by a high powered Board of Censors . . . is not a piece of utter consequence. It is relevant material, . . . though not infallible in its verdict. But the Court is not barred from trying the case because the certificate is not conclusive. Nevertheless, the magistrate shall not brush aside what another tribunal, has for similar purpose found."[60] While considering the case from Madhya Pradesh, the Supreme Court changed this decision and asked the Delhi High Court to take a note of its new decision, which in effect made the certificate an iron-clad defense.

Stardom appears to be absent from official legal discussions on *Satyam shivam sundaram*, but it clearly functioned at a more informal level to shape these discussions. Given the backlog of cases in India, Kapoor's stature and stardom must have assisted him in procuring the Supreme Court's attention toward not one but two cases in a short period of time— for a few months later a second case involving *Satyam shivam sundaram* appeared before the Supreme Court, again under special leave. Claiming to be "the President of a Youth Organisation devoted to defending Indian cultural standards," a resident of Madhya Pradesh named Laxman launched a unique *pro bono publico* case "against the unceasing waves of celluloid anti-culture, arraigning, together with the theatre owner, the producer, actors and photographer of a sensationally captioned and loudly publicised film by name *Satyam shivam Sundaram*, under Sections 292, 293, and 34 Indian Penal Code . . . for alleged punitive prurience, moral depravity and shocking erosion of public decency."[61] Like the audiences who concluded from the film's title that they would be viewing a mythological film, the litigant also felt tricked and cheated by the film and found "the fascinating title was misleadingly foul and beguiled the guileless into degeneracy."[62]

Kapoor attempted to quash these proceedings by presenting the state-issued certificate in his defense, but the High Court rejected this argument. Appealing against the High Court's decision, Kapoor took the case to the Supreme Court, contending that since the film was "certified under the [the Cinematograph Act], he was absolved in law under section 79, IPC in exhibiting it to the public."[63] Judge Krishna Iyer, ruling in favor of Raj Kapoor, cited Section 79, which stated that "an offence is a non-offence only when the offending act is actually justified by law or is *bona fide* believed by mistake of fact to be so justified."[64] Iyer elaborated: "if an expert body like the Board of Censors, acting within their jurisdiction and on an application made and pursued in good faith, sanctions the public exhibition, the producer and connected agencies are protected because Section 79 exonerates them at least in view of their *bona fide* belief that the certificate is justificatory."[65] From these observations, Iyer concluded that the case against Kapoor was not sustainable.

The events following *Satyam shivam sundaram*'s exhibition and reception made the film an allegory of its own narrative. In the film Rajiv and Rupa survive the flood by holding on to the temple's spire. The temple is a sacred site, built on a solid foundation impervious to floods. Similarly, when Kapoor was threatened by the waves of public litigation, he reached out to the Supreme Court, the pinnacle of law and justice, which then rescued him. The film bears the message that Rupa's scar is not unseemly because it is God's work, and God's creation cannot be a blemish. Similarly, Iyer's judgment affirms that *Satyam shivam sundaram* is not a blemish, a scar on the surface of Indian culture, because it has been sanctioned by the state. The case highlights an unusual effect of state censorship, namely, its beneficial consequences for the film industry. To a large extent, the process of certification protects it from litigation. Perhaps this explains why only a few members of the film industry have ever demanded the eradication of the CBFC. Many believe that would be an unwise cut.

6

An Anomalous Dilemma

To Ban or to Certify the Self-Sacrificial Wife in Pati parmeshwar

A Pedestrian Tale

Released in 1989 after a long court battle, *Pati parmeshwar* (A Husband Is Like God) is an anomaly in the history of Indian censorship, because the debates in which it was enmeshed sought to define what kinds of cinematic representations constitute woman's servility. For decades, committees of the Central Board of Film Certification and its predecessor had consistently overlooked representations of this kind and focused on censoring sexually explicit images, such as close-ups of women's bosoms, thighs, and gyrating hips. While the unusual content of *Gupt gyan* and *Satyam shivam sundaram* produced debate within both the state and the public, in the case of *Pati parmeshwar* the CBFC banned a film that employed a figure ubiquitous in Hindi film, the self-sacrificial wife. In this chapter I examine this anomalous act and its subsequent consequences, showing how competing visions of tradition and modernity shape the construction of the "Indian state" and the "Indian woman."

Pati parmeshwar narrates the story of a con man, Vijay (played by Shekhar Suman), who dupes parents of eligible daughters by promising marriage and then vanishing with their money on the day of the wedding. Vijay seeks to run this scam on Rekha (Sudha Chandran) and her father (Om Shivipuri); on realizing that her father is very wealthy, however, Vijay decides to marry her. As soon as Rekha arrives at her in-laws' home, physical and mental abuse begins. Her mother- and sister-in-law humiliate and beat her. Her husband becomes enamored of a courtesan named Tara/

Despite a poor performance in its theatrical avatar, *Pati parmeshwar* continues to circulate in a VCD version. A small, smudged version of the state-issued certificate, along with triangle indicating that the film was subject to cuts, appears on the back cover.

Durga (Dimple Kapadia), who is actually one of the many victims of his previous con jobs and who seeks him out to take revenge.

When Rekha discovers her husband's affair with Tara, she is hurt and angry but eventually decides to save her marriage. Consequently, she endures further humiliations at the hands of her in-laws and husband, all the while praying for her husband's redemption. When Rekha's father attempts to intervene, she sends him back, recalling what he told her on her wedding day: that her *pati* (husband) is her *parmeshwar* (god). During this period, she helps an old man (played by Alok Nath) who turns out to be another victim of her husband's previous scams. The old man is grateful for Rekha's help and urges Vijay not to pursue the courtesan. When Vijay demurs, the old man proclaims that God will punish him. The next day, Vijay is paralyzed from the waist down; Rekha cares for him and, for his recovery, undertakes a fast to death. When Vijay becomes delirious and pines for Tara, Rekha takes him to her place since he is unable to walk there. When Rekha's in-laws discover that Vijay is paralyzed, they decide that both Vijay and Rekha are useless to them and unsuccessfully attempt to kill Rekha by poisoning her. The old man arrives on the scene and threatens to call the police, but Rekha stops him. He then goes to Tara's place to champion Rekha's cause and discovers that Tara is none other than his daughter Durga. He alerts Tara/Durga that the real victim of her vengeance is Rekha, which leads her to jilt Vijay. Later, a distraught Vijay is saved from a life-threatening accident by the old man, who reveals Tara's true identity and urges him to reform and return to his devoted wife. Vijay arrives at a temple where Rekha is challenging the deity to cure him, failing which she will kill herself. Lightning bolts seemingly dispatched by the deity strike Vijay's legs, curing his paralysis. The movie ends with a recovered and reformed Vijay, a reunited couple, and forgiven in-laws—a consummately happy family. Instead of the usual "The End," the last words emblazoned on the screen are "Your wife is your destiny."

Like *Gupt gyan*, *Pati parmeshwar* boasted neither a stellar production staff nor, except for Dimple Kapadia, a famous cast.[1] It was produced by R. K. Nayyar, who began his career as an assistant director on *Boot Polish* (1954) and *Aah* (1953) for Raj Kapoor's RK Films. Shashadhar Mukherjee, a prominent producer, gave him the opportunity to direct his first film, *Love in Simla* (1960), which was a box-office hit and made Sadhana and Joy Mukherjee into stars. His directorial efforts in the 1960s, which ranged from successful to moderately successful, followed the dominant formula of the time, combining tourism, romance, and action. In 1974 he produced Sadhana's last hit, *Geeta mera naam*. After a twelve year hiatus, he made a thriller entitled *Qatl* (1986) and soon thereafter wrote and produced *Pati parmeshwar*. Nayyar hired Madan Joshi, who had worked under him when he made *Intequam* (1969), to direct the film. Joshi had primarily worked as a dialogue writer and had also appeared on the "big screen" in bit roles. The film's heroine, the self-sacrificial wife, was played by Sudha Chandran. Chandran, a former classical dancer, had turned to acting following the loss of a leg in an accident in 1982. Before beginning *Pati parmeshwar*, she had starred only in a Telugu film, *Mayuri* (1984), and its Hindi remake, *Nacche mayuri* (1986), with a plot inspired by her life story. While Chandran was relatively unknown in the Hindi film industry, the film's "other woman," Dimple Kapadia, had made a famed debut in Raj Kapoor's blockbuster *Bobby* (1973) and exited the film industry after marrying the superstar Rajesh Khanna. In 1984 Kapadia left Khanna and returned to acting. Alok Nath, who plays Dimple Kapadia's downtrodden father (a role he would continue to play in subsequent films), had acted in a few films but earned success in the television serial *Buniyaad* (1987). Shekhar Suman was cast as the dishonest husband. He had begun his career as a television actor in the serial *Wah janab* (1984). Prior to *Pati parmeshwar*, Suman had worked in a few films, including *Naache mayuri* (1986), with Sudha Chandran.[2]

In an era dominated by action films, including the "avenging woman" genre,[3] Nayyar chose to put his money in a different kind of film, the family melodrama. The inspiration for *Pati parmeshwar* appears to have come from the Telugu director T. Rama Rao, who enjoyed a virtually uninterrupted run of successes by rendering the "Madras movie" in Hindi. Rao first tasted success in Telugu cinema with "his crude variations upon L. V. Prasad-Pratyagatma's family drama theme, relying on dialogue, rapid cutting and spectacle."[4] He went on to adopt Telugu cinema's successful family melodramas and cheaper shooting styles for films in Hindi. His Hindi oeuvre included *Maang bharo sajana* (1980), *Judaai* (1980), *Ek hi bhool* (1981), *Jeevan dhara* (1982), *Mujhe insaaf chahiye* (1983), *Sadaa suhagan* (1986), and *Naseeb apna apna* (1986), which, as I discuss later, would become a benchmark for Nayyar.[5]

Like *Naseeb apna apna* (To Each His Own Destiny), *Pati parmeshwar* deals with the problem of a wayward husband, a familiar theme in Hindi cinema.[6] Nayyar's heroine, Rekha, follows the course of devotion, love, and prayer to reform both her husband and her in-laws. Considering that narratives in which women resolve family disputes via self-sacrifice pervade Hindi cinema, the CBFC's decision to ban this film appears unusual. Certainly Nayyar did not think he had produced an atypical film; he was simply following a tried-and-true Hindi film formula. To understand the CBFC's decision, we need to consider the context of the film's reception. The CBFC examined the film at a time when Indian feminist activists were vociferously campaigning against dowry, violence against women, and demeaning portrayals of women in the media. During this period, the Indecent Representation of Women (Prohibition) Act, 1986, which barred images that depict women as sexual objects, was passed by the Indian Parliament.[7] In addition, Doordarshan, the state-sponsored television channel, introduced a new guideline for advertisers in 1987, requiring that "women not be portrayed in a manner that emphasizes passive, submissive qualities and encourages them to play a subordinate, secondary role in the family and society."[8]

Two defining events of the 1980s were the volatile controversies surrounding the Shah Bano and Roop Kanwar cases. Debates on these cases raised concerns about women's agency, rights, and relationship to tradition, as well as the role of the state vis-à-vis women, religious community, and family; the *Pati parmeshwar* case harnessed those concerns and *re-presented* them. To understand the anomaly of the film, then, we must understand these two events.

The Shah Bano case, brought before the Supreme Court in 1985, foregrounded the state's relationship to Muslim personal law (*shariat*). In 1978 Shah Bano, an elderly woman whose husband had divorced her, filed a petition in the Indore Magistrate's Court asking that he "be ordered to pay her maintenance." While the court did rule in her favor, it provided only a meager sum. Shah Bano "went on to appeal to the Madhya Pradesh High Court[,] which raised the amount." At this point, her former husband went to the Supreme Court, arguing that the judgment "exceeded [the high court's] jurisdiction and violated Muslim personal law as stated by the *Shariat*." The Supreme Court eventually ruled in favor of Shah Bano, stating that she was entitled to maintenance by her husband. The judgment became controversial because it seemed to suggest that Muslim personal law was ethically deficient and that "the 'Muslim community' preferred unjust laws[,] so somebody (in this case the State) would have to impose 'justness' on them."[9] In the end, the tremendous pressure that her family and sections of the wider Muslim community put on Shah Bano led her to ask the Supreme Court to record that she stood against the petition it had upheld and to refuse the maintenance the court had accorded her.

In September 1987 the death of Roop Kanwar incited a furious debate on *sati* (widow immolation). Roop Kanwar's husband died soon after their marriage. After his death, his family decided that the widow would become a *sati*:

> [T]he impending event was announced in advance, because *sati* is always a public spectacle. Yet, her family was not informed about this event. Evidence which trickled out pointed to murder: some of her neighbors said that Roop Kanwar had tried to run away and to hide in a barn before the ceremony, but was dragged out, pumped full of drugs, dressed in her bridal finery and put on the pyre. . . . The pyre itself was lit by her brother-in-law, a minor.[10]

Soon thereafter, the site of this immolation became a popular pilgrimage destination, with vendors selling mementos showing Roop Kanwar smiling blissfully on the pyre as well as devotional songs. Her father in-law formed an organization "to run the site and collect donations."[11] There were demonstrations both against and for the immolation. Neither the local, the state, nor the central government intervened to punish Roop Kanwar's in-laws, the doctor who had drugged her, or the persons who had profited from her death.[12]

Unusual Decisions

Pati parmeshwar came up for certification the same month that the debate on Roop Kanwar erupted in the media. Nayyar first applied to the

CBFC for certification on September 30, 1987. After viewing *Pati parmesh-war*, the examining committee unanimously concluded that it could not issue a certificate for its exhibition. In an official letter to Nayyar, Anna Dani, the regional officer at the CBFC, gave the following reasons for refusing to certify the film:

> The film upholds traditional subjugation of women as a positively desirable moral asset. In the process, woman has been shown as totally servile and this servility has been glorified both in dialogues, visuals and recurring refrains of songs, highlighting this character-istic as a positive aspect of Indian culture. By such portrayal the film trivialises the genuine serious and tragic consequences of socio-economic crimes against women. Despite official pronouncements about the undesirability of dowry, mal-treatment of wives and sati, the film presents a retrograde view on this issue. While bride burn-ing and deaths of wives at the hands of their in-laws in current day Indian society has been condemned by progressive sections of the society, the film shows in an episode that Rekha barely escapes death by poisoning at her in-laws' hands. However[,] Rekha states that they have done no wrong and that the police should not be called. There are several other objectionable dialogues, visuals promoting this servility. But the most reprehensible was the sequence where Rekha takes her husband to a prostitute since he is unable to walk himself. The film becomes all the more objectionable when this servility is contrasted against the character of the husband. This makes Rekha's attitude all the more insulting and demeaning to all women. Hence it has been refused a certificate under guidelines 2 (iv) (a), keeping in mind that the medium of film should be responsive to the values and standards of society.[13]

Dani invoked guideline 2(iv)(a), which was introduced in May 1983, to deny certification. This guideline asks committees to ensure that "visu-als or words depicting women in ignoble servility to man and glorifying such servility as a praiseworthy quality in women are not presented."[14] Her later comments in a writ petition, quoted below, suggest that this guide-line was in some measure a result of pressure that women's organizations had placed on the CBFC:

> From time to time the Board has received complaints from the pub-lic and Women's Organisations and also questions were raised in

Parliament regarding the portrayal of women in films especially depicting women in servility to men or glorifying such servility as [a] praiseworthy quality in women. In the Constitution it is stressed that equality of status should be given to woman and [the] portrayal of women in films in ignoble servility to men does not fulfill the objective mentioned in the Constitution and such portrayal gives a wrong impression to the viewers in a progressive society and such portrayals do not show a desirable social change in values. As early as 1981, the recognised association of film producers and other film bodies were informed that the Board will not pass films which show woman as servile to man and portrayal of women in any denigrating manner will not be certified after the present guideline 2 (iv)(a) was introduced in May 1983. With this background, the film "Pati Parmeshwar" was examined and a certificate was refused.[15]

Dani's letter and her comments in the writ petition suggest that the Roop Kanwar case and ongoing agitations by women's groups put pressure on the CBFC to take a stance on women's representation. In articulating this stance, Dani invoked the tenets of the modern Nehruvian state, which viewed socioeconomic crimes against women as an impediment to establishing a modern India.

Appeal to the Revising Committee

Upon receiving Dani's letter refusing certification, Nayyar took his film to the next level of CBFC bureaucracy, the revising committee. In his appeal to the revising committee, Nayyar systematically countered the examining committee's objections, asserting that its members had misread the film. The concept of tradition played a central role in Nayyar's argument. According to him, the film commended Indian women for upholding the "glorious" Indian tradition:

Among the very first reasons given by you is that the film "upholds traditional subjugation of women as a positively desirable moral asset." The emphasis is on the word **TRADITIONAL**. . . . This one word is the solitary sentinel safeguarding our cultural heritage. . . . **TRADITION** alone has enabled us to bear the thunderbolts of history stoically and with equanimity and still hold our heads high in the Community of Nations. . . . Pati Parmeshwar believes in **TRADITION**, particularly the tradition of Indian housewife's valiant efforts through the centuries to preserve and protect the sanctity and unity of her home.[16] [boldface in original]

Nayyar puts forward "tradition" as that which forms India's unique cultural identity and power, and he equates it with the preservation of "home"—that is, kinship relations, family, and marriage. Indian women are cast as the guardians and protectors of this tradition. Rekha, Nayyar explained, simply follows in the footsteps of women revered in Hindu tradition, such as "Savitri, Anusya, Gandhari of *Mahabharatha*, and Sita of *Ramayana*."[17] Any condemnation of such tradition, he claimed, was tantamount to "sacrilege."[18] Nayyar's invocation of these virtuous figures as empowering examples of Indian womanhood was not new. Since the end of the nineteenth century, Rochana Majumdar writes, "[t]hese mythical names became iconic and routine in what was written about women's emancipation."[19] For those like Nayyar, they recalled "a history of women's agency and respect in Indian society"; for others, they were "totems of patriarchal oppression and deprivation" that needed to be overcome.[20]

Combining moral and constitutional challenges, Nayyar not only charged the examining committee with sacrilege but also accused its members of religious discrimination. Alluding to the extant discussions on personal law and civil code (which included the Shah Bano case), Nayyar asserted that as a "Hindu film producer," he should be allowed to represent Hindu traditions:

India is one country and no two different religions are to be meted out different treatments. If the highest office of this country can be forced by Muslims to have a separate law for themselves based on their scriptures written a thousand years back, surely, the Censor Board should have no objection if a Hindu film producer merely extols the virtue of a woman who lives up to her religious traditions especially when her deep religious attitude benefits everybody and hurts none.[21]

Thus, as a citizen Nayyar demanded the Indian state live up to its secular promise and treat all religions equally. In constructing this statement, he drew on an argument common to Hindu nationalist discourse, namely, that the Muslim minority in India had been given privileges denied to the Hindu majority; this imbalance between the two was unjust and should be rectified. Though the debate ostensibly centered on censorship, it (re)produced communal discourse,[22] for women's conduct and tradition were combined to construct unified Hindu and Muslim communities separate from each other.

Nayyar claimed that in producing *Pati parmeshwar*, he had followed in the footsteps of other great films that had represented Hindu tradition. He asserted that his "valiant" efforts at upholding India's cinematic tradition were analogous to the "noble" efforts of Rekha in maintaining the "tradition of the Indian housewife." Only a "perverse logic," Nayyar contended, could interpret this "noble" film as one that degraded women. If the committee wished to ban ignoble representations of women, Nayyar indignantly noted, then they should have prohibited films such as *Naseeb apna apna*, in which "the heroine [played by Radhika], married to Rishi Kapoor, actually begs him to let her stay in his house as a maid-servant and serve him and his mistress Farha. . . . That was SERVILITY."[23] Contrasting such servile conduct with the actions of *Pati parmeshwar's* heroine, Nayyar stated that Rekha voluntarily chooses "to follow the traditional Indian Woman's role and make a sincere effort to make her marriage work and win back her husband." Emphasizing the heroine's agency, he added, "[i]t is an uphill task and she puts up a valiant fight and finally succeeds. Would anyone call it servility?"[24]

Nayyar was not wrong in questioning the board's decision to ban his film while giving a U certificate to *Naseeb apna apna*. *Pati parmeshwar* is similar to *Naseeb apna apna* in the tactics employed by the heroines. In both films, the heroines seek to reform their wayward husbands through prayer and devotion. In *Naseeb apna apna*, Kishan (played by Rishi Kapoor), a record company executive, is forced into an arranged marriage with a homely village girl, Chanda, by his father. He abandons his wife soon afterward and marries an attractive, urbane colleague, Radha (Farha Naaz). His first wife arrives at his new home and discovers that he is married to another woman; Chanda decides to stay in their house as a "servant." When Chanda's father-in-law discovers her servile status, he seethes with anger, promising to straighten out his son. Chanda begs him to leave and let her handle the situation. While in the house, Chanda cooks and cleans for the couple and teaches Radha marital traditions such as *karva chauth* (a fast that married women in North India generally observe for the well-being of their husbands). Eventually, with Radha's help, Chanda transforms into a well-groomed woman, a suitable wife for an executive. Chanda's transformation is noticed by Radha's brother, who expresses a romantic interest in her. This interest arouses Kishan's jealousy. He realizes his mistake and returns to his first wife. In the end, Radha kills herself to make way for the "real" married couple.

Applying the CBFC's interpretation of the guidelines, one could argue that *Naseeb apna apna* also glorifies women's servility, but its director, T. Rama Rao, had greater stature than Nayyar, and Rishi Kapoor and Farha Naaz were established stars. My earlier analyses of *Gupt gyan* and *Satyam shivam sundaram* highlight the pivotal roles of stardom and stature in navigating state censorship, which supports Nayyar's later arguments to the Bombay High Court that the CBFC's decisions depended on "who the hero is and/or who the producer is and/or at times even who the story writer is . . . who at the time are the panel members and who at his sweet will and pleasure, wields the censor's scissors."[25] Nayyar's frustration with the CBFC's arbitrariness pervades his many petitions. Instead of seeing this arbitrariness as a flaw, however, we might profitably view it as constitutive of the state's operations. After all, it is this very arbitrariness in the state's decision-making process that enabled Nayyar's film to be certified in the end.

In addition to exposing the CBFC's capricious nature, Nayyar used *Naseeb apna apna* as a foil to demonstrate that Rekha is an active agent rather than a subjugated woman. In this instance as well as in later appeals, Nayyar drew on a liberal democratic discourse, underscoring Rekha's will, choice, and volition:

> She has choices; options. . . . She voluntarily and willingly undertakes the journey. . . . All her actions in the film are voluntary and of free will and choice. . . . Despite various options before her she voluntarily chooses on her own to stand firm on her marriage vows. . . . She is not shown doing any act, I repeat once again, against free will . . . [;] the entire theme of the said film is one which depicts the wife Rekha undertaking all her actions totally voluntarily and without coercion, whatsoever. . . . She is affluent and educated, a woman of the world, who elects to adopt the role of the traditional wife. . . . [S]he elects, once again, to devote herself to placing her misguided husband on the correct path.[26]

By mobilizing this discourse, Nayyar seeks to depict Rekha as an ethical, liberal subject, not a subjugated woman who needs to be rescued by liberal democracy. He failed to convince the revising committee, however, for a majority of its members viewed Rekha's behavior as servile.

In the initial discussion after the screening, the revising committee refused to certify the film, by a four-to-three majority:

Four members (Prof. Vanamali, Ms. Gandhi, Smt. [Mrs.] Phatak and Smt. Ganjawalla) felt that the film clearly, completely and overtly violated guidelines 2(iv)(a) read with 1(c) and 3 (ii). The woman is shown in [a] totally "conditioned" and servile attitude and the servility practised by the heroine is glorified from the beginning to the end which promotes totally negative, undesirable and out-dated values. The film tries to say that an Indian wife has no status or identity without her husband who at all times is her God. These four members, therefore, felt that the film should be refused a certificate. The remaining three members (Shri Sippy, Smt. Sinha and Shri Sharma) did not subscribe to these views. They felt that the heroine, who is brought up in a traditional family background, is shown trying to bring her husband to the right path with love, devotion and constant prayers. Ultimately her efforts are fruitful. These three members, therefore, did not consider the role of the heroine to be servile. They felt that the film could be granted a "U" certificate with some cuts.[27]

The four-to-three split regarding Nayyar's arguments demonstrates the fissures in state practices; this division focused on what constitutes women's servility. "Self-interest" and "self-sacrifice," Rochana Majumdar argues, define the historiography of women's rights in India: "Women came to be depicted either as capable of sacrificing their interests and therefore, being virtuous, or as interest bearing subjects who were disadvantaged precisely through talk of self-sacrifice."[28] The arguments of the majority and the minority on the committee coalesce around these two nodal points.

As a routine practice, the official letter sent to Nayyar focused on the revising committee's decision and did not recount its deliberations. By screening the committee's operations and not disclosing the dissenting voices, the letter effectively presents the committee, and by extension the state, as a unified entity. The majority, who concurred with the examining committee's decision, claimed that Nayyar's appeal did not address the "thrust of the objections raised by the Examining Committee by merely stating that India's 'tradition' is glorious and distorting the meaning of 'tradition.' The film is not responsive to the social change in our country and shows woman in total servility."[29] According to these members, it was Nayyar's logic that was "perverse," for he had simply twisted India's tradition to suit his purposes.

Interestingly, the three dissenting members disagreed about the six cuts they proposed.[30] A cut recommended by Mr. Sippy and Mr. Sharma is noteworthy, because it involved deleting "the visual of 'Sati'" in a painting. Nayyar replied that the subject of *sati* was "not even remotely connected with any scene, song, dialogues or visuals of [his] film"; he speculated that the committee "might have misunderstood the still-visual of Seeta's Agni Pariksha as Sati."[31] Mr. Sippy and Mr. Sharma's (mis)reading of the painting indicated a preoccupation with widow burning, which demonstrates the effect of the political context—in this instance, the Roop Kanwar case—on the committee's decision. Indeed, the cases of many of the films I discuss (e.g., the impact of underworld shootings on the committee's evaluation of a comic scene in *Deewana mastana*, the effect of the Emergency on *Gupt gyan*, and the role of economic liberalization in *Khalnayak*'s public debate and government response) underscore the extent to which context plays a pivotal role in shaping not only CBFC judgments but also public discussions.

Appeal to the Film Certification Appellate Tribunal

Undaunted by the revising committee's refusal to certify his film, Nayyar appealed to the next level of bureaucracy, the Film Certification Appellate Tribunal (set up in 1981 to hear appeals against CBFC decisions, the tribunal is located in New Delhi). At the outset, he submitted that the guidelines under which *Pati parmeshwar* had been refused certification were unconstitutional, going "beyond the scope of . . . Section 5, sub-sections 5-B (1) and 5-B (2)."[32] Furthermore, he argued that the decisions of the examining and revising committees had been "incorrect" on the following grounds:

> My film, as I understand it, is being refused a certificate, not on
> the grounds of any gruesome violence, or scene of obscene sex, but
> because it presents a point of view about a woman's role, and the way
> in which a marriage should be saved, which happens to be at vari-
> ance with that of the members of the Examining Committee and the
> Revising Committee. This, I submit, is being unfair to me.[33]

In refusing to certify a film that did not transgress the limits of violence, decency, and morality, Nayyar contended, the committees had unjustly violated his constitutional right to free expression. Nayyar thus equated morality and decency with the prohibition of sexually explicit representations. Having failed to convince the revising committee, Nayyar shifted his argument from tradition to freedom of expression. Invoking the discourse of liberal democracy, he appealed to the state as a citizen, demanding his rights.

Nayyar felt that as an "Indian and as a film-maker" he had the right to "express a point of view, an attitude, which is at variance and does not concur with the official point of view."[34] Explaining his stance, Nayyar noted:

> Today, I can say the world is divided into two kinds of societies, broadly speaking, on the issue of how to deal with a situation where a woman happens to be married to an undesirable character as shown in my film. The so-called modern or Western society would perhaps instantly advise divorce proceedings and a chance for the woman to start life again. A traditional society would recommend or appreciate a woman who through her love, devotion, and loyalty patiently tries to reform the husband, open his eyes and return him to a path of goodness. . . . The point of view on which *Pati Parmeshwar* is based is only taken from the scriptures and hallowed by tradition. It is a point of view which psychiatrists, psychologists, educationists, moral and religious leaders, are re-examining in the light of today's tension filled times and millions of broken homes scarring the face of a permissive society. It is a POINT OF VIEW that is valid today and is needed to be emphatically restated in today's times.[35]

Deploying oft-heard arguments, Nayyar accused modern or Western society and the women's liberation movement of contributing to the dissolution of marriage and family life. In contrast, he contended, the traditional values presented in *Pati parmeshwar* sustain both marriage and family life. According to Nayyar, the West (marked as modern) was morally bankrupt and required the assistance of tradition to stop its decay. An example of such decay was the women's liberation movement, which had yielded broken homes and families. Nayyar argued:

> The Board has described the voluntary devotion, love, sacrifice, forgiveness and loyalty of a wife to her husband as a symbol of woman's servility to man. In the same way, I, too can be justified by describing their upholding of modern and so-called progressive values as exemplified in smooth granting of a certificate to films like KAASH showing a wife walking out on her husband at the first provocation as making a direct contribution to breaking up of homes. . . . At a time when films advocating violence, vendetta, vengeance, viciousness and salaciousness, unrestricted and [abundant] sex are freely being shown, I feel that a film like "Pati Parmeshwar" has all the more reasons to be encouraged to fight the wrong values above-mentioned, and to restore

a sense of appreciation, of basic nobility, goodness and forgiveness which alone can fight the disturbing social trends of today.[36]

Nayyar counters the CBFC's interpretation that *Pati parmeshwar* depicts women's servility by contrasting it with the films that the CBFC had certified. Later, in a writ petition to the Bombay High Court, he explicitly states that the CBFC is in effect advocating divorce and violence, which are destructive to the social fabric,[37] whereas, he asserted, his film taught values that preserve marriage and family life and consequently was relevant to contemporary society.

Nayyar proceeded to narrate the story of this "noble" film and to provide an interpretation that highlighted its "valuable" lessons. In his continuing effort to challenge the view that the film glorifies women's subjugation, Nayyar cast Rekha as a Gandhian "passive" resister, thereby consolidating her role as an ethical subject:

> Rekha finds herself tricked into marriage with a cheat who is deeply
> enamoured of other women. Her choice is to make good of her
> marriage. . . . It is an uphill task and she puts up a valiant fight with
> the weapon of passive resistance and succeeds. . . . Rekha aims at
> total and complete transformation of her husband. The concept
> of her Gandhian Philosophy is the remission of his sins through
> her forbearing. If forbearance is crime or ignoble, Jesus Christ and
> Mahatma Gandhi died in vain and what Gautama preached was
> wrong. Rekha does suffer in the process. But to a Hindu Rekha suf-
> fering is the best form of prayer. Her upbringing has taught her that
> to suffer is to pray and to pray is to suffer. . . . [India's] traditions like
> self-abnegation, self-sacrifice and non-violence are considered its
> prime virtue. Sehan Shakti is not a weakness. It is unequalled power
> SHAKTI means power.[38]

Combining ethics and politics, Gandhi had forged a new form of resistance against British colonialism. In doing so, he drew on the theme, widespread in India, of attaining what one seeks through self-abnegation (fasting, prayer, pilgrimage, and nonviolent persuasion through impeccable behavior). In fact, he often reiterated that he had learned "passive resistance" from observing Indian women. As Nayyar equates Rekha's domestic struggle with Gandhi's anticolonial resistance, the domestic space transforms into a political terrain—and Rekha becomes a politico-ethical subject who employs tactics such as self-sacrifice, devotion, and prayer to reform her husband. Casting Rekha as this politico-ethical subject allows Nayyar to say that *"the film is, in fact[,] a feminist film,* underlining the importance of marriage and the bliss in its permanence, one that should be viewed particularly by men, to caution themselves against the consequence of unreasonable dominance and lack of compassion" (emphasis added).[39] At first reading, I cringed and rolled my eyes at Nayyar's claim that *Pati parmeshwar* is a feminist film. My immediate thought was, "How could this be a feminist film?" Upon later reflection, however, I realized that while the film invites such knee-jerk responses, it also compels us to think about what feminism might mean for a range of women. For many women in India who are invested in kinship and socially sanctioned relations (e.g., marriage or the joint family) and interested in maintaining them, Rekha might be viewed as an agent (i.e., a feminist) who is able to reform her husband and in-laws and live a happily married life.

Genre, the State, and the Divine

The appellate tribunal, however, was not receptive to Nayyar's arguments. Cementing the views of the examining committee and the majority on the revising committee, members of the tribunal stated: "the film is full of scenes showing a servile role for women and glorifying such a role in a male dominated society. . . . The message given to women is that they should meekly submit to humiliations, cruelties and sufferings inflicted by wicked husbands and their family."[40] In the tribunal's view, the film sought to "resurrect" and promote "anachronistic customs" that hindered women's progress. As an example of this, they cited the film's conclusion:

> [I]n the end is shown the divine miracle curing the husband's paralysed legs which fuels superstitious beliefs. There is a real danger that credulous women seeing the film might begin to believe that going on a fast and praying devoutly could effect miraculous cures when all systems of medicine prove ineffective—as shown in the film. Since this film is a "social" and not a "mythological," such statements go against the very grain of a scientific, rational approach we are asked to uphold.[41]

The tribunal's decision suggested that films should avoid "superstitious beliefs," "miraculous cures," and "derogatory representations of women" because they hindered the formation of a modern India. While the tribunal argued that it had to uphold "a scientific and rational approach," however, this criterion is not listed in the censorship guidelines. More-over, it implies that a "social" (i.e., a film dealing with social issues) should adopt this approach; in the process, it attempts to reproduce the vision of a Nehruvian state within a film genre. But the "social," which emerged in the 1950s, was not committed to a scientific, rational approach; rather, it drew on various genres in constructing its narratives. It eluded a strict defini-tion beyond the fact that it was "set in contemporary times and generated societal images."[42] Most Hindi films, including socials, contained "divine" elements, as Nayyar notes in his appeal to the Bombay High Court: "the impugned order in holding that the said film values superstitious beliefs and will be a danger to credulous women, is clearly discriminatory since almost every Hindi movie portrays an entreaty made to divine power to which there is positive response."[43] Owing to promiscuous and in this case serendipitous filing practices, when I inspected the CBFC's *Pati parmesh-war* file, it contained material related to another film, *The Bed Room Story* (1988), in which another tribunal expressed similar anxieties about super-natural elements:

> Certifying a film having some elements of superstitions and super-natural would not justify certifying films which have excess of these. A line is necessarily to be drawn beyond which these phenomena will contravene the guidelines. Again, no hard and fast rule can pos-sibly be laid down and it is left to the intelligence of the members of the Board and its advisory panels and the Tribunal to decide the same keeping in view the overall impact a film is likely to have over the prevailing standards and the sensitivities of the society with a view to make the society move forward and prevent it from sliding into the old backwardness.[44]

These anxieties echo concerns raised in the CBFC's deliberations dur-ing the early 1980s. In her writ petition to the Bombay High Court, Dani points out that in 1981 the CBFC had decided to generate new rules gov-erning the censorship of antiscientific and antirational representations in addition to the portrayal of women as servile:

> The Board felt that films whose total impact on the audience was clearly negative in so far as progressive social change was concerned should be discouraged and that the Board should keep in mind the constitutional obligation enjoined on all citizens to develop the scientific temper. Accordingly the Board resolved that careful

attention should be given to the following points while censoring films: (i) Does the film induce or strengthen irrational and superstitious beliefs and have the effect of promoting cults and customs that invoke supernatural agencies that are claimed to reward believers and harm non-believers?[45]

While a directive prohibiting "antiscientific" representations, whether visuals or dialogue, does not appear in the guidelines until 1991, the issue seems to have influenced the decision-making process well before that, as is demonstrated in the cases of *Pati parmeshwar* and *The Bed Room Story*.

The CBFC's apprehensions compel us to consider the role of miracles and the divine in *Pati parmeshwar*. In undertaking this investigation, I draw on Philip Lutgendorf's insights in his analysis of the superhit "mythological" *Jai Santoshi maa* (In Praise of Goddess Santoshi). Lutgendorf offers an alternative construction of women's agency by demonstrating how the divine empowers and enables the film's heroine, Satyavati, to negotiate and resolve problems associated with entry into a new household, such as mistreatment by in-laws and the burdens of housework.[46] Unlike the 1970s' "angry young man," Satyavati employs prayer rather than violence to achieve her goals. Furthermore, she is not a transgressive figure but a "humble, submissive woman who overtly asks little for herself. While appearing to adhere to the code of a conservative extended family (the systemic abuses of which are dramatically highlighted), Satyavati nevertheless quietly achieves goals, shared by many women, that subvert this code."[47] Like *Jai Santoshi maa*, *Pati parmeshwar* poses a set of contemporary concerns for women: arranged marriage, marital infidelity, and the difficulties of moving to a new household (which might include demands for money, pressures to do housework, and mental as well as physical abuse by in-laws). It posits and then discards both Rekha's father and allopathic and traditional medicine as potential cures for the problems of marital dispute and paralysis, respectively. More important, the state plays no role at all in *Pati parmeshwar*, even though the film deals with concerns, such as gender inequality and violence against women, that were central to the Nehruvian state. In fact, in the single instance in the film when a character (Tara/Durga's father) threatens to call the police, Rekha urges him not to do so. It is the divine that propels the narrative and resolves problems (e.g., Vijay is punished and then cured, the in-laws' attempt to kill Rekha is foiled, and the divine reunites the couple as well as the larger family). The turn to the divine in this "social" points to the limits of a secular, rational order dear to the Nehruvian state.

Rekha, who is the prime beneficiary and agent of the divine in *Pati parmeshwar*, parallels Satyavati, the heroine of *Jai Santoshi maa*, in that she is oppressed and abides by a conservative code but nevertheless triumphs. While the film's title might be *Pati Parmeshwar*, its central character is not the husband but the devoted wife who accomplishes what the male hero normally does in a Hindi film—resolve problems and unite the family. Moreover, she attains success via a novel approach. Generally, both the male heroes in the action genre, which dominated the 1980s, and the heroines in the "avenging woman" genre transgressed the laws of the state, pursuing a course of violence to achieve their ends. The female characters in contemporaneous middle-brow and art cinema often flouted dominant social norms governing community, kinship, and marital relations. In contrast, Rekha stays within the *lakshman-rekha* (i.e., the bounds of society)[48] and achieves her goals through forms of self-abnegation (e.g., fasting, prayer, and nonviolent persuasion through model behavior).

The tribunal felt the divine belonged not in the contemporary social film but in the "golden" past. Opposing Nayyar's contention that Rekha's actions are analogous to Sita's, Savitri's, and Anasuya's, they argued:

> The conduct of their husbands was exemplary and therefore the love and affection of the wives was also ideal. They were not servile to their husbands. But it is a historical fact that in the last hundreds of years women lost their identity and were treated as chattel. However, in this century great strides have been made in this country to give women their due place.[49]

The tribunal's narrative constructs a golden age of exemplary marital behavior from which there is a fall and asserts that the modern state, through laws and policies, is addressing this fall by providing women with agency. In a writ petition to the Bombay High Court, Nayyar challenged the tribunal's views:

> The Tribunal's order incorrectly states that the husband of Seeta and Anasuya showed exemplary conducts. Rama, husband of Seeta, on mere hearsay, compelled her to go through Agni-Preeksha [trial by fire] and then later when he was crowned the King and ascended the throne, banished his wife Seeta[,] who was pregnant[,] to the forest on the mere unproven words of a washerman. Seeta obeyed willingly. Anasuya's husband in Hindu mythology was a drunkard and a womanizer. He finally contracted leprosy which incapacitated him totally.

Despite all their husband's misdeeds and behaviour, their respected wives Seeta and Anasuya behaved in a manner comparable to that of Rekha which the Tribunal considers not only servile but as a sign of weakness.[50]

Nayyar disputes the tribunal's linear narrative, which enshrines and seals tradition, robbing it of any political force. He argues that Hindus gods are not "ideal"; rather, they are portrayed as unfaithful and unreliable, needing to be cajoled. He likens Rekha to Hindu goddesses, suggesting that both need to employ traditional tactics to deal with errant partners and marital difficulties. Unlike the tribunal, he emphatically argues that tradition can be the site of female agency.

Bombay High Court

Unbowed by the tribunal's judgment, Nayyar, with the support of the Film Federation of India,[51] petitioned against the decision in the Bombay High Court, alleging that the CBFC and the tribunal's orders had been discriminatory and unconstitutional. After watching the film, reviewing the script, and listening to the submissions and arguments on both sides, Justice S. C. Pratap ruled that "the total ban of this film" was unjustified and that "with cuts, deletions, substitutions and modifications," it deserved a U certificate.[52] Pratap justified his ruling by quoting official figures who had emphasized that cinematic representations should be "true to Indian culture; true to Indian tradition; and true to Indian womanhood."[53] In Justice Pratap's view, the representation of Rekha had abided by these strictures:

> Rekha has been true to all these. She exemplifies the inner strength
> and character of Indian womanhood. She asserts and ultimately suc-
> ceeds in bringing down her husband to the path of righteousness
> and virtue. It is the triumph and victory of Indian womanhood, not-
> withstanding the ups and downs of matrimonial life and the storms
> which it not infrequently passes through.[54]

Pratrap felt that in choosing to stay with her husband, Rekha had preserved and abided by "traditions of Hindu society which believes in maintaining the sanctity and piousness inherent in the sacred institution of marriage."[55] In Pratap, Nayyar had finally found a sympathetic reader who concurred with his view that Rekha is an agent who manages to reform her husband via devotion. Like Nayyar, Pratap felt that the decision to ban the film had been unduly "harsh," "discriminatory," and "arbitrary," especially when compared to the decisions regarding films "of recent and current origin and release" that had been granted certificates, such as *Shahenshah* (1988), *Ghunghat* (1988), *Kab tak chup rahungi* (1988) and *Aaage ki soch* (1988).[56]

In supporting Nayyar, Pratap strayed beyond his juridical purview and into the CBFC's and the tribunal's domains, as evidenced by the CBFC's subsequent appeal against his decision. For example, Pratap asked Nayyar to make changes in the film and then screen it for select members of the CBFC—ones he himself would select. Suspicious of the constitution of previous committees, as well as "the mode and manner of reaching a decision," Pratap "prepared a list of seven persons from the [CBFC] panel and gave liberty to the [CBFC] to select any five to see the film and forward their opinion to the Court."[57] Upon receiving these decisions, Justice Pratap, "out of deference to the views of the committee members," directed further cuts and ruled that the film be issued a UA certificate as a "compromise," since an equal number of members had recommended A, U, and UA certificates.[58] In entering the domain of the CBFC, Pratap unwittingly questioned formal state divisions that designated censorship to be specifically the duty of the censors.

After rendering his judgment, Justice Pratap offered the following "off-the-bench" observation:

> [U]nlike many in this modern world always turning westward for everything, the heroine Rekha is not colour blind to basic Hindu culture, heritage and traditions. She exemplifies the inner strength and character of Indian womanhood. Her commitment to marriage is total and supreme and she honours it in full measure in the true spirit of Hindu ethos. Being a rich father's daughter, she was not helpless. She need not have accepted and passed through what is part and parcel of the web of Hindu life. . . . A true *saubhagyavati*, she steadfastly holds on to the higher values which, in many a matrimonial home today, are seen falling by the wayside.[59]

Pratap constructs a dichotomy between the East and the West in which the East is morally superior; moreover, he defines and glorifies Hindu tradition. Recall the context in which this decision was rendered: the rise of Hindu nationalism. The Sangh Parivar,[60] for example, advocated nation building by mobilizing Hindu tradition, a discourse in which women were largely defined as wives and mothers, dutiful and sacrificing, who deployed their *matrishakti* (literally, power of motherhood) in service of family, community, and the nation.

Modifications

After viewing *Pati parmeshwar*, Pratap "*directed* several cuts, deletions, modifications, substitutions and modifications [be made] both in the scenes and in the scripts/dialogues"[61] (emphasis added). Pratap's actions echo those of the officials at the Ministry of Information and Broadcasting who, after viewing *Gupt gyan*, suggested that Adarsh needed to mute its garish colors. In ordering these revisions, Justice Pratap was in a sense contributing to the film's direction and editing and therefore participating in a creative endeavor. Thus Pratap's actions can be read as both authoritative and creative, contributing to the production of the film. I would like to underscore the porous nature of practices. The cases of both *Gupt gyan* and *Pati parmeshwar* demonstrate that creativity is not the sole domain of the director.

In a scene added to the film at Pratap's direction, Rekha has a conversation with her conscience (figured as an image in a mirror) about her husband's wayward habits and manages to convince this alter ego that her decision to save her marriage is the correct one. Pratap suggested that this addition would highlight "Rekha's determination to save her marriage without losing self-respect."[62] Interestingly, the final version of the film has a different version of the scene; specifically, the roles of the conscience and Rekha are reversed, with the former seeking to convince the latter to save her marriage. The scene takes place after Rekha discovers that Vijay loves Tara. The sequence is a compilation of ten shots and a fade-out followed by another twenty shots and a fade-out. The fast-paced cuts supplemented by the wailing and mournful violins on the soundtrack highlight Rekha's agitated and distraught state of mind. The agitation conveyed through film grammar is verbalized in the exchange that takes place between Rekha and her conscience. Initially, Rekha appears stunned by the magnitude of Vijay's betrayal, but her grief and shock quickly turn to anger as she vows not to put up with such abusive behavior. The camera cuts to her conscience, who appears in a mirror. Wearing a simple white sari, a red *bindi* on her forehead, and a *mangalsutra* around her neck, Rekha's mirror image appears calm and firm as she asks about Rekha's course of action. Rekha stridently replies that she plans to leave Vijay if he does not stop pursuing Tara. In a horror-struck voice, the conscience demands, "What? You'll ask for a DIVORCE?"[63] The word *divorce* reverberates seven times as the camera zooms in and out on Rekha's face, as if striking her—and the audience—with the force of it. The soundtrack issues loud claps of thunder, constructing divorce as a calamity.

The thought of walking out on Vijay disturbs Rekha, but she still manages to retain some composure, replying, "Why not? I'm a modern woman. If my husband behaves this way, then the law has given me the right to demand divorce." Her conscience concedes, "Of course the law has given you this right, but after marriage, you become a wife and your duty is to your husband." The camera cuts to Rekha as she interjects, "I'm not willing to believe in such a notion of duty, one that doesn't treat men and women equally." In the subsequent exchange, the conscience challenges Rekha's understanding of gender by defining a "good" Hindu woman's role:

CONSCIENCE: Our religion gives much more respect to women—as it should. After all, a woman gives life; she gives birth to man and that's why she's worshiped. Our many temples in which goddesses are worshiped testify to the respect accorded to women in this land.

REKHA: They are worshiped only in temples, in the form of mothers—not in the form of wives.

CONSCIENCE: After all, it is the wife who becomes the mother.

REKHA: But I want my rights as a wife from my husband. I'm not a weak woman, and I won't suffer any abuse from my husband.

CONSCIENCE: To suffer defeat silently is weakness but to warn the person who's abusing you, to fight this abuse with the strength of your mind—and through nonviolence to see the end of this abuse—is not weakness but power.

REKHA: Power? How is that power?

CONSCIENCE: Why is a woman compared to Earth? Because a woman possesses the same positive attributes as the Earth. The Earth endures so much—plowing, wars, tornadoes, earthquakes—but she doesn't rebel; she doesn't ask for a divorce. She gives human beings so much. Even after such abuse, she gives human beings space to live, to flourish, and even her lap to die. That is the victory of the Earth. You also must be victorious by bringing your straying husband to the right path.

Unlike the doubling and splitting in *Satyam shivam sundaram* (Rupa as both wife and mistress), which draws our attention to Hindi cinema's questionable resolution to the woman question, the splitting in *Pati parmeshwar* is deployed to (re)produce a figure central to the narratives of Hindi cinema, namely, the self-sacrificial woman. In splitting Rekha, the filmic narrative reproduces a dichotomy between self-interest (i.e., rights) and self-sacrifice, which, as Majumdar notes, is central to the historiography of women's emancipation.[64] Self-sacrifice yields to self-interest, as Rekha is convinced that, as a good Hindu woman, she must try to save her marriage. Notably, this dichotomy is repeated in the contrast between the heroine Rekha and the courtesan Tara, another dyad ubiquitous in Hindi cinema. Unlike *Satyam shivam sundaram*, which problematizes this binary opposition (and splitting in general), *Pati parmeshwar* largely showcases it. While Rekha chooses a life of self-abnegation, Tara attempts to avenge the wrongs committed against her family. Once more self-sacrifice triumphs, as Tara stops her quest for vengeance once her father shows her that her real victim is the devoted Rekha.

In the exchange between Rekha and her conscience, both Rekha and the audience are invited to view the image in the mirror, which advocates self-sacrifice, as an ideal representation and to emulate this representation. For the audience, this exchange is further complicated by the mediating technologies of the screen and the camera. In fact, the mirror in which Rekha sees her conscience parallels the screen on which the audience witnesses this scene. The audience is invited not only to view the image in the mirror as ideal but also to see this film as an ideal representation of Hindu tradition, or in Nayyar's words, as "one of the cleanest, most acceptable, most respectable, and most noble movies produced in Bombay in recent years."[65] This reading is bolstered by the fact that the objections raised by the CBFC and the tribunal are included in this carefully scripted dialogue. As Rekha voices their objections by asserting her rights as a modern woman, her conscience counters them by reminding her of supposedly more important roles as a Hindu woman: wife and mother.

As the story of *Pati parmeshwar*'s trials is (re)presented in this dialogue, the members of the CBFC suffer defeat not only within the space of the courtroom but also within the diegetic space. In fact, it seems possible even to trace the successive moments that constitute this defeat by tracing the *but* that marks the relation between the law and its negation, between the mirror and Rekha, and thus between the audience and the screen. *But* as pivot point, as point and granule of resistance, is worn away, and with its dissolution the audience by extension ceases to utter the formal *but* that is the mark, perhaps, of its suspension of belief, the mark of its knowledge of its own fantasy.[66]

The Central Board of Film Certification's Appeal

The CBFC appealed Pratap's decision, requesting the Bombay High Court to review the case. The board contended that the "judgment and order dated 22nd June 1988 passed by His Lordship Mr. Justice S. C. Pratap [was] arbitrary, illegal, unconstitutional and in excess of his jurisdiction."[67] Elaborating on this claim, it stated that this court had no jurisdiction either to constitute a committee to examine the film or "to grant such certificate on the basis of certain cuts suggested" by the justice; instead, Pratap should have followed procedure and returned the film to the CBFC for reassessment. Pratap's decision, the board argued, contravened the film censorship guidelines as well as the Constitution of India:

> The Learned judge failed to appreciate that to picturise a married woman in ignoble servility and to glorify the said servility as a quality of the woman is indecent and immoral and to take into account the contemporary standards of the country and the people in India and the values and standards of the society and so also the needs for social change and improvement of status of women, as contemplated under Article 19 (2) of the Constitution of India.[68]

In disregarding the judgment of the tribunal, Pratap had undermined the status and work of a "constitutional body."

The case of *Pati parmeshwar* illustrates the difficulty of reaching a both political and cultural consensus. Bombay High Court Justices Agarwal and Lentin, who considered the CBFC's appeal, had diametrically opposite views of the case. While Justice Agarwal questioned the constitutional validity of guideline 2(iv)(a), Justice Lentin asserted that it fell squarely within the scope of "indecency and morality" regulation as stated in the Cinematograph Act and the Constitution of India. Agarwal claimed that even if one accepted the constitutional validity of this guideline, Rekha's depiction did not violate it. He argued that her servility is not "ignoble" but rather "enobling," for it abides by Hindu tradition: "Justice Agarwal sees the film as an exaltation of traditional Hindu values. He appears to read into the guideline a caveat saying that it is to be applied to films about Hindu tradition which are shown to Hindu audiences."[69] Conversely, Lentin maintained that Rekha's portrayal contravened guideline 2(iv)(a) and that the film was not "responsive to social change" as stated in the guidelines. Because of this difference of opinion, the case was sent to a third judge, Justice P. S. Shah. Although Justice Shah concurred with Lentin with respect to the constitutional validity of guideline 2(iv)(a), he disagreed with Lentin's interpretation of Rekha's depiction. Justice Shah declared, "because the film was seen by a primarily Hindu audience, there was nothing wrong with Rekha's 'ignoble servility.'"[70] Thus, the CBFC's appeal was unsuccessful.

The limited scholarship on *Pati parmeshwar* has focused on the judgments of the Bombay High Court. It concurs with Justice Lentin's views and draws our attention to the communal nature of Shah's and Agarwal's judgments, which construct a homogeneous, majority "Hindu audience" who share cultural attitudes and viewing practices.[71] By extending this scholarship, we see that the screen and the theater transform into political sites for the (un)democratic play of majority and minority politics. This scholarship, however, fails to examine the film itself and other materials related to the case; as a result, it overlooks alternative constructions of women's agency and neglects any analysis of the mechanisms of censorship.

The comments and decisions of the examining committee, revising committee, Film Appellate Tribunal, and Bombay High Court judges reveal competing visions of the Indian state, even among those who reside within its ambit. These visions underscore that the state is not a monolithic entity. Rather, the unequal play of these opposing and overlapping visions produces the state. On the one hand, many of the officials' statements concur with the project of the modern Nehruvian state, to which economic and social development were central. In this project, tradition was largely associated with caste and gender inequalities, as well as religious excesses, which were viewed as regressive; thus, tradition had to be regulated or overcome so that it would not become an obstacle to progress. On the other hand, officials such as the minority within the revising committee and some of the judges disagreed with the place allotted to tradition in the Nehruvian vision. They viewed tradition as a commitment to cultural heritage, religious beliefs, and the sanctity of marriage and family. They concurred with Nayyar's arguments that Hindu tradition is not opposed to progress, development, or women's agency; while embodying tradition, Hindu women have also mobilized it to empower themselves. These views drew on and contributed to the rising discourses of Hindu nationalism and communalism.

The CBFC attempted to appeal the Bombay High Court's decision to certify the film and to take the case to the Supreme Court to settle the question of jurisdiction:

[T]he case involves a substantial question of law of general importance regarding the powers of the Film Censor Board to arrive at a conclusion as per the guidelines and the limits of the judicial scrutiny of this judgment made by Tribunal on facts presided over by Retired Chief Justice. Hence, this question of interference by the High Court in the discretion and finality of findings given by the Tribunal is often coming before the courts. So to have the law on the subject crystallized finally, a decision by the highest court is necessary.[72]

The board was unsuccessful, and the film was granted a UA certificate contingent on the filmmakers' enacting the cuts and substitutions recommended by the ad hoc committee convened by Justice Pratap. There is some documentation suggesting that Bikram Singh, the chairperson of the CBFC, was asked to resign in 1989 partly because the CBFC had pursued the *Pati parmeshwar* case, but he could simply have been a casualty of coalition politics and a change in the government, bringing in its wake shifting views about what do to with cinema and the CBFC.[73] During the period when *Pati parmeshwar* was examined, the central government directed the CBFC to pursue issues related to the representation of women. When a new government took power following elections, the board was informally advised to stop pursuing the *Pati parmeshwar* case. The CBFC flouted this directive, however, and followed the earlier policy, stating that it had not received the new directive in writing.[74] Contrary to an often expressed belief, this demonstrates that coalition politics (which perhaps enables such subversive challenges) is not or at least need not be a sign of a weak state. Rather, it should remind us that the state is neither a monolithic nor a fixed entity.

In reading the "failure" of the CBFC and the tribunal, we should take into account their unusual decisions, which drew attention to a "normal" representation, namely, the self-sacrificial woman. In questioning this representation and reading it as "the glorification of woman's subjugation," the CBFC and the tribunal added to discourses on the role of women, matrimony, and family relations. The act of regulating representations, then, has an impact on broader areas. Such micropractices engender decisions that are supported and challenged both within and beyond the ambit of the state, thereby contributing to state formation.

Alternative Reading

The trail of documents in the *Pati parmeshwar* case, which focus almost exclusively on Rekha's depiction, sediments the discourse on the film on the issue of women's subjugation. To unsettle the focus of these documents, I turn to an alternative site for reading this film by examining the role of the other major female character, Tara/Durga. In his appeal to the tribunal, Nayyar draws our attention to this character:

> The film does not[,] as alleged, ignore women's independence and sense of identity. In fact there is a parallel character to Rekha, that of Tara alias Durga, whose defiance to male chauvinism is strongly shown in the film. . . . Both [Rekha and Tara] are educated and are of independent mind. One chooses marital bliss and the other vengeance. . . . I emphasise strongly that the two women in my film are neither subjugated, nor servile and are not treated ignobly.[75]

In his decision Pratap also refers to Tara:

> Coming to the mujra girl Tara, she is strongly motivated by her fully justified desire for revenge. She's out to avenge her betrayal. She is bold, independent and strong willed. There is no question at all of any servility on her part. On the contrary, by her charm and will, it is she who renders Vijay total[ly] servile to her. And, what is more, she gives him nothing in return.[76]

Pati parmeshwar deployed the familiar dyad of the wife and the courtesan. Unlike her predecessors, however, Tara has a heart not made of gold but filled with vengeance, gesturing to the "avenging woman" genre of the 1980s. Through her spectacular dances and sensuous performance, she overshadows Rekha, paralleling the prominence of Dimple Kapadia over Sudha Chandran. Both the character Tara/Durga and the star Dimple Kapadia, a single mother of two daughters who separated from her famous husband and returned to work in the film industry, become important sites for assessing social norms such as marriage and family inside and outside the diegetic space.

In the film, vengeance is arrested by self-sacrifice, a prominent feature of family melodrama, as Tara stops pursuing vengeance once she learns of the devoted Rekha's plight, which may well be read as solidarity between two women. Indeed, it is partly because they overlooked the character of Tara that many of the officials involved viewed *Pati parmeshwar* simply as a film about women's subjugation and then set out to regulate its representation. In questioning this reading of the film, Nayyar does offer an alternative construction of women's agency; however, his interpretation rests on normative roles for women (specifically Hindu women) as wives and mothers and overlooks figures such as Tara/Durga, and by extension Dimple Kapadia, who challenge such notions.

(Un)spectacular Effects

While *Pati Parmeshwar* gained a lot of attention from the CBFC, the tribunal, and the courts, as the thick file of official documents about it attests, it passed unnoticed at the box office. Unlike its effect on *Khalnayak*, which I discuss next, the act of censorship did not mark *Pati Parmeshwar* as a desirable text; put simply, prohibition did not produce desire. By ignoring this film, however, the Indian audiences were not necessarily rejecting patriarchal values, though some might have been. The rejection more likely concerned the largely unappealing cast (with Dimple Kapadia the exception) and camerawork, as well as the mediocre songs. Ironically, *Pati parmeshwar* failed at performing a *traditional* Hindi film formula.[77]

7 Tracking the Twists and Turns in the *Khalnayak* Debates on Censorship

In 1993 the song "Choli ke peeche kya hai?" ("What is behind the blouse?") from Subhash Ghai's film *Khalnayak* (1993; The Villain) plunged India into a debate about morality. The teaser line, "Choli ke peeche kya hai," stood accused of transmitting improper sexual mores and encouraging immoral acts. As in the case of *Satyam shivam sundaram*, this debate emerged at the site of reception. It was stoked by anxieties related to the impact of economic liberalization on Indian culture and Indian tradition. As I noted in Chapter 2, the entry of satellite and cable television (due to economic liberalization) gave audiences access to Western programs, generating concerns about the impact of foreign values on Indian audiences. The song caught my attention when I visited Delhi in the summer of 1993, as it was ubiquitous in both public and private spaces, playing on cassette players as well as satellite and cable channels.[1] My interest was piqued because of this heated controversy and because the song was picturized on Madhuri Dixit, the reigning Hindi film star of the 1990s. The themes of stardom, sound, and sexuality that animate my analysis of the production and reception of *Satyam shivam sundaram* also guide my examination of *Khalnayak*'s infamous song. I track the song through the filmic narrative, R. P. Chugh's legal petition, public reception, music and film industries, and the Central Board of Film Certification and demonstrate how it transforms, depending on the context, into a lure, a legal entity, a commodity, a transgressive object, and a piece of entertainment. In charting these varied terrains, I show how the articulation of female desire generates anxieties about the status of Indian culture and the moral virtue of the nation.

Central Players

As in the case of *Satyam shivam sundaram*, the extratextual mechanism of stardom shapes the readings of *Khalnayak*, albeit in a less-discordant fashion. A lavish, big-budget Hindi film, *Khalnayak* was Subhash Ghai's twelfth directorial effort. Like Raj Kapoor, Ghai was a prominent and well-respected director. A product of the prestigious Film and Television Institute, Ghai began his career as an actor in 1970 and moved successfully to direction in 1976 with *Kalicharan*. In 1983 he became an independent producer by establishing his company Mukta Arts. Ghai was one of the top producer-directors of the 1980s, helming many successful films. His production team for *Khalnayak* included well-known members of the film industry, such as the lyricist Anand Bakshi, the music-composing duo Laxmikant-Pyarelal, the choreographer Saroj Khan, and the cinematographer Ashok Mehta. As did Kapoor's for *Satyam shivam sundaram*, Ghai's fame contributed to his film's relatively safe journey through the CBFC.

The stellar cast of *Khalnayak* comprised Madhuri Dixit (as Ganga), Sanjay Dutt (Ballu), and Jackie Shroff (Ram Sinha). Dixit and Dutt were pivotal figures in the two renditions of "Choli ke peeche kya hai?" The son of the illustrious actors Nargis and Sunil Dutt, Sanjay Dutt entered the family profession. From the beginning of his career, film magazines reported his troubled history with drugs and his frequent love affairs, casting him as a wayward son. Dutt's star persona dovetailed with Ballu, his on-screen character in *Khalnayak*, who is led astray by evil individuals and adopts a villainous path. During the making of *Khalnayak*, Dutt added a real-life twist to his on-screen role as an absconding criminal: he was arrested in connection with the March 1993 bombings in Bombay, which had fueled tensions between Hindus and Muslims. The discussion that followed his arrest brought to the surface the Bombay film industry's connection to the "underworld."

Dutt's costar, Dixit, with whom he had also been romantically linked, lacked a film pedigree. After acting in a few mediocre films, she had been catapulted to success by her riveting dance performance[2] in *Tezaab's*(1988) film song "Ek, do, teen" ("One, two, three"). As I noted in the chapter on *Pati parmeshwar*, action films dominated the Hindi film industry during the 1980s. This genre is hero driven, and traditionally the narrative is dominated by the male action hero. Through her spectacular dance performances, Dixit commandeered screen space in a way that seriously challenged the position of the male hero. People frequently entered theaters to watch her dance routines and left when the story started. The media hailed her as the "female Bachchan," comparing her to Amitabh Bachchan, the Hindi film industry's foremost male action hero and superstar, who enjoyed unparalleled success in the 1970s. Whether the genre was action or family melodrama, Dixit's screen presence easily overshadowed her male costars; in the popular press, for example, the two major hits of the 1990s, *Beta* (1992; The Son) and *Raja* (1995; The King), were often referred to as *Beti* (The Daughter) and *Rani* (The Queen). Dixit brought an enticing combination of innocence, comedy, and sensuality to her performances. Like Aman, she also drew on the gestures and dress of the vamp, though this poaching was largely limited to her dance performances.

While many argue that Dixit's performances were far more sensual than her predecessors,[3] Dixit, unlike Aman, managed to escape the sex-symbol tag. Whereas Aman's screen roles served to affirm her status as a "Westernized," "uninhibited" heroine, Dixit's dance performances stood in stark contrast to her conservative public persona. Articles in film magazines and newspapers emphasized her classical dance training as well as her middle-class, Maharashtrian background, duly noting that her mother managed her love life (according to the gossip mill, Dixit's mother singlehandedly broke up the romance between Dixit and her "nefarious" costar Sanjay Dutt). In interviews Dixit confirmed her image as a "good, middle-class Indian daughter" who would follow her parents' guidance and willingly accept an arranged marriage (which she eventually did). As I will later show, this public identity effectively mediated her relationship with her middle-class female fans. Unlike Dixit, Neena Gupta, her costar in the dance sequence, had a rather colorful history. A well-known television and film actress and director, Gupta primarily performed supporting character roles in film. She shot to the limelight in 1989 after declaring her out-of-wedlock pregnancy on national television; her decision to embrace single parenthood shocked many. Later, journalists exposed the name of the baby's father, the famous and married West Indian cricketer Vivian Richards, adding to the scandal. Given Gupta's public history, she was the proper choice for the brief but feisty role of Champa, who aggressively inquires, "Choli ke peeche kya hai?"

Both Dixit's and Gupta's voice-mates in the song sequence matched their off-screen personas. Dixit was paired with Alka Yagnik, who along with Dixit rode to fame on the success of "Ek, do, teen." Film magazines record that Yagnik followed in her mother's footsteps, obtaining training in classical Indian music. She began her career singing *bhajans*, or devotional songs, on Calcutta Radio at the tender age of six and eventually entered the film industry in the late 1970s. As I noted elsewhere, the emergence of cassette technology proved to be a pivotal development for Hindi film; the medium allowed new singers to enter the industry and thus broke the hegemonic hold of stalwarts such as Lata Mangeshkar and Asha Bhosle.[4] Yagnik exudes a feminine, middle-class ethos through her soft, high-pitched voice and subdued attire, wearing modest *salwaar kameezes* and *saris*. In contrast, the husky Ila Arun, who sings for Gupta, projects an assertive and flamboyant personality. An antithesis to Yagnik and even more to Mangeshkar, she is often photographed wearing flowing, sequined *ghaghras* and *cholis* with large *bindis* and chunky jewelry. Her vibrant clothing and accessories serve to consolidate her image as a typical Rajasthani folksinger—a fact that assumes importance in discussions about *Khalnayak*. Unlike Kapoor, who both mobilized and challenged Mangeskhar's and Aman's star personas, Ghai shrewdly relied on and augmented established images. What were the consequences of these seamless matches as opposed to the dissonance we encounter in *Satyam shivam Sundaram*? I contend that in *simultaneously* mobilizing Dixit, Arun, and Gupta's star personas, Ghai compounded the sexual charge of "Choli ke peeche kya hai?" which then evoked demands for cutting at the level of reception. Ironically, these demands led to increased profits for both Ghai and Tips Industries, the music distributor for *Khalnayak*.

The Object of Controversy: "Choli Ke Peeche Kya Hai?"

The song's first appearance is set up in the film as follows. The villain Ballu kills a politician and is captured by the hero, the intelligence officer Ram Sinha. While Ram is visiting his girlfriend, Subinspector Ganga, in Hindi cinema's version of an Indian village, Ballu escapes from prison, and Ram is bombarded with accusations of incompetence.[5] In fact, one reporter suggests that Ram failed to fulfill his duty as an intelligence officer because "he was having a good time with Ganga." Ganga, then, becomes the temptress who leads Ram astray from his duty and causes his failure. To redeem himself in the eyes of the police force, he must regulate his desire for her. Consequently, Ram vows to remain unmarried until he recaptures Ballu. Seeking to salvage her fiancé's reputation as well as her own—for the townspeople have begun to wonder about Ganga's relations with Ram, since he has not married her—Ganga disguises herself as a folk dancer and sings the song "Choli ke peeche kya hai?" to seduce Ballu so that she can join his gang and bring him to justice.

Like *Pati parmeshwar* and *Satyam shivam sundaram*, *Khalnayak* relies on the device of impersonation to develop its narrative and to stage spectacle.[6] In all three cases, the spectator is made aware of the legitimate reasons for the pretense. How does this knowledge affect the staging of spectacle, or in Mulveyian terms, of putting female bodies on display?[7] For *Satyam shivam sundaram*, the knowledge of Rupa's status as scarred wife interrupts the spectator's complete enjoyment of Rupa as mistress, but both *Pati parmeshwar* and *Khalnayak* provide the spectator with pleasure in knowing and pleasure in looking. In other words, the spectator delights in viewing Kapadia's and Dixit's performances and in the privileged knowledge that the performance is an *act* undertaken to avenge personal injuries and crimes against the state, respectively. These twin pleasures hinge on an implicit understanding that the spectacle and impersonation will eventually end and moral equilibrium will be restored.

In *Khalnayak*, Ganga's guise as a dancer constructs the expression of her sexuality as a masquerade. We as privileged spectators know that behind this guise is a "pure" Ganga who loves Ram and who is enacting this role from a sense of duty. At the beginning of the song sequence, which comprises 114 shots, a veiled Ganga, swaying to the sinuous rhythm of a flute, enters a room that combines facets of Hindi cinema's brothel and cabaret. Unlike the all-male audience that watches Ganga's entry, the spectators know that she is a representative of the police force and thus a danger to the criminal world. Interestingly, within the domain of criminals, Ganga is also constructed as the object of desire and as a lure that can destroy this world if she is not controlled.[8] As Ganga, dressed in an itsy-bitsy red-sequined blouse, glides across the floor, the camera salaciously focuses on different parts of her body. In this case, the technology of the camera and the editing processes construct Ganga as a desirable object. They also position the male audience members within the diegetic space as voyeurs and extend the same position to the spectators in the theater. Although the camera and editing processes construct Ganga as a sexual object, the privileged spectators, unlike the all-male diegetic audience, know that she is a subinspector and therefore an agent of the Law. This transgressive casting of woman as an agent of the state unsettles claims made by Mulvey, who invokes the Law theoretically via the Freudian psychoanalytic model and the law literally (e.g., the policeman in *Vertigo*) to buttress the authority of the male characters she discusses and to demonstrate the female characters' disempowered status.[9]

After marking Ganga's entry, the camera cuts to another dancer, Champa (Neena Gupta), as she demands "Choli ke peeche kya hai? Chunari ke neeche kya hai?" (What is behind the blouse? What is under the veil?)[10] Employing a shot/reverse shot, the camera turns to Ganga, focusing on her blouse, as she slowly unveils and answers "Choli mein dil hai mera, chunari mein dil hai mera, yeh dil mein doongi mere yaar ko, mere pyar ko" (My heart is in my blouse, my heart is under veil, I'll give this heart to my lover).[11] The camera lingers over Ganga's blouse and makes the double entendre visible. The reference is not only to Ganga's heart but also to her breasts. After showing this interaction between Ganga and Champa, the camera cuts and zooms in on the smirking figure of Ballu, the villain who is simultaneously the desiring male subject and the criminal object under Ganga's surveillance. Ganga's twin role as dancer and subinspector complicates Mulvey's well-known argument about "the gaze," where men are endowed with the active power of looking and women are merely passive objects to be looked at.[12] By extension, this dual identity also invites a spectatorial response more complicated than the simple acquiescence to masculine subjectivity for which Mulvey argues. The spectator is encouraged to identify with two subjects, Ganga and Ballu, and thus to partake in both pleasure in knowing and pleasure in looking. Our privileged knowledge about Ganga's ruse and the extradiegetic knowledge that Dixit is a virtuous daughter generate a moral cocoon. While we might view Ganga just as Ballu and his gang do, we are not fully aligned with them, and we can therefore fully enjoy the dance performance without feeling complicit in an illicit activity.

The fact that the song is a performance—a ruse—to capture the villain is embedded in the dance; using minute head movements, Champa gestures to Ganga to move closer to Ballu and to the goal of infiltrating his gang. Furthermore, the multiple close-ups of Ballu in the sequence highlight his dual status as male client and police target. Thus, what Ballu does not realize and the privileged spectator does is that behind the blouse and behind the veil is a representative of the police force masquerading as an object of desire. The law is not positioned against desire. Rather, through the act of impersonation, the Law is made desirable—a fact confirmed by the film's ending, when Ballu places his weapons at Ram's feet.

Intermission: Interrupting Female Desire

While the first rendition of the "Choli ke peeche" created much furor and discussion, its second rendition did not attract the attention of the public or the CBFC. The song reappears in the film after an intermission, a staple of Hindi cinema. In most cases, the intermission comes at a climatic point halfway through the film. Like song-and-dance sequences, the intermission breaks the linear flow of narrative dear to Hollywood classical cinema.

Directors edit their films to include this productive break—or cut—which increases the profits of theaters, since they sell snacks and drinks during it. In addition to buying food and visiting the restroom, however, audience members also discuss the film and form judgments at this time; sometimes these discussions prompt them to leave, to "cut out."[13]

In addition to linking "film audiences to adjacent economies," the intermission also constitutes an "indispensable structuring device for the film."[14] Generally, the intermission partitions a film into two related segments. The first segment of *Khalnayak*, before the intermission, sets up problems or puzzles, and the second offers resolutions.[15] Following this model, the first rendition of the song, which appears in the first half of the film, constructs female desire and sexuality as a "problem." The second half of the film, which features the second rendition of the song, resolves this "problem" through the strategy of parody, among other mechanisms.[16]

After the intermission, both Ganga and the audience find out that Ballu discovered Ganga's true identity at their first meeting, soon after she finished singing the song. This discovery not only unveils Ganga's identity as a subinspector but, more important, reveals that her display of sexuality was a masquerade and that behind this masquerade is a pure Ganga. When Ganga realizes that she is being held hostage, she protests her imprisonment by not eating. Ballu and his gang sing the song to coax her to eat. In a sequence composed of twenty-eight shots, Ballu and his gang don dancing attire—*ghaghras* and *dupattas* (scarves) worn over their trousers and shirts (no revealing clothing for them)—and attempt to entertain Ganga. In ill-fitting costumes, Ballu and his gang clonk across the floor, parodying the earlier performance. This half-drag show unmasks Ganga's earlier performance as an act. In its excess, the performance also unwittingly reveals gender/sex to be a performance that is naturalized in cinema through the work of technology. The editing processes and camera angles do not sexualize the men's bodies as they imitate the earlier performance. Whereas the women's performance is spectacular and riveting, the men's performance is comical and ungainly. The men fail miserably at being either sexy or alluring. This failure is aptly visualized when Ganga plants a resounding slap on one of the gang members' faces, cutting short their less than impressive performance.

Whereas Ballu and his gang are depicted as voyeurs during the first picturization of the song, the camera does not construct Ganga as a voyeur when she refuses to watch the men's performance. By the same token, the camera does not extend this position to the spectators in the audience during the scene. What, then, is behind the men's failure to perform as "good" lures and Ganga's failure to act as a "good" voyeur? Behind these failures is a social convention, one that supports a patriarchal status quo. It is only women, especially "bad" women, who can be good lures; men are obviously the subjects of desire, not sexual objects. The second rendition uses humor to defuse the threat of female desire and sexuality.

Although the song occurs twice in the film and on the audiocassettes, only the first version became the focus of public controversy. Why did the second version fail to attract attention from the public or the censors? Was it the spectacular representation of sexualized female bodies in the trailer and the film that arrested the public's and the examining committee's gaze? Did the refrain "Choli ke peeche kya hai?" become less vulgar when, in its comic iteration, it was sung by Vinod Rathod and enacted by Ballu and his gang? Were the lyrics more obscene and threatening when sung by female singers and performed by female characters in a more "serious" context? The answer turns on agency: the first rendition of the song was disruptive because the visual and verbal representation combined to produce female sexual desire. The articulation of this desire was the problem, for it posited that women are not only sexual objects but also sexual subjects.

In this context, it will be worthwhile to revisit a central concept in feminist film theory, namely, spectacle. While many scholars have challenged Mulvey's arguments about "the gaze," less attention has been devoted to her deployment of the term *spectacle*.[17] Mulvey employs the dichotomy of narrative versus spectacle to advance her argument about the disempowered position of women within dominant Hollywood narratives:

> [T]he split between spectacle and narrative supports the man's role
> as the active one of forwarding the story, making things happen. The
> man controls the film phantasy and also emerges as the representa-
> tive of power in a further sense: as the bearer of the look of the spec-
> tator, transferring it behind the screen to neutralise the extra-diegetic
> tendencies represented by woman as spectacle.[18]

For Mulvey, spectacle is primarily a visual event that halts the story, whereas the narrative drives it forward: "The presence of woman is an indispensable element of spectacle in normal narrative film, yet her visual presence tends to work against the development of a story-line, to freeze the flow of action in moments of erotic contemplation."[19] By characterizing spectacle and, by extension, woman as mute, immobile, and inert, Mulvey strips them of agency and thereby re(produces) the very disempowerment and "fetishistic reduction that she herself imputes to the patriarchal mechanisms of film apparatus."[20] She writes, "Woman displayed as sexual object is the leitmotif of erotic spectacle . . . [;] she holds the look, and plays to and signifies male desire."[21] For Mulvey, then, woman either is on display for the pleasure of the male character and the masculine spectator or is punished, as was Marlene Dietrich, for her performance.

Mulvey conflates the cinematic apparatus with the image and fails to examine the role of sound. For her, visual spectacle embodies all that is problematic with this apparatus. Like Mulvey, Kaja Silverman also argues that the image as constructed by Hollywood cinema shrinks women to the status of mute bodies. Thus Silverman turns to the disembodied voice, in which she hears the possibilities of women's agency:

> To allow her to be heard without being seen would be even more dangerous, since it would disrupt the specular regime upon which dominant cinema relies; it would put her beyond the reach of the male gaze (which stands in here for the cultural "camera") and release her voice from the signifying obligations which that gaze enforces. It would liberate the female subject from the interrogation about her place, her time, and her desires which constantly resecures her. Finally, to disembody the female voice in this way would be to challenge every conception by means of which we have previously known woman within Hollywood film, since it is precisely *as body* that she is constructed there.[22]

In Mulvey's and Silverman's analyses, female characters' relationship to the image is reduced to the process of fetishzation.[23] Their arguments fail to consider four crucial points central to examining "Choli ke peeche kya hai?" specifically and song-and-dance sequences in Hindi cinema generally. First, neither of them attends to the female body's ability to speak through gesture and movement, especially as a woman dances. Second, both of them overlook the aural dimension of spectacle and thus fail to examine how sound (voice, language, and music) shapes it. Third, they neglect the roles that aural and visual stardom play in our understanding of spectacle. Last, in maintaining a focus on the film text, they do not consider the role of spectacle in an industrial context.

In *Khalnayak* specifically, and in Hindi popular cinema more generally, song-and-dance sequences have a complex relationship to the narrative. For example, although "Choli ke peeche kya hai?" is a visual feast and invites a voyeuristic gaze, this spectacle works with rather than against the narrative's agenda (i.e., capturing the criminal); in fact, it is pivotal to the story. Through this spectacular performance, Ganga infiltrates the gang and takes charge of bringing Ballu to justice. Meanwhile, Ram pursues Ballu through more formal means, as well as through clues Ganga leaves behind. This wresting of agency at the level of narrative is repeated at the level of cinema. As are many other industries, the film industry is dominated by men—in this case, male directors and male actors. Through her dance routine, however, Dixit literally seizes screen space; moreover, extratextual knowledge about Dixit's virtuous middle-class background interrupts the simple construction of her as a sexual object. Like Dixit, Saroj Khan took charge of the film in the process of choreographing and directing "Choli ke peeche kya hai?"[24] As song and dance grew increasingly important during the 1990s, Khan, a much desired choreographer, had the Hindi film industry dancing to her direction. Furthermore, by supplementing the diegesis with extratextual knowledge about Gupta and Arun, we can read spectacle as a signifier of sexual agency rather than the site of oppression. Finally, while Silverman and Mulvey read spectacle as a visual event, the fact that both the public debate and the examining committee focused on the "obscene" lyrics sung by female singers and lip-synched and enacted by female characters compels us to read this spectacle as a narrative event rather than merely a visual performance.

To elaborate on my critique of Silverman and Mulvey, I return to the song's first rendition. In the stanzas following the infamous refrain, Ganga, prompted by Champa's queries, bemoans that she has not yet found a suitable lover to whom she can give her heart. She adds that even though she veils her face when walking about town, men continue to chase her (possibly because she lifts her expensive skirt to avoid soiling it and in the process exposes her shapely legs). Champa obliquely looks at the camera, asking someone to save Ganga, and the camera quickly cuts to Ballu, establishing him as the potential savior. Ganga chimes in, saying that she is unable to bear her loneliness and wishes to get married because she does not want to be either an ascetic or a mere mistress. In another stanza, she once more expresses her feelings of loneliness. Parting her legs, she croons that she sleeps with her door open and longs for her "Prince Charming" to return. The lyrics combined with the dance movements manifest her sexual desire. Presumably, to satisfy this desire, Ganga arrives at Ballu's table, inviting him to become the ornaments that her adorn her body, asking him to do her bidding and to be her slave. By the end of the song, Ballu is quite willing to undertake this task and follows Ganga to her dressing room. The public debate and examining committee's evaluation focused exclusively on the refrain, reading it as stripping of woman and of culture.

In the process, the debate and the evaluation disavow the articulation of female desire in the stanzas and dance movements, a disavowal repeated in the narrative.

In *Khalnayak*, while spectacle gives Ganga agency, the filmic narrative slowly shackles her, reinscribing her as a pure woman. Ganga protects Ballu from the police during a shootout by inserting herself between the two. When Ballu escapes again, Ganga is arrested for aiding a criminal. She is accused of consorting with a criminal and is placed on trial for betraying the police service. While the police charge Ganga with treason, newspapers accuse her of a greater crime—namely, being unfaithful to her lover—and only Ballu can save Ganga's tarnished reputation. The film ends with Ballu's dramatic entry into the courtroom. He declares that Ganga is "pure": she has betrayed neither her lover nor the police service. In fact, he announces that her purity compelled him to return and surrender. While the film's conclusion upholds purity as virtue, particularly for women, the abject figure of Ganga sitting in the dock testifies to a silenced sexuality.

Music Industry and Censorship

The filmic context in which I have anchored my analysis was not the context in which the public first encountered "Choli ke peeche kya hai?" The song was first released on audiocassette, then appeared on cable and satellite television and film trailer, and finally (re)surfaced in the film itself; this temporal order affected its public reception. According to common market practice, Tips, an established company primarily involved in film music, released an audiocassette of songs from *Khalnayak* while the film was still in production. "Choli ke peeche kya hai?" could be heard on the radio and cassette players and on the "top-ten" shows in the form of music videos created from publicity clips from *Khalnayak*. In India the success of a popular film is often connected to the popularity of its music.[25] The audiocassettes and music videos not only serve to advertise the film but also generate profits for the music companies, with some of those profits often passed along to the film producers. Since the introduction of tape-cassette technology in the mid-1970s, the music industry has both expanded and flourished. By 1993 "over thirty [Indian] companies were active in the field of film music," and countrywide street sales of audiocassettes were estimated at Rs 5 billion ($157,728,707) annually, ensuring that composers and music producers were happily singing all the way to the bank.[26] During this period, approximately 150 Hindi music titles were released every year, with sales across India estimated at 1 million cassettes a day—inclusive of piracy. The music industry thus entered the business of filmmaking as a financial giant. In its new avatar as a major commercial film financier, the music industry had transformed the practice of commercial filmmaking, in particular, the production and distribution of songs.

In a letter written to the Ministry of Information and Broadcasting, Pandit Gautam Kaul, a concerned citizen, enumerated the adverse effects of the mushrooming music industry. Kaul cataloged the detrimental effects resulting from this transformation:

> Recording of songs are completed even before the film goes into pro-duction and recording companies, without waiting for the release of the film, exploit the songs as investments. It is also noticed that there are some cases now where the songs of a movie announced for pro-duction proved immensely popular and the film remained unknown even after its release. There are possibilities that a full album of songs can be released, and the film may never be made. In such cases, the songs would be given nomenclature as "private songs."[27]

For Kaul, these *new* forms of production and distribution of film songs warranted immediate attention because they were circumventing state scrutiny. He suggested that the state tackle this issue by compelling producers to submit film songs to examining committees before being released and by creating offices for the certification of "private" and film music to regulate the burgeoning music industry.[28] Kaul's letter provides us an instructive lesson about the nature of power: simply put, power is not unidirectional. While state censorship (in)forms filmmaking, prac-tices of film production and distribution also affect state censorship. In the process of drawing attention to the implications of a growing music industry for the practice of censorship, Kaul unwittingly demonstrated how technology, in this case audiocassettes, can reveal the limits of state authority. As a medium not subject to state censorship, audiocassettes could circulate and carry potentially subversive or, as Kaul feared, *vulgar* messages freely.

A Legal Petition against *Khalnayak*

As "Choli ke peeche kya hai?" circulated on cassettes, R. P Chugh, an attorney and a Bharatiya Janata Party (BJP) supporter,[29] was among the many who heard it. On April 6, 1993, Chugh wrote to the Ministry of

Information and Broadcasting protesting the song's circulation; this letter was forwarded to the CBFC. He also sent a letter to Ghai demanding the deletion of "Choli ke peeche kya hai?" These letters did not produce the desired results; consequently, Chugh adopted more forceful measures and filed a legal petition in Delhi decrying the song: "[It] is obscene, defamatory to women community and is likely to incite the commission of offence. The song is grossly indecent and is being sung through cassettes at public places, annoying the people at large, the undersigned specially."[30] Like Kaul, Chugh was annoyed by the song's unhindered circulation via audiocassette. Both Kaul and Chugh objected to the song's lyrics; in other words, sound was deemed "indecent." In Chugh's eyes, moreover, the veiled sexual reference made the song not only obscene but derogatory to women. As a result, he objected to the song's unhindered circulation. Chugh's cluster of complaints drew together three specific assumptions about sexuality common to patriarchal discourse in India: first, that sexuality is obscene; second, that sexual references dishonor women; and third, that sexuality's entry into public space disrupts social boundaries. Chugh's petition was a means for seeking redress against such affronts.

The legal petition produced a juridical relation among Chugh, the court, and the addressees of the complaint. Such a relation constructed Chugh as a juridical subject and citizen who, by calling on it to adjudicate, hailed the court as arbitrator in a dispute against other subjects, "the defendants," who included Tips Cassettes, the CBFC, Subhash Ghai and Mukta Arts, and the Ministry of Information and Broadcasting. In short, as in the cases of *Satyam shivam sundaram* and *Pati parmeshwar*, the legal petition both drew on and reproduced a juridical apparatus constitutive of the state. What requests did Chugh make as a juridical subject? First, he called on Subhash Ghai, the film's producer, and the CBFC to remove the song from the film. Second, he demanded that Tips be restrained from selling cassettes including it. Third, he requested that the CBFC forbid the exhibition of *Khalnayak* until the song was deleted. Fourth, he asked that the Ministry of Information and Broadcasting bar the song from airing on state-run television. Chugh's requests reveal how concerns about the film song's aural incarnation were haunted by its visual avatar. They also highlight the fact that that in the theater of censorship—especially music censorship, because music enjoys complex distribution networks—multiple entities are involved in the play of power.

What are the effects of a scenario in which multiple entities are involved in the play of power in general and the act of cutting in particular? While the CBFC could excise "Choli ke peeche kya hai?" from the film *Khalnayak*, it had no authority to prohibit the sale of audiocassettes; it could exercise authority only over *films*, as stated in the Cinematograph Act of 1952. In this case, then, the technology of audiocassettes revealed the limits of the CBFC's authority, and so too did Chugh's request to the Ministry of Information and Broadcasting. The regulation of state television was allocated to the ministry, not the CBFC, which meant that Chugh had to contend with another technology, television, and the quirks of another authority, the Ministry of Information and Broadcasting. As does the case of *Pati parmeshwar*, these circumstances reveal the distribution of power that is constitutive of the state. The state is not a coherent body but an effect of a series of practices.

The advent of liberalization in the 1990s added a new twist to Chugh's request to prohibit the song on state-run television. As I noted earlier, the rise of satellite television and innumerable privately owned cable channels, which were not regulated by the state, meant that even if programs were prohibited on state-run television, viewers could easily watch them on private channels. For example, while the trailer for *Khalnayak* had to be certified before it could be screened on state-run television, there was no such requirement for its airing on satellite and cable television. These new technologies revealed the fragility of national boundaries and state authority.

My archival work foregrounds the splitting of the song from the filmic narrative. Economic liberalization enabled decontextualization. As the song traveled via audio and televisual technologies, it acquired meanings distinct from those in the filmic text. In the latter, female desire is portrayed as a ruse. Untethered from this context, the song bears no hint that the desiring female voice embodies the state surveillance system, thus allowing it to suggests the more subversive possibility of an authentic female desire. This desiring female voice lies outside not only sociosexual conventions but also the panoptic state. Because it was concerned about the growing menace of television, which facilitated the circulation of televisual texts such as "Choli ke peeche kya?" the state moved to reassert and expand its authority by enacting laws in 1994 and 1995 to regulate cable and satellite television.

Chugh's allegations were contested by Subhash Ghai. In their legal defense of the song, Ghai and Mukta Arts highlighted the state's regulatory apparatus:

[The defendants] submitted that the film *Khalnayak* was examined by the Examining Committee in accordance with the procedure

prescribed in the Cinematograph Act and the rules made there under
and also in the light of guidelines issued by the Central Board of Film
Certification under Section 5B (2) of the Cinematograph Act. It is not
out of place to mention here that the Examining Committee consist
of members from different fields which include social workers, wom-
en's organisations, film critics, advocates, doctors, students, different
unions and many others along with members of the committee [state
officials]. The film was duly certified and was given a UA Certificate.
It is denied that while granting the certificate the guidelines issued by
the Central Govt. are ignored or in violation of Section 5-B of Cinematograph Act. . . . It is, however[,] submitted that the song is sung
by a Rajasthani Tribe girl and in the context in which the song has
been depicted in the film is not against public decency and morality
and defamatory for women. . . . It is[,] however, submitted that the
said suit is filed by the plaintiff with the sole aim of gaining cheap
publicity and is filed not in the public interest but in his own interest
as stated above and with some ulterior motives.[31]

The Supreme Court's landmark judgment in Raj Kapoor's case clearly sets
a precedent, for Ghai first and foremost cites the film's certification by
the CBFC in challenging Chugh's charges. Second, he points to the varied
makeup of the examining committees, which are drawn from the public;
thus they not only regulate but also represent public opinion. Ghai's comments highlight the fact that examining committees include both state
functionaries and members of the general public. This double role calls
attention to the public's participation in the internal workings of censorship, challenging both scholarly and political boundaries between the
state and civil society. Last, Ghai relocates the song within the film's context to argue against charges of "vulgarity" and "indecency." In doing so,
he contains the threat of a mobile female desire, enveloping it within the
fold of the narrative and enclosing it in the figure of the traditional Rajasthani tribal girl. As in *Satyam shivam sundaram*, where Kapoor invokes the
authentic dress of the *Adivasi* woman in order to minimally clothe Aman,
Ghai invokes the figure of the female tribal to simultaneously represent
and rein in sexuality.

Fortunately or unfortunately, neither the status of state authority nor the
court's ability to be a just arbitrator was tested severely in this legal drama.
On the day of the trial, R. P. Chugh failed to arrive in court on time, and
the case was dismissed. Drawing on Foucault's insights, we can see in this
comic turn of events the subordination of law to order. In this case, it was

not justice but the clock that prevailed. Subsequently, however, politicians took up the controversy, which led to a stricter approach by the CBFC.[32]

Public Debate

Although Chugh's petition failed in legal terms, it succeeded in escalating the public debate on the representation of sex in cinema. Shakti Samanta, then the chairman of the CBFC, received approximately two hundred letters for and against removing the song from the film and its trailer.[33] An overwhelming majority urged Samanta to retain it in the film; at the same time, a small but powerful minority that included members of the Bharatiya Janata Party, a Hindu nationalist organization, demanded the song's removal. The domain of culture was central to the BJP's (re) vision of India. The party proposed to ward off the dangers of economic liberalization, promising to "[g]lobalize but in the Indian way."[34] In advancing its agenda, the BJP foregrounded voices of women who passionately spoke from within the bounds of tradition—as wives, mothers, and sisters—demanding the prohibition of such vulgar songs. In a letter supporting Chugh's petition, the president of the BJP's Women's Wing in New Delhi wrote: "'Choli ke peeche kya hai' is an obscene song and as a result of which new anti-social elements have got the excuse of singing this song on seeing girls. Many incidents of eve-teasing [sexual harassment of women] have occurred. The film song singers only just to earn money are shamelessly singing such type of songs which are against the public interest."[35] According to this woman, "Choli ke peeche kya hai" benefited the singers at the cost of the sexual harassment of women. Shankar Chugh, another member of the BJP, reiterated her views, adding that the song undermined laws protecting women:

> On the one hand, [a] number of steps have been taken for the welfare and security of women, on the other hand persons like Subhash Ghai have been giving song to the anti-social elements like *choli ke peeche kya hai* and it has become very difficult for girls and women to go out. In case the above song is going to continue, the next song would be: *kachi ke peeche* [behind the underwear] and *peti cot ke peeche* [behind the petticoat], etc.[36]

Vineet Kumar, who filed a case against *Khalnayak* at the Consumer Redressal Forum[37] in Faridabad, cited an "instance in Sambhal where a young man namely Raju, son of Shri Nazar resident of Miyan Sarai used to tease girls of respectable families by singing this un-parliamentry song." Kumar argued that the song should be deleted from the film on the grounds that it was "against the culture, convention[s] and moral[s] of Indian society."[38]

Concurring with Kumar's sentiments, an affronted Ashok Kumar from the Integrity and Welfare Society wrote: "One doesn't understand what the director Subhash Ghai wants to say to a cultured nation like India by showing songs with double meaning[s]. When one's sisters and daughters are around and songs like these are played, one feels ashamed and embarrassed."[39] Adding to the list of the song's detrimental effects, Mrs. Ram Gupta from the Women's Branch of the Citizen's Association against Corruption drew attention to the song's circulation via Star TV, MTV, and Zee TV. She indignantly inquired what kind of culture and tradition children would learn from watching such a song:

In thinking about the audiences of contemporary Indian films, we cannot ignore that children form an important part of this audience. . . . [In films,] action, violence, rape, [and] vulgar songs are becoming normal for children. And Dish Star TV, MTV, Zee TV—sweet poisons—have already inserted themselves into children's minds. Given that they have strayed so far from their culture, when these children grow up, what contribution will they be able to make to their society and country[?] What kind of culture and society will exist in their future? . . . Today the song from *Khalnayak*, "Choli ke peeche kya hai, Chunnari ke neeche kya hai," has become quite popular. From its popularity, one can gauge in which direction kids are being pulled.[40]

Shweta Sanjay, too, expressed her concern about the song's effects on "innocent minds":

The audio playing of the said song has been disturbing parents and innocent minds throughout the nation. The said audio song should have been banned immediately on its release. . . . I fail to understand as to how will parents feel while viewing the said film with their children and more so when they ask about the meaning of the said words.[41]

Like Chugh's petition, Sanjay's letter and the other correspondence disclose anxieties related to the song's aural incarnation as well as its visual avatar. According to Sanjay, the song's vulgarity (present in the lyrics) would only be amplified by the visual spectacle, prompting her to record her distress and apprehensions. In general, the letters against the song reveal concerns about the song's aural and visual impact on familial relations, women, children, and Indian culture. According to the letters, these entities need to be shielded from that which is corrupting, violent, and obscene—in short, from sexuality. The letters align the family, women, children, and Indian culture, situating them in opposition to sexuality.

Such views about the song and its effects did not stand unchallenged. The song's many proponents included exhibitors, a number of whom wrote letters from Rajasthan that clearly drew on a common text and pointed to an organized effort similar to that of their BJP opponents. In the letters, they urged the CBFC to retain "Choli ke peeche kya hai?" in the trailer for *Khalnayak*:

> Our cinema is situated in Jaipur capital of Rajasthan. We have come to know from Trade papers that you have asked to delete the song "CHOLI KE PEECHE from the Trailor of Picture Khalnayak. The above song is a very popular folk song of Rajasthan. It can be heard during Holi and other festivals in Rajasthan. We do not find anything vulgar in the above song. In fact we have seen many ladies singing the song. If the song was vulgar then the ladies would have never liked it. Also, looking in the past record of Mr. Subhash Ghai we are sure he will never give us anything vulgar or obscene. Under these circumstances, we request you to go through the above song once again before giving your decision and allow us to enjoy the beautiful song.[42]

> Our Cinema is situated in Ramganj Mani district Kota, Rajasthan. We have read that you have asked to delete the song Choli Ke Peeche Kiya Hai from the Trailor of the picture KHAL NAYAK. This song is a folk song of Rajasthan and it is very popular during festivals in Rajasthan. We do not find any thing vulgor in the above song. If the song was vulgor than the ladies would like the song. I have seen the song on Zee TV and when I compared the words with the visuals I found nothing vulgor in it. The picturisation is also quite sober and we can enjoy with the family. We will request you to go through the song before giving us your decision and allow us to enjoy the beautiful song.[43]

Whereas the song's opponents had argued that the lyrics conflicted with Indian tradition, its proponents cited its traditional pedigree as well as its director-producer's impeccable reputation in order to dissociate it from the charge of vulgarity. The fact that Ila Arun, a self-proclaimed Rajasthani singer, had lent her voice to the song and that Ghai had claimed the character to be a "Rajasthani tribal girl" bolstered their assertion that it was a Rajasthani folk song. Interestingly, no one interrogated this contention even though Anand Bakshi, a Punjabi, was credited for penning the song's lyrics.

Given that these letters come from exhibitors, it is important to situate their arguments not only in the domain of public morality but also in that of the market. In arguing that the song neither disrupted familial relations nor denigrated women, the exhibitors sought to (re)claim valuable markets that the songs' opponents might have alienated. To make their argument, they invoked and reinscribed a common market understanding that women and families generally stay away from "vulgar" films (notwithstanding the second letter's Freudian slip). Recall the case of *Satyam shivam sundaram*, whose failure was attributed to the A certificate that ostensibly kept away women and children. One reviewer invoked female audiences as a specific demographic, indicating that women were upset by the representation of sexuality in *Satyam shivam sundaram*. Both instances indicate how conservative moral ideology structures the market. One can argue that the issue was not that women avoided A-rated or vulgar films featuring nonreproductive or illicit sexuality; rather, it was deemed necessary that they steer clear of such films to protect the traditional, patriarchal family, for on-screen desires might infect female viewers and, by extension, destroy the family.

Writing in *India Today*, Arun Katiyar confirmed that "folk traditions, especially in Punjab, Gujarat, Rajasthan and Uttar Pradesh[,] have spawned wicked lyrics." Such songs, however, are sung in *specific contexts*, such as prenuptial ceremonies; when "women sing what is commonly called ladies' *sangeet* [songs] in Punjab," he explained, "it is done more in fun than as a come-on."[44] According to Katiyar, "Choli ke peeche kya hai?" had been dislodged from this context of prenuptial ceremonies—in other words, the site of tradition. The problem was not the song but its placement in the film. Indeed, as was noted earlier, the setting of the song's first rendition fuses elements from Hindi cinema's brothel and its cabaret—the obverse of prenuptial ceremonies and, by extension, socially sanctioned tradition.

Tradition, sexuality, and women are intertwined in these discussions. The detractors claimed that "Choli ke peeche kya hai?" contributed to sexual harassment, constructing women as victims. Conversely, its proponents suggested that it could not be vulgar since women had been seen singing it. Last, Katiyar confirmed the song's traditional pedigree but contended that it had been displaced from its context. These positions (re) produce an "Indian tradition" in which women are either sexual victims or guardians of morality and tradition, but they shirk from representing women as sexually active beings.

S. Nayyar (an interested citizen) and the director of the Nirman Theatre both supported the claims of the Rajasthani exhibitors by pointing to the arbitrary nature of public debate and censorship:

> I fail to understand why such a hue and cry is being raised over the song "choli ke peeche" and asking for it to be banned etc. If the reason for this is the so-called vulgarity and suggestiveness of the lyrics then it seems only right to point out that this is not the only song by far to have such lyrics. And this is a folk song—which means that it has been sung for decades and maybe centuries! While other songs which abound in double entendre and innuendo cannot even claim that distinction and have been written purely for the titillation of the masses. All these great moralists and puritans who have woken up so suddenly did not have much to say for the banning of other songs. My advice to them is to take the literal meaning of the song and forget about the so-called vulgarity. It's all minds anyway. And my request to you, sir, is that you will not let some narrow minded people with double standards influence you into taking such rash action.[45]

> It is very astonishing that Censor has raised objections to the song "Choli ke Peeche." Video Cassettes of Khal-Nayak has already been shown frequently through the Tips and has been enjoyed by every class of public. So far no one has ever objected regarding the wordings or picturisation of songs. It will not be befitting to give the disappointment to the music lovers to enjoy this song. In the past Indian screen has already experienced make it worded [sexually explicit] songs like "Ik Chumma De De" [Give me a kiss]; Ik pappi De De [Give me a kiss], why this song has been singled out? Hope you will not object and keep the song intact in the trailors. We are regular exhibitors of Subhash Ghai who never tried to plunge into the dirty games in order to meant money and keeps his image in all pictures. In view of this please don't touch the song and let it be enjoyed by the general population.[46]

Both letters noted that examining committees had passed salacious songs previously, and those songs had not been subject to public censure. The letters thus draw attention to the pivotal role of context—in this case economic liberalization—in shaping public debates and the CBFC's decisions. In addition, the letter written by the director of the Nirman Theatre underscored that neither the song's aural nor its visual incarnation was a threat; both were merely objects of entertainment. The director also expressed two points implicit in the earlier letters written by exhibitors from Rajasthan: their formal associations with Ghai had prompted the exhibitors to write the letters, and through these letters, the exhibitors sought to protect their own investments.

The most articulate and lengthy letter in the CBFC case file on *Khalnayak* in support of the song was written by the *Cine Darshak Manch* (Film Viewers Group) and signed by 115 members. It builds its case by employing many of the arguments made in the previously quoted letters: it cites Ghai's stature and pedigree, states that "Choli ke peeche kya hai?" is a folk song, notes the song's popularity and wide circulation in public spaces and ceremonies, and points to other songs passed by the examining committees that were far more vulgar than "Choli ke peeche kya hai?" was. In addition to reproducing these now familiar arguments, their letter contended that the song had become a tool to settle political scores and advance political agendas, gesturing to the BJP supporters who had written letters to the CBFC and a BJP politician who had raised a question regarding the song during a parliamentary session. In closing, they stated: "If respected members still find the song to be vulgar, we would request that they apply their scissors to the vulgar image as opposed to the popular song. 'Choli ke peeche kya hai' is a Rajasthani folk song and folk songs like these are often sung during weddings in Bihar and Uttar Pradesh."[47] This curious concluding note splits the image and the soundtrack, characterizing the former as vulgar and the latter as both popular and traditional. Through its formulation, the letter highlights the visual and aural stakes in this dispute.

The Examining Committee's Report on *Khalnayak*

The "nearly complete" *Khalnayak* and its trailer appeared before an examining committee in Bombay during the course of Chugh's petition and the public debate. The trailer was submitted for certification a few days before the film. Initially, the examining committee ordered that the words "Choli ke peeche kya hai" be deleted from the trailer because they violated censorship guidelines—specifically, 2(vii), which states that "human sensibilities are not [to be] offended by vulgarity, obscenity or depravity."[48] After examining the entire film, however, the committee passed the trailer without cuts because it was satisfied that the line did

The DVD cover of *Khalnayak* features stills from the first rendition of "Choli ke peeche kya hai?" As seen on the back cover, the British Board of Film Classification rates the film suitable for those fifteen years of age or older. From *Khalnayak*.

not violate the guidelines in the context of the song as a whole. This happy ending did not take place immediately. As in any good *masala* film, certain obstacles had to be overcome first.

After the committee members watched *Khalnayak*, they discussed their reactions to the film:

> The members felt the theme of the film, the song sequences, and fights would be better understood by children with parental guidance. The members therefore unanimously felt the film should be granted an "UA" certificate with some cuts. The Examining Officer then informed the committee about the various letters received by CBFC for and against the film. The members after further discussion felt that the visuals in the song sequence were not vulgar, but the words "Choli ke peeche kya hai" could be deleted.[49]

Public debate informed the committee's decision to grant *Khalnayak* a UA certificate subject to seven cuts, three of which pertained to the *first picturization of the song*. The committee recommended the following visual and verbal cuts in the song sequence:

> Cut No. 5 Reel No. 6: Delete the words "Choli Ke Peeche Kya Hai, Chunari ke Neeche Kya hai" from the song sequence.
>
> Cut No. 6 Reel No. 6: Delete the visuals of Ganga pointing at her breast in the song where she sings the song "Jogan bana na jay kya karu" [I can't bear being an ascetic so what should I do?].
>
> Cut. No. 7 Reel no. 6: Delete the close visuals of pelvic jerks of dancing girls in the beginning of the song "Choli ke peeche" 2(vii).[50]

The committee informed the applicant, Subhash Ghai, of its decision. He accepted most of the committee's recommendations but appealed the demands for cuts 5 and 7. The committee reconsidered its decision and unanimously waived cut 5, which was directed at the refrain "Choli ke peeche kya hai, Chunari ke neeche kya," but retained cut 7, which focused on the visual performance. Ghai agreed to this compromise. The report does not note why the committee decided to waive cut 5, revealing the limits of archival research. Perhaps Ghai's fame as an A-list producer influenced their decision. Or perhaps they altered their initial judgment of vulgarity when they reconsidered the song sequence in the context of the film, where the expression of sexuality is a ruse and the heroine is actually a police officer. Although the film had been examined, the final editing for *Khalnayak* was still in progress. After its completion, Ghai sent the committee several additions and deletions; all were certified.

These events show that censorship is not simply the domain of the state; rather, it is a site at which relations among the state, citizenry, and film industry are negotiated. Furthermore, an analysis of the filmic narrative and these negotiations reveals that censors are not the only ones who cut films. I would like to highlight two instances of cutting: editing and censoring. While the former is part of the "creative" process, the latter is viewed as an imposition of state authority. I contend that both instances contribute to the production of meaning, in short, to the way the film is understood in its total social moment (the reception of a film as well as the events surrounding its production). In addition, the process of censorship is not limited to cutting. For example, *Khalnayak* was given a UA certificate. What prompted this decision was the committee's uncertainty about whether children would be able to acquire a *proper* understanding of the film—specifically, sequences containing sex and violence—without parental guidance. The certification served as signpost to parents, urging them to exert their authority, and regulated how the film was understood.

Partly because of this controversy, "Choli ke peeche kya hai?" became a smash hit. In eastern India alone, the song sold over seven hundred thousand cassettes. According to market estimates, Tips invested Rs 12.5 million ($394,322), including publicity, in the *Khalnayak* soundtrack, and sold over 5 million tapes, making the company a profit of Rs 30 million ($946,372). The company probably shared these profits with the producers of *Khalnayak*.[51] Considering the sums at stake, an editorial in the *Sunday Times of India* suggested that the "Choli ke peeche kya hai" controversy was a marketing strategy engineered by the showman Subhash Ghai.[52] The legal petition to censor the song and the ensuing debate contributed to constructing it as an object of controversy.[53] When this controversial text entered the public domain, it became a marketable property through its lure as a forbidden object, and its status as a forbidden object was constructed by the known act of censorship. Censorship, in this case, fueled desire. An effect of this desire was an increase in profits for the film producer and the music industry. For *Khalnayak*, then, censorship augmented the song and the film's success, but the differing fortunes of *Satyam shivam sundaram* and *Pati parmeshwar* demonstrate that the known act of censorship does not guarantee profits.

Reflections

My analysis of "Choli ke peeche kya hai?" reveals that this controversy concerned more than just controlling representations and articulations of sexuality; it concerned the moral virtue of the Indian nation, too. The female body and voice became the site and focus for a debate on virtue— and the role of sex in Indian tradition. The debates on Indian tradition have been further complicated by the specific function the film industry assumes in a growing capitalist market. Some members of the film and music industries claimed that "Choli ke peeche kya hai?" was a "folk song" and hence a part of Indian tradition, but such traditions are easily manufactured, packaged, publicized, and sold in the capitalist market. In *Khalnayak* this film and "folk" song becomes a conduit for the commodified presentation of the female body. Bombay cinema's highly sexualized version of the "village belle" is sold in theaters and video stores for huge profits. Thus, the film industry plays a crucial role in the commodification of female sexuality.

In considering this controversy, we should problematize both the repression of female sexuality and the commodification of female sexuality in the name of Indian tradition—and further explore the possibility of women's sexual agency, a possibility than can be illuminated by rethinking the role of spectacle (as I have done earlier), revisiting the intermission, and attending to this film's reception. As I noted earlier, the intermission in *Khalnayak* punctuates the filmic narrative, dividing it into the "problem" and the resolution. In doing so, it establishes a causal link between the two segments. But the intermission also creates a temporal and spatial break as audience members leave their seats to buy snacks, go to the lavatory, or converse with one another. In doing so, it can break the "spell of the narrative"[54] and by extension break the causal link between the two segments. By seizing on this break, we can explore other strategies of reading, ones not dependent on the ending or the resolution.

I turn now to a reading of the song by Dixit's fans, in particular the middle-class women in urban India who enjoyed "Choli ke peeche kya hai?" During the period when this film was released, Dixit became the highest-paid film actress in popular Hindi cinema. Among her many fans (including myself), Dixit was known for her stunning and sexy dance performances, and it is easy to see why India's middle-class urban women would enjoy these performances.[55] These women often receive gender training from their families and from society at large. They are told how to dress and how to speak, and by and large they are warned that any public expression of sexuality on their part will lead to sexual violation. Whether women pay heed to these precautionary measures does not seem to matter, for they are generally subjected to sexual harassment in any case. In an atmosphere where the consequences of any sexual expression are sexual violation or harassment, many of Dixit's middle-class female fans find her performances pleasurable because they associate them with sexual agency.[56] Their identification with Dixit is mediated by the comforting extratextual knowledge that she too was raised in a middle-class household.[57]

Janice Radway's insights help us in interpreting these responses. By attending to viewers' responses in a context, we can see that "although ideology is extraordinarily pervasive and continually determines social life, it does not preclude the possibility . . . of limited resistance."[58] This resistance is carried out by viewers who "appropriate otherwise ideologically conservative forms in order to better their lives, which have been controlled and dictated by their place in the social structure."[59] By reading films such as *Khalnayak* against the grain, we will not only discover "'a code of prohibition and denial'—in the sense that cinema supplies what reality denies"—but also "recognise the wounds that the 'code of prohibition and denial' have inflicted on desire itself—wounds that are not external to but within the iconographic system . . . that expresses rather than represses."[60] The song's circulation independent of the film combined with Madhuri Dixit's star persona enable us to read the song as an articulation of female desire by a knowing female subject, thereby generating a space for women's sexual agency.

8 | *Dilwale dulhania le jayenge*
Certifying a "Family Love" Story

I do believe love stories are immensely liked by audiences in India
and abroad. In the West, there are better action and offbeat films.
But when it comes to love stories, I believe we're unbeatable. . . .
I think we tell love tales from our heart. That's why they work
so well.
    —SHAH RUKH KHAN, ONLINE INTERVIEW, JUNE 24, 2005

[Dilwale dulhania le jayenge is] correct cinema because it didn't
have the condom scene in the film.
                    —SHAH RUKH KHAN, INTERVIEWED ON
                    THE *Dilwale dulhania le jayenge* DVD

On October 20, 1995, Aditya Chopra's *Dilwale dulhania le jay-*
enge (The Brave-hearted Will Take Away the Bride), affectionately
referred to as *DDLJ*, was released in theaters nationwide and in
overseas territories. Chopra, the twenty-four-year-old son of the
famed director-producer Yash Chopra, was dubbed a prodigy. He
received lavish praise for his first effort at direction and screenplay
writing. He was commended for the script, cinematography, picturization of songs in scenic European locales, and most important,
creating a good family film, one devoid of vulgarity and violence.
DDLJ became an "all-time blockbuster" and bagged an unprecedented ten *Filmfare* awards—the Oscars of India.[1] In his heartfelt
acceptance speech for the best director award, Chopra thanked his
"parents for bringing [him] up the way they did . . . for instilling in
[him] correct values, which is what *DDLJ* is about."[2] In equally moving words, Yash Raj Chopra, while accepting the best film award,

lavishly praised his son, thanking him for this precious gift (i.e., *DDLJ*) on the eve of Yash Raj Films' twenty-fifth anniversary. Thus, the value of family was hailed at the level not only of narrative but also of cinema itself, with the *Filmfare* function highlighting the centrality of family (in particular, patriarchal family) to the functioning of the Bombay film industry.

It was not only members of the film industry, audiences, and film critics who applauded *DDLJ*'s family values; the state gave it the 1996 National Film Award for "Best Popular Film Providing Wholesome Entertainment."[3] As a 1996 "National Award" winner, *DDLJ* was also exempt from taxation. Relieved of this charge, ranging from 25 to 60 percent, depending on the state involved, *DDLJ* could be enjoyed for a reasonable price. In 2001 *DDLJ* broke *Sholay*'s (1975) record for the longest-running film in India. By February 2010 *DDLJ* had run continuously for 750 weeks at Bombay's Martha Mandir theater.[4] Despite having seen *DDLJ* several times, families, couples, and individual fans continue to queue up for tickets "to relive their romance with a film . . . whose dream run has not been shaken by anything released thereafter."[5]

While most scholarship on *DDLJ* focuses on textual analysis, in the following account I link questions of representation to state censorship and widen the scope of investigation into the film's impact.[6] Moreover, in turning to a discussion of a "family love story"—an unlikely candidate for a study on censorship—I seek to extend our understanding of censorship, too.

Like *Khalnayak*, *DDLJ* was released during the initial years of economic liberalization. Whereas *Khalnayak*'s "Choli ke peeche kya hai?" fueled anxieties about the status of Indian culture and tradition, *DDLJ*, as many scholars have argued, alleviated these concerns by offering a happy union of "wholesome tradition" and "consumerist modernity."[7] In sharp contrast to *Khalnayak*, *DDLJ* was showered with praise and accolades by the state and audiences. *DDLJ*, along with its highly successful predecessor *Hum aapke hain koun?* (What Is My Relation to You?) were forerunners of the most successful genre of the 1990s, what the Indian state, media, and audiences approvingly referred to as "family films." This extremely profitable genre emerged at a crucial historical conjuncture. The Indian government opened up its economy 1990s and sought to woo multinationals and foreign as well as Non-Resident Indian (NRI) investors. Around the same time, the Bombay film industry sought a greater international presence, especially turning toward the valuable diasporic market. These family films appeared to meet the twin goals of the state and the Bombay film industry. They affirmed India's moral foundations by representing its traditions and announced India's triumphant entry into the global market by persistently including a wide array of multinational brand names in their narratives. In films such as *Hum aapke hain koun? DDLJ*, and their subsequent reincarnations, the state appeared to have found allies for combating the "vulgarity," "obscenity," and "depravity" that plagued Indian screens and were both audible and visible in songs such as *Khalnayak*'s "Choli peeche kya hai?" as well as "Sexy, sexy, sexy, mujhe log bole" (People say I am sexy, sexy, sexy), from *Khuddar* (1993; Self-Respecting Person); "Meri pant bhi sexy" (My pant is sexy), from *Dulaara* (1993; The Loved One); and "Sarkayleo khatiya jara lage" (Bring your cot closer, I am feeling cold), from *Raja babu* (1993; His Lordship). Family films helped the Bombay film industry secure its domestic market and reach the diasporic market while educating Indian nationals, both at home and abroad, in Indian traditions.[8] Moreover, they reconciled the tensions between Indian traditions and multinational consumerism by making consumption a family value.

Analyses and accounts of film censorship largely focus on films that have been cut by the state or ones that have generated controversy. Unlike *Khalnayak*, which encountered obstacles at the level of the state and public reception, *DDLJ* sailed smoothly through the Central Board of Film Certification, which granted it a clear U certificate.[9] Thus, one could argue that DDLJ was not censored if one thinks of censorship *only* as a process of excision whereby some topics are forbidden expression in representation. By including *DDLJ* in a book on film censorship, I break with this scholarly tradition and broaden the conceptualization of censorship by drawing attention to four other processes: first, the less-highlighted functions of the CBFC, certification and classification; second, the ways in which the film industry itself cuts or otherwise alters films, that is, editing both the screenplay and film footage, inserting an intermission, and adding deleted scenes on DVDs; third, the excisions instituted by exhibitors to accommodate a regimented screening menu and schedule; and fourth, the selection and consumption of films by audiences. I show how the (re) production of the on-screen family in *DDLJ* and its unanimous off-screen celebration in the era of economic liberalization is indebted not only to the reconciliation of tradition and modernity but also to a critique of the family. This (re)production is secured through all the state, industry, and audience practices just listed.

Constructing a Family Love Story

As I already noted, *DDLJ* was given a clear U certificate allowing all audiences to see the film. How was this process of certification productive?

During the course of my fieldwork in Bombay, I asked an official at the CBFC whether the examining committee members had voiced any concerns about the film; the official quickly replied, "No, everyone liked the film." The examining committee's report confirmed this response, noting, "Subsequent to the screening of the film and initial reactions, members felt the film is made for the family audience and there is nothing objectionable in the film hence the film may be recommended a clear 'U' certificate."[10] In granting this certification, the examining committee abided by the censorship guidelines reissued by the Ministry of Information and Broadcasting in 1992, which urged the CBFC to ensure that any film granted a U certificate be "suitable for family viewing, that is to say, the film should be such that all the members of the family including children can view it together."[11] Unlike *Khalnayak*'s "Choli ke peeche kya hai?" which defied state guidelines and, according to some, could not be watched in a family setting, *DDLJ* clearly conformed to state guidelines and enabled family viewing. As I show later, by encouraging such collective viewing, the U certificate enabled the intergenerational transmission of cinephilia.

While a clear A certificate shrank the potential market for *Satyam shivam sundaram*, DDLJ's clear U certificate helped generate the widest possible market for that film; this fact surely appealed to distributors, who did not have to worry about delays at the level of the CBFC or public controversies. Unlike Raj Kapoor, who had to contend with possibly alienating family or female audiences, the Chopras were assured that the much desired U certificate would attract both. The rating, which appeared in newspaper listings, signaled audiences that the film was appropriate for family viewing. Moreover, this state-conferred stamp appeared at the onset of *DDLJ*'s screening and framed its reading. Thus, as I demonstrate in my analysis of *Satyam shivam sundaram*, mechanisms of censorship regulate not just morality but also the film's potential market; furthermore, they contribute to the way a film is interpreted. The U certificate was valuable for the Chopras not only for the present but also for the future. If the Chopras decided to sell the film to state-run or satellite television, they wouldn't have to make another trip to the CBFC to recertify the film (and as I noted in Chapter 3, state-run television and, after 1995, satellite television can show films only if they have a U certificate). These visits cost time and hence money. Furthermore, there is always the possibility that the new committee watching the film might decide that more cuts are warranted, which can entail dealing with various levels of bureaucracy.

In this case, a U certificate was valuable in terms of time and money and marked *DDLJ* as a film suitable for the entire family. Such classification begs a central question: what kind of film is considered suitable for the family, specifically, the Indian family? Consider this summary of the film provided by the examining committee:

> The film is a family love story. Raj and Simran fall in love when they meet each other in Europe. Baldev father of Simran believes in arranged marriage and wants Simran to marry Kuljeet son of his friend. Simran is heart broken but Raj travels all the way to Punjab from London. As the marriage preparations for Simran and Kuljeet's wedding begin, Raj enters the family as a stranger friend and wins the confidence of all the family members with his friendly behaviour. Finally Baldev becomes very angry knowing the intention of Raj. However, he agrees at the end to give away his daughter to Raj when he knows that his daughter is really in love with Raj and not Kuljeet.[12]

The examining committee members refer to the film as a "family love story"—an interesting appellation considering that love stories in popular Hindi films generally take place against the wishes of the family, as does the one in *DDLJ* itself. In what way, then, is this film a "family love story"? By considering *DDLJ* in the context of film production in India in the late 1980s and the early 1990s, the answer becomes clearer. While the love story had been a prominent feature in Hindi films in general, a palpable shift occurred at this time. The romantic pair moved to the forefront so decisively that it diminished the role of other characters and relations, specifically, those of the family.[13]

Unlike most of its contemporaries, *DDLJ* reestablishes the importance of familial relations even as it appears to imagine their transgression. *DDLJ* differs from these other stories because it reconciles the family and the love story, establishing the importance of family relations in its narrative. The family's prominent position is reinforced by the amount of screen time given to characters who play aunts, uncles, parents, siblings, and grandparents. The story (especially the second half) accords the family significance and value. For example, Raj, the hero of the film, refuses to elope with Simran, his lover, despite her many pleadings. He repeatedly tells her that their union must be blessed by her family, particularly her father. While the love story normally draws on elements of the action genre by including chase sequences, kidnappings, and encounters with the law or goons to foreground obstacles generated by larger forces (e.g., the family), *DDLJ*, for the most part, refuses this generic turn; its unconventional romantic hero, Raj, follows the path of "emotion" rather than

LIVERPOOL JOHN MOORES UNIVERSITY
LEARNING SERVICES

"action," adopting the strategy of love to secure his relationship not only with his girlfriend but also with her family.

Finally, the references within *DDLJ* to previous commercial films—in other words, intertexuality[14]—weave a relation between Bombay cinema present and past, constructing *DDLJ*'s genealogy and in the process producing Bombay cinema as familial. The film's title comes from a Hindi film song in *Chor machaye shor* (1974; The Boisterous Thief), and at one point the family members play *antakshari* (a collective singing game) that refers to older film songs. The most moving reference to Bombay cinema's past occurs when, during the prenuptial festivities, Baldev sings his wife a song from Yash Chopra's *Waqt* (1965; Time).[15] *Waqt* in turn is an evocative film about a Punjabi Hindu family separated after an earthquake but eventually reunited. This reference is made more poignant by the knowledge that Achla Sachdev, who plays Baldev's mother in *DDLJ*, was the heroine in *Waqt* to whom the song was sung. Moreover, it underscores filmmaking as a family profession. Like *Waqt*, which Yash Chopra directed under his elder brother B. R. Chopra's banner, *DDLJ* was a family effort, with Pamela Chopra (Aditya Chopra's mother), Uday Chopra (his younger brother), and most of all Yash Chopra extending their full support—financial, professional, and emotional—to Aditya Chopra's maiden effort.[16] *DDLJ* is read as a film that attends to both the family and the love story—hence the appellation "family love story."

The examining committee's apt naming of this film was affirmed by *DDLJ*'s audiences. At its three-hundredth-week celebrations at the Martha Mandir theater in Bombay, many repeat viewers, who declared they had seen *DDLJ* from 5 to 255 times, proffered several reasons for liking the film, including its representation of North Indian culture; sequences shot in beautiful European locations; hummable, nonvulgar songs; the way Raj (Shah Rukh) woos the family members; and the fact that it is "youth-oriented" and tells "every boy and girl's story."[17] One young male viewer emphatically stated that *DDLJ* showed that "[n]o matter how much we love another person, we need to respect our parents' feelings."[18] The viewers' responses demonstrate the film's wide-ranging appeal, which engaged viewers with both modern and traditional sensibilities.

The Good Indian Daughter and Virginity; or, The Honor of an Indian Woman

What kind of a family and love story are we presented? Unfortunately, the examining committee report provides us only a bald summary, shorn of details. Nevertheless, this summary warrants consideration since it claims to tell us about the salient events and characters that form the film. For the most part, it informs us that the film's active players are Simran's father, Baldev, and her lover, Raj. The summary reveals that patriarchal desires dominate the film—and the summary itself. While patriarchal desires do dominate the film, however, they are not all-inclusive. Foucault reminds us that power is a relation, and an agonistic relation at that, which is to say, one characterized by resistance.

I seek to explore this relation and its articulation(s) by closely analyzing *DDLJ*, paying particular attention to scenes containing conversations about virginity, honor, and familial duty. These scenes would not be characterized as "sexual," at least not in the eyes of examining or revising committees, film industry professionals, or audiences, for they do not contain any drenched, unclad, or gyrating heroines. As Freud has taught us, however, the field of sexuality is not limited to genital acts or the anticipation of them, and in an agonistic manner, Foucault has explained the operation of sexuality as the nexus for the social organization of pleasure and power. In the light of these insights, I resituate sexuality within the field of unequal gender and kinship relations, which are generally slighted in discussions about the censorship of sexuality in film. For the most part, they pass unnoticed, and films including them are easily certified by examining committees, which identify them as suitable and appropriate for unrestricted viewing. In overlooking such relations, conventional discussions about the censorship of sexuality accept the terms on which sexuality is conceived by censorship. They unwittingly reproduce the apparatus of censorship they describe and sometimes oppose. To reconceive censorship, we must rethink the field of sexuality that it posits as its raison d'être.

The first scene that I will examine takes place early in the narrative. Composed of twelve shots, the sequence opens with the postman's arrival at Baldev and Lajjo's house with a letter from India. After accepting the letter, Baldev enthusiastically runs into the kitchen announcing that a letter from his friend in Punjab has arrived.[19] Strains of "Ghar aaja pardesi" (Come home, foreigner) play in the background as Baldev twirls Lajjo around, telling her to smell the fragrance of Punjab, which envelops the letter. The dialogue, the music, and Baldev's excitement indicate that even though he has lived in London for twenty years, he is still quite attached to "India"; for him, India is a series of cultural values and traditions largely associated with Punjab.

Baldev, Lajjo, and Chutki (the younger sister) gather around Simran in what appears to be a picture-perfect family portrait as she begins to read the letter. Simran's crisp and clear Hindi pronunciation establishes that

Surrounded by her family, Simran reads the letter that has arrived from Punjab. From *Dilwale dulhania le jayenge.*

Simran quickly turns to her mother after reading about her impending marriage. From *Dilwale dulhania le jayenge.*

despite being raised in London, she is literate in her "mother tongue."[20] Her smooth reading falters when she arrives at the section of the letter where Baldev is asked to honor a promise made between the two friends: that Baldev's daughter would marry his friend's son—that is, the reproduction of tradition. She ceases to speak in her mother tongue at the moment when the totality of which it is a part—Indian tradition—threatens to envelop her, or more precisely, her desire. It is a traumatic moment. Simran's voice fades, and the camera pans to the left, briefly holding Lajjo and Simran in a frame. Simran shoots a troubled glance at her mother and hands her the crumpled letter before quickly exiting the living room. Baldev misses this glance because he is positioned in such a way that her reaction does not fall within his field of view. The framing suggests that a relation, one of mother and daughter, enables *insight*; we as privileged spectators are shown this insight and are invited to sympathize with Simran's predicament.

Blind to his daughter's state of mind, Baldev is thrilled by the proposal and interprets his daughter's unwillingness to meet his eyes and her exit not only as consent to the marriage but also as a sign of modesty. He misreads her refusal to embody the promise, and by extension tradition, as its very opposite: the extension of tradition, its reproduction. In his view, she exhibits a "proper" reaction—embarrassment—when the topic of marriage is raised in the company of her father. He proudly declares to Lajjo that even though Simran has been raised in London, her embarrassed reaction demonstrates that he has succeeded in raising a good Indian daughter. In this case, discourses of visuality, patriarchy, sexuality, and nation combine to produce not only a "good Indian daughter" but also a "good Indian father." In short, Simran's identity as a "good Indian daughter" is crucial for constituting Baldev as a "good Indian father."

Lajjo, however, is more cognizant of their daughter's troubled state of mind, and she suggests to Baldev that he ask Simran's opinion about the proposal. He quickly brushes off her remark, saying that Simran has known about this engagement all her life. Unable to persuade her husband, Lajjo goes to console her daughter. The soundtrack softly plays "Mere khwabon mein jo aaye" (The one who comes into my dreams) as Simran slowly tears up an identically titled romantic poem that she had written and read to her mother. When her mother inquires what she is doing, she responds sadly, "I forgot that I wasn't supposed to even dream."[21] Cradling her daughter, Lajjo remarks consolingly, "You can dream, just don't expect your dreams to come true. And perhaps Kuljeet is your dream." This sequence demonstrates how discourses of visuality, patriarchy, sexuality, and nation are knitted together to produce an "Indian family," one in which the centrality of Baldev's wishes and promises is affirmed. But this centrality does not go unchallenged. Simran's distressed state, Lajjo's unsuccessful attempt to persuade her husband, and the poignant conversation between mother and daughter can be read as challenges to this centrality, albeit failed ones. They effectively show that patriarchy is a relation and not an all-pervasive force. The process of certification reproduces such unequal relations.

While one consequence of Baldev's promise to his friend is Simran's imminent engagement, another is a Eurail trip on which Simran will meet Raj, her dream lover. Simran asks her father to send her on a Eurail trip with her friends so that she can enjoy their company before departing for

India to marry a stranger. On this trip, she encounters Raj. While both Simran and Raj have been raised in London, gender and class inform their upbringing. Simran, whose father runs a small convenience store, is a dutiful middle-class daughter; it is clear that father and daughter love each other, but their relationship is formal, burdened by the weight of tradition. In contrast, Raj is a rich, fun-loving flirt who has a far more easy-going relationship with his entrepreneur father, Dharam Veer. One of the film's most humorous sequences occurs when Dharam Veer discovers that Raj has not passed his college exams. He gives his son a tour of family portraits, tells him that all his forefathers had similarly failed, and then congratulates Raj for not only continuing but advancing this family tradition; after all, his ancestors had failed only at lower ranks (the eighth, tenth, and twelfth grades) in India, but Raj has failed college in Britain. Dharam Veer happily sends his son off on the Eurail trip, urging him to live life fully.

Raj and Simran meet on the train. On the trip, Raj continually harasses and annoys Simran. As in the letter scene, we are once more privileged spectators, for we know from the previous song sequence that Raj is her dream lover. Thus, we are invited to read Raj's pranks not as signs of sexual harassment but as rituals of courtship. One such event takes place when Simran and Raj accidentally miss the train and spend a night in Switzerland. After Simran drinks too much cognac,[22] Raj brings her to a bed-and-breakfast. When she wakes up, she notices that she is wearing a man's shirt—and the camera slowly pans across the room to show us her strewn clothes. Simran's confusion is heightened when Raj enters the room with a tea tray and a rose. In a series of tight close-ups, the camera makes Simran's

Raj reveals lipstick marks as evidence that Simran and he spent the night together. From *Dilwale dulhania le jayenge.*

distress visible as she begs Raj to relate the previous night's events. He insinuates that they slept together, and when she does not believe him, he displays lipstick marks on his chest as evidence.

The camera shows us Raj's suppressed laughter, but Simran is not granted this view. Our privileged glimpse enables us not only to read the scenario as yet another prank but also to see that Simran has retained her "honor," that is, her virginity. Meanwhile, Simran believes that she made the marks and is thus herself "marked": she is no longer a "virgin surface" and is cut off from tradition. When Simran begins to cry, Raj realizes the joke has gone too far and quickly tells her that he stole the lipstick from her purse and painted his chest and that nothing happened between them the previous night. Through Raj's confession, tradition is reaffirmed: Simran is still a virgin, still within the scope of tradition. When Simran continues to wail, Raj pulls her head back and asserts:

> Listen to me, Simran. Listen to me. I know what you think about me. You think I'm a no-good, low-down creep, but I'm not a creep. I'm a *Hindustani*. I know what a *Hindustani*[23] girl's honor means to her. I would never even imagine doing such a thing to you. I'm telling you the truth: nothing happened last night. It was a joke. [my emphasis]

Raj's explanation hinges on gendered cultural values. As a Hindustani man, he could not have taken Simran's virginity because he knows what her honor means to a Hindustani girl. In this gendered version of Hindustani cultural values, a woman's honor is lodged in her body; sexual purity

Raj tries to convince Simran that they did not have sex. From *Dilwale dulhania le jayenge.*

constitutes her as a Hindustani woman. And a Hindustani man is one who recognizes the importance of sexual purity.

Raj's explanation reinforces an old patriarchal association of sexuality, honor, and the female body. This association is fueled by both Simran's initial distress and her subsequent relief on hearing Raj's explanation. Embracing Raj, she tells him, "Don't ever joke like that. You don't know what I would have done." This scene underscores the value of virginity for a woman while neglecting the value of virginity for the (re)production of patriarchy. Raj validates his identity as an honorable and respectful Hindustani man by claiming to value Simran's virginity. This show of respect is an effect of an asymmetrical power relation, one that locates a woman's honor in her body and a man's honor in his deeds and words. Later in the film, Raj gains access to Simran's family and her future in-laws by posing as an NRI entrepreneur who wants to open a Stroh's Beer factory in Punjab. As Mankekar notes, *DDLJ* reestablishes the male hero as an agent by constructing him as an NRI investor as well as the guardian of an Indian woman's sexual purity and, by extension, the virtue of the nation.[24]

Within the context of *DDLJ*, this emotionally charged sequence invites spectators to invest in gendered conceptions of honor. In contrast, on October 18, 1995, two days prior to the film's release, the documentary *The Making of Dilwale Dulhania Le Jayenge*, which aired nationwide on Doordarshan, offered spectators a more comical vantage point for viewing this scene. This new spectatorial position sought to entice audiences who perhaps did not subscribe to traditional mores. Like *DDLJ*, the documentary would have been subject to state approval, for Doordarshan—state-run television—in India shows only U-rated material. While the trailers for *Khalnayak* and audiocassettes of its music circumvented state scrutiny and thereby generated controversy, desire, and profits, the documentary subscribed to state rules and by acquiescing reached national audiences and produced *DDLJ*'s status as a family film. Unlike the audiocassettes, theatrical trailers, posters, and television promos that filmmakers had regularly used to entice audiences, this documentary was an innovative—"never been done before"—marketing strategy employed by Aditya Chopra. According to Anupama Chopra, "[i]t created a splash. In places like Assam, shops closed because people thought that they were showing the actual film."[25]

In a brilliant maneuver, the documentary, like the film, mapped out multiple viewing positions to attract audiences of varied dispositions. The carefully edited show, reduced from eight hours of tape to a thirty-minute program, showcased *DDLJ* as a family film through interviews with the cast and crew as well as behind-the-scenes footage. Many of the enthusiastic and happy cast members declared that they had greatly enjoyed shooting the film because of the congenial atmosphere during production, which made them feel as if they were a part of a "household."[26] While the documentary highlighted this familial environment through its female stars, Farida Jalal and Kajol (who play mother and daughter, respectively), it also initiated a critique of traditional patriarchal values at the level of both narrative and cinema; this ambivalence was not accidental but crucial to attracting both "traditional" and "modern" spectators, as well as many between these two poles.[27] Bursting into laughter, Kajol recalls the zipper and lipstick-marks sequence: "The whole shot it was so funny! You won't find it so funny when you see it on screen. I can't explain it to you; we both started laughing. Adi got very angry. Nobody else was laughing. I was supposed to be crying. I was laughing my guts out." Shah Rukh Khan confirms Kajol's comments, stating that this scene took the most takes—forty, to be precise.[28] The documentary intercuts the Kajol and Shah Rukh interviews with one of the takes, showing both of them dissolving into laughter and falling on each other as an annoyed Aditya Chopra watches them.

Although at this point in the documentary Kajol says she cannot explain why she laughed, her earlier comments about enacting this character may provide some insight: "Simran's basically a prude. I don't know how I've managed to portray her; I hope I've managed to portray her. She's totally unlike me. I definitely don't believe in her character at all; I really don't understand her at times, I don't identify with her at times. She's very much the traditional woman."[29] Later in the show, the lipstick marks resurface as a sign of Kajol's labor for the film. This extrafilmic information reveals the scene and therefore gendered conceptions of honor as performance. In making visible both the labor required to put together such performances (forty takes and numerous outlines of lip marks) and its leading lady's detachment from the character she played, the program offered spectators with more "modern" sensibilities a more humorous and distant position from which to view this sequence. In doing so, the documentary suggested that even if "you" were not invested in these traditional values, this film was nevertheless for "you," because even the cast and crew involved in its production had an ambivalent relationship to those values. In contrast to Kapoor, who alienated audiences by showing how a film is put together, Aditya Chopra forged emotional alliances not only with family audiences but also with audiences unreceptive to traditional notions of the family.

Joining the Love and Family Story, (Re)producing the Self-Sacrificial Woman

Like the documentary about the film, its intermission serves as a crucial avenue for consolidating *DDLJ*'s narrative and viewership. With respect to the intermission, a structural analysis buttresses a textual reading of the film. Simran eventually falls in love with Raj during the rail trip. When she returns home, her father accidentally discovers this fact. He promptly decides to take his entire family back to Punjab so that Simran can be married to Kuljeet and not indulge in further escapades that would endanger his honor. Soon afterward, Raj arrives at her doorstep and vows to pursue her. Subsequently, the word *Intermission* appears on the screen. Like the U certificate, the intermission announcement is a framing device; it conveys to audiences that the film has reached its midpoint and that at this juncture viewers may go to buy snacks, take a restroom break, or talk to one another. In *Khalnayak*, as I noted earlier, the intermission serves a crucial narrative function, setting up a problem-solution scheme in which the film's second half serves to police female desire. In *DDLJ* the intermission serves to connect the love story to the family one, as well as diasporic Indians to "native" Indians.[30] The first half of the film takes place mostly in outdoor locations throughout Western Europe. The diasporic Indians Raj and Simran live in London with their nuclear families. During the course of the train trip, Raj woos Simran, and they fall in love. The film's second half is set largely in Baldev's family home in Punjab, where Raj undertakes the task of winning over Simran's entire family. Thus, the love story is brought into the fold of the joint family, and the diasporic Indians are enveloped in the national family.

Intermission also marks a shift in Simran and Raj's personalities. In the first half, the narrative foregrounds Simran's spunky nature through her expression of desire in the song sequence of "Meri khwabon mein ko aaye"; her skillful negotiation with her father to obtain permission to go to on a much desired Eurail trip; and her charged encounters with Raj, who is largely portrayed as a flirtatious prankster. In the second half, Raj takes control of the action and transforms into a more serious romantic hero. Meanwhile, Simran grows more passive, becoming largely dependent on Raj to ensure that their love story is not extinguished by the patriarchal joint family. In addition to structuring the narrative, intermission provides a moment when audience members discuss the film and even, if the film does not appeal to them, leave the theater. In *DDLJ* this break clearly cemented the film's appeal, whereas in other cases (*Satyam shivam sundaram* appears to be a likely example given the viewers' violent responses) the space of the interval reinforced the viewers' dislike of the film. There is, then, a diffusion of power in both public assent and public dissent.

A few minutes after intermission, what Khan calls a "buffer scene" appears. Generally, directors insert a buffer scene between two charged scenes to cushion their impact. Placed as it was, however, this buffer scene was designed not to balance the narrative's emotional chords but, as Khan puts it, to "settle audiences."[31] In other words, the scene's task was to deal with the disruptive effects of intermission and resuture audiences, a task it unquestionably accomplishes, showing us how astutely *DDLJ* was made. Before this scene, we see that Simran's family and future in-laws have begun the prenuptial festivities. Simran is not reconciled to her fate and still longs for Raj. Dejected, she sits by the window while her younger sister distributes gifts to relatives. At this point her mother walks in and sees her melancholic daughter. The window[32] serves as the site for a poignant interchange in which Lajjo requests Simran to forget Raj. In a scene composed of twenty cuts, mainly in a shot/reverse shot format, Lajjo tells her daughter:

> Simran, when I was young, your grandfather used to say that there
> was no difference between men and women: what was the right
> of the one was the right of the other. Throughout my childhood, I
> believed this, but when I grew older, I realized that it wasn't true. My
> education was stopped because my brother's education was consid-
> ered more important—that was my first sacrifice. After that, at every
> turn, sometimes as a daughter, as a sister, as a wife, I kept sacrificing
> my happiness. But when you were born, when I held you in my arms,
> I promised myself that what happened with me wouldn't happen
> with my daughter. She would not sacrifice her happiness as a daugh-
> ter, sister, or mother; she would live life according to her wishes;
> she would get every bit of happiness that was rightfully hers. But I
> was wrong, Simran. I had forgotten that a woman has no right to
> promise. She is born so that she can simply sacrifice herself for men
> because a man will never sacrifice himself for a woman. That's why
> I've come to ask you for your happiness. Forget him, forget him. Your
> father won't understand your tears. So, for everyone's peace of mind,
> I beg you to forget him.

The sniffles in the theater when this scene was projected—during my multiple viewings—attest to its evocative abilities. It corroborates the sentiments and experiences of many men and women. It resonates with an

Lajjo narrates her life story as Simran looks out the window. From *Dilwale dulhania e jayenge.*

emotional reality that has been often visualized in Hindi cinema but rarely articulated.

Recounting a legacy of patriarchal practices, Lajjo tells Simran that little has changed with respect to the role of women. While lip service is paid to equality, women continue to bear the burden of sacrifice in kinship relations. In effect, the united family depends on the sacrifice of Simran's happiness. At the level of dialogue, then, Lajjo both criticizes patriarchal practices and advocates resigned acceptance, but what occurs at the level of film grammar? Consider two aspects of it, framing and the shot/reverse shot. The window that serves as the site of the conversation mirrors the screen, revealing the practice of framing. This practice points to the constructed nature not only of film composition but also of patriarchy.[33] While patriarchal practices frame Lajjo's and Simran's lives, they are not all-encompassing, as Lajjo's critique reveals; in short, resistance remains possible. The movements that together constitute this resistance are enacted through the shot/reverse shot format. This technique typically involves an eye-line match to indicate that a dialogue is taking place. Early in this scene, though, there is no eye-line match, as Simran continues to look out the window at other possibilities and, by extension, at a screen other than the one on which she appears. By the end of the scene, however, Simran agrees to her mother's wishes.

The very narrative that reveals the cost women bear in accommodating patriarchal desires also reproduces patriarchy by invoking emotional and kinship attachments. More specifically, when Simran consents to her mother's request and agrees to marry Kuljeet, she does not suffer from false consciousness; she is fully conscious of her father's dominance. Her consent is related to the way she is constituted as a subject, the way she has learned to recognize herself—namely, as her parents' daughter. More simply, she consents because she is emotionally attached to her parents. The camera also attempts to establish a relationship between Lajjo and the audience that is homologous to the diegetic one between Lajjo and Simran. The camera invites the audience to become daughters of the screen. These sentiments seek to relink the audience with Bombay cinema, making both Bombay cinema's practices and patriarchy palatable.

The self-sacrificing woman, a familiar trope in popular Hindi films, is constitutive both of the cinematic representation of the Indian family and of Bombay cinema. Let me suggest then that there is another layer to this scene, the economy of Bombay cinema and its hiring practices. In a canny interview shown in *The Making of Dilwale Dulhania Le Jayenge*, Farida Jalal, who plays Lajjo, declares:

> It's one of the best roles I've done. Mother's role okay . . . it's another
> mother's role for me, but then it's different in two or three scenes that
> are not the typical Indian mother's scenes. I'm playing my age in the
> film. I didn't have to put white in my hair. . . . After how many years,
> I really danced on the sets of *Dilwale Dulhania Le Jayenge*.

Whereas Lajjo explicitly critiques the patriarchal Indian family, Jalal, in a more implicit fashion, draws our attention to the dearth of roles for older women in Hindi commercial films, even in the 1990s, given that Bombay cinema slots older actresses in roles of long-suffering, sacrificial mothers. In effect, Jalal, the older actress, reveals to Kajol, the younger actress, the unfortunate and not-so-distant future awaiting her, given the short shelf life of heroines. Put simply, this scene points to the play of power not only at the level of filmic narrative but also, more fundamentally, at the level of cinema itself.

Given that the theme of self-sacrifice, in particular women's self-sacrifice, is central to *DDLJ*, one could ask why *DDLJ* was not subject to the CBFC's rebuke and ire, as *Pati parmeshwar* had been. After all, if Rekha is oppressed by her husband and in-laws, Simran is equally coerced to do her father's bidding. Certainly, context plays a crucial role in the disparate evaluations of the two films. The examination of *Pati parmeshwar* took place around the time of Roop Kanwar's murder and Shah Bano's divorce case; as I show in my analysis, many of the officials contended that *Pati parmeshwar* paralleled these events in undermining the development of women and India's status as a modern nation. The assessment of *Dilwale dulhania le jayenge*, however, occurred during economic liberalization, when examining committee members and officials were grappling with the threat to tradition from forces of "Westernization." The differences in evaluation could also be attributed to the stature of the director-producers, as well as to the varied composition of the examining committees. Aditya Chopra's easy journey through the CBFC could be accorded to the repute of his father, Yash Chopra, whereas R. K. Nayyar and Madan Joshi enjoyed no such connections. Finally, the committee members who determined *Pati parmeshwar's* fate might simply have been more sensitive to women's normative roles.

However that may be, these dissimilar judgments hinged as well on *DDLJ's* reformulation of tradition, family, and sacrifice. Unlike Rekha, who only embraces tradition, Simran overtly and covertly resists it even as she remains within its scope. For example, both Rekha and Simran perform *karva chauth*, the fast married women often undertake to ensure their husbands' long lives. While Rekha fasts for her wayward and abusive husband, Simran undertakes it for her lover, Raj, who treads an unconventional path by joining her in the fast. In fact, to ensure that Raj breaks her fast, Simran pretends to faint. An unknowing Raj quickly steps forward to grab her and gives her water; she opens her eyes and slyly winks at him. Moreover, although Rekha and Simran are equally superstitious, Simran can use such beliefs to her own ends. For example, she declares that she will not allow Kuljeet to place the engagement ring on the appropriate finger, for doing so would give him access to her heart, and so she invokes tradition to circumvent it. By feigning to have injured her ring finger, Simran achieves her goal. While Simran performs such acts for "modern" love, Rekha does them to save her traditional arranged marriage.

In *Pati parmeshwar* tradition is associated with the backward practices of arranged marriage, such as physical and mental abuse by in-laws and the groom, or the reliance on superstitions (as when Vijay is miraculously cured, apparently by divine intervention). Given these circumstances, Rekha's decision to adopt the path of self-sacrifice appeared regressive to many officials and committee members. In *Pati parmeshwar* self-sacrifice assumes a bodily form: it is visualized through Rekha's fasting, her continual washing of clothes and dishes, and her treks with Vijay to his mistress's house, despite her weakened condition. Lajjo articulates the labor of sacrifice, but in *Pati parmeshwar* we witness its deleterious effects on Rekha's body. *Pati parmeshwar* draws attention to Rekha's abject body rendered weak and haggard through the forces of tradition. While sacrifice might mark Simran and her mother's souls, it is not similarly visible on their bodies. Suffering in *DDLJ* assumes a resistant yet compliant aural incarnation rather than an oppressive physical one.

Pati parmeshwar primarily showcases the drudgeries of tradition, whereas *DDLJ*, while staging tradition in its more stifling forms, such as honor, patriarchal authority, and arranged marriage, also depicts it in more sumptuous and spectacular forms: exquisite silk saris, sequined *lehenga* (skirt) and *choli* outfits, flying multicolored *dupattas*, and pleasurable (and sanitized) *mehndi* (henna) and *sangeet* ceremonies. Unlike the decontextualized bawdy "traditional" lyrics of "Choli ke peeche kya hai?" in *Khalnayak*, the marriage songs in *DDLJ* appear in their proper context and are appropriate for family viewing. Furthermore, Chopra humanizes the joint family and almost entirely erases villainy from the narrative. For example, Baldev is a stern yet loving father. We are invited to empathize with his nostalgia for India and the difficulties of raising a family in a foreign land. Thus, Chopra makes both tradition and family desirable, and this desire is central to reconciling the family story and the love story and to ensuring spectatorial investment in the film. After all, we must go along with Raj's plan to woo the family rather than assent to Simran and Lajjo's pleas to elope if we wish to continue to enjoy the pleasures of tradition.

Constructing an Honorable Hindustani Hero

Aditya Chopra masterfully uses the character of Raj to both solidify and challenge tradition (i.e., the patriarchal family) by making him the meeting point for the love story and the family. Raj first encounters Baldev in London when he goes to buy beer at Baldev's convenience store. When Raj and his friends enter the shop, Baldev is closing up and refuses to sell the beer. The meeting quickly turns sour. After Raj and his friends throw money at the counter and rush off with the beer, Baldev returns home cursing British-born Indians for lacking Indian cultural values and manners. Anupama Chopra writes that in Aditya Chopra's screenplay, Raj goes to Baldev's store to buy condoms; "later, Aditya thought condoms would be too much of a transgression, so in the film, Raj only wants beer."[34] Chopra's decision to excise condoms likely rested on the belief that spectators and censors might be willing to accept that beer, at least when swigged by the film's hero, is not a sign of complete immoral, Western degeneracy (as portrayed in numerous Hindi films), but condoms would not generate such a forgiving response. Unlike in *Gupt gyan*, where the presence of condoms replicated the state discourse of development aimed at reducing the size of the family and the population, in *DDLJ* they would have signaled the presence of nonreproductive and unregulated sexuality, thereby endangering the film's family narrative, its clear U certificate, and its hero's reputation as a Hindustani. After all, as a condom consumer or an NRI who wished to open a condom factory instead of a Stroh's Beer plant, it would have been quite difficult for Raj to argue that he was an honorable Hindustani. Thus, on the eve of *DDLJ*'s three-hundredth-week celebrations, Khan, while wishing that Aditya had not substituted beer for condoms, shrewdly noted, "it's a correct film. . . . [I]t's correct cinema because it didn't have the condom scene in the film."[35]

After intermission, Raj, in his pursuit of Simran, arrives in Punjab. Initially Raj gains access to Baldev's home by "saving" Kuljeet, Simran's fiancé, who invites him to join the groom's party.[36] Upon his admission, however, Raj quickly switches allegiance to Simran's family. More specifically, he allies himself with the bride's family, which in the hierarchy of arranged marriages generally occupies a position below the groom's side, for the bride's side is expected to provide a dowry and to bear the larger burden of the wedding expenses. As Anupama Chopra astutely notes:

> Given these grim realities . . . Raj's behaviour is radical. . . . [H]e takes
> a tray of sweets from Lajjo's hand and starts serving the guests. . . .
> In later scenes, he helps Baldev's younger sister pick an appropri-
> ate sari, serves drinks [to guests] and brings bushels of grain to the
> kitchen. Raj is the only male to enter these female spaces. He sits in
> the kitchen and peels carrots while he talks. . . . In his participation
> in these female rituals [e.g., *karva chauth*], and in his easy movement
> through spaces inhabited by women, Raj is quite unlike most Hindi
> film heroes, and especially unlike the angry young men who domi-
> nated the cinema in the 1970s and 1980s.[37]

The narrative thus showcases Raj as behaving favorably, in contrast to the stern Baldev and the aggressive Kuljeet; Raj becomes the sensitive man who not only understands women's emotions and burdens but also is willing to participate in their worlds. At the level of the narrative, Raj successfully courts the female members of the household, cannily concluding that they will be his most likely allies. Equally at the level of the cinema, such sequences allowed Khan (and Aditya Chopra) to shrewdly woo female audiences, who constitute a crucial market.[38] Raj's success is visible when Lajjo, on discovering that Simran loves Raj, urges them to elope. But Raj takes the high road and refuses to run away. In a scene once

more framed by the window, Raj kneels at Lajjo's feet and tells her that
"[t]here are always two roads, . . . the right one and the wrong one. And
though the wrong route is seductive in its ease, he will take the more difficult, correct path. Because, he says, he doesn't want to snatch steal Simran.
He wants to marry her with the approval of the family [i.e., her father]."[39]
Spectators, along with Lajjo and Simran, are invited to assent to Raj's moving moral stance. In the film this path bears favorable results, for Baldev
eventually allows Simran to marry Raj. This happy ending underscores
the value of the "correct path." In a *Filmfare* interview after winning the
magazine's best actor award, Khan, citing his own love story, also emphasized the importance of following the "correct path." He stated that like
Raj, he too courted his Hindu girlfriend's family and eventually attained
their approval for the marriage.[40] If Kajol distanced herself from Simran,
Khan embraced his on-screen role, seamlessly suturing his off-screen persona with his on-screen avatar. In a later interview, he boldly declared,
"Heroes generally say I became Raj, Rahul etc. Raj is Shah Rukh. I'm like
Raj. Raj is me. There is no character."[41] Khan's claim to sameness offers
an instance to contemplate another aspect of tradition, namely, religion.
Khan's assertion can be interpreted as "a Hindu man is a like Muslim man.
A Muslim man is like a Hindu man." This assertion challenges the divisive
and hierarchal vision of India—that is, the national family—as imagined
by Hindu nationalists.

Deleted Scenes

In January 2002, nearly six and a half years into *DDLJ*'s theatrical exhibition, Yash Raj Films released the double-disc official DVD of *DDLJ*. Like
the theatrical film, the DVD was granted a U certificate. While the censorship rules stipulate that producers must reapply for a certificate when
releasing DVDs, it is unclear whether either the feature film or the discs'
bonus features were (re)examined.[42] As I noted in Chapter 5, for an applicant requesting the same certificate as originally conferred and submitting
a disc containing the unaltered version of the feature film, the Cinematograph Rules allow the regional officer, with prior approval of the chairperson, to issue a certificate without constituting a committee to review the
film. The state certificate appears on the DVD cover of *DDLJ* and at the
beginning of the feature film, though it does not frame the entry into the
bonus features, suggesting that they might have escaped state scrutiny.

By the time the DVD version of *DDLJ* was released, the film had enjoyed
a stupendous theatrical run and several television airings. It was also

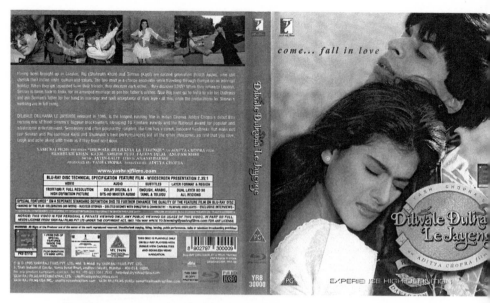

The Blu-ray version of *DDLJ* features both the Indian U rating and the PG rating given by the British Board of Film Classification. *From Dilwale dulhania le jayenge.* (Mumbai: Yash Raj Films, 2009).

widely available as pirated DVDs, VCDs, and videocassettes. To ensure the DVD's sales, the production house packed the set with special features including the film's original theatrical trailer; four television promos; the made-for-television documentary *The Making of Dilwale Dulhania Le Jayenge*; "Success Story," which contains clips from *DDLJ*'s premiere in 1995 to its thee-hundredth-week celebrations at Bombay's Martha Mandir theater, with effusive comments from devoted fans; "Highlights from the 1995 *Filmfare* Awards," which showcases moving acceptance speeches; interviews with Khan, Kajol, and Yash Chopra, conducted in 2001 for the three-hundredth-week celebrations, in which they reflect on their experiences of the film and express their thoughts about its unmatched success; and seven deleted scenes with optional commentary by the film's director, Aditya Chopra, to guide our viewing. Often DVDs feature a "director's cut" that restores the "original" object by reinserting footage excised at the behest of producers or censors. In the case of *DDLJ*, however, the deleted scenes are supplements to a beloved object. Thus, cutting emerges as addition rather than subtraction. These scenes offer cinephiles the pleasure of elongating their experience of the film and, through Chopra's commentary, the pleasure in knowing how the film is put together.[43]

How do these scenes affect the representation of the family and the love story? Most of the deletions that Chopra shares on the DVD are directed at the family, leaving the love story intact. Thus, the family emerges as a locus of concern not only for the examining committee or state censorship but also for Chopra and more generally the film industry, especially in the era of economic liberalization. In his commentary Chopra states that he removed the scene entitled "Simran's original introduction" because when he initially wrote the film, he was planning on casting fresh actors. He therefore wanted to tease audiences before unveiling this new heroine. Later, however, he decided that he required more established actors for the roles. In retrospect, he notes, the heroine's introduction appeared too long, for audiences would have been familiar with Kajol.

This scene begins with a view of Simran as she sits in a chair with her head covered by a yellow towel. When Simran asks her mother Lajjo to pass her some face cream, Lajjo lightly rebukes her, stating that Simran has no need for a beauty regimen because she is not in the running to be the next Queen Elizabeth. Rather, Simran will return to India, where people like wheat-colored skin. While Lajjo's comments on face cream gesture to extant racism in the United Kingdom, they simultaneously screen a common Indian fetish with fair skin. Later, Lajjo notes that as a young girl she never used creams or rouge; she simply pinched her cheeks to make them red, a fact that made Baldev spill over with laughter. Simran's voice is laced with surprise as she inquires whether there was time when her father actually laughed. Her mother sadly replies that his boomerang laughter used to cross rivers in Punjab, but it died once they moved to London because a fellow Indian fleeced them and then absconded to Africa. Lajjo's remarks invite spectators to sympathize with Baldev.

In the train-station scene, cut to reduce the film's length, spectators also witness a more favorable representation of Baldev as he expresses his anxieties about Simran's upcoming journey and urges her not to do anything that might dishonor him or her; Simran dutifully assents. This scene establishes Baldev as the protective father, but it also underscores Simran as the repository of her father's honor and her need to guard this honor to maintain their relationship. In his commentary, Chopra tells us that this was one of his favorite scenes and movingly elaborates on Baldev's concerns, providing spectators with privileged insight into the father's apprehensions about sending his daughter on a trip with friends who may not have had similar upbringings and could lead her astray. Chopra's voice-over compounds the sympathetic portrayal of Baldev in the diegesis and reveals his own emotional investments in the patriarchal family. In cutting these two scenes, however, Chopra decreases spectators' affinity with Baldev and the patriarchal family.

The train-station scene may showcase Simran as a dutiful daughter, but an earlier scene, also deleted to trim the film's length, represents her as less than ideal. It establishes that Simran is a habitual latecomer to *pooja* (prayer) and is linked to a later scene when Simran completes *pooja* before her father's arrival and then requests his permission to go on the Eurail trip. Chopra suggests that the earlier scene was intended to heighten the emotional charge of the later scene. Perhaps so, but its presence also increases the artful negotiation she does later, so that its removal mutes Simran's resistance to and negotiation with her father.

A terrace scene that Chopra deleted in yet another effort to decrease the film's length tailors Raj's character, too. The scene takes place soon after Raj meets Simran's family members in Punjab and realizes that her father is the convenience store owner with whom he had an altercation in London. Raj initially tells Simran that he is planning to leave, for he will not be able to persuade her family, especially her father, given his unpleasant encounter with him. As a shocked Simran stares at him and begins to cry, he announces that he was simply joking and that he intends to woo all her family member, even her old man. In his commentary Chopra tells us that this scene had bothered him even before filming it because it did not fit well with an upcoming scene in which Raj, like Baldev, is shown feeding pigeons. When the film's length became a problem, Chopra excised this scene first. For Chopra, this cut enabled the more seamless joining of Raj's entry into the family home and the sequence in which Baldev comes upon Raj as he is feeding the pigeons and forgives him for his misbehavior in London. In removing this scene, Chopra reduces Raj's irreverent, prankster persona and heightens his transformation into a good Hindustani who respects his elders, especially Simran's father. After all, Raj's ability to convince Baldev (and some spectators) that he would be a better son-in-law than Kuljeet rests on this transformation.

Another entertaining deleted scene, removed for time considerations, takes place before Lajjo urges Simran and Raj to run away. It shows Raj secretly narrating his love story to a rapt all-female audience in the kitchen. Later, in a scene from a *mela* (fair) sequence that Chopra cut because he deemed it unnecessary, Raj tells Kuljeet, "[W]hen you are unable to win a girl's heart with action, you need to employ emotion." Both scenes draw attention to Raj's canny knowledge of women's feelings. They also make visible the film's (and the film industry's) explicit attempt to woo female audiences by turning away from "action" and toward "emotion." In cutting these scenes, Chopra eliminated the film's canniness about the market without sacrificing the sobs.

In his commentary on the scene from the *mela* sequence, Chopra states that although he decided that the sequence was superfluous while editing the film, he nonetheless wanted to share a scene from it because the crew and cast had a lot of fun shooting the sequence. He contritely notes that this deletion affected the development of Preeti's character (Kuljeet's sister) and upset Mandira Bedi, who played this role. Chopra's comments draw attention to two significant points. First, the deleted scenes included on the DVD were culled from a larger lot. Thus, as spectators, we are once more privy to scenes that the director has selected and would like us to see; in other words, our vision is still carefully being guided. Second, we are reminded that the editing table tailors not just the narrative but also the careers of film stars. Gossip magazines tell us that stars often fight to retain scenes that feature them because they rightly equate screen time with their professional success. Khan's fledging career, for example, was consolidated at the editing table when Aditya Chopra viewed the rushes of *Darr* (1993; Fear) and decided to give to him greater presence in the film, in the process alienating the established star Sunny Deol, who played the film's hero.

Chopra sadly tells us that the final scene he cut from the film was quite dear to him. In fact, he deleted it only after the first copy was printed; hence, unlike the other scenes, this one includes the background score. Once again, Chopra cites length as a decisive factor in its removal. Chopra reveals that he liked the scene because it was well acted and enhanced the drama. In addition, it sharply contrasted Baldev's stubbornness with Raj's more easygoing nature. Moreover, he states the scene shows that Lajjo, as a good wife, attempts to persuade her husband before she tells the lovers to leave. The scene takes place after Lajjo discovers that Simran loves Raj. Composed of four shots, including two shot/reverse shot sequences, the scene begins with a medium shot showing Baldev closing his closet door. It slowly zooms to a close-up as Lajjo helps a smiling Baldev with his coat and carefully broaches her topic. As she hesitatingly revisits a conversation about Simran in which she remarked that their daughter would slowly forget Raj, Baldev's face slowly freezes and assumes an intractable form. The escalating violins in the background heighten the charged nature of the conversation and alert us to Baldev's brewing anger. As privileged viewers, we are able to see (and hear) Baldev's reaction; Lajjo, who is placed behind him and unable to do so, continues to speak, telling Baldev that she was wrong: Simran still loves Raj.

Baldev slowly turns around and in a menacing voice demands to know exactly what she is trying to say. With a mixture of dread and confidence, Lajjo persists: "If Simran loves this man so much, then don't you think we should at least ask her about him? Perhaps he might be a really nice person. After all, this is a question concerning Simran's entire life. Perhaps we are making a wrong decision."[44] Initially, as Lajjo surreptitiously begins pleading Simran's case, the strumming sitar in the background matches her sympathetic tone, but it quickly returns to its earlier heated mode as Baldev turns around to lambaste Lajjo for doubting his ability to make decisions about this daughter's life. When Lajjo attempts to deny this, Baldev raises his hand to silence her. As Baldev and Lajjo are framed by a claustrophobic close-up, he leans in, moving closer to Lajjo's face, and sternly tells her:

> More than Simran, you've embarrassed and insulted me. I know exactly what I am doing. I know that a boy who has no knowledge of our culture and our land would never be able to make Simran happy. Simran will only marry Kuljeet. This is the reality and no one, no matter how strong, can change this reality. You should understand this and ensure that your daughter also understands this.

Throughout Baldev's speech, we hear brief, protesting grunts from Lajjo's throat. After Baldev departs, a determined look appears on her face, and Lajjo immediately goes to Simran and Raj, urging them to elope.

As was mentioned previously, Raj refuses to run away, persuasively citing the value of the correct path and implicitly promising that this path will lead to a happy ending. Our assent to Raj's plan—the correct path—to a large extent rests on the deletion of the scene just described, for it decisively demonstrates that this path does not always yield fruit, at least not when women follow it. In cutting this scene, Chopra eliminates the film's most trenchant critique of the correct path, paving the way for the reproduction of the patriarchal family. The presence of this scene on the DVD as well as Chopra's initial resistance to cutting it alerts us to *DDLJ*'s ambivalence about the patriarchal family—an ambivalence crucial to its continued and wide-ranging appeal.[45]

Reducing *DDLJ*'s Length

Unlike examining committees, which, following official censorship guidelines, cite decency, state security, and communal harmony in deciding which scenes should be excised, Chopra attributes his deletions to informal reasons centering on length, continuity, tight narrative, and cast; among these factors, length emerges as the most significant reason for cutting many of the scenes, for the film originally exceeded three hours and twenty minutes. In her book on *DDLJ*, Anupama Chopra notes that film's length "perturbed" Yash Chopra, who "helped Aditya shave off two and a half minutes."[46] Nonetheless, both Anupama and Aditya fail to explain why the film's length is a problem or cause for worry.

To understand this problem, we need to move from the site of film production to film exhibition. During the period of *DDLJ*'s release, single-screen theaters still dominated India, and they followed a conventional screening schedule of 12–3:00 p.m., 3–6:00, 6–9:00, and 9–12:00 a.m.; habitual audiences knew this schedule and planned their viewings accordingly. This regimented schedule generally accommodated the screening of trailers, Films Division shorts,[47] the feature film, advertisements, and the intermission. Both Aditya and Yash Chopra would have known that the film's length would raise concerns at the sites of exhibition, where a longer film would reduce the number of screenings and consequently the film's revenues. Moreover, it would have tampered with viewer expectations regarding screening times and risked losing its audience; in addition, a lengthy narrative might have generated restlessness among potential viewers. The Chopras' concerns demonstrate that the auteurist vision is subject to the forces of the market.

Despite Chopra's cuts, the film still ran for three hours and ten minutes, well over the conventional length. A personal anecdote sheds further light on the persisting problem of length and the theme of family viewing. *DDLJ* was released in India during the course of my fieldwork. I saw it four times with relatives and friends at the Plaza, a well-known Delhi theater and a favorite childhood haunt where I had viewed numerous films with family members; I initiated all those viewings. While I am not always eager to share films that I enjoy with most relatives, or for that matter friends, I felt that *DDLJ* would charm both groups. After all, it artfully combines melodrama and comedy and even includes a brief action sequence. It offers sensual yet sanitized song sequences, the entertaining *jodi* (pairing) of Shah Rukh Khan and Kajol, beautiful cinematography capturing European locales, a sumptuous display of Indian traditions, reverence for the family combined with sympathy for the romantic pair, and an engaging and well-enacted story, as well as moments of feminist critique. Moreover, I could watch the film comfortably with either group, without squirming in my chair at the appearance of an explicit sex sequence. My own experience underscored the extent to which the film could entice individuals of varying sensibilities and encourage collective viewing, which was partly made possible by the U certificate.

On October 20, 1995, *DDLJ*'s opening day, my cousin and I arrived at the Plaza intending to buy tickets for the following week's show. To our surprise, tickets were available for the noon show, but the film, the ticket seller told us, had already started. Delighted at obtaining first-day, first-show tickets, I quickly purchased them and did not bother to inquire what time the screening had begun; I thought we would have missed at most the opening credits and a scene or two. By the time we rushed in and took our seats, however, the screen showed Simran running to catch her train at Victoria Station. I later realized that I had missed approximately thirty minutes of the film because the show had started at 11:30 a.m. rather than the conventional time of noon—an unfortunate cut, one might say. The second time, knowing that *DDLJ* is longer than the usual films, I arrived early and impatiently waited for my mother to arrive so that we could go inside. This time I saw the entire film, at least to my knowledge. The next two times that I saw the film, I noticed that scenes had been cut, making me doubt that I had ever seen the full version. In the interest of a regimented schedule and timely screenings, the exhibitors apparently decided to arbitrarily chop scenes that they deemed irrelevant.

Segmented Viewings

Interestingly, *DDLJ*'s airing on television multiple times, its wide circulation on videocassette and VCD, and its official release on DVD have not cut short its theatrical run. As mentioned earlier, by February 2010 it had run at the Martha Mandir theater for 750 continuous weeks, and as of this writing, it is still running there. Anupama Chopra tells us: "*DDLJ* 'regulars' saunter in even half an hour late for the movie, and leave after their favourite scene or song is over. The pleasure is no longer in the tale itself, but in the telling of it."[48] Such segmented viewings, prior to the VCD/DVD moment, were not limited to *DDLJ*. As I noted in my discussion of *Khalnayak*, fans of Madhuri Dixit would often enter the theater to see her dance and walk out once those sequences were over. These cinephiles choose to lavish their attention on the segment, timing their entries so they can catch their beloved scene, dialogue, or song. Within the ambit of state censorship, cutting is cast as prohibition, while here, cutting signifies pleasure—a pleasure that adds to *DDLJ*'s profits. Both censors and cinephiles choose segments to which they devote their energy and time. Both forms of selection, I argue, are exercises of power to which a study of censorship must attend.

9 From Censorship to Selections

My old man used to say, Always finish what you start. It's a sound principle, but it can't work in this cafe. If life is truly a song, then what we've got here is just snatches of a few melodies. All these folks are in transition; they come midway in their stories and go on. —GLORIA NAYLOR, *BAILEY'S CAFE*

Picture abhi baaki hai mere dost [More of the film is still to come, my friend]. —*OM SHANTI OM* (2007)

On April 5, 2001, Dev Anand's *Censor* was released in theaters in India with a UA certificate that was granted only after cuts had been made.[1] The film was crammed with both veteran and faded stars, including Rekha as a regional officer in the CBFC (an uncharacteristic role, given the complex sexual resonances of her star image), Hema Malini, Raj Babbar, Shammi Kapoor, Randhir Kapoor, Jackie Shroff, Govinda, Mamta Kulkarni, Ayesha Jhulka, and Dev Anand himself. These stars no longer commanded box-office clout in 2001. The film's production values were similarly dated. The film recounts the tale of a well-known director named Vikram (Dev Anand) whose "modern" and provocative film *Aane waala kal* (The Arriving Future) is subject to the trials and tribulations of state censorship. At its outset, *Censor* foregrounds the historical moment of liberalization by staging a debate in the Indian Parliament about the impact of satellite television on "Indian culture," specifically, the explicit depictions of sex and violence, as well as the glorification of alcohol. While two vocal members of

Parliament emphatically argue for greater censorship to protect "Indian culture," others propose that censorship should move in step with the changing times. This debate generates stricter censorship guidelines, which are sent to the CBFC, where members are expected to follow them.

Later, the film shows how satellite television affects the family. This new medium creates intergenerational strife, with the younger generation championing progress (i.e., short dresses, discotheques, dating, and the right to view sexually explicit shows) while the older generation stresses the value of tradition and regards satellite television as a challenge to its authority. This battle between "tradition" and "modern" sensibilities is staged in an outlandish sequence in Vikram's *Aane waala kal*. A college lecturer (played by Heenee Kaushik) invites her female students to debate the position of women in contemporary India, to name women they admire, and to discuss which careers they wish to pursue. The students immediately call out names of women whom they respect—Indira Gandhi, Razia Sultan, and Jhansi ki Raani (the queen of Jhansi), all important political figures in Indian history. Most of the students express a desire to work outside the home, as a pilot, a singer, an actress, an astronaut, or a police officer. Two women, clearly in the minority, state a preference for less "modern" paths. One believes that woman's place lies with her husband as his helpmate. Another meekly states that she plans to follow her dead grandfather's wishes and have an arranged marriage; if her husband dies, she plans to become a *sati*. Their fellow classmates ridicule and berate their choices.

In stark contrast to the conservative position of the two women, a fellow student named Parveen (Mink Singh) declares that she wishes to become a famous belly dancer. At the urging of her classmates, she agrees to give a demonstration of her dancing skills. Parveen unbuttons her jacket and with a flourish throws it at one of the "regressive" women. Now, clad in a white-sequined bikini top and a short white skirt, she climbs on her desk and provocatively swings her hips. A classmate who plans to become an actress, Pooja (Pooja Batra), joins Parveen. Before mounting the desk, Pooja similarly removes her black wrap and tosses it at the "traditional" women. In her black-and-white striped tank top and miniskirt, Pooja matches Parveen's erotic moves. The camera angles and editing processes construct both women as desirable sexual objects. While the rest of the classmates cheer the two girls, the two conservative women are horrified by their performance and urge them to stop, declaring that they are degrading Indian culture. Parveen and Pooja continue to revel in their sexual display, asserting that women's power lies in their ability to effectively deploy their sexuality. As shown in this sequence and in the narrative at large, female sexuality (or more specifically, the exposure of the female body and its gyrations) emerges as the point of contention in and as central to discussions of Indian culture, tradition, and censorship.

Before screening *Aane waala kal* for a CBFC examining committee, Vikram holds a trial show of his film for a diverse audience. He invites the audience to be his film's "censors" by penning their reactions without consulting one another. The audience offers glowing reviews of the film. In fact, Maggie (Archana Puran Singh), who is a member of the Academy of Motion Picture Arts and Science's Awards Committee, gushingly praises the film and offers to begin proceedings to nominate the film for the U.S. organization's Best Foreign Film Award. A delighted Vikram rushes to the CBFC to get a certificate so that he can promptly send his film to the United States. After the screening, the regional officer, Mrs. Srivastav (Rekha), tells Vikram that the majority of the examining committee members found the film to be too bold for Indian audiences and gave it an A certificate contingent on his making thirteen cuts. While we are not informed about the nature of the cuts, it is implied that they deal with sex and violence.

A devastated Vikram begs Mrs. Srivastav and the committee members to reconsider, stating that the A certificate will restrict the film's audience and the cuts will mangle it; however, they refuse to change their decision. We learn that two committee members hold personal grudges against Vikram and attempt to exact revenge by strictly censoring his film. A third member dislikes Vikram because his films have "corrupted" his daughter, leading her to defy his authority. Vikram informally meets with the committee members and attempts to sway them. When he fails, he informally pressures the minister of information and broadcasting in Delhi to view the film, bypassing any revising committee. Unfortunately for Vikram, the minister proves to be even more severe in his judgment, for he gives the film an A certificate—and that subject to eighteen cuts being made. The film foregrounds the crucial role of Vikram's stardom in the institutional operations of censorship. Vikram leverages his stardom to pressure the members of the examining committee and the minister to change their minds. While he fails in these endeavors, the film highlights the fact that Vikram's stardom enables him to initiate these conversations. Later, his fame assists him in mobilizing viewers to support his battle against state censorship.

At this juncture in *Censor*, to meet the Academy Awards' nomination deadline, Vikram smuggles a print of the film out of India and names Maggie a coproducer so that the film can be screened in the United States sans the Indian state certificate, thereby circumventing state censorship. He tells his devoted wife (played by Hema Malini) that he will challenge the CBFC and the minister's decisions by taking his case to court because the excisions pertaining to scenes of sex and violence would destroy his film's "soul." As in the case of Kapoor's *Satyam shivam sundaram*, the body emerges as the film's "soul." Moreover, the film is viewed as a complete, untouched object prior to the hacking it receives at the hands of the CBFC. In court Vikram undermines the testimonies of three committee members who voted to delete scenes from his film and give it an A certificate. He shows that while the two male members advocate sexual restraint and preach about tradition publicly, they engage in extramarital affairs privately. He also points out that one of the male members is by no stretch of the imagination the epitome of tradition given that he physically abused his daughter and later failed to attend her wedding when she married someone of her own choosing. Finally, he proves that a third member is merely a scorned starlet.

To further bolster his case, he submits his trial-show notebook to the judge and brings all the viewers from that screening as witnesses to demonstrate that his film has the support of the masses. Prior to receiving a verdict on the case, Vikram and his crew fly to the United States, where he wins the Best Foreign Film and Best Director awards for that year. This ceremony is avidly watched by the Indian public, examining committee members, and the case judge. In his speech Vikram applauds American freedom, which has enabled his film to be viewed and thus to win these awards. He also profusely thanks his loyal and dedicated wife, who has supported him. The pressure to demonstrate that India, like the United States, is a democratic nation-state compels the judge to grant *Aane waala kal* a clear U certificate. The judge declares that now the film is free from the shackles of censorship so that it can be viewed intact, as it was viewed in the United States. A victorious Vikram is given a standing ovation by the court (at the behest of the judge) and is triumphantly carried out.

Like Vasudev's *Liberty and Licence in the Indian Cinema*, which I examined in Chapter 1, Dev Anand's *Censor* delineates the various state institutions involved in the exercise of censorship. It departs from Vasudev's account by making three significant new observations about this process. It points to the audiences as potential "censors" (albeit clearly more friendly ones than the state-appointed censors) and highlights the roles of stardom and informal practices in the operations of censorship. Unfortunately, these observations are not mobilized to visualize a new tale of censorship. Instead, the narrative succumbs to commercial cinema's pressure to produce heroes and villains and thus formulaically constructs censorship as a process of excision or restriction enforced by the state. In doing so, it underscores how resilient Vasudev's binary argument is even in 2001. In the film the much-maligned censors are the ones who cut films and reduce its audience, thereby hindering a director's creativity and freedom of expression as well as limiting public access to films. It is assumed that the film is a "whole" object before the state cuts it, thereby screening the processes of film production. This film demonstrates how a hierarchical and linear understanding of censorship can be so persistent that it assumes cinematic form. Moreover, this vision becomes so pervasive that it defines relations of power in the narrative, that is, the heroes and villains.

I have been questioning such formulas by demonstrating that the practice of cutting is not limited to the censors and by highlighting oft-slighted aspects of censorship, namely, certification and classification. For example, if the possibility of cutting and an A certificate hamper Vikram's *Aane waala kal* in *Censor*, the U certificate emerges as its savior, for it allows all audiences to view the film and paints India as a liberal democracy like the United States. Interrogating this account, I show through my case studies how certification generally, and U certification more specifically, involves an exercise of power. In contrast to the narratives of censorship presented in Vasudev's work and in *Censor*, my argument casts censorship as more than simply a prohibition dictated by the state. In the film we see how such a vision of censorship affects the representation of female heterosexuality, reducing it to two binary choices: if state censorship seeks to cover up and control women's bodies, then resistance and agency, as I have shown with respect to the *Aane waala kal* sequence, assume the form of stripping and flaunting one's sexual attractions.

I demonstrate that censorship is not a Manichean struggle between artist and censor; rather, it plays out on a wider terrain, as attending to film production and reception makes visible. Thus, my analysis illuminates the knotty processes of selection. For example, while a conventional account of censorship would consider *Gupt gyan* simply a casualty of the Emergency and underscore the imprint of state power, I show through an analysis of film and booklet, examining and revising committee reports, correspondence, and Adarsh's informal interventions how power is a negotiated relation, albeit an uneven one. Moreover, I point to the ways in which state censorship changes its practices in the face of new genres. While a film such as *Gupt gyan* would appear in a study on film censorship, a blockbuster noncontroversial film such as *Dilwale dulhania le jayenge* would not be examined within the domain of state censorship. By analyzing this film, I demonstrate the importance of the process of certification and attend to the practice of cutting at the sites of film production, exhibition, and reception. My eclectic filmography brings a diverse set of films and relations of power in conversation with one another, revealing the complexity of the field of censorship. A fruitful political intervention needs to take account of this complexity so that it does not reproduce the terms that it seeks to challenge.

Tracking *My Name Is Khan*

My theoretical model, which attends to mobile practices of cutting, certification, and classification at sites of film production, reception, and exhibition, makes possible new objects of study. A brief analysis of Karan Johar's *My Name Is Khan* (2010) will delineate such an object and show the continued relevance of this analytical framework. In late January 2010, mere weeks away from its much anticipated release, *My Name Is Khan* (*MNIK*) was subject to the ire of Shiv Sena, which threatened to ban its exhibition. Shiv Sena, a formidable Hindu Right group located in Bombay, has played a major role in policing cinema since the 1990s.[2] It instigated the protests against Mani Ratnam's *Bombay* (1995), objecting to that film's representation of the Hindu-Muslim riots in Bombay. Its members violently blocked the screenings of Deepa Mehta's *Fire* (1997), decrying the film's explicit portrayal of lesbianism as well as its use of Indian mythological names for its protagonists. More recently, Shiv Sainiks targeted the film posters of *Kurbaan* (2009), which displayed the nude back of its heroine, played by Kareena Kapoor, alleging that it was obscene; in fact, to make their point, some Sainiks used a sari to cover up an image of Kapoor's back that appeared on a poster in Juhu, Bombay.

Given this history, one might analyze the events surrounding the release of *MNIK* by focusing solely on Shiv Sena's coercive tactics, which were given ample time and space in the media and incited much debate. Such an analysis would limit the discussion to Shiv Sena and those who resisted it. It would confirm the exercise of censorship as a supreme act of power synonymous with prohibition. In contrast, my theoretical model offers an understanding of power as diffuse by tracking *MNIK* through the filmic narrative and film production, reception, and distribution (e.g., as theatrical release, VCD, or DVD). The framework produces a new object of study by generating a dialogue among these sites, which are generally analyzed in isolation, for they are bracketed under textual analysis, censorship, or the institutional operations of the film industry.

The much-publicized *MNIK* reunited the blockbuster team of Karan Johar, Kajol, and Shah Rukh Khan eight years after their previous film.[3] Through this film, Johar sought to prove that he was not merely a "bubble-gum romance" filmmaker but a serious director who could tackle issues such as 9/11 and racial discrimination. *MNIK*, according to Johar, cemented his "familial relations" with Shah Rukh, for Red Chillies Entertainment (Khan's production house) came on board as coproducer. Johar stressed the significance of such familial relations (i.e., the informal modes and pro-cesses of production) even as he along with other members of the Bombay film industry pursued more formal partnerships with corporations enter-ing the industry. Johar and Khan signed a first-time contract with one such corporation, Fox Searchlight Pictures, which acquired the rights to distrib-ute *MNIK* in India and worldwide. Johar underscored the import of this tie by noting that Fox would open new territories for Hindi films, taking them beyond the usual domestic and NRI South Asian markets. The film's pub-licity actively advertised its "Islam-friendly narrative" as well as its Muslim star cast and playback singers in order to reach Muslims in India's hinter-lands and across the globe. Television shows that Johar and Khan attended during this period, such as *Bingo* and *Music ka maha muqabala* (Super Music Challenge), quite deliberately either increased Muslim members in the audience or were edited to highlight the presence of such viewers.

MNIK recounts the story of Rizvan Khan (played by Shah Rukh Khan), who suffers from Asperger's syndrome, a form of autism. Khan grows up in a lower-middle-class neighborhood in Bombay under the shelter of a doting mother (Zarine Wahab) who defends him against insults, nurtures his talents, and teaches him to judge human beings according to their actions rather than their religion, race, or nationality. After his mother's death, Rizvan goes to San Francisco to live with Zakir (Jimmy Shergill) and his wife, Haseena (Sonya Jehan). During a stint selling beauty prod-ucts, he meets Mandira (Kajol), a divorced Hindu mother who works as a hairdresser. In a moving sequence, Rizvan, who shirks from physical con-tact, insists that Mandira cut his hair. For him, this is equivalent to shout-ing his love from rooftops.[4] At this juncture and later in the film, when Mandira cuts a bow to inaugurate her salon in a small town in California, cutting signifies romantic love and heralds a perfect suburban family life after Rizvan and Mandira's marriage.

Then 9/11 arrives and irrevocably disrupts the lives of Mandira, Riz-van, and their son, Sameer: their business dwindles and their neighbors treat them as pariahs. Moreover, Sameer, called Sam by his friends (the truncated name presumably enables him to blend easily into American life and easily rolls off American tongues), is mercilessly teased at school and eventually killed by his classmates. His death ruptures Mandira and Rizvan's mixed-religion marriage, for she attributes her son's death to his newly adopted surname: Khan. To repair his marriage, Khan travels across the country to meet the U.S. president and tell him, "My name is Khan and I am not a terrorist."

Throughout this journey, Rizvan encounters American state institutions that subject him to invasive security checks, sentence him to prison without any substantial proof of wrongdoing, and torture him to obtain information about al-Qaeda. While the American state is largely presented as violent (or, in the case of finding Sameer's killers or assisting victims of the "Wilhelmina flood disaster"—the film's stand-in for Hurricane Katrina—simply ineffectual), the media, which track Rizvan's moves, become his allies. The media, in fact, record how Rizvan, along with his family and supporters, helps the African American victims of the Wilhelmina disaster, thereby drawing the attention of a presidential candidate (the gesture here is to President Barack Obama).

Compelled by Rizvan's sincerity and love, her friend Sara's urging, and a closure to Sameer's death (she finds his killers), Mandira appears at the Wilhelmina disaster site. Before Rizvan and Mandira can unite, however, Rizvan is knifed by a Muslim fanatic who blames him for the arrest of an important leader. The cut on the screen is matched by a cut in editing, recalling the famous *Psycho* shower sequence. This cutting produces Rizvan as both messiah and hero. Later, Rizvan is able both to reunite with his wife and to meet the president. While the film provides a happy ending, it is triumphant in neither tone nor color; the melancholic blue palette is still visible in the end. And it cannot be triumphant: Sameer is dead, and his best friend, Reese, is complicit in his murder. Even though Sara brings her son, Reese, to Mandira so that he can confess his role in Sameer's murder, and Mandira, for Sara's sake, requests a more lenient sentence for Reese, this act ends the two women's friendship. As Rizvan's poignant placard— "Almost Repair Anything"—reminds us, some things cannot be repaired.

Uncannily, the themes of race, discrimination, and religion central to the film shadowed its production and exhibition. The film faced a temporary setback during late December 2008 when the actor Amir Bashir was denied a visa to the United States.[5] He was eventually replaced by Jimmy Shergill as Khan's younger brother. Despite pleading with local authorities that his film would not promote "anti-social values," Johar was not permitted to shoot a scene at a Los Angeles mosque, and eventually a set was erected at a club in Bombay to shoot the sequence.[6] On August 14, 2009,

Khan came to the United States to participate in promotional events, and much like his character Rizvan, he was pulled aside and interrogated by immigration officers at Newark Airport. In February 2010, when Khan went to the United Kingdom to promote *MNIK*, he alleged that the security staff had used a newly installed scanner to photograph his naked body.[7]

Approximately two weeks prior to the film's release, on February 12, 2010, the film plunged into controversy after Khan, who is an owner of the cricket team *Kolkata Knight Riders*, stated that Pakistani players should have been allowed to participate in the Indian Premier League cricket tournament. Shiv Sena immediately called on Khan to apologize for this antinationalist statement, threatening to ban his upcoming film if he did not comply. Vishwa Hindu Parishad also questioned Khan's patriotism, alleging that as a Muslim, Khan was sympathetic to Pakistan (recalling the accusations against the character Khan played in *Chak de India* [2007]). In an unprecedented move, Khan categorically refused to apologize for his statement. As the release date of his film approached, he made conciliatory gestures but stayed short of an outright apology.

Shiv Sena appeared to change its position and declared that it would not block the film's exhibition. A few days prior to the film's release, however, when theaters in Bombay opened to take advance orders for tickets, members of Shiv Sena attacked and vandalized at least nine of them, leading at least sixty out of seventy theaters to close advance sales of tickets for the film. The Bombay police detained 1,600 party workers, arresting 59 on charges of vandalism, and Chief Minister Ashok Chauvan promised security at all the exhibition venues. Most exhibitors were frightened, however, and did not wish to screen the film. A panicked Johar and the team from Fox's Indian subsidiary, Star Studios, had lengthy late-night meetings with exhibitors to convince them to show the film.[8]

Amid this raging controversy, the film was quietly examined by the Central Board of Film Certification, which classified it as a "social" and gave it a UA certificate on conditions of deletions only in sound.[9] (The on-line newspapers and web sites did not indicate the nature of these aural deletions.)[10] And *MNIK* required "certification" to circulate in other nations. For example, the film was rated PG-13 in the United States; in the United Kingdom and the Irish Republic, it was classified 12A; in Australia, it was categorized M; and in Canada as well as Singapore, it was rated PG. There was no discussion or debate over the film's domestic or international certification. In different national contexts, these ratings regulated who could view the film and framed viewers' entries into the film. A cursory look at the web site of the British Board of Film Classification (BBFC), which includes the categorization of *MNIK*, demonstrates the significance of certification. The BBFC generated classifications for fourteen separate items, displaying an astonishing bureaucratic exactitude in its bid to manage *MNIK*, its ancillary materials, and its audiences: a U for a short version of the theatrical trailer, a PG for three longer versions of theatrical trailer and the video trailer, a 12A for the theatrical film, a 12 for the film's video release, a U for video material featuring the music of *My Name Is Khan*, a PG for video material featuring the story of *My Name Is Khan*, a 12 for additional descriptive material, a U for the "Tere Naina" (Your eyes) and "Sajda" (Worship) music promos, and a U for additional video material entitled "Changing face of Bollywood."[11] An attention to certification within a transnational context compels us to question distinctions between state censorship and nongovernment regulation. State censorship, especially in "developing" countries, is viewed as a sign of political repression. In contrast, self-regulation or regulation via nongovernmental bodies, especially in "developed" nations, is regarded as characteristic of a mature democracy. A focus on certification not only points to the exercise of power in each case but also enables us to see how the discourse of development both generates and thrives on distinctions such as state censorship versus nongovernmental regulation.

Upon its release on February 12, 2010, *MNIK* received largely positive reviews in India and abroad.[12] Many reviews lauded Khan's restrained performance while criticizing Johar's over-the-top Wilhelmina flood sequence. In a bid to oppose Shiv Sena's chauvinistic rhetoric, the majority of the Indian media outlets formed a united front, showcasing "houseful signs" as well as appreciative viewers who were not cowed by Shiv Sena's threats. While the media suggested that despite the dangers, Indians generally and Bombayites particularly were going to the theaters in droves to see the film, the availability of tickets on the Internet, especially for shows in Bombay, suggested otherwise. The controversy may have galvanized audiences in other parts of India, but it depleted ticket sales in the Bombay territory, a major distribution territory. Given that the majority of a film's business today rests on its first week's take, this constituted a major setback.[13] In India, then, the film did not break records, as it had been expected to do, but overseas its performance was noteworthy.

On April 21, 2010, Reliance Big Home Video released a VCD version of *My Name Is Khan*, as well as a collector's edition containing two DVDS. Like the film's theatrical version, both the VCD and DVD versions were subject to state censorship, receiving UA certificates. While the VCD version included only the film, the DVD version boasted bonus features,

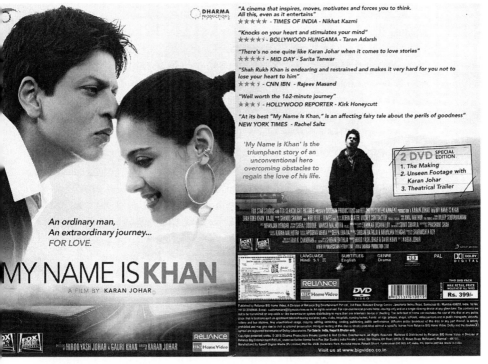

The DVD of *MNIK* features a miniature version of the UA state certificate on the bottom of the back cover. From *My Name Is Khan*.

including the theatrical trailer, material about the making of *MNIK*, and forty-five minutes of "[u]nseen footage with Karan Johar." Interestingly, no state-issued certificate precedes the material about the production of the film or the footage with Johar. As in the case of *DDLJ*, it is unclear whether these bonus features were examined by the CBFC, suggesting that they might have escaped the state's panoptic gaze.[14]

At the outset of his commentary for the "unseen footage," Johar informs his viewers that he has included all of the film's deleted scenes on the DVD. This footage includes alternative versions of the nondiegetic songs "Tere Naina" and "Sajda," scenes from Rizvan's childhood and his relationship with Mandira, incidents of racial discrimination following 9/11, Mandira's attempt to find her son's killers, and scenes from the Wilhelmina sequence. These additional scenes are directed at cinephiles, extending their enjoyment of and engagement with the film. This viewing pleasure is further supplemented by the knowledge that they, as did the production team, have access to the entire film.

Adopting a friendly, pedagogical style, Johar explains the reasons for cutting these scenes. This commentary both provides insight into the production process and offers a critical vocabulary for understanding the narrative and filmmaking.[15] At the outset, he tells us that sequences showing Rizvan's childhood needed to be reduced so that the film could arrive quickly at the story of the adult Rizvan and showcase the talents of the superstar Shah Rukh Khan. In explaining the decision to trim scenes of Mandira and Rizvan's romance, Johar divides the film into two halves, a love story and political drama. While a formal intermission is not present in the DVD, it structures Johar's thoughts on the film. He stresses that the love story of Mandira and Rizvan in the first half of the film provides the emotional syntax for the political drama in the second. According to Johar, the love story needed to be truncated to pave the way for Rizvan's heroic journey. Johar tell us that the political drama in the second portion could have followed either Mandira's quest for justice or Rizvan's epic trek across the country. Johar chose the latter because to narrate both tales would have been "too much." His decision demonstrates that male stars and male-driven narratives are still viewed by members of the industry as pivotal to a film's success. Johar's decisions significantly decreased Kajol's role in the film. Beyond upsetting Kajol—who, the material about the making of *My Name Is Khan* makes clear, expected the film to focus on Mandira and Rizvan, not on Rizvan's solitary journey—this reduction likely had an impact on the film's reception. Viewers who were savoring the prospect of watching the SRK-Kajol *jodi* (pair) were surely disappointed.

The previously unseen footage concludes with an eight-minute sequence that was cut from the much-abused Wilhelmina material. Johar prefaces this sequence by noting, as he did in interviews after the film, that it troubled him and his crew during production, after production, and after the film's release. Nonetheless, he felt that the narrative required a larger-than-life event that would compel the president of the United States to recognize and meet Rizvan. Through the DVD commentary, Johar is able both to address criticism pertaining to this portion of the film and to make his viewers aware of the cost and effort of shooting this sequence. The commentary constructs Johar as a committed and transparent producer-director who is able to instruct us without screening either the film's or his flaws.

After the release of the DVD and VCD in India, Fox, following an unusual distribution strategy, released an "international director's cut" of *MNIK* in select theaters in New York and Los Angeles on May 7, 2010.[16] This reedited version was not crafted by Johar; rather, it was initiated by Fox, which hired Allan Edward Bell, a well-known Hollywood editor, to work with Deepa Bhatia, Johar's editor, to produce a version of *MNIK* suited to nontraditional markets. Fox stated that it would distribute this version of *MNIK* more widely in the United States if it proved successful at the limited venues.[17] The original film, which clocked at 161 minutes, was reduced by 34 minutes to generate the "international" cut.[18] Through editing Fox intended to transform the commercial film into an "art-house" version, trimming Indian excesses and tailoring it to international tastes and U.S. norms governing running times.[19] It is also worth noting that there was no intermission when the original version was screened in U.S. theaters, which attracted diverse clienteles. This mode of exhibition also mimicked customary U.S. screening practices.

Pirated prints on the Internet and in stores, the official DVD and VCD editions, and the reedited version of *MNIK* were in circulation. In addition, *MNIK* in its "original" theatrical form was screened in theaters in Poland in April 2010, in France and Spain in May 2010, in Germany in June 2010, in Kazakhstan and Russia in September 2010, and in China in November 2010. In late May and early June 2010 the film was premiered on direct-to-home television, and in August 2010 Fox released yet another DVD of *MNIK*. The multiple versions of *MNIK* currently circulating demonstrate that certification is not a linear process. Moreover, these versions involve differing screening and viewing practices. Thus, viewers have access to different texts and contexts for watching and making sense of the film. To elaborate on these points and their consequences, I offer a personal anecdote about my own access to the film. Living in Ithaca, New York, on February 12, 2010, I would have needed to drive to Syracuse, which is about seventy-five minutes away, in order to see *MNIK* in a theater. Unfortunately I wasn't able to attend any of the screenings at Syracuse. Soon after the film's premiere, pirated copies circulated on the Internet, but I did not want to see a fuzzy print accompanied by a muffled soundtrack on my fourteen-inch laptop while potentially subjecting the computer to viruses. Moreover, I had recently discovered that pirated copies were at times edited to enable uploading. So I waited and religiously followed *MNIK* via reviews and commentary on the Internet. I knew the film's story (including spoilers), varied versions of its box-office fate, and numerous viewers' as well as critics' responses. And I engaged in lengthy discussions about *MNIK* with friends who had viewed it.

When the DVD and VCD copies were released in India, I scoured the Internet for the DVD, which, unlike its meager VCD cousin, included bonus features. I could have purchased the DVD via the Internet, but I decided not to risk the vagaries of the postal service. Instead, I waited for a colleague who was serendipitously traveling from Delhi to New York City to bring it. I collected the DVD during a trip to New York City in late May. The version of the film I saw at home had received a UA certificate from India; the certificate appeared both on the DVD box and prior to the film itself on disc 1.

The easy availability of the DVD of *MNIK*, as well as the effortless access to information about the film, delighted me; it was all a click and credit card away. Here, it is important to note that although I was able to find a lot of information about *MNIK* while in Ithaca, I was unable to obtain the CBFC case file. The DVD is an organized archive, featuring ordered bonus features; labeled deleted scenes; and prepared commentary that offers insight into the process of filmmaking, provides a vocabulary for analyzing the content, and suggests new paths of inquiry. It demonstrated that the film industry has been assuming an important role in archiving its history. In contrast, the archives that I encountered in my fieldwork were restricted (the case reports at the CBFC) or chaotic (the room at the Film and Television Institute with unlabeled cans of film cuts) or required hours of traveling and waiting for officials or librarians. As I mentioned in Chapters 1 and 3, my fieldwork was often frustrating and daunting. I had to compile and categorize material while learning new terms (e.g., legal ones) and research techniques (conducting interviews or observing examining committees) that were not as user friendly as the DVD or the Internet is. I close, mulling over the possibilities and limits of these new archives: Are their accessibility and legibility obscuring other archives that are more arduous to reach and comprehend? How are they shaping our objects of study? How are they defining our *selections*?

NOTE: *I have copied the information that appears in these appendices from the Ministry of Information and Broadcasting website, www.mib.nic.in.*

GOVERNMENT OF INDIA
MINISTRY OF INFORMATION AND BROADCASTING
New Delhi, the 6th December, 1991.

NOTIFICATION

S.O. 836-(E) In exercise of the power conferred by sub-section (2) of section 5 B of the Cinematograph Act, 1952 (37 of 1952) and in supersession of the notification of the Government of India in the Ministry of Information and Broadcasting No. S.O. 9(E), dated 7th January 1978, except as respects things done or omitted to be done before such superssion, the Central Government hereby directs that in sanctioning films for public exhibition, the Board of Film Certification shall be guided by the following principles:

1. The objectives of film certification will be ensure that—

(a) the medium of film remains responsible and sensitive to the values and standards of society;

(b) artistic expression and creative freedom are not unduly curbed;

(c) certification is responsive to social change;

(d) the medium of film provides clean and healthy entertainment; and

(e) as far as possible, the film is of aesthetic value and cinematically of a good standard.

2. In pursuance of the above objectives, the Board of Film Certification shall ensure that—

(i) anti-social activities such as violence are not glorified or justified.

(ii) the modus operandi of criminals, other visuals or words likely to incite the commission of any offence are not depicted;

(iii) Scenes—

(a) showing involvement of children in violence as victims or as perpetrators or as
forced witness to violence, or showing children as being subjected to any form of child abuse;

(b) Showing abuse or ridicule of physically and mentally handicapped persons; and

(c) showing cruelty to, or abuse of, animals, are not presented needlessly;

(iv) pointless or avoidable scenes of violence, cruelty and horror, scenes of violence primarily intended to provide entertainment and such scenes as may have the effect of desensitising or dehumanising people are not shown;

(v) scenes which have the effect of justifying or glorifying drinking are not shown;

(vi) Scenes tending to encourage, justify or glamorise drug addiction are not shown;

(vi-a) Scenes tending to encourage, justify or glamorise consumption of tobacco or smoking are not shown;

(vii) human sensibilities are not offended by vulgarity, obscenity or depravity;

(viii) such dual meaning words as obviously cater to baser instincts are not allowed;

(ix) scenes degrading or denigrating women in any manner are not presented;

(x) scenes involving sexual violence against women like attempt to rape, rape or any form of molestation, or scenes of similar nature are avoided, and if any such incident is germane to the theme, they shall be reduced to the minimum and no details are shown;

(xi) scenes showing sexual perversions shall be avoided and if such matters are germane to the theme, they shall be reduced to the minimum and no details are shown;

(xii) visuals or words contemptuous of racial, religious or other groups are not presented;

(xiii) visuals or words which promote communal, obscurantism, anti-scientific and anti-national attitudes are not presented;

(xiv) the sovereignty and integrity of India is not called in question;

(xv) the security of the State is not jeopardised or endangered;

(xvi) friendly relations with foreign States are not strained;

(xvii) public order is not endangered;

(xviii) visuals or words involving defamation of an individual or a body of individuals, or contempt of court are not presented;

EXPLANATION: Scenes that tend to create scorn, disgrace or disregard of rules or undermine the dignity of court will come under the term "contempt of Court" and

(xix) National symbols and emblems are not shown except in accordance with the provisions of the Emblems and Names (Prevention of Improper Use) Act, 1950 (12 of 1950).

3. The Board of Film Certification shall also ensure that the film—

(i) is judged in its entirety from the point of view of its overall impact; and

(ii) is examined in the light of the period depicted in the film and the contemporary standards of the country and the people to which the film relates, provided that the film does not deprave the morality of the audience.

4. Films that meet the above-mentioned criteria but are considered unsuitable for exhibition to non-adults shall be certified for exhibition to adult audience only.

5. (1) While certifying films for unrestricted public exhibition, the Board shall ensure that the film is suitable for family viewing, that is to say, the film should be such that all the members of the family including children can view it together.

(2) If the Board, having regard to the nature, content and theme of the film, is of the opinion that it is necessary to caution the parents/guardian to consider as to whether any child below the age of twelve years may be allowed to see such a film, the film shall be certified for unrestricted public exhibition with an endorsement to that effect.

(3) If the Board, having regard to the nature, content and theme of the film, is of the opinion that the exhibition of the film should be restricted to members of any profession or any class of persons, the film shall be certified for public exhibition restricted to the specialised audiences to be specified by the Board in this behalf.

6. The Board shall scrutinise the titles of the films carefully and ensure

that they are not provocative, vulgar, offensive or violative of any of the above-mentioned guidelines.

_____
_____
_____

Foot-note: Notification No. 5/5/77-F(C) dated 7.1.78 published in the Extraordinary Gazette of India Part II, Section 3 sub-section (ii) dated 7.1.98 as S.O. 9(E).
Amended by—
(i) Notification No.5/5/770F(C) dated 27.1.79 published as S.O. 618 in the Gazette of India Part II Section 3 sub-section (ii) dated 17.2.79
(ii) Notification No. 805/2/83-F(C) dated 7.5.83 published as S.O. 356(E) in the Gazette of India Extraordinary Part II Section 3, sub-section (ii) dated 7.5.83.
(iii) Notification No. 805/4/89-F(C) dated 11.8.89 published as S.O. 2179 in the gazette of India, Part II, Section 3, sub-section (ii) dated 9.9.89.

Form I

Form of application for certification for public exhibition of a film produced in India.

No. and date of application (to be entered by Board's office)
To
The Central Board of Film Certification through the Regional Officer at
_____.

Application for certification for public exhibition of a film produced in India at _____.

1. (a) Name of the film
   (b) Language of the film
   (c) Length of the film in ft
   _____ meter
   (d) Number of reels
   (e) Gauge of the film
   (f) Type of the film i.e. whether it is 2-D, 3-D, cinemascope, vistavision etc.
   (g) Whether the film is silent or a talkie
   (h) Colour of the film
   (i) Name and address of the producer
   (j) Name of the director
2. State whether the film is a newsreel/documentary/scientific/educational/feature/advertisement film.

2. (a) Specify the certificate requested "U" "UA" "A" or "S".

3. State separately the number of negative and positive prints of the film.

    (a) produced (negative _____

       positive _____)

    (b) in the applicant's possession (negative _____

       Positive _____)

    (c) Name and address of the processing laboratory.

4. (a) Whether the present film is a dubbed version or a remake of any other film? If so, state the particulars along with full details of certificates issued to that film.

    (b) Whether any pre-censorship advice was obtained and if so the details thereof.

    (c) Whether permission for any shooting abroad was obtained and, if so, the details thereof.

    (d) Whether the film contains any dialogue/commentary in any language other than the language of the film and, if so specify the language and the reels in which they occur.

5. Has any pervious application been made to certify this film as suitable for public exhibition in India? If so,

    (a) Where and to whom was it made

    (b) What was the result of the application

    *(i) A "U"/"UA"/An "A"/"S" certificate

    No _____ dated was granted

       subject to the following cuts _____

    * (ii) Certificate was refused.

6. Has the exhibition of this film been at any time suspended or the film declared uncertified by the Central or any State Government? State particulars.

7. Does the film contain any dialogue, song, poem, speech or commentary in any language other than English or an Indian language?

    If so, specify that reel or reels in which the dialogue, song, poem speech or commentary occurs and, the language or language used.

8. Amount of fee accompanying the application of account of the fee prescribed in Rule 36.

8(A). [Whether any animal has been used in shooting of the film? If so, whether declaration specified in clause (bb) of sub-rule (3) of rule 21 has been filled?][1]

Vide (i) Receipt No. _____ dated _____

    (ii) Bank draft No._____ dated _____ on

_____ Bank.

(iii) Postal Order No. _____ dated _____ on
_____ Post Office

9. Name, address and telephone number, if any of the applicant Telephone No:

10. I declare that the print of the film is ready for examination by the Board and the Statements recorded above are true in every particular.

Date _____ Signature of applicant _____

* Score out the word or words which are not applicable.
[1] Inserted as per notification dated 12.11.97.

MINISTRY OF INFORMATION AND BROADCASTING
"A" Wing, Shastri Bhavan, New Delhi-110 001.

Dated: 17th January, 2006

OFFICE MEMORANDUM

Subject: Policy for certification of films for film festivals.

In accordance with Section 9 of the Cinematograph Act, 1952, the Central Government may, by order in writing exempt, subject to such conditions and restrictions, if any, as it may impose, the exhibition of any film or class of film from any of the provisions or any rules made thereunder. The Ministry of Information and Broadcasting has been receiving requests from various festival authorities for according exemption from the process of certification for films for exhibition in their festivals. A need was felt for framing a concrete policy drawing up detailed guidelines on the issue. Accordingly, a broad based Committee was constituted comprising film-makers, academicians, etc. to recommend a policy framework to the Government on the matter.

2. After detailed deliberations, the Committee submitted its report to the Government on 16.11.2005 with certain recommendations which have since been accepted. The following guidelines are notified with immediate effect:

(i)   In those festivals which are non-commercial in nature and viewership is confined to delegates (definition of delegates would include filmmakers, media students, critics, film theorists, film lovers and all those associated with the production and business of film and members of the press duly registered with the festival authorities as well as its jury), the Government would grant exemption for both Indian and foreign films. However, the exemption would be subject to fulfillment of the conditions prescribed in para 3 below.

(ii) The request for exemption from the process of certification will be disposed of within 15 days from the date of receipt of the proposal complete in all respects from the Director of the Festival.

(iii) In exceptional cases, the Ministry of I&B will have the powers to reject, for reasons to be recorded in writing, the request for exemption to any film(s) if, in its opinion, it would impinge on the security or integrity of the country or affect law and order or affect relations with other countries.

(iv) In case of rejection, the Director of the Festival shall have the option to appeal to the next higher authority in the Ministry of I&B i.e., the Additional Secretary/Secretary, as the case may be, who shall dispose of the appeal within 15 days from the date of receipt in the Ministry.

3. In order to consider the request for exemption from the process of certification for films to be screened in festivals, the following documents shall be sent by the Director of the Festival addressed to Joint Secretary (Films) along with the request for exemption:
  (i)   List of films to be screened in the festival.
  (ii) Synopsis of each of the films.
  (iii) Composition of the Preview Committee, which should comprise persons who are related to the film industry or are critics/writers connected with films.
  (iv) Report of the Preview Committee certifying that the films have been recommended for exhibition at the festival.
  (v)   Certificate from the Director of the Festival to the effect that the screening of such films would be limited to delegates (definition of delegates would include film-makers, media students, critics, film theorists, film lovers and all those associated with the production and business of film and members of the press duly registered with the festival authorities as well as its jury).

(vi)   Certificate from the Director of the Festival to the effect that the festival is non-commercial in nature.

4. The above mentioned guidelines may also be accessed through this Ministry's website www.mib.nic.in.

CHAPTER 1

1. For an insightful consideration of queer sexualities, see Brinda Bose and Sub-habrata Bhattacharyya, eds., *The Phobic and the Erotic: The Politics of Sexualities in Contemporary India* (London: Seagull Books, 2007). For a compelling discussion of queer sexuality within the context of South Asian diasporas, see Gayatri Gopinath's *Impossible Desires: Queer Diasporas and South Asian Public Cultures* (Durham, N.C.: Duke University Press, 2005). Gopinath's work and Bose and Bhattacharyya's edited collection refer to the censorship controversy related to Deepa Mehta's *Fire* (1996). Many other scholars have also examined *Fire*, and I provide citations for some of this scholarship in the bibliography.

2. These sources reveal that knowledge comes in many hues: evidence, proof, hints, possibilities, speculations, rumors, and gossip. The sources themselves are valued differentially, as was attested by the inevitable smiles that greeted me when I revealed that I read *Filmfare*, a popular film magazine, to conduct scholarly research.

3. Relevant works by Michel Foucault include *The History of Sexuality, Vol. 1: An Introduction*, trans. Robert Hurley (New York: Pantheon, 1978); *Power/Knowledge: Selected Interviews and Other Writings, 1972–1977*, ed. Colin Gordon (New York: Pantheon, 1980); *The Foucault Reader*, ed. Paul Rabinow (New York: Pantheon, 1984); *The History of Sexuality, Vol. 2: The Use of Pleasure*, trans. Robert Hurley (New York: Random House, 1985); *The History of Sexuality, Vol. 3: The Care of the Self*, trans. Robert Hurley (New York: Random House, 1986); *Ethics: Subjectivity and Truth*, ed. Paul Rabinow, vol. 1 of *Essential Works of Foucault, 1945–1984* (New York: New Press, 1997); *Aesthetics, Method, and Epistemology*, ed. James D. Faubion, vol. 2 of *Essential Works of Foucault, 1945–1984* (New York: New Press, 1998); *Power*, ed. Colin Gordon, vol. 3 of *Essential Works of Foucault, 1945–1984* (New York: New Press, 1999); *Politics, Philosophy, Culture: Interviews and Other Writings*, ed. Lawrence Kritzman, trans. Alan Sheridan (London: Routledge, 1990).

4. Michel Foucault, "Afterword: Subject and Power," in *Michel Foucault: Beyond Structuralism and Hermeneutics*, ed. Hubert L. Dreyfus and Paul Rainbow, 208–226 (Chicago: University of Chicago Press, 1983).

5. For examples, see the articles in *Velvet Light Trap* 63 (Spring 2009). Relevant works concerning South Asia include Mallika Ariyal, "Official Arbiters," *Himal South Asian*, September 2009, http://www.himalmag.com/himaledition=2009-09-01; Someswar Bhowmik, *Cinema and Censorship: The Politics of Control in India* (New Delhi: Orient Longman, 2009); Nandana Bose, "Between the Godfather and the Mafia: Situating Right-Wing Interventions in the Bombay Film Industry (2002)," *Journal of South Asian Film and Media* 1, no. 1: 23–43; Nandana Bose, "The Hindu Right and the Politics of Censorship: Three Case Studies Policing Hindi Cinema, 1992–2002," *Velvet Light Trap* 63 (Spring 2009): 22–33; Shohini Ghosh, "The Troubled Existence of Sex and Sexuality: Feminists Engage with Censorship," in *Image Journeys: Audio-Visual Media and Cultural Change in India*, ed. Christiane Brious and Melissa Butcher, 233–260 (New Delhi: Sage, 1999); Lalitha Gopalan, *Cinema of Interruptions: Action Genres in Contemporary Indian Cinema* (London: British Film Institute, 2002); Julie Marsh and Howard Brasted, "*Fire*, the BJP and Moral Society," in *Hindu Nationalism and Governance*, ed. John McGuire and Ian Copland, 283–302 (New Delhi: Oxford University Press, 2007); Edwina Mason, "The *Water* Controversy and the Politics of Hindu Nationalism," in *Hindu Nationalism and Governance*, ed. John McGuire and Ian Copland, 303–315 (New Delhi: Oxford University Press, 2007); Shammi Nanda, "Censorship and Indian Cinema: The Case of *War and Peace*," *Bright Lights Film Journal* 38 (Nov. 2002), http://www.brightlightsfilm.com/38/indiacensor.htm; Tejaswini Gianti, "The Limits of Decency and the Decency of Limits: Censorship and the Bombay Film Industry," in *Censorship in South Asia: Cultural Regulation from Sedition to Seduction*, ed. Raminder Kaur and William Mazzarella, 87–121 (Bloomington: Indiana University Press, 2009); Manjunath Pendakur, "Censorship," in *Gender and Censorship*, ed. Brinda Bose, 19–30 (New Delhi: Women Unlimited, 2006); Aruna Vasudev, *Liberty and Licence in the Indian Cinema* (New Delhi: Vikas, 1978). See n. 39 to this chapter for further scholarly and journalistic references.

6. See Annette Kuhn, *Censorship, State and Sexuality, 1909–1925* (New York: Routledge, 1988). My study is deeply indebted to Kuhn's work, and I make both explicit and implicit references to it throughout this book.

7. "Introduction," *Velvet Light Trap* 63 (Spring 2009): 1.

8. Theresa Cronin, "Media Effects and the Subjectification of Film Regulation," *Velvet Light Trap* 63 (Spring 2009): 5.

9. Laura Cook Kenna, "Exemplary Consumer-Citizens and Protective State Stewards: How Reformers Shaped Censorship Outcomes Regarding *The Untouchables*," *Velvet Light Trap* 63 (Spring 2009): 38.

10. Nandana Bose, "The Hindu Right and the Politics of Censorship: Three Case Studies of Policing Hindi Cinema, 1992–2002," *Velvet Light Trap* 63 (Spring 2009): 30.

11. Tessa Dwyer and Iona Uricaru, "Slashings and Subtitles: Romanian Media Piracy, Censorship, and Translation," *Velvet Light Trap* 63 (Spring 2009): 47–48.

12. In Chapter 8, on *Dilwale dulhania le jayenge*, I show how the practice of certification assists in (re)generating the Indian family, bringing the diasporic community into the Indian nation and promoting intergenerational cinephilia.

13. In the 1990s and early 2000s, many cities in India chose to adopt their precolonial names. Calcutta became Kolkata, Madras reverted to Chennai, Trivandrum changed to Thiruvananthapuram, and Bombay was transformed into Mumbai. With regard to most of these cities, I have used their colonial names for the sake of consistency. In case of Bombay, I have additional reasons for using the colonial name. First, during the historical period that this book covers, namely 1970-1995, the city was known as "Bombay"; its name was officially changed in 1995. Second, my use of the phrase "Bombay cinema" gestures to a cinema aesthetic that cannot be captured by saying "Mumbai cinema." Last, by using "Bombay," I express political solidarity with groups that have been protesting Shiv Sena's mobilization of "Mumbai" to promote a violent, ethnocentric politics. With the exception of some citations where the publisher or the corporation has used the term "Mumbai," I choose to employ the term "Bombay" in the main text and the notes.

14. See nn. 5 and 39 to this chapter.

15. Most of these studies assume an implicit theoretical framework of censorship but do not investigate it explicitly.

16. Paul R. Brass, *Politics of India since Independence* (Cambridge: Cambridge University Press, 1994), 40.

17. According to official figures, at least 2,000 deaths occurred because of these drives.

18. Vasudev, *Liberty and Licence*, ix.

19. Ibid., x.

20. Ibid., 149.

21. Ibid., xv.

22. Ibid., 116.

23. Ibid., 203.

24. Ibid.

25. Ibid., 103.

26. Ibid.

27. Ibid., 105.

28. Ibid.

29. Ibid.

30. Ibid., 203.

31. Vasudev urges the state to police the *content* of Bombay cinema and does not explicitly demand the censorship of the *form* of these narratives, in particular, their "fantastical features." Her critique of Bombay cinema, however, suggests that she believes these "fantastical features" assist in propagating regressive values, ones that conflict with the goals of the state. In contrast, she voices her approval of art cinema and the realist aesthetic often deployed in its narratives. In her view, these narratives are socially progressive.

32. In the case of *Garam hawa* (1974), the certification board was concerned that the film might incite communal violence, so it forwarded the case to the central government, which ruled in favor of certifying the film. With *Samskara* (1970), the

Madras Regional Board refused to certify the film on the grounds that it would offend the Brahmins of a particular sect. This decision was appealed, and the central government overruled the regional board's decision.

33. Kuhn, *Censorship*, 1.

34. Ibid., 4.

35. Ibid., 3.

36. Ibid., 2.

37. These categories have changed over time. During my fieldwork, I had access to some examining committee forms from 1974 to 1997. The categories noted are culled from these forms. Since I did not have unrestricted access to these forms, I was unable to track the changes closely.

38. Discussions of genre have focused on the semantic elements through which one can identify a genre, genre as a site of negotiation between the film industry and audience, and genre as reflective of ideology or a particular historical period. For a discussion on the concept of genre as well as an excellent bibliography, see Barry Keith Grant, ed., *Film Genre Reader III* (Austin: University of Texas Press, 2003). Also see the compelling argument on genre in Christine Gledhill's "Rethinking Genre," in *Reinventing Film Studies*, ed. Christine Gledhill and Linda Williams, 221–243 (London: Arnold, 2000).

39. My arguments regarding debates on film censorship are based on my research at the National Film Archive of India, Nehru Memorial Library, the Ministry of Information and Broadcasting, the Indian Law Institute, and the Indian Institute of Mass Communication. Works that touch on these topics include Enquiry Committee on Film Censorship, *Report of the Enquiry Committee on Film Censorship* (New Delhi: Government of India Press, 1969); Film Enquiry Committee, *Report of the Film Enquiry Committee 1951* (New Delhi: Government of India Press, 1951); Working Group on National Film Policy, *Report of the Working Group on National Film Policy* (New Delhi: Government of India Press, 1980); Chidananda Das Gupta, *Talking about Films* (New Delhi: Orient Longman, 1981); G. D. Khosla, "Why Do We Need Film Censorship?" *Statesman*, Feb. 9, 1986; Ratna Kapur, "Who Draws the Line? Feminist Reflections on Speech and Censorship," *Economic and Political Weekly* 31, nos. 16-17 (Apr. 20, 1996): WS 15-WS 30; Amita Malik, "A Kiss Is but a Kiss," *Statesman*, Jan. 16, 1978; Khalid Mohamed, "Film Censorship: Corrupt, Confused and Castrating," *The Times of India*, Oct. 29, 1978; M. Madhava Prasad, "Cinema and the Desire for Modernity," *Journal of Arts and Ideas* 25-26 (1995): 71-86; T. M. Ramachandran, ed., *Seventy Years of Indian Cinema (1913-1983)* (Bombay: CINEMA-India International, 1985); Firoze Rangoonwalla, "Conviction Gap between Censors and Government," *Star and Style*, 1977; Firoze Rangoonwalla, "Kissing-Hindi Film Style," *The Illustrated Weekly of India*, May 26, 1974; K. Sarkar, *Indian Cinema Today* (New Delhi: Sterling, 1975); Kobita Sarkar, *You Can't Please Everyone: Film Censorship, the Inside Story* (Bombay: India Book House, 1982); Sunil Sethi et al., "Who's Afraid of Censorship?" *India Today*, Oct. 1980; Bikram Singh, "Film Censorship," *Indian Express*, Mar. 3, 1990; Aruna Vasudev, *Liberty and Licence*; Ravi Vasudevan, "Bombay and Its Public," *Journal of Arts and Ideas* 29 (1996). Also see note 5.

40. For discussions on the concept of national cinema, see Mette Hjort and Scott Mackenzie, eds., *Cinema and Nation* (London: Routledge, 2000); Valentina Vitali and Paul Willemen, eds., *Theorising National Cinema* (London: British Film Institute, 2006).

41. K. Sarkar, *You Can't Please Everyone*, 30–31.

42. Ibid., 31.

43. Firoze Rangoonwalla, "Editorial," *Star and Style*, Oct. 6–19, 1978.

44. While films from many parts of the world are screened in India, the "double standard" debate is primarily concerned with films from the West.

45. Qtd. in Dr. C. G. Thakur, "Is There a Double Standard as the Industry Alleges?" *Star and Style*, Sept. 1967, 34.

46. C. K. Razdan, ed., *Bare Breasts and Bare Bottoms* (Bombay: Jaico, 1975), 6.

47. Das Gupta, *Talking about Films*, 47. Das Gupta was one of the founders of the Calcutta Film Society in 1947. He has been writing on cinema since the midforties and has published many articles on film in newspapers, magazines, and journals.

48. Ibid.

49. I am drawing on my conversations with the members of examining committees in concluding that the censors share the art/commerce hierarchy. The members noted that art films could depict sexuality without being vulgar or exploitative, whereas commercial films often fell short of this goal. The depiction of sexuality in commercial films tended to be more vulgar or obscene. Hence, such films were subject to more cuts.

50. K. Sarkar, *Indian Cinema Today*, 46.

51. Bruce Michael Boyd, "Film Censorship in India and Reasonable Restriction," *Journal of Indian Law Institute* 14, no. 4 (1972): 530.

52. Throughout this book, I explicitly and implicitly draw on works in postcolonial, feminist, and South Asian studies that have documented the ways in which the figure of woman, tradition, and sexuality have been knitted together in debates on the nation and nation building. These valuable analyses have demonstrated how women have been constructed as guardians of national traditions; how their bodies have been marked by elaborate codes of male honor and are employed in marking boundaries between communities; how their bodies, their behavior, their dress, and their decorum have raised questions regarding respectability and propriety; and how the accepted role of the mother, one that yokes female sexuality to reproduction and that evokes "feminine" virtues such as caretaking and self-sacrifice, has been rendered iconic in the representation of the nation. Relevant references from postcolonial and feminist studies focusing on the historical context of South Asia include Urvashi Butalia, "Community, State and Gender: On Women's Agency during Partition," *Economic and Political Weekly* 28, no. 17 (Apr. 24, 1993): WS 12-WS 24; Ritu Menon and Kamla Bhasin, "Recovery, Rupture, Resistance: Indian State and Abduction of Women during Partition," *Economic and Political Weekly* 28, no. 17 (Apr. 24, 1993): WS 2-WS 11; Partha Chatterjee, *Nationalist Thought and the Colonial World: A Derivative Discourse?* (London: Zed, 1986); Partha Chatterjee, *The Nation and Its Fragments: Colonial and Postcolonial Histories* (Princeton, N.J.: Princeton University

Press, 1993); Madhu Kishwar, "Gandhi on Women," *Economic and Political Weekly* 20, no. 40 (Oct. 5, 1985): 1691-1702; Madhu Kishwar, "Gandhi on Women," *Economic and Political Weekly* 20, no. 41 (Oct. 12, 1985): 1753-1758; Radha Kumar, *The History of Doing* (Delhi: Kali for Women, 1993); Shahida Lateef, *Muslim Women in India: Political and Private Realities* (London: Zed, 1990); Ashis Nandy, *The Intimate Enemy: Loss and Recovery of Self under Colonialism* (Delhi: Oxford University Press, 1983); Santi Rozario, *Purity and Communal Boundaries* (London: Zed, 1992); Kumkum Sangari and Sudesh Vaid, eds., *Recasting Women: Essays in Indian Colonial History* (New Delhi: Kali for Women, 1989.

53. Although film censorship is clearly part of the apparatus of sexuality, Foucault does not discuss it.

54. Foucault, *History of Sexuality*, 1:57.

55. Ibid.

56. Ibid., 58.

57. Kum Kum Roy, "Unravelling the *Kamasutra*," in *A Question of Silence? The Sexual Economies of Modern India*, ed. Mary E. John and Janaki Nayar, 368-390 (New Delhi: Kali for Women, 1998), 52–76.

58. Works that engage questions of gender and sexuality in the context of the mass media include Bose, ed., *Gender and Censorship*; Bose and Bhattacharyya, eds., *The Phobic and the Erotic*; Sumita S. Chakravarty, *National Identity in Indian Popular Cinema 1947–1987* (Austin: University of Texas Press, 1993); Gopalan, *Cinema of Interruptions*; Mary E. John, "Globalisation, Sexuality and the Visual Field: Issues and Non-issues for Cultural Critique," in *A Question of Silence? The Sexual Economies of Modern India*, ed. Mary E. John and Janaki Nair, 368-390 (New Delhi: Kali for Women, 1998); Shohini Ghosh, "The Pleasures and Politics of Pornography," *Himal South Asian*, September 2009, http://www.himalmag.com/himaledition=2009-09-01; Ghosh, "Troubled Existence of Sex"; Neepa Majumdar, *Wanted Cultured Ladies Only! Female Stardom and Cinema in India, 1930s-1950s* (Urbana: University of Illinois Press, 2009); Purnima Mankekar, *Screening Cultures, Viewing Politics* (Durham, N.C.: Duke University Press, 1999); Ratna Kapur, "Cultural Politics of *Fire*," *Economic and Political Weekly* 34, no. 21 (May 28, 1999): 1297-1299; Tejaswini Niranjana, "Banning 'Bombayi': Nationalism, Communalism and Gender," *Economic and Political Weekly* 30, no. 22 (June 3, 1995): 1291-1292; M. Madhava Prasad, *Ideology of the Hindi Film: A Historical Construction* (New Delhi: Oxford University Press, 1998); Ravi Vasudevan, "Sexuality and the Film Apparatus: Continuity, Non-Continuity and Dis-Continuity in Bombay Cinema," in *A Question of Silence? The Sexual Economies of Modern India*, ed. Mary E. John and Janaki Nair (New Delhi: Kali for Women, 1998), 192–215; Ravi Vasudevan, "'You Cannot Live in Society—and Ignore It': Nationhood and Female Modernity in *Andaz*," in *Social Reform, Sexuality and the State*, ed. Patricia Uberoi (New Delhi: Sage, 1996), 83–108; Jyotika Virdi, *The Cinematic ImagiNation*. (New Brunswick, N.J.: Rutgers University Press, 2003).

59. John and Nair provide a succinct and eloquent review of the ways in which scholars and activists have engaged with questions of gender and sexuality on screen.

NOTES TO PAGES 22-29

See Mary E. John and Janaki Nair, "A Question of Silence: An Introduction," in *A Question of Silence? The Sexual Economies of Modern India*, ed. John and Nair, 1–51 (New Delhi: Kali for Women, 1998).

60. John and Nair, "Question of Silence," 1–2.

CHAPTER 2

1. A more comprehensive historical account of film censorship in India, along the lines of Vasudev's work, can be found in Someswar Bhowmik's *Cinema and Censorship: The Politics of Control in India* (New Delhi: Orient Longman, 2009).

2. Relevant works that take a globalist perspective include Priya Jaikumar, *Cinema at the End of Empire: A Politics of Transition in Britain and India* (Durham, N.C.: Duke University Press, 2006); Hamid Naficy, *An Accented Cinema: Exilic and Diasporic Filmmaking* (Princeton, N.J.: Princeton University Press, 2001); Ella Shohat and Robert Stam, *Unthinking Eurocentrism: Multiculturalism and the Media* (New York: Routledge, 1994).

3. See Annette Kuhn, *Censorship, State and Sexuality, 1909-1925* (New York: Routledge, 1988); Theresa Cronin, "Media Effects and the Subjectfication of Film Regulation," *Velvet Light Trap* 63 (Spring 2009): 3–21.

4. Film censorship was not the only site where techniques of classification and codification were applied; Benedict Anderson notes that "three institutions of power—the census, the map, and the museum"—played a role in the making of India, for they "profoundly shaped the way in which the colonial state imagined its dominion—the nature of the human beings it ruled, the geography of its domain, and the legitimacy of its ancestry." By classifying and codifying, the colonial state was able to take account of the colonial terrain and its subjects. See Benedict Anderson, *Imagined Communities* (New York: Verso, 1992), 163–185.

5. Legislative Council Debate, September 5, 1917, qtd. in Aruna Vasudev, *Liberty and Licence in the Indian Cinema* (New Delhi: Vikas, 1978), 12. According to Vasudev, while films were subject to regulation prior to 1917, the "laws whereby control was exercised came under the Indian Penal Code and the Criminal Procedure Code" (11).

6. Aruna Vasudev, *Liberty and Licence in the Indian Cinema* (New Delhi: Vikas, 1978), 12.

7. Ibid., 14–15. Vasudev also notes that the composition of the boards varied. Her list shows that the head of each board was the commissioner of police. Thus, while a new law was instituted for the cinematograph, it was still being administered by the police. The procedure for selecting board members remains unclear. In the postcolonial era, these guidelines have been periodically revised. For further details about these shifts, see Bhowmik's *Cinema and Censorship*.

8. For further discussion on censorship and its links to racial anxieties, see Poonam Arora, "'Imperiling the Prestige of the White Woman': Colonial Anxiety and Film Censorship in British India," *Visual Anthropology Review* 11, no. 2 (Fall 1995): 36–50; Prem Chowdhry, *Colonial India and the Making of Empire Cinema:*

Image, Ideology, and Identity (Manchester, U.K.: Manchester University Press, 2000); Priya Jaikumar, "More Than Morality: The Indian Cinematograph Committee Interviews (1927)," *Moving Image* 3, no. 1 (2003): 82–89.

9. Ann Stoler, "Educating Desire in Colonial Southeast Asia: Foucault, Freud, and Imperial Sexualities," in *Sites of Desire, Economies of Pleasure: Sexualities in Asia and the Pacific*, ed. Lenore Manderson and Margaret Jolly, 27–47 (Chicago: University of Chicago Press, 1997).

10. Jaikumar, "More Than Morality," 82–109. Also see Vasudev, *Liberty and Licence*, 20–35. For an analysis of the 1927 Quota Act regulation, see Priya Jaikumar, "An Act of Transition: Empire and the Making of a National British Film Industry, 1927," *Screen* 43, no. 2 (Summer 2002): 119–138. For more analyses of British colonialism and film censorship in India, see Stephen Hughes, "Policing Silent Film Exhibition in Colonial South India," in *Making Meaning in Indian Cinema*, ed. Ravi S. Vasudevan, 39–64 (New Delhi: Oxford University Press, 2000); William Mazzarella, "Making Sense of the Cinema in Late Colonial India," in *Censorship in South Asia: Cultural Regulation from Sedition to Seduction*, ed. Raminder Kaur and William Mazzarella, 63–86 (Bloomington: Indiana University Press, 2009); Miriam Sharma, "Censoring India," *South Asia Research* 29, no. 1 (2009): 41–73.

11. Jaikumar, *Cinema at the End of Empire*, 5.

12. Ibid.

13. The committee was led by an extremely sharp chairperson, as the interviews demonstrate. During the course of one interview, a witness remarked that criminals were learning new tricks of the trade from watching films. Rangachariar quickly retorted that if criminals could enhance their skills and methods from watching films, the police should be capable of following suit. Rangachariar also dealt astutely with the vexed question of the Imperial Bill, which if enacted would have curtailed the exhibition of American films and increased the exhibition of imperial productions. The colonial state wanted to pass the bill and, conflating imperial and indigenous productions, righteously asserted that imperial or indigenous productions required the support of the colonial *state*. An observant Rangachariar pointed to this conflation and unbraided one from the other. He responded to the assertion by urging the state to support an Indian film industry rather than an American or British one if it truly wanted to develop an "indigenous film industry." Rangachariar's comments were often thoughtful and provocative, making critical interventions within the committee.

14. Indian Cinematograph Committee, *Report of the Indian Cinematograph Committee, 1927–1928* (Madras: Government Press, 1928), 110.

15. Ibid., 4–5.

16. Ibid., 151.

17. Ibid., 5.

18. Ibid., 112.

19. Manishita Dass, "The Crowd outside the Lettered City: Imagining the Mass Audience in 1920s India," *Cinema Journal* 48, no. 4 (Summer 2009): 77–98.

20. Ibid., 79.

21. *Report of Cinematograph Committee*, 11.

22. Ibid., 155.

23. Ibid., 134–136.

24. Ibid.

25. Timothy Mitchell, "The Limits of the State: Beyond Statist Approaches and Their Critics," *American Political Science Review* 85, no. 1 (1991): 77–96. Mitchell's work is exemplary in showing how political boundaries between civil society and the state enable lucrative oversights. For an updated version of Mitchell's article, see Timothy Mitchell, "Society, Economy, and the State Effect," in *State/Culture: State Formation after the Cultural Turn*, ed. George Steinmetz, 76–97 (Ithaca, N.Y.: Cornell University Press, 1999). As a whole, this is a useful collection on state and culture, containing rich contributions as well as a comprehensive and insightful introduction.

26. Jaikumar, "More Than Morality."

27. The entire history of censorship of art and literature lies beyond the scope of this work. For a discussion on the censorship of art and literature in colonial and postcolonial India, see N. Gerald Barrier, *Banned: Controversial Literature and Political Control in British India, 1907–1947* (Columbia: University of Missouri Press, 1974); Shohini Ghosh, "Censorship Myths and Imagined Harms," in *SARAI Reader: Crisis/Media*, 447–454 (New Delhi: SARAI, 2004); Timothy Brennan, *Salman Rushdie and the Third World: Myths of a Nation* (London: Macmillan, 1989); Lisa Appignanesi and Sara Maitland, eds., *The Rushdie File* (Syracuse, N.Y.: Syracuse University Press, 1990); Henry Schwarz, "Aesthetic Imperialism: Literature and the Conquest of India," *Modern Language Quarterly* 61, no. 4 (Dec. 2000): 563–586. Unlike books or artworks, films are subject to censorship before they enter the public domain in India. The producer must submit a film for certification before it can be screened in public. The mechanism of censorship thus affects the film even when it is in production, because the producer has a general idea of what is likely to be censored.

28. R. M. Ray, *Film Seminar Report* (New Delhi: Sangeet Natak Akademi, 1956), 75–76.

29. I am grateful to John Mowitt's comments in developing this point. See Mitchell, "Limits of the State," for further discussion on the formation of the state. As Mitchell's work shows, Foucault's concept of governmentality has played an important role in rethinking the operations and formation of the state. While I recognize the importance of this concept, Foucault's earlier insights on power and micropractices proved more valuable for my project. These earlier Foucauldian insights enabled me to conceptualize censorship as a set of practices performed at the sites not just of state censorship but also of film production, distribution, and reception; governmentality would have restricted me to examining the operations of the state.

30. *The Cinematograph Act, 1952 (37 of 1952) and Censorship Guidelines* (New Delhi: Rakesh, 1992). The act also gave the government the power to exempt films from censorship in special case, e.g., when they circulated in film festivals.

31. Rajya Sabha debates, November 26, 1954, qtd. in Vasudev, *Liberty and Licence*, 107.

32. Jawaharlal Nehru, *SIFCC Bulletin*, August 1954, qtd. in Vasudev, *Liberty and Licence*, 107.

33. After independence, the postcolonial state was more interested in modernizing industries that would help the nation become "developed"; at this time, cinema was considered to be such an industry. The differences between Nehru and Mohandas Gandhi with regard to modernization are important to remember. Not only was Gandhi wary of industrialization, but he framed the process of industrialization in specifically moral terms. He argued that it was fueled by and in turn contributed to increasing desire. This rampant desire did not take into account the needs and conditions of the 80 percent of India's population who lived in villages. Nehru, however, enthusiastically supported industrialization and did not view it as an object of moral contestation. See Mahatma Gandhi, *Cent per cent Swadeshi, or, The Economics of Village Industries* (Ahmedabad: Navajivan, 1948). For a compelling discussion of the discourse of development's central role in forming postcolonial India, see Akhil Gupta, *Postcolonial Developments: Agriculture in the Making of Modern India* (Durham, N.C.: Duke University Press, 1998).

34. Gupta, *Postcolonial Developments*, 105.

35. Lilavati Munshi, *Journal of the Film Industry*, March 1952, 24, qtd. in Vasudev, *Liberty and Licence*, 106.

36. *Journal of the Bengal Motion Picture Association*, November 1954, qtd. in Vasudev, *Liberty and Licence*, 104.

37. I am indebted to John Mowitt's comments in developing this point.

38. *Filmfare* was launched in 1952. It is printed in English with a Hindi edition.

39. *Filmfare*, March 4, 1955, 14.

40. I am indebted to Ravi Vasudevan's comments about the character of *Filmfare* in the 1950s.

41. I was able to look at only the English edition of *Filmfare*. I do not know whether the editors printed all the letters that they received; I presume they did not. For my analysis, I chose a few of these letters based on the ways they both approached and expanded the discussion on censorship.

42. Jal Jehangir, "Letter," *Filmfare*, April 29, 1955, 14.

43. Anant Kumar Suri, "Letter," *Filmfare*, May 27, 1955, 18.

44. This variation in opinion had and continues to have financial consequences for the film industry. Until 1998, when film was accorded industry status in India, the commercial cinema received no financial aid from the state; in fact, it was heavily taxed because it was classified as an *entertainment* industry. For further discussion on the industry status granted to film, see Monika Mehta, "Globalizing Bombay Cinema: Reproducing the Indian State and Family," *Cultural Dynamics* 17, no. 2 (2005): 135–154.

45. Mr. Majumdar and S. Mukerjea, "Letter," *Filmfare*, May 27, 1955, 19.

46. I am grateful to John Mowitt for drawing my attention to this point. During my fieldwork, both officials and directors noted that in order to certify films, directors bribe members of the examining committees. I discuss this further in Chapter 3.

47. Leelabai Gambhue, "Letter," *Filmfare*, May 27, 1955, 19.

48. Kadani Venkatao Rao, "Letter," *Filmfare*, May 27, 1955, 18.

49. H. Suryanarayana, "Letter," *Filmfare*, May 27, 1955, 19.

50. *K. A. Abbas v. Union of India* (1971) 2 SCR 446, 481–482.

51. G. N. Bhattacharya, "Letter," *Filmfare*, May 27, 1955, 18.

52. The notion that "Western films" are made for educated middle-class audiences and commercial Bombay films are made for the "masses" is a common one.

53. *Filmfare*, September, 26, 1969, 35.

54. Enquiry Committee on Film Censoship, *Report of the Enquiry Committee on Film Censorship* (New Delhi: Government of India Press, 1969), 122.

55. *Filmfare*, September 26, 1969, 35.

56. *Filmfare*, June 20, 1969. This controversy prompted one enterprising director, I. S. Johar, to begin making a short film tracing the history of the kiss. Unfortunately, the archives do not indicate whether it was ever completed.

57. P. I. John, "Letter," *Filmfare*, July 4, 1969, 51.

58. Vijaya Subramaniam, "Letter," *Filmfare*, October, 24, 1969. Vatsayana is the author of the *Kamasutra*.

59. Ibid.

60. This argument can be traced to nineteenth-century nationalists who believed that they were morally and culturally superior but had been conquered by the British because of India's poor performance in the material world, i.e., in terms of industrialization and technology. See Partha Chatterjee, *Nationalist Thought and the Colonial World: A Derivative Discourse?* (London: Zed Books, 1986).

61. Dikes Mills, "Letter," *Filmfare*, August 15, 1969.

62. *Filmfare*, September 12, 1969, 45.

63. For further discussion about M. G. Ramachandran's star persona, see M. S. S. Pandian, *The Image Trap: M G Ramachandran in Film and Politics* (New Delhi: Sage, 1992). It would be productive to consider how censorship practices have shaped star images. More recently, despite the reemergence of the on-screen kiss, the superstar Shah Rukh Khan, whose phenomenal rise has been associated with his family-friendly image both on and off the screen, has refused to kiss on-screen.

64. Interestingly, the Tamil and the Hindi cinema share codes about sexuality and gender, as the discussions about censorship reveal.

65. A. K. Singhal, "Letter," *Filmfare*, October 24, 1969.

66. For a discussion on female stardom in the context of Hindi cinema, see Behroze Gandhy and Rosie Thomas, "Three Indian Film Stars," in *Stardom: Industry of Desire*, ed. Christine Gledhill, 107–131 (New York: Routledge, 1991); Neepa Majumdar, *Wanted Cultured Ladies Only! Female Stardom and Cinema in India, 1930s–1950s* (Urbana: University of Illinois Press, 2009); Rosie Thomas, "Sanctity and Scandal: The Mythologization of Mother India," *Quarterly Review of Film and Video* 11, no. 3 (1989): 11–30; Ravi Vasudevan, "'You Cannot Live in Society—and Ignore It': Nationhood and Female Modernity in *Andaz*," in *Social Reform, Sexuality and the State*, ed. Patricia Uberoi, 83–108 (New Delhi: Sage, 1996), 104–106.

67. Singhal, "Letter."

68. C. K. Razdan, ed., *Bare Breasts and Bare Bottoms* (Bombay: Jaico, 1975), 3.

69. In my hunt for discussions about the kiss, the last reference that I came across

concerned the 1942 Marathi film *Pahili mangalagaur* (First night), directed by R. S. Junnarkar.

70. M. Madhava Prasad, *Ideology of the Hindi Film: A Historical Construction* (New Delhi: Oxford University Press, 1998), 88–116.

71. Sangita Gopal, "Sentimental Symptoms: The Films of Karan Johar and Bombay Cinema," in *Bollywood and Globalization: Indian Popular Cinema, Nation, and Diaspora*, ed. Rini Bhattacharya Mehta and Rajeshwari V. Pandharipande, 15–34 (London: Anthem, 2010).

72. "Kiss-Kiss, Smooch-Smooch, Bollywood Is No Longer Shy," *India Forums*, July 23, 2009, http://www.bollycurry.com/news/hot-n-happening/10172-kiss-kiss -smooch-smooch-bollywood-is-no-longer-shy.htm (accessed Aug. 12, 2010).

73. N. N. Satchitanand, "The Nude Wave and the Indian Cinema," *Star and Style*, October 2, 1969, 7.

74. *Abbas v. Union of India*.

75. Ibid.

76. *Ranjit D. Udeshi v. State of Maharashtra*, AIR 1965 S.C. 881. In rendering their judgment, the court cited laws and legal cases from the British colonial era, the United States, the contemporary United Kingdom, and postindependence India.

77. For guidelines before and after the Emergency, see Kobita Sarkar, *You Can't Please Everyone: Film Censorship, the Inside Story* (Bombay: India Book House, 1982).

78. *Filmfare*, August 1978. During a press conference in Pune soon after the Janata government came to power, L. K. Advani, the union minister for information and broadcasting, announced that "he was not averse to allowing kissing in Indian films provided it was a happy marriage. . . . Kissing, in his view, was a peripheral aspect which always received undue attention from the censors. The main problem was obscenity, which, he said, brooked no compromise" (ibid.). Advani's liberal comments came under heavy attack by public and official sectors, who berated him for undermining India's culture and tradition.

79. The case of the film *Kissa kursi ka* (The Case of the Chair) makes for interesting reading in this regard.

80. The group was headed by Dr. K. S. Karanth, who had been given six months to submit the report. By the time the report was presented, however, the Congress Party had once more assumed power.

81. Working Group on National Film Policy, *Report of the Working Group on National Film Policy* (New Delhi: Government of India Press, 1980).

82. Nandana Bose, "Between the Godfather and the Mafia: Situating Right-Wing Interventions in the Bombay Film Industry (1992–2002)," *South Asian Film and Media* 1, no. 1 (2009): 23–43.

83. In film lore, Raj Kapoor's *Bobby* (1973) marks the emergence of teen sexuality on the screen.

84. In 1994 the state announced the Cable Television Networks Rules, and in 1995 the state passed the Cable Television Networks (Regulation) Act to regulate the

influence of cable television. See Cable Television Networks Rules, 1994, *http://www.nfdcindia.com/copyright.html.*

85. See the 1984 amendment on videos, *http://www.nfdcindia.com/copyright.html.*

86. Ministry of Information and Broadcasting, Government of India, *Film Censorship: What Everyone Should Know* (Delhi: Bengal Printing Press, 1992), 8–9.

87. In fact, as I show in my analysis of *Pati parmeshwar*, objections against such representations arose from within the ranks of the examining and revising committees; such protests from these committees, however, were anomalous. Moreover, when women's organizations drew attention to such images, they did not generate controversy.

88. *Bandit Queen* also contained caste and sexual violence as well as explicit language. It has a very colorful history both pre- and postproduction.

89. "Banned, Banned and Banned Again!" *Queer India*, May 19, 2006, http://queerindia.blogspot.com/2006/05/banned-banned-and-banned-again.html (accessed Aug. 14, 2010).

90. Interestingly, films such as Amol Palekar's *Daayara* (1997; Circle) and Kalpana Lajmi's *Darmiyaan* (1997; In-between), which similarly interrogated normative constructions of gender and sexuality, received little public or scholarly attention.

91. I make this point in my commentary piece in *Velvet Light Trap* as well. See "Re-framing Censorship," *Velvet Light Trap* 63 (Spring 2009): 66–69.

92. See Mazzarella's interview with Anand in William Mazzarella, "The Obscenity of Censorship: Rethinking a Middle-Class Technology," Department of Anthropology, University of Chicago, http://anthropology.uchicago.edu/pdfs/mazz_obscenity.pdf (accessed Aug. 12, 2010).

93. Geeta Seshu, "Pornography: Certification vs. Censorship," *Boloji.com*, August 11, 2002, http://www.boloji.com/wfs/wfs067.htm (quotation) (accessed Aug. 14, 2010); Siddharth Narrain, "Exit, Anupam Kher," *Frontline*, November 6–19, 2004, http://hinduonnet.com/fline/fl2123/stories/20041119008112600.htm (accessed Aug. 14, 2010).

94. As I discuss elsewhere, under Kher, there was debate on the music video of the remixed song "Kaanta laga" (A thorn hurt me) that took place not only within national space but also on the Internet, highlighting technology's role in expanding debates on censorship. See Nilanjana Bhattacharyja and Monika Mehta, "From Bombay to Bollywood: Tracking Cinematic and Musical Tours," in *Global Bollywood: Travels of Hindi Song and Dance*, ed. Sangita Gopal and Sujata Moorti, 105–131 (Minneapolis: University of Minnesota Press, 2008).

95. Dr. T. Subbarami Reddy, M.P, "The Cinematograph (Amendment), 2002: A Bill to Further Amend the Cinematograph Act, 1952," to be introduced in the Rajya Sabha, http://mpa.nic.in/aro3-04/append7.htm (accessed July 5, 2009). The Rajya Sabha is the upper house of the Indian Parliament, containing both appointed specialists and elected members. A more innovative amendment, submitted in 2005, sought to introduce new guidelines that would prohibit scenes involving "damage of food items, public property, crops etc." on the grounds that India was a "poor

country" and many lacked such essential amenities, which were "wasted/dam-aged" in films. The new guidelines also sought to restrict any scene where currency is burned "because it was disrespectful and in bad taste." See Shri Subodh Mohite, M.P., "The Cinematograph (Amendment), 2005: A Bill to further amend the Cinematograph Act, 1952," as introduced in the Lok Sabha, http://mpa.nic.in/ar06-07/appendix.pdf (accessed July 5, 2009).

96. Members of the Alternative Law Forum responded to this call. They wrote a detailed and insightful letter that offered cogent criticisms and suggestions for the new bill. See "Comments on Draft Cinematograph Act, 2010," <http://www.altlaw forum.org/law-and-media/campaigns/cinematograph-act-final%20submission.doc /view> (accessed Aug. 7, 2010).

97. A productive line of inquiry would be to study the regulation of narratives concerning communal violence, which were equally important in this period.

98. Vinay Lal, "Travails of the Nation," *Third Text* 19, no. 2 (Mar. 2005): 177–187.

99. See Appendix C.

100. Ministry of Information and Broadcasting, Government of India, "Draft Cinematograph Bill, 2010," Acts and Rules [Films], Introduction (unnumbered first page). http://mib.nic.in/ShowContent.aspx?uid1=7&uid2=49&uid3=0&uid4=0&uid5 =0&uid6=0&uid7=0.

101. Ibid.

102. Ibid., 2.

103. Ibid., 3.

104. Ibid., 4 and 6. The current act does have a "quota" for women on advisory panels; the exact numbers differ as presented in different places within the act. I refer to this earlier "quota" in Chapter 3.

105. Ibid.

106. Ibid., 7.

CHAPTER 3

1. Hannah Arendt, *Eichmann in Jerusalem: A Report on the Banality of Evil* (New York: Viking, 1965). I want to underscore that I am not equating the film censors with the Nazis but rather using Arendt's insights to think through another context.

2. Initially, there were only three branches, located in Bombay, Calcutta, and Madras, which are important film-industry centers. Later, as film industries in other states flourished, more offices were added.

3. These guidelines have been revised a number of times since Independence. I refer to some of these changes in the context of my analyses. Appendix A presents the current guidelines, which were in use during my fieldwork.

4. Central Board of Film Certification, Government of India, "Highlights," *Annual Report 1996* (Mumbai: Central Board of Film Certification, n.d.).

5. See Appendix A.

6. For many in India's middle and upper-middle classes, viewing Hindi films was

a guilty pleasure at this juncture. Toward the mid- to late nineties, more members of these classes begin to embrace Hindi cinema publicly. This shift can be attributed to a number of factors, such as the emergence of the multiplex and new genres, as well as a growing interest in "Bollywood" in the West.

7. Though the project falls outside the scope of this book, a comparative study of state censorship, examining these processes and guidelines and the composition of members, would likely yield significant results. For example, one could look at this process in India and China.

8. Kobita Sarkar, *You Can't Please Everyone: Film Censorship, the Inside Story* (Bombay: IBH, 1982).

9. See Appendix B.

10. Both "illegal films" and those shown at film festivals evade state censorship. In the former case, the directors or producers simply forge the certificate. The latter has a more complicated history. For the most part, governments have not required state certification for festival films because they have presumed that these films will be viewed by middle- or upper-class audiences.

11. For foreign films, their point of entry into India dictates where they will be examined, although the CBFC chairperson has the authority to relocate films. There is also a separate application form for foreign films.

12. Raj Kapoor has commented that the first time he included a background score was when he submitted *Satyam shivam sundaram* to the CBFC, which indicates that this requirement has been flexible and could bend to accommodate influential forces.

13. Report of member of examining/revising committee, 1997, CBFCB.

14. Ibid.

15. Central Board, *Annual Report 1996*, 7.

16. Nitin Govil discusses the role of the informal within the Indian film industry; see Govil, "Bollywood and the Frictions of Global Mobility," in *Media on the Move: Global Flow and Contra-flow*, ed. Daya Kishen Thussu, 84–98 (London and New York: Routledge, 2007).

17. The film was granted an A certificate. I'm not sure whether it was cut, for I had no access to the records.

18. Ministry of Information and Broadcasting, Government of India, *Film Censorship: What Everyone Should Know* (Delhi: Bengal Printing Press, 1992), 8.

19. See appendix A.

20. Ministry of Information, *Film Censorship*, 8.

21. Section 292, Indian Penal Code (1860).

22. The film was granted a U certificate subject to cuts.

23. The entry of "dons" into the film industry dates back to the mid-1970s, when the mobster Haji Mastan made two C-grade films with a starlet called Sona. Initially, members of the underworld viewed the film industry as a perfect site for laundering money, since huge amounts of it could be written off as production costs. The 1980s witnessed the increase of the clout of dons, in particular Dawood Ibrahim.

Depending on the situation, these dons act as financiers, extortionists, and "protectors." They generally keep tabs on the financial transactions within the industry, pressure film stars to give dates for shooting films, force producers and directors to hire particular stars, and demand that film stars perform at their *mehfils* (gatherings). In the past few years, the highly publicized murders of the director-producer Mukesh Duggal and Tips Cassettes owner Gulshan Kumar, extortion threats against the producers Rajiv Rai and Subhash Ghai, and the recent attempt on the producer Rakesh Roshan's life have generated great anxiety and fear within the film industry. While this spate of violence certainly sent the industry a message about "cooperating" with the underworld, it also galvanized the Bombay police, who were given yet another chance to uproot corruption and establish their credentials as champions of justice. Unfortunately, the film industry was the grudging recipient of this attention; they perhaps found the choice between the underworld and the Bombay police a difficult one, considering the little difference between their practices. The industry responded to the threats of the underworld in two ways. First, industry professionals became more careful about revealing financial information, making it more difficult for the extortionists to extract money. Second, the industry intensified its efforts to gain state support for financing its productions.

24. Dawood Ibrahim is one of the more powerful "underworld dons."

25. Central Board, "Highlights."

26. Although English is one of India's two official languages, it is not considered to be a "vernacular" language. English is spoken by approximately 5 percent of the Indian population, basically the upper and middle classes. The vernacular languages include Hindi (the other official language), Telugu, and Tamil, among others.

27. For further discussion on interpolations, see Amit Rai, *Untimely Bollywood: Globalization and India's New Media Assemblage* (Durham, N.C.: Duke University Press, 2009); Amit Kumar, "The Lower Stall: The Sleaze-Sex Film Industry in India, an Introduction," *Spectator: The University of Southern California Journal of Film and Television* 26, no. 2 (Fall 2006): 27–41.

28. The CBFC requires that only one negative print be processed and that negatives of all cuts be deposited at the certification board before a certificate is issued. Enforcement of this requirement is based largely on trust, which can always be violated.

29. I use the term *resistance* and its cognates with some discomfort because they evoke heroism and, perhaps, progressive politics. Resistance need not be either heroic or progressive. In judging resistance, one must consider who is resisting what, by what means, and to what effect. Such judgments are by no means easy, complete, or fixed; they are at best fragile, based on some faith, some information, and some analysis.

30. In this context, the word translates, as "okay."

31. These people asked about my family and my marital status, too.

CHAPTER 4

1. Ministry of Information and Broadcasting to chairman of the Central Board of Film Censors, October 11, 1973, *Gupt gyan* file, CBFCB.

2. For these guidelines, see Kobita Sarkar, *You Can't Please Everyone: Film Censorship, the Inside Story* (Bombay: India Book House, 1982), 111–115. The guidelines applicable then testify to Britain's engagement with the sex-hygiene films discussed in Annette Kuhn's work. The guidelines continued into the postcolonial era. For further discussion about censorship guidelines, see Someswar Bhowmik, *Cinema and Censorship: The Politics of Control in India* (New Delhi: Orient Longman, 2009).

3. See note 52 in Chapter 1.

4. Sanjay Srivastava, *Passionate Modernity: Sexuality, Class, and Consumption in India* (New Delhi: Routledge, 2007), 47.

5. Partha Chatterjee, "The Nationalist Resolution of the Women's Question," in *Recasting Women: Essays in Indian Colonial History*, ed. Kumkum Sangari and Sudesh Vaid, 233-253 (New Delhi: Kali for Women, 1989).

6. Ibid., 238–239.

7. Also see Partha Chatterjee, *The Nation and Its Fragments: Colonial and Postcolonial Histories* (Princeton, N.J.: Princeton University Press, 1993), 120–121.

8. Swart writes that *darsan* plays an important role in the way that images, holy or authority figures, and sacred spaces are mobilized to organize our vision. This concept has interesting effects for theories of spectatorship and voyeurism, for it is based on the idea that the object looks back, and does so with powerful consequences. See Patricia Swart, "Darson, Visuality and Indian Cinema," http://www.newschool.edu/mediastudies/conference/visual_culture/patricia_swart.htm, accessed October 29, 2009. For further discussion on *darsan*, see Diana Eck, *Darsan: Seeing the Divine Image in India*, 3d ed. (New York: Columbia University Press, 1998); Ravi Vasudevan, "The Politics of Cultural Address in a 'Transitional' Cinema: A Case Study of Popular Indian Cinema," in *Reinventing Film Studies*, ed. Christine Gledhill and Linda Williams, 130–164 (London: Arnold, 2000).

9. B. K. Adarsh to chairman of the Central Board of Film Censors, December 6, 1973, *Gupt gyan* file, CBFCB.

10. Entry on Jaymala, British Film Institrute web site, http://ftvdb.bfi.org.uk/sift/individual/748602.

11. Author's interview with Shakti Samanta, film producer and chairman of the Central Board of Film Certification, July 22, 1996. *Bobby* was released in 1973 by Raj Kapoor, a well-established commercial filmmaker. After the release of this fairly successful film, which represented teenage sexuality, many producers came out with similar films.

12. For a historical account of this period, see Paul Brass, *Politics of India since Independence* (Cambridge: Cambridge University Press, 1994).

13. Madhava Prasad, *Ideology of the Hindi Film: A Historical Construction* (New Delhi: Oxford University Press, 1998).

14. Srivastava, *Passionate Modernity*, 103–105. While Srivastava suggests that this figure disappears after the 1960s, the appearance of an "FYP hero" in *Gupt gyan* and in *Satyam shivam sundaram* (1978) suggests that this protagonist did not disappear but rather was eclipsed by the figure of the "angry young man." The persistence of such protagonists suggests a continued engagement with the Nehruvian vision of the Indian state.

15. Sumanta Banerjee, *Family Planning Communication: A Critique of the Indian Programme* (New Delhi: Radiant, 1979), 17–18.

16. While the state had included some measures to control venereal diseases in the Five-Year Plans, the resources earmarked for this project were considerably less than those for family planning. In fact, between 1957 and 1982 only two films were made on venereal diseases (*Vicious Enemy* [1957] and *Sexually Transmitted Diseases* [1982]), whereas 700 films made during this period focused on family planning. See the Films Division web site, http://www.filmsdivision.org; Devender Mohan Thapa, "The Evolution of Venerology in India," *Indian Journal of Dermatology, Venereology, Leprology* 73, no. 3 (May–June 2006): 187–196.

17. B. K. Adarsh, *Gupt gyan* booklet, in *Gupt gyan* file, CBFCB.

18. Ibid.

19. Ibid.

20. Interview with Samanta. For a short period in the 1970s, the All India Film Producers' Council attempted to exercise self-regulation. A producer would show a film to other, well-established producers and seek their approval for it before sending the film to examining committees. The certificates issued by the council indicated that it took into consideration the Cinematograph Act 1952 and its associated rules.

21. S. E. Hassnain, personal report, included in revising committee report on *Gupt gyan*, *Gupt gyan* file, CBFCB.

22. *Gupt gyan* (1973), dir. B. K. Adarsh, VCD (New Delhi: Bhola Plastic, 2007).

23. Ibid.

24. Eric Schaefer, *"Bold! Daring! Shocking! True!" A History of Exploitation Films, 1919–1959* (Durham, N.C.: Duke University Press, 1991), 31.

25. Ibid.; for Kuhn's argument, see Annette Kuhn, *The Power of Image: Essays on Representation and Sexuality* (London: Routledge and Kegan Paul, 1985).

26. The term "footpath literature" refers to inexpensive and cheaply produced pulp fiction as well as pamphlets on taboo issues (written by nonexperts). These are often sold on footpaths. For further discussion on footpath literature, see Srivastava, *Passionate Modernity*.

27. As I noted in Chapter 1, while Foucault places "India" under the category of "ars erotica," *Gupt gyan* demonstrates the ways in which Foucault's arguments about modern sexuality are pertinent to thinking about these discussions and practices in India.

28. The government favored the use of IUDs, but women often lacked proper follow-up care and consequently developed other illnesses. For further discussion, see Banerjee, *Family Planning*.

29. See Roger Eberwein, *Sex Ed: Film, Video, and the Framework of Desire* (New Brunswick, N.J.: Rutgers University Press, 1999). My analysis of *Gupt gyan* is indebted to Eberwein's arguments and close readings of U.S. sex-education films.

30. Adarsh may have been articulating his own conformist vision through the film, but his choices may also reflect his need to account for the opinions of the officials and audiences who would be watching the film.

31. Rape sequences are common in Hindi cinema.
32. Examining committee report on *Gupt gyan*, 1973, *Gupt gyan* file, CBFCB.
33. Ibid. The following rules are those that Varma said the film violated:

I It is not desirable that a film shall be certified as suitable for public exhibition, either unrestricted or restricted to adults which: (D) exhibit the human form, actually or in shadowgraphs: (i) in a state of nudity; II In addition to the matter dealt with generally in Section I, the following subjects may be objectionable in a context in which they either amount to indecency, immorality, illegality or incitement to commit a breach of law: (i) confinements (ii) details of surgical operations, (iii) venereal disease or other loathsome disease such as leprosy or sores, (vii) indecent dress, conduct, speech, song or theme, or indecent portrayal of national institutions, traditions, customs or culture, (xix) horror as a predominant element, (xxiii) intimate biological studies & (xxiv) crippled limbs or malformations. [Examining committee report; Varma did not mention specific instances in the film that violated these directives.]

The guidelines are from the copy of the Cinematograph Act of 1952 (as modified up to June 1, 1959). In 1978 the Janata-led government issued new rules. For both sets of guidelines, see K. Sarkar, *You Can't Please Everyone*, 113–114.
34. Examining committee report on *Gupt gyan*, 1973.
35. Ibid.
36. Ibid.
37. Revising committee report on *Gupt gyan*, 1973, *Gupt gyan* file, CBFCB.
38. Ibid.
39. Ibid.
40. Ibid.
41. In his letter to the Ministry of Information and Broadcasting, Vyas included reports of foreign feature films on sex education passed by the board: *Sins of the Father* (1954), *Because of Eve* (1954), and *The Case of Dr. Laurent* (1964). The first two films were decertified in 1956; Vyas's letter does not indicate why. After examining *The Case of Dr. Laurent*, the committee asked for the removal of a childbirth sequence; once that was done, the film was passed.
42. Ministry of Information and Broadcasting to the chairman of Central Board of Film Censors, October 11, 1973, *Gupt gyan* file, CBFCB.
43. Ibid.
44. Ibid.
45. Ibid.
46. The specific demands were as follows:

[1.] Reduce the scene in which Chanchal entices Dinesh in his study, deleting the beginning of the scene. [2.] Reduce considerably the reproductive organs in the sequence showing the Venereal Diseases, deleting completely the shots which are gruesome. [3.] From the Seth and stenographer scene, cut all shots from the dialogue "I am not that type . . ." to eliminate suggestions of molestation. [4.] (i) Delete the repetitions of the close-ups of the genital from the sequence in which the loop is inserted; (ii) Delete entirely the Vasectomy operation; (iii) Delete entirely the Tubectomy operation; (iv) From the sequence related to the two kinds of abortion, delete all the live shots of the vacuum sucker method and the Caesarean method. [5.] From the scene in which the Seth tries to molest Radhia, delete the portions after the dialogue of Radhia "chale jayiye . . ." [Go away] and her giving back the money. [6.] Reduce close-ups of Dinesh's father, suffering from venereal disease, on the death bed. [7.] Delete all surgical details of the Tubectomy (Vaginal) operation and also all the portions after the stitching are over. [8.] From the sequence of child birth by psychosomatic medication, delete all shots after baby is born. [9.] Delete the underlined words from the following sentence "Aaj family planning par karodon rupaya karch ho raha hai. Doctoron ki poor army lagi hui hai, parivar niyojan ke peeche, *lekin safalta nahin mil saki* [Today, the government is spending millions on family planning. An army of doctors is supporting these efforts, *however their efforts have not been successful so far*]. [10.] Delete the underlined words from the following sentence: "Homosexualities, yaani ek mard ka doosre mard ke saath sambhog, ek aurat ka doosri aurat ke saath sambandh. *Iska matlab hota hai apne khoon ke saath sambhog karma. Jaise ki ek baap ka beti ke saath, baap ka apne bete ke saath, bhai ka apni bhain ke saath* [Homosexualities, that is to say, a man having sex with another man, a woman having sex with another woman. This is akin to incest. Like a father having sex with his daughter, a father having sex with his son, a brother having sex with his sister.] [11.] Delete the following words in the dialogue by Chanchal "Doctor ke paas kaise aate hain *apna badan dikhane*" [You go to doctor to show him your body]. [Bombay, Central Board of Film Certification, Examining Committee Report on *Gupt Gyan*, 1973; the bracketed English translations are mine.]

47. Regional Officer, Central Board of Film Censors, to Adarsh Arts, December 6, 1973, *Gupt gyan* file, CBFCB. While the demand for cut 11 (see previous note) was sustained, two other demands were modified to read as follows.: "4(i) Delete the repetitions of the close-ups of the genital from the sequence in which the loop is inserted (There is no objection to the first shot of the vagina being shown). 4(iv) Modified to read as '[f]rom the sequence relating to the two kinds of abortion, delete all live shots of the vacuum sucker method and the Caesarian method' (There is no objection to the first shot of the vacuum sucker being allowed.)"

48. Aruna Vasudev, *Liberty and Licence in the Indian Cinema* (New Delhi: Vikas, 1978), 89–91. After independence, the new government revised the Cinematograph Act and the associated Censorship Rules. Vasudev explains, "[in] exercise of its powers under Rule 32 (4) of these Cinematograph Rules 1951, the Board decided to grant exemption of part of the examination fee in respect to films that were not of an

educational nature in the technical sense, but which nevertheless fulfilled an educational purpose. Films certified as being of a predominantly educational (PE) nature were divided into two categories—1. Films useful as visual aids to instruction in the classroom. 2. Films not included in Category 1, but which are informative and educational in the general sense." This decision to make a film tax free, however, is subject to each state's approval. For more information on the PE certificate, see K. Sarkar, *You Can't Please Everyone*, 68–69. The history of the PE certificate is not well documented, so that questions with regard to its emergence and the subsequent changes remain unanswered. During the course of my fieldwork, the officials whom I interviewed were unable to provide information on it.

49. B. K. Adarsh to chairman of the Central Board of Film Censors, March 11, 1974, *Gupt gyan* file, CBFCB.

50. PE committee report for *Gupt gyan*, 1974, *Gupt gyan* file, CBFCB.

51. Ibid.

52. Ibid. Adarsh was notified of the committee's decision on April 30, 1974.

53. Virendra D. Vyas, chairman of the Central Board of Film Censors, to Shri L. Dayal, Ministry of Information and Broadcasting, April 20, 1976, CBFCB. There was no further information available on the discussion of the working group or on the reason Vyas changed his views.

54. *Picture Post*, July 1977; the Lok Sabha is the lower house of the Indian Parliament.

55. For a thoughtful discussion on sterilization and the Emergency, see Emma Tarlo, *Unsettling Memories: Narratives of the Emergency in Delhi* (Berkeley: University of California Press, 2003).

56. Examining committee report on *Gupt gyan*, 1978, *Gupt gyan* file, CBFCB.

57. B. K. Adarsh to chairman of the Central Board of Censors, May 4, 1978, *Gupt gyan* file, CBFCB.

58. Ibid.

59. Ibid. The underlining is Adarsh's.

60. Revising committee report, May 10, 1978, *Gupt gyan* file, CBFCB.

61. K. Sarkar, *You Can't Please Everyone*. Sarkar also notes that it is unclear how this new certificate would be enforced.

62. *The Cinematograph Act, 1952 (37 of 1952): Cinematograph Certification Rules 1983 and Certification Guidelines* (New Delhi: Rakesh, 1992), 31, 34-35. In 1997 the phrase "compact disc" was inserted in reference to VCDs, and it applies to DVDs, too. The Cinematograph Act and its associated rules, as well as the application forms, refer to all nontheatrical versions as "video films."

CHAPTER 5

1. For a discussion of the kiss in Hindi cinema, see Chapter 1 and M. Madhava Prasad, *Ideology of the Hindi Film: A Historical Construction* (New Delhi: Oxford University Press, 1998).

LIVERPOOL JOHN MOORES UNIVERSITY
LEARNING SERVICES

2. Neepa Majumdar, "The Embodied Voice: Song Sequences and Stardom in Popular Hindi Cinema," in *Soundtrack Available: Essays on Film and Popular Music*, ed. Pamela Roberston Wojcik and Arthur Knight, 161–181 (Durham, N.C.: Duke University Press, 2001). Majumdar makes the useful distinction between "visual" and "aural" stardom and insightfully plots the trajectory of the latter in Hindi cinema. For discussions on female stardom, see Neepa Majumdar, *Wanted Cultured Ladies Only! Female Stardom and Cinema in India, 1930s–1950s* (Urbana: University of Illinois Press, 2009); and Rosie Thomas, "Sanctity and Scandal: The Mythologization of Mother India," *Quarterly Review of Film and Video* 2 (1989): 11–30.

3. For an extensive list of sources on Raj Kapoor, see www.therajkapoorproject. com/sources.php. Scholarship on Kapoor primarily focuses on his work in the 1950s, paying close attention to his films with Nargis, his heroine, collaborator, and mistress. For many scholars, journalists, and biographers, *Satyam shivam sundaram* falls on the wrong side of his oeuvre, a part of his post-Nargis work, when he purportedly acquiesced to his libidinal and commercial desires. These writings appear to affirm Kapoor's statement that Nargis was the "mother of his films," implying that the rest of his leading ladies were mere mistresses. This division of Kapoor's oeuvre is tantalizing given this chapter's investment in exploring the concepts of splitting as well as the dyads of wife versus mistress, and heroine versus vamp.

4. In his cinematic efforts, Raj Kapoor was supported by his father, an established thespian and film actor who managed the film careers of his three sons. Generations of the Kapoor clan have worked and continue to work in the Bombay film industry.

5. Khalid Mohamed, "Everything for Sale," undated, Raj Kapoor article file, NFAI.

6. Ibid.

7. Sunil Sethi et al., "Who's Afraid of Film Censorship," *India Today*, October 1–15, 1980, 61.

8. Rauf Ahmed, "Raj Kapoor: Between Hope and Despair," *Super*, May 1978, 15.

9. Bunny Reuben, "Satyam Shivam Sundaram," *Illustrated Weekly of India*, May 7, 1978; Bunny Reuben, *Raj Kapoor: The Fabulous Showman* (New Delhi: Virgo, 1988), 273.

10. Reuben, *Raj Kapoor*, 247.

11. Ibid., 251–252, 278.

12. Qtd. in Ingrid Albuquerque, "Will 'Satyam . . .' Be Raj Kapoor Swan Song?" undated, Raj Kapoor article file, NFAI.

13. Ibid.

14. Ibid.

15. Ahmed, "Between Hope and Despair," 15.

16. Kushwant Singh, "We Sell Them Dreams," *New York Times Magazine*, October 31, 1976, 42.

17. Reuben, *Raj Kapoor*, 278.

18. Reuben, "Satyam Shivam Sundaram"; Reuben, *Raj Kapoor*, 258–259. In his biography of Kapoor, Reuben refers to a less scandalous and salacious audition,

one that Aman confirmed in a television interview (*Star Talk*, with Vir Sanghvi; see http://www.youtube.com/watch?v=dY50SHSGrYo). In this version, Aman appears before Kapoor with a burn scar and wearing a *ghaghra choli* (a long skirt and blouse outfit)—a vision of a hard-working actress (as opposed to sex symbol)—attempting to obtain the much desired role. In his biography Reuben suggests that this was a second audition, not the one that actually got Aman the coveted role.

19. D. B. Gaekwad, letter to the editor, *Filmfare*, August 16, 1978.

20. A *mangalsutra* is a pendant given at the time of marriage, and *sindoor* is vermilion powder. These two symbols of Hindu marriage are generally worn by women. The reference is to Hindi cinema's extensive use of these symbols to depict the sanctity of matrimony for women.

21. Deepa Gahlot, "Out of Sync: What Went Wrong with Zeenat's Career," *Filmfare*, December 15, 1984.

22. Ibid. Also see Olga Tellis, "How Zeenat Won the Rat Race," *Sunday*, October 9, 1977, 15–17.

23. Tish Malhotra, "The King of Romance," *Patriot News*, June 3, 1988, Raj Kapoor article file, NFAI.

24. Ahmed, "Between Hope and Despair," 15. Kapoor draws on a familiar industry argument: that the realistic rendering of a character—in this case, an "*Adivasi*" (tribal)—demands this state of undress. The argument thus sexualizes the figure of the female tribal. She is constructed as closer to nature, unfettered by social mores. The oxymoronic nature of an *Adivasi* girl belonging to a Brahmin household does not appear to disturb Kapoor's realist vision.

25. Raju Bharatan, *Lata Mangeshkar: A Biography* (New Delhi: UBSPD, 1995), 85.

26. Malhotra, "King of Romance."

27. Ahmed, "Between Hope and Despair."

28. Mary Doane, "The Voice in the Cinema: The Articulation of Body and Space," in *Theory and Practice: Film and Sound*, ed. Elizabeth Weis and John Belton, 162–176 (New York: Columbia University Press, 1985).

29. Partha Chatterjee, "When Melody Ruled the Day," *Indian Horizons* 44, no. 1 (1995): 57.

30. N. Majumdar, "Embodied Voice," 163.

31. Sanjay Srivastava, *Passionate Modernity: Sexuality, Class, and Consumption in India* (New Delhi: Routledge, 2007), 86; see also 80–91, 108.

32. Michel Chion, *The Voice in Cinema*, ed. and trans. Claudia Gorbman (New York: Columbia University Press, 1999), 156, 161.

33. Bharatan, *Lata Mangeshkar*, 110.

34. Reuben, *Raj Kapoor*, 271.

35. Madhu Jain, *The Kapoors: The First Family of Indian Cinema* (New Delhi: Viking, 2005), 145-146.

36. Bharatan, *Lata Mangeshkar*, 89.

37. Ibid., 85–86, 143–144.

38. In South Asia, picturization of a song refers to the on-screen rendering of it.

39. During this period, Hema Malini was involved with a well-known married star, Dharmendra. This fact did not appear to impact Mangeshkar's vision of her, since Malini's star persona included elements of both "Indianness" and "respectability."

40. Bharatan, *Lata Mangeshkar*, 87.

41. Ibid.

42. See Rick Altman, ed., *Sound Theory and Sound Practice* (New York: Routledge, 1992); Elisabeth Weis and John Belton, eds., *Theory and Practice: Film Sound* (New York: Columbia University Press, 1985); N. Majumdar, "Embodied Voice"; Kaja Silverman, *The Acoustic Mirror: The Female Voice in Psychoanalysis and Cinema* (Bloomington: Indiana University Press, 1988).

43. N. Majumdar, "Embodied Voice," 161–181.

44. For articles and letters criticizing *Satyam shivam sundaram*, see letters to *Star and Style*, August 11–24, October 1–19, and November 17–30, 1978; T. G. Vaidynathan, "*Satyam Shivam Sundaram*," *Deccan Herald*, July 9, 1978; "Talk of the Town," *Amrit Bazar Patrika*, July 16, 1978; "Review Point," *Star and Style*, July 13, 1978; Anil Dharker, "Dirty Old Man," *Debonair*, June 1978; Gautam Kundu, "Tits Sublime," *Sunday*, October 29, 1978; Girija Rajendran, "What the Camera Missed," *Hindustan Times*, June 11, 1978. For letters and articles supporting the film, see "Cinema: New Releases," *The Times of India*, June 12, 1978; "*Satyam Shivam sundaram*," *Poona Herald*, March 31, 1978.

45. "Talk of Town," *Amrit Bazar Patrika*, July 16, 1978.

46. "Cinema: New Releases," *The Times of India*, June 12, 1978; "*Satyam Shivam Sundaram*," *Poona Herald*, March 31, 1978.

47. "Talk of the Town," *Amrit Bazar Patrika*, July 16, 1978.

48. Khalid Mohamed, "Everything for Sale," undated, Raj Kapoor article file, NFAI.

49. "Talk of the Town," *Amrit Bazar Patrika*, July 16, 1978.

50. Kundu, "Tits Sublime."

51. Letters to the editor, *Filmfare*, August 1978.

52. Letters to the editor, *Star and Style*, August 11–24, October 1–19, and November 17–30, 1978.

53. Ramraj Deshmukh, letter to the editor, *Star and Style*, August 11–24, 1978, 21. The complaints also drew attention to film publicity and sought to bring it under the surveillance of the state. Viewers noted that while the public exhibition of A-rated films was restricted to those eighteen or older, a film's publicity was not similarly regulated, so that hoardings and posters for A-rated films abounded. The government responded to these objections by bringing film publicity under its surveillance. In November 1978 the central government approved an ordinance enforcing the regulation of obscene posters. See letters to the editor in *Star and Style*, November 17–30, 1978, and in *Picture Post*, November 1978.

54. These marches are important because they contributed to larger discussions about women's representation that would find their constitutional resolution in the formation and the institution of the Indecent Representation of Women

Act (Prohibition) of 1987, which I will discuss in the subsequent chapter on *Pati parmeshwar*.

55. "Film Censorship: Corrupt, Confused, Castrating," *The Times of India*, October 29, 1978.

56. *Picture Post*, January 1979.

In another survey, conducted only in Bombay through the Federation of Film Societies and in which about 1,500 movie-goers registered their views on the certification of SSS, 51.43 percent stated that the censors were correct in certifying the film in the "A" category. Further 22.29 percent opined that the film should have had some cuts along with the "A" certificate. 9.14 percent said the film should have been given a "U" certificate with some cuts. 8 percent said that the films should have been given a clear "U" certificate and 9.14 percent were of the view that the film should have been refused a certificate. [Ibid.]

57. Ibid.

58. "Fresh Warrant on Film Star," *Poona Herald*, September 15, 1978; *Picture Post*, Oct. 1978.

59. *Raj Kapoor and Others vs. State and Others*, 1980 SCR (1) 1081; "Quick Disposal of Raj Kapoor's Plea," *The Times of India*, October 29, 1979.

60. *Raj Kapoor and Others vs. State and Others*, 1980 SCR (1) 1081.

61. *Raj Kapoor v. Laxman*, 1980 SCR (2) 512.

62. Ibid.

63. Ibid.

64. Ibid.

65. Ibid.

CHAPTER 6

1. *Pati parmeshwar's* production values were better than *Gupt gyan's*. Given Nayyar's background, his stature in the film industry would have been a notch above Adarsh's, albeit far below Raj Kapoor's.

2. During the making of *Love in Simla*, Nayyar and Sadhana fell in love; despite her mother's objections, they tied the knot six years after the film's release. For R. K. Nayyar, see http://indianfilmtrade.com/services/filmdatabase/actor_details.php?actor_id=22615; Dinesh Raheja, "Sadhana's Song," http://www.rediff.com/entertai/2002/feb/11dinesh.htmp.176. For Sadhana Shivdasani, R. K. Nayyar, Madan Joshi, Sudha Chandran, Alok Nath, and Shekhar Suman, see the entries under their individual names at www.imdb.com.

3. For a more detailed examination of the avenging woman and the action genres, see Lalitha Gopalan, *Cinema of Interruptions: Action Genres in Contemporary Indian Cinema* (London: British Film Institute, 2002); M. Madhava Prasad, *Ideology of a Hindi Film: A Historical Construction* (New Delhi: Oxford University Press, 1998);

Rajeswari Sundar Rajan, *Real and Imagined Women: Gender, Culture and Postcolonialism* (London: Routledge, 1993); Jyotika Virdi, *The Cinematic ImagiNation: Indian Popular Films as Social History* (New Brunswick, N.J.: Rutgers University Press, 2003).

4. Ashish Rajadhyaksha and Paul Willemen, "Tatineni Rama Rao," *Encyclopedia on Indian Cinema* (New Delhi: Oxford University Press, 1995), 176. An anonymous reviewer brought to my attention that "from the 1970s there had been a strong intervention from the south through producers like B. Nagi Reddy and Dasari Narayana Rao which exalted the devoted wife and domestic values."

5. Ibid.

6. Some other films of note that have a reform or self-sacrifice theme include *Gunsundari* (1927, 1934), *Dulhan wahi jo piya man bhaye* (1977), and *Main tulsi tere angan ki* (1978).

7. Geetanjali Gangoli, *Indian Feminisms: Law, Patriarchies and Violence in India* (Hampshire, U.K.: Ashgate, 2007), 70. Feminists argue that this act did not address the concerns and aspirations of women's campaigns. Rather, it bolstered state authority and enabled the state to further regulate citizens' lives.

8. Ibid., 70–71; "Code for Commercial Advertising on Doordarshan," http://www.ddindia.gov.in/Business/Commercial+And+Sales/Code+for+Commercial+Advertisements.htm.

9. Radha Kumar, *History of Doing: An Illustrated Account of Movements for Women's Rights and Feminism in India, 1800-1990* (Delhi: Kali for Women, 1993), 161, 163.

10. Ibid., 174–175.

11. Ibid., 175.

12. For further discussion on the Shah Bano and Roop Kanwar cases, see ibid., 160–181. For a more detailed examination of the historical conjuncture of feminism, Hindu nationalism, and the initial questioning of the Nehruvian paradigm, see Paola Bacchetta, *Gender in the Hindu Nation: RSS Women as Ideologues* (New Delhi: Women Unlimited, 2004); Mary E. John, "Gender and Development in India, 1970–1990s: Some Reflections on the Constitutive Role of Contexts," in *Feminism in India*, ed. Maitreyee Chaudhuri, 246-258 (New Delhi: Kali for Women and Women Unlimited, 2004); Sucheta Mazumdar, "Moving Away from a Secular Vision? Women, Nation, and the Cultural Construction of Hindu India," in *Identity Politics and Women: Cultural Reassertions and Feminisms in International Perspectives*, ed. Valentine Moghadam, 243-273 (Boulder, Colo.: Westview, 1994); Sucheta Mazumdar, "Women on the March: Right-wing Mobilization in Contemporary India," *Feminist Review* 49, no. 1 (1995): 1–28; Tanika Sarkar, *Hindu Wife, Hindu Nation: Community, Religion, and Cultural Nationalism* (Bloomington: Indiana University Press, 2001); Rajan, *Real and Imagined Women*; Susie Tharu and Tejaswini Niranjana, "Problems for a Contemporary Theory of Gender," in *Writings in South Asian History and Society*, ed. Shahid Amin and Dipesh Chakrabarty, 232-260 (New Delhi: Oxford University Press, 1996).

13. Examining committee report on *Pati parmeshwar*, October 12, 1987, *Pati parmeshwar* file, CBFCB. The official letter was sent to Nayyar on October 15, 1987.

14. Censorship Guidelines, 1983, *Pati Parmeshwar* file, CBFC.

15. In the High Court of Judicature at Bombay, Writ Petition No. 38 of 1988, the Film Federation of India & Another vs Union of India & Others, Affidavit, Anna Dani, Regional Officer, Feb. 17, 1988, *Pati parmeshwar* file, CBFCB.

16. R. K. Nayyar to the CBFC, October 20, 1987, *Pati parmeshwar* file, CBFCB.

17. Ibid.

18. Ibid.

19. Rochona Majumdar, "'Self-Sacrifice' versus 'Self-Interest': A Non-Historicist Reading of the History of Women's Rights in India," *Comparative Studies of South Asia, Africa and the Middle East* 33, nos. 1–2 (2002): 20–35.

20. Ibid.

21. R. K. Nayyar to the CBFC, October 20, 1987.

22. Communalism, Pandey writes, is "a product of colonial knowledge." This product, Bipin Chandra reminds us, presumes that a person's religious identity determines his or her social, political, and economic interests. By privileging religious identity, this concept reduces the complex formation of a person's identity into a palatable category. This form of categorization in the case of India has had significant political and social consequences, for example, the destruction of the Babri Masjid in 1992. It is therefore important to trace the construction of this concept and to situate it within a wide field. As Pandey explains, communalism "stands for the puerile and the primitive—all that colonialism in its own reckoning was not. The paradox is that the nationalists have zealously worked to corroborate this conception." Pandey indicates that the formation of communalism cannot be attributed simply to the colonizers but must be situated within a wider field if we are to contend with the rise of Hindu nationalism in India today (Gyanendra Pandey, *The Construction of Communalism in Colonial North India* [New Delhi: Oxford University Press, 1990], 6; see also Bipin Chandra, *Communalism in India* [New Delhi: Vikas, 1984]).

23. R. K. Nayyar to the CBFC, October 20, 1987.

24. Ibid.

25. In the High Court of Judicature at Bombay, Writ Petition No. 38 of 1988, the Film Federation of India & Another Vs Union of India & Others, Coram: S.C. Pratap J., June 22, 1988, *Pati parmeshwar* file, CBFCB.

26. R. K. Nayyar to the CBFC, October 20, 1987; R. K. Nayyar to the Film Certification Appellate Tribunal, October 30, 1987; In the High Court of Judicature at Bombay, Writ Petition No. 38 of 1988, the Film Federation of India & Another Vs Union of India & Others, January 6, 1988; In the High Court of Judicature at Bombay, Writ Petition No. 38 of 1988, the Film Federation of India & Another Vs Union of India & Others, Affidavit, R. K. Nayyar, February 23, 1988, all in *Pati parmeshwar* file, CBFCB.

27. Revising committee report on *Pati Parmeshwar*, October 20, 1987, *Pati parmeshwar* file, CBFCB. See Film Censorship Guidelines, 1984, *Pati parmeshwar* file, CBFCB; rule 1(c) states, "censorship is responsive to social change"; and rule 3(ii)

states a film is to be "examined in the light of contemporary standards of the country and the people to which the film related."

28. Majumdar, "'Self-Interest,'" 21.

29. Revising committee report on *Pati Parmeshwar*. These dissenting voices do not appear in the letter sent to R. K. Nayyar on October 29, 1987, informing him of the majority decision.

30. The cuts focused evenly on removing "vulgar" and "servile" images and dialogues from the film.

31. R. K. Nayyar to Film Certification Appellate Tribunal, October 30, 1987.

32. Ibid. The Cinematograph Act, 1952, Section 5-B(1), states, "A film shall not be certified for public exhibition if, in the opinion of the authority competent to grant the certificate, the film or any part of it is against the interests of the sovereignty and integrity of India, the security of the State, friendly relations with foreign States, public order, decency or morality, or involves defamation or contempt of court or is likely to incite the commission of any offence." Section 5-B(2) states, "Subject to the provisions in sub-section (1), the Central Government may issue such directions as it may think fit setting out the principles which shall guide the authority competent to grant certificates under this Act in sanctioning films for exhibition."

33. R. K. Nayyar to Film Certification Appellate Tribunal, October 30, 1987.

34. Ibid.

35. Ibid.

36. Ibid.

37. In the High Court of Judicature at Bombay, Writ Petition No. 38 of 1988, the Film Federation of India & Another Vs Union of India & Others, January 6, 1988, *Pati parmeshwar* file, CBFCB.

38. R. K. Nayyar to the CBFC, October 20, 1987.

39. Film Certification Appellate Tribunal Order, December 29, 1987, *Pati parmeshwar* file, CBFCB.

40. Ibid.

41. Ibid.

42. Prasad, *Ideology of the Hindi Film*, 46–47; Ravi Vasudevan, "The Melodramatic Mode and the Commercial Hindi Cinema," *Screen* 30 (Summer 1989): 30; Rosie Thomas, "Mythologies and Modern India," in *World Cinema since 1945*, ed. William Luhr, 301-329 (New York: Ungar, 1987), 304.

43. In the High Court of Judicature at Bombay, Writ Petition No. 38 of 1988, the Film Federation of India & Another Vs Union of India & Others, Affidavit, R. K. Nayyar, February 23, 1988, *Pati parmeshwar* file, CBFCB.

44. In the High Court of Judicature at Bombay, Writ Petition No. 1904 of 1986, Ramanlal Lalbhai Desai vs. The Central Board of Film Certification and Others India, Coram: S. M. Daud, J., January 20, 1988, *Pati parmeshwar* file, CBFCB.

45. "Proposal for amendment of the guidelines with reference to portrayal of women in films and supernaturalism," Ministry of Information and Broadcasting F (C), file no. 805/2/82-F (C), 22 March, 1982, *Pati parmeshwar* file, CBFCB.

46. Philip Lutgendorf, "*Jai Santoshi Maa* Revisited: On Seeing a Hindu 'Myth-

ological' Film," in *Representing Religion in World Cinema: Mythmaking, Culture Making, Filmmaking*, ed. S. Brent Plate, 19–42 (New York: Palgrave/St. Martin's, 2003).

47. Ibid., 27.

48. In some versions of the *Ramayana, Lakshman-rekha* refers to a line Lakshman drew around the forest dwelling he shared with his brother Rama and Rama's wife, Sita. The line was meant to protect Sita while he was away searching for Rama. In modern usage, it is viewed as a strict social boundary or limit that is crossed at one's peril. http://en.wikipedia.org/wiki/Ramacharitamanas.

49. Film Certification Appellate Tribunal Order, December 29, 1987.

50. In the High Court of Judicature at Bombay, Writ Petition No. 38 of 1988, the Film Federation of India & Another Vs Union of India & Others, January 6, 1988, *Pati parmeshwar* file, CBFCB.

51. The Film Federation of India (FFI) was formed in 1951. The apex body of the film industry, it negotiates and intervenes on behalf of members of the industry as required.

52. In the High Court of Judicature at Bombay, Writ Petition No. 38 of 1988, the Film Federation of India & Another Vs Union of India & Others, Coram: S.C. Pratap J., May 10, 1988, *Pati parmeshwar* file, CBFCB.

53. Ibid.

54. Ibid.

55. Ibid.

56. Ibid.

57. Ibid.

58. In the High Court of Judicature at Bombay, Writ Petition No. 38 of 1988, the Film Federation of India & Another Vs Union of India & Others, Coram: S. C. Pratap J., June 22, 1988, *Pati parmeshwar* file, CBFCB.

59. Ibid. The term *saubhayavati* refers to a blessing given by elders to women for a happy married life, central to which is her husband's long life.

60. Sangh Parivar refers to a family of Hindu organizations that promote Hindu nationalism. They include the Bharatiya Janata Party (BJP), Vishwa Hindu Parishad (VHP), and Rashtriya Swayamsevak Sangh (RSS).

61. In the High Court of Judicature at Bombay, Writ Petition No. 38 of 1988, the Film Federation of India & Another Vs Union of India & Others, Coram: S.C. Pratap J., May 10, 1988, *Pati parmeshwar* file, CBFCB.

62. Ibid.

63. *Pati Parmeshwar*, VCD, dir. Madan Joshi (1989) (Mumbai: Ultra Distributors, 2002). All translations are mine.

64. R. Majumdar, "'Self-Interest.'"

65. R. K. Nayyar to the CBFC, October 20, 1987.

66. I wish to thank Adam Sitze for making this point.

67. In the High Court of Judicature at Bombay, Writ Petition No. 38 of 1988, Union of India and Others Versus The Film Federation of India & Another, July 12, 1988, *Pati parmeshwar* file, CBFCB.

68. Ibid.

69. Indira Jaising and Andrea Wolfe, "The 'Ignoble Servility' of *Pati Parmeshwar* towards Equality of Women," in *Gender and Censorship*, ed. Brinda Bose, 127–137 (New Delhi: Kali for Women, 2006), 132.

70. Ibid., 130–131.

71. Gangoli, *Indian Feminisms*; Jaising and Wolfe, "'Ignoble Servility'"; Ann Stewart, "Debating Gender Justice in India," *Social and Legal Studies* 4 (1995): 253–274; Aruna Vasudev, "Women Beware Men," *Index on Censorship* 20, no. 3 (1991): 7–8. Gangoli and Stewart largely cite and repeat Jaising and Wolfe's arguments.

72. CBFC to Ministry of Law and Justice, Bombay, Ref: U.O. no. 3545, vol. 2, October 1988, *Pati parmeshwar* file, CBFCB.

73. Ajit Pillai, "Govt. Takeover of Censor Board Imminent," *Indian Post*, February 25, 1989.

74. Ibid.

75. R. K. Nayyar to the Film Certification Appellate Tribunal, October 30, 1987.

76. In the High Court of Judicature at Bombay, Writ Petition No. 38 of 1988, the Film Federation of India & Another Vs Union of India & Others, Coram: S. C. Pratap J., June 22, 1988, *Pati parmeshwar* file, CBFCB.

77. Vasudev, "Women Beware Men."

CHAPTER 7

1. On the political front during this period, the businessman Harshad Mehta accused Prime Minister Narasimha Rao of accepting Rs 10 million ($315,457) ostensibly as a "donation" to the Congress Party but actually as a bribe to help Mehta out of his legal troubles, and the newspapers were asking another equally tantalizing question: *Suitcase ke andar kya hai* (what is inside the suitcase)? This question plunged the nation into a discussion about the contents of the suitcase delivered to the prime minister. Like the song, this controversy raised concerns about morality. The prime minister stood accused of letting greed interfere with meeting his moral duty as the nation's leader. Thus, the prime minister was characterized as incompetent and nearly forced to resign to preserve the reputation of his party.

2. Within the Hindi film industry, song-and-dance sequences such as the one featuring "Choli ke peeche kya hai?" have occupied a pivotal function in both film production and narrative. Producers often spend lavishly in crafting visual feasts to entice audiences. In the 1990s such spectacles were on the rise, giving more prominence to Saroj Khan and other choreographers. Budding actors and actresses increasingly found their dancing skills being evaluated, for these performances were crucial to drawing audiences.

3. Ashish Rajadhyaksha and Paul Willemen, *Encyclopedia of Indian Cinema* (New Delhi: Oxford University Press, 1995), 87.

4. Nilanjana Bhattacharya and Monika Mehta, "From Bombay to Bollywood: Tracking Cinematic and Musical Tours," in *Global Bollywood: Travels of Hindi Song*

and Dance, ed. Sangita Gopal and Sujata Moorti, 105–131 (Minneapolis: University of Minnesota Press, 2008), 110.

5. Hindi commercial cinema frequently uses names of religious and mythical figures as signposts for its audience. The names of the characters Ram, Ballu (an abbreviation of Balram), and Ganga refer to the *Ramayana*'s dutiful Rama; to Balram, who is easily angered; and to the goddess/river Ganga, respectively. The river Ganga (the Ganges) is supposed to be pure and wash away the sins of those who take a dip in it; in fact, it is quite polluted.

6. Sumita Chakravarty's *National Identity in Popular Hindi Cinema 1947–1987* (Austin: University of Texas Press, 1993) offers a more sustained discussion and deployment of impersonation within the context of Hindi cinema.

7. Laura Mulvey, "Visual Pleasure and Narrative Cinema," in *Feminism and Film*, ed. E. Ann Kaplan, 34–47 (Oxford: Oxford University Press, 2000).

8. During the course of the song, the gang members look at Ballu uneasily, afraid that he may be too smitten by the folk dancer and that his desire for her might harm the gang.

9. Mulvey, "Visual Pleasure," 44–45.

10. *Khalnayak*, DVD, dir. Subhash Ghai (1993) (London: Eros Entertainment, 2003).

11. Ibid.

12. Mulvey, "Visual Pleasure," 39–40.

13. Lalitha Gopalan, *Cinema of Interruptions: Action Genres in Contemporary Indian Cinema* (London: British Film Institute, 2002). I am indebted to Gopalan's theorization of the intermission/interval, on which I rely in this chapter and elsewhere.

14. Ibid., 70.

15. I am drawing on an innovative description of the "classic scripting theory of a Hindi film" offered by Prem Panicker, who writes, "First, put a man up a tree. Then throw things at him. Then get him down off the tree, and let the audience go home. In other words, the three-act structure of a movie is: Create the problem/conflict, escalate the problem, resolve the problem" (Prem Panicker "The Second Coming," *Rediff*, September 7, 2000, http://www.rediff.com/entertai/2000/sep/07fiza.htm).

16. Research on the function of parody in the context of gendered representation of state and criminality would likely be worthwhile. In addition to constructing female desire and sexuality as a problem, the first half of the film posits criminality, too, as a problem. By singing the song, Ganga, a police officer, hopes to join the gang and capture the villain. But why represent the state as an alluring, sexy woman? Furthermore, to the extent that the first half of the film poses criminality as a "problem," how does the second half of the film resolve this problem? More specifically, how does the song figure into this resolution? In the process of parodying the earlier performance, Ballu and his gang slip into both a visible feminine identity by wearing *ghaghras* and *dupattas* and the invisible garb of the state. How does one understand this parody of the state? By not sexualizing the bodies of criminals, is the song suggesting that criminality is not sexy? Is the song also defusing the threat posed

by criminality in the second rendition? Certainly the ending of the film, in which Ballu surrenders to the state, suggests that it is the state and not criminality that is alluring.

17. See Elena del Rio, *Deleuze and the Cinemas of Performance: Powers of Affection* (Edinburgh: Edinburgh University Press, 2009), for a compelling critique of Mulvey's use of the spectacle.

18. Mulvey, "Visual Pleasure," 41.

19. Ibid., 40.

20. Del Rio, *Deleuze*, 32.

21. Mulvey, "Visual Pleasure," 40.

22. Kaja Silverman, *The Acoustic Mirror: The Female Voice in Psychoanalysis and Cinema* (Bloomington: Indiana University Press, 1988), 164.

23. Elena del Rio makes a similar argument in her work *Deleuze and the Cinemas of Performance*.

24. For the most part, the director is formally in charge in Hindi film production, but segments involving action and choreography are put together by experts in those fields.

25. The rise of the film song in the 1930s in India coincided with the advent of the sound in film. The film industry realized it had access to technology that would allow it to reproduce songs; thus, it would have access to larger markets and greater profits. Therefore, classical songs such as *ghazals* were restructured to match the new medium. In Indian classical music musicians improvise, altering both melodies and tempos depending on the context, but the medium of the film demands uniformity, reproducibility, and repeatability to sell this product at a centralized scale. Through the wide reach of radio and phonograph recordings, film songs rapidly displaced both classical and folk music in popular culture. Thus the film song is linked to the project of building a modern nation-state. As the "traditional" folk song is linked to the "community," the modern form of popular Indian culture, the film song, is associated with the nation. In fact, the success of a popular film was (and is) largely connected to the popularity of its music, which was (and is) played on radios, phonographs, and tape players months before the film itself is released. See Bhaskar Chandravarkar, "Indian Film Song," in *Seventy Years of Indian Cinema (1913–1983)*, ed. T. M. Ramachandran, 244–251 (Bombay: CINEMA India-International, 1983); Sanjeev Prakash, "Music, Dance and the Popular Film: Indian Fantasies, Indian Repressions," in *Indian Cinema Superbazaar*, ed. Philippe Lenglet and Aruna Vasudev, 114–118 (New Delhi: Vikas, 1983); M. A. Mannan, "Hitting the Right Notes," *India Today*, November 30, 1993, 50–53.

26. Bhattacharyja and Mehta, "From Bombay to Bollywood," 110.

27. Pandit Gautam Kaul to Shri Bhargava, May 19, 1993.

28. Shakti Samanta to Shri Brij Sethi, June 25, 1993, *Khalnayak* file, CBFCB. Shakti Samanta, then the CBFC chair, was sent Pandit Gautam Kaul's remarks and suggestions but refused to consider them, citing the board's functions as outlined in the Cinematograph Act of 1952 in support of his action. In his response, he stressed

that the CBFC's sole task was to review films for the purpose of certification for public exhibition; it was not asked to attend to film financing or audio certification practices.

29. This piece of information becomes significant in the light of letters received by various Bharatiya Janata Party (BJP) wings in support of Chugh's petition.

30. R. P. Chugh, legal notice sent to Subhash Ghai, Tips Cassettes and Records Company, Central Board of Film Certification, minister of information and broadcasting, and director of Doordarshsan, June 4, 1993, *Khalnayak* file, CBFCB.

31. See Legal Petition, August 3, 1993, filed in court by Subhash Ghai and Mukta Arts in the court of Brijesh Sethi, subjudge, Delhi, *Khalnayak* file, CBFCB.

32. Usha Rai, "Censor Board for Ending Denigration of Ministers, Officials in Films," *Indian Express*, July 3, 1994.

33. The committees certify films as well as their trailers. With the advent of satellite television, the trailers did not require certification from the state for exhibition on privately owned channels. They did, however, require certification for exhibition in theaters and on state-run television.

34. As Shohini Ghosh and Ratna Kapur have astutely pointed out, the efforts of feminists and the BJP to prohibit screenings of "vulgar" songs such as "Choli ke peeche kya hai?" sometimes overlapped; they themselves, however, argue for more "speech" rather than prohibition. See Shohini Ghosh and Ratna Kapur, "The Violence of Censoring," in *Gender and Censorship*, ed. Brinda Bose, 94-98 (New Delhi: Women Unlimited, 2006); Shohini Ghosh, "The Troubled Existence of Sex and Sexuality: Feminists Engage with Censorship," in *Image Journeys: Audio-Visual Media and Cultural Change in India*, ed. Christiane Brosius and Melissa Butcher, 233–260 (New Delhi: Sage, 1999); Ratna Kapur, "Who Draws the Line? Feminist Reflections on Speech and Censorship?" *Economic and Political Weekly* 31, nos. 16–17 (Apr. 20, 1996): WS 15–WS 30. For works focusing on the interventions of the Bharatiya Janata Party in the media, see Nandana Bose, "Between the Godfather and the Mafia: Situating Right-Wing Interventions in the Bombay Film Industry (2002)," *Journal of South Asian Film and Media* 1, no. 1 (2009): 23–43; Nandana Bose, "The Hindu Right and the Politics of Censorship: Three Case Studies Policing Hindi Cinema, 1992–2002," *Velvet Light Trap* 63 (Spring 2009): 22–33; Ratna Kapur, "Cultural Politics of *Fire*," *Economic and Political Weekly* 34, no. 21 (May 28, 1999): 1297–1299; Mary E. John and Tejaswini Niranjana, "Mirror Politics: *Fire*, Hindutva and Indian Culture," *Economic and Political Weekly* 34, nos. 10–11 (Mar. 12, 1999): 581–585; Julie Marsh and Howard Brasted, "*Fire*, the BJP and Moral Society," in *Hindu Nationalism and Governance*, ed. John McGuire and Ian Copland, 283–302 (New Delhi: Oxford University Press, 2007); Edwina Mason, "The *Water* Controversy and the Politics of Hindu Nationalism," in *Hindu Nationalism and Governance*, ed. McGuire and Copland, 303–315; Arvind Rajagopal, *Politics after Television: Hindu Nationalism and the Reshaping of the Public in India* (Cambridge: Cambridge University Press, 2001); Carol Upadhya, "Set This House on Fire," *Economic and Political Weekly* 33, no. 50 (Dec. 12, 1998): 3176–3177.

35. President of the Women's Wing of BJP to female members of Parliament, July 25, 1993, *Khalnayak* file, CBFCB.

36. Shankar Chugh to the union minister of information and broadcasting, New Delhi, 25 July 1993, *Khalnayak* file, CBFCB. The translations are mine.

37. The legal procedure under which the case could be filed was the Consumer Protection Act.

38. See the legal petition filed by Vineet Kumar, *Khalnayak* file, CBFCB. The outcome of the petition was unavailable.

39. Ashok Kumar to Shakti Samanta, April 30, 1993, *Khalnayak* file, CBFCB. My translation from Hindi.

40. Mrs. Rama Gupta to Shakti Samanta, April 27, 1993, *Khalnayak* file, CBFCB. My translation from Hindi.

41. Shweta Sanjay to Shakti Samanta, April 4, 1993, *Khalnayak* file, CBFCB.

42. Paras Cinema (Jaipur, Rajasthan) to Shakti Samanta, May 12, 1993, *Khalnayak* file, CBFCB. This text was repeated almost verbatim in Bharat Talkies (Chomu, Jaipur) to Shakti Samanta, May 12, 1993, and Preeti Palace (Anupgarh, District Sriganganagar) to Shakti Samanta, May 8, 1993, both in *Khalnayak* file, CBFCB.

43. Rajesh Talkies (Ramganj, Rajasthan) to Shakti Samanta, May 10, 1993, *Khalnayak* file, CBFCB. The delicious Freudian slips in this letter include misspelling the song title as "Choli Ke Peeche Kiya Hai," which means "I've done it behind the veil," and forgetting to include the crucial "not" in the sentence "If the song was vulgor than the ladies would like the song."

44. Arun Katiyar, "Obscene Overtures," *India Today*, January 15, 1994, 158.

45. S. Nayyar to Shakti Samanta, May 12, 1993, *Khalnayak* file, CBFCB.

46. Director of Nirman Theatre to Shakti Samanta, May 7, 1993.

47. Cine Darshak Vichar Manch (Muzzafarpur, Bihar) to chairperson of CBFC, May 24, 1993, *Khalnayak* file, CBFCB.

48. *The Cinematograph Act, 1952*. See Appendix A for a list of film censorship guidelines.

49. Examining committee report on *Khalnayak*, 1993, *Khalnayak* file, CBFCB.

50. Ibid.

51. Mannan, "Hitting the Right Notes," 51–53.

52. Saibal Chatterjee, "Strange Objects of Desire," *The Sunday Times of India*, January 2, 1994, 13. Following the fiscal success of "Choli ke peeche kya hai," a series of similar songs were produced to cash in on the current fad. According to one estimate, songs with the word *choli* in them or those boasting Ghai's rustic melody could have collectively sold about 1.45 million tapes. Sawan Kumar's *Khal-naaikaa* (The villainess), Mohan Prasad's *Dosti ki saugandh* (On the honor of friendship), and Ajay Kashyap's *Pathrila rasta* (A rocky path) all feature a *choli* song. See Arun Katiyar, "The Choli Craze: Raunchy Rhymes," *India Today*, July 31, 1993, 107.

53. I am drawing on Kuhn's discussion of the construction of controversy. See Annette Kuhn, *Cinema, Censorship, and Sexuality 1909–1925* (New York: Routledge, 1988), 96.

54. Gopalan, *Cinema of Interruptions*, 69.

55. I focus on middle-class women and urban India simply because of my familiarity with both.

56. I am drawing on the film entitled *Memories of Fear* and the discussion that took place after this film's screening at a film appreciation course at the National Film Archive that I attended in June 1996. Also see Jyoti Puri, *Woman, Body, Desire in Post-colonial India: Narratives of Gender and Sexuality* (New York: Routledge, 1999). Chandan Arora's *Main Madhuri Dixit banna chahti hoon* (2003) effectively captures this "Madhuri-philia"; this film is an homage to Madhuri that explicitly cites her as an example of female agency—the film's female character, a Madhuri fan, finds in the actress and dancer the inspiration to pursue her own dreams.

57. In contrast, identification with either Aman, Gupta, or Arun would be more difficult given their star personas.

58. Janice Radway, *Reading the Romance: Women, Patriarchy, and Popular Literature* (Chapel Hill: University of North Carolina Press, 1984), 17.

59. Ibid., 17–18.

60. Gertrud Koch, "The Body's Shadow Realm," in *Dirty Looks: Women, Pornography, Power*, ed. Pamela Church Gibson and Roma Gibson, 22–45 (London: British Film Institute, 1993), 36.

CHAPTER 8

1. "DDLJ Completes Continuous Run of 700 Weeks," Yash Raj Films, http://www.yashrajfilms.com/ (available by searching the web site under the film's title). The film won the following *Filmfare* Awards. Best Film: Yash Chopra (producer); Best Director: Aditya Chopra; Best Actor: Shah Rukh Khan; Best Actress: Kajol; Best Supporting Actress: Farida Jalal; Best Comedian: Anupam Kher; Best Lyricist: Anand Bakshi ("Tujhe dekha to"); Best Playback Singer (male): Udit Narayan ("Mehndi Lagake rakhna"); Best Dialogue Writer: Aditya Chopra/Javed Siddiqui; Best Screenplay Writer: Aditya Chopra.

2. "Highlights of *Filmfare* Awards," *Dilwale dulhania le jayenge*, DVD (Mumbai: Yash Raj Films, 2002).

3. "DDLJ Completes Continuous Run."

4. "DDLJ Completes 750 Weeks," *Indian Express*, February 27, 2010. On-line blogs and articles suggest that in the past few years, the number of viewers who watch the film has dwindled considerably; some say that at times the only viewers are the theater's security guards or projectionists. Despite this, the film continues to play at the theater because of the low rental cost and the cheaply priced tickets, which make exhibitors and audiences happy. Because of this continued exhibition, the Chopras accrue cultural capital.

5. Rajeev Masand, "City Keeps Romance with DDLJ Alive," *Indian Express*, March 6, 2000, *http://www.expressindia.com/bin/click/clickthru/ie_story_topstp3*. Film revenues in India depend a great deal on a film's "repeat value," that is, the number of times viewers go to see the film.

6. See, among other works, Philip Lutgendorf, "Hum Aapke Hain Kaoun," Iowa University, http://www.uiowa.edu/~incinema/humaapke.html (accessed Nov. 24, 2009); Purnima Mankekar, "Brides Who Travel: Gender, Transnationalism, and Nationalism in Hindi Film," *Positions* 7, no. 3 (1999): 731–762; Vijay Mishra, *Bollywood Cinema: Temples of Desire* (New York: Routledge, 2002); Jenny Sharpe, "Gender, Nation, and Globalization in *Monsoon Wedding* and *Dilwale Dulhania Le Jayenge*," *Meridians: Feminism, Race, Transnationalism* 6, no. 1 (2005): 58–81.; Patricia Uberoi, "The Diaspora Comes Home: Disciplining Desire in *DDLJ*," *Contributions to Indian Sociology* 32, no. 2 (1998): 305–336; Jyotika Virdi, *The Cinematic ImagiNation* (New Brunswick, N.J.: Rutgers University Press, 2003).

7. Lutgendorf, "Hum Aapke Hain Koun." Many other scholars have also emphasized the happy marriage of tradition and modern in *Dilwale dulhania le jayenge*; see, among other works, Anupama Chopra, *Dilwale Dulhania Le Jayenge* (London: British Film Institute, 2002); Jigna Desai, *Beyond Bollywood: The Cultural Politics of South Asian Diasporic Film* (New York: Routledge, 2004); Mankekar, "Brides Who Travel"; Mishra, *Bollywood Cinema*; Sharpe, "Gender, Nation, and Globalization"; Uberoi, "The Diaspora Comes Home"; Virdi, *Cinematic ImagiNation*.

8. Monika Mehta, "Globalizing Bombay Cinema: Reproducing the Indian State and Family," *Cultural Dynamics* 17, no. 2 (2005): 135–154.

9. Examining committee report on *Dilwale dulhania le jayenge*, 1995, DDLJ file, CBFCB.

10. Ibid.

11. *The Cinematograph Act of 1952 (37 of 1952) and Censorship Guidelines* (New Delhi: Rakesh, 1992), 67.

12. Examining committee report on *Dilwale dulhania le jayenge*, 1995. The summary's concluding sentence misrepresents the film's ending. The reason Baldev finally allows Simran to go with Raj is because he realizes that Raj is worthy of this daughter, that he is a Hindustani. The misreading does accord a value to Simran's love that is not present in this sequence.

13. In a scene deleted from the film, Raj explains to Kuljeet the value of "emotion" versus "action" in winning women's affections.

14. While intertexuality in India was not a new phenomenon in the 1990s, this phenomenon increased considerably. For example, titles of films are constructed from past film songs, music scores include phrases from past music scores, and dialogue and lyrics include references to past films. These prolific references demand from the spectators a level of pop literacy.

15. Yash Chopra won his first Best Director *Filmfare* award for *Waqt*.

16. Yash Chopra's stature and reputation made this journey relatively easy for Aditya Chopra. For more detailed work on Yash Chopra, see Rachel Dwyer, *Yash Chopra* (London: British Film Institute, 2002).

17. "Success Story," *Dilwale dulhania le jayenge*, DVD.

18. Ibid.

19. Immigrants from the Indian state of Punjab have been important contributors to the Bombay film industry.

20. The question of language is interesting here, for Hindi is India's official language, not Punjab's. Following the Partition, however, many Punjabis claimed Hindi rather than Punjabi to be their mother tongue. In doing so, they distinguished themselves from both Muslim and Sikh Punjabis. Language in this case was linked to religion: Urdu for Muslims, Hindi for Hindus, and Punjabi for Sikhs. For a compelling study on India's Partition and Indian cinema, see Bhaskar Sarkar, *Mourning the Nation: Indian Cinema in the Wake of Partition* (Durham, N.C.: Duke University Press, 2009).

21. *Dilwale dulhania le jayenge*, dir. Aditya Chopra, 1995. All quotations from this film come from the 2002 DVD; the transcriptions and translations are mine.

22. In this scene, Simran at first refuses to drink alcohol and scolds Raj for drinking in front of a woman. Presumably, Indian women do not drink. In commercial films this theme is a device for distinguishing the "vamp," the "Western" or "Westernized" woman, from the "Indian" woman.

23. *Hindustani* is commonly translated as "Indian." More specifically, the word refers to a person who lives in Hindustan, namely, the place of Hindus.

24. Mankekar, "Brides Who Travel," 753–754.

25. Chopra, *Dilwale Dulhania Le Jayenge*, 48.

26. *The Making of Dilwale Dulhania Le Jayenge*, dir. Karan Johar and Uday Chopra, included in the *Dilwale dulhania le jayenge* DVD; as with the film itself, all quotations from the documentary come from the 2002 DVD, and all transcriptions and translations are my own.

27. I discuss the interview with Farida Jalal later in the chapter.

28. In her monograph *Dilwale Dulhania Le Jayenge* Anupama Chopra tells us that it took forty takes.

29. Ibid.

30. A detailed analysis of Hindi cinema and questions of diaspora and transnationalism falls beyond the scope of this chapter. For compelling arguments on these issues, see, among other works, Jigna Desai, "Bollywood Abroad: South Asian Diasporic Cosmopolitanism and Indian Cinema," in *New Cosmopolitanisms: South Asians in the US*, ed. Gita Rajan and Shailja Sharma, 115–137 (Stanford, Calif.: Stanford University Press, 2006); Jigna Desai, "Planet Bollywood: Indian Cinema in Asian America," in *East Main Street: Asian American Popular Culture*, ed. Shilpa Davé, LeiLani Nishime, and Tasha Oren, 55–71 (New York: NYU Press, 2005); Gayatri Gopinath, *Impossible Desires: Queer Diasporas and South Asian Public Cultures* (Durham, N.C.: Duke University Press, 2005); Mankekar, "Brides Who Travel."

31. Shah Rukh Khan interview by Uday Chopra, "Interviews," *Dilwale dulhania le jayenge* DVD.

32. The window that serves as the backdrop for this conversation echoes an earlier moment in the narrative when Simran is singing and dreaming about her unseen lover near a window.

33. Christian Metz, "The Impersonal Enunciation, or the Site of Film," in *The Film Spectator: From Sign to Mind*, ed. Warren Buckland, 140–163 (Amsterdam: Amsterdam University Press, 1995).

34. Chopra, *Dilwale Dulhania Le Jayenge*, 63.

35. Shah Rukh Khan interview.

36. In the film, Raj sets up Kuljeet's accidents and then "saves" him. When Kuljeet asks what he is doing in the area, Raj states that he is scouting locations for a Stroh's Beer factory.

37. Chopra, *Dilwale Dulhania Le Jayenge*, 77–79.

38. Ibid., 36. According to Anupama Chopra, in order to persuade Shah Rukh Khan to play Raj, Aditya Chopra passionately argued that Khan would "never achieve superstar status unless he was every woman's dream man and every mother's dream son." Following *Dilwale dulhania le jayenge*, Khan did become a superstar; he is deeply indebted to his ardent female fans for this status, a fact he clearly recognizes given his constant loving and respectful references in interviews to women in general and to his wife and mother in particular.

39. Ibid., 76.

40. Jitesh Pillai, "Shah Rukh Best Actor," *Filmfare*, April 1996.

41. Shah Rukh Khan interview.

42. Regulations requiring certification for "compact discs" (i.e., VCDs), which also later applied to DVDs, were introduced in 1997.

43. Mostly, the deleted scenes on the DVD follow the order in which they would have appeared in the film, enabling cinephiles to mentally insert a scene in its proper place if they wish to do so.

44. "Deleted Scenes," *Dilwale dulhania le jayenge* DVD.

45. A delicious coda to *DDLJ* appears in *Heyy Babyy* (2007), where we learn that from Raj's father that Simran has run away, so that he's seeking a new bride for his son.

46. Chopra, *Dilwale Dulhania Le Jayenge*, 47.

47. K. L. Khandpur, "Compulsory Screening of Documentaries in India," in *Seventy Years of Indian Cinema (1913–1983)*, ed. T. M. Ramachandran, 505–511 (Bombay: CINEMA India-International, 1985), 507. The national government adopted the colonial policy of "compulsory exhibition" ostensibly to mitigate commercial cinema's pernicious influence and to promote "development." This policy forced cinema houses to pay for and show "approved" documentary films and newsreels made by the Films Division before screening a main feature film. The colonial state introduced compulsory exhibition during World War II to boost the war effort and to gain assistance of colonial subjects. After independence, the postcolonial state retained the policy to project national programs and policies via this medium. Khandpur argues that compulsory exhibition in India was productive, for it led to the growth of documentary films in India that otherwise would not have been produced, much less screened.

48. Chopra, *Dilwale Dulhania Le Jayenge*, 9.

CHAPTER 9

1. I did not have access to the examining committee's report, but an interview available on the Internet suggests that the committee members had objected to some

nude scenes. See I. C. Jagan, "Dev Anand's Censor Problems," *Bollywood World*, January 28, 2001, http://www.bollywoodworld.com/interviews/yo129.shtml.

2. While Shiv Sena, as well as its offshoot, Maharashtra Navnirman Sena, has received a lot of attention from both the media and scholars for their coercive tactics, it would be useful to examine more generally the rising role of community in debates on censorship. For example, in the case of *Singh Is Kinng* (2008), Vipul Shah screened his film for the Sikh community in order to ensure that it did not offend them and to obtain their stamp of approval. In 2007 the Utter Pradesh chief minister led the charge against the use of the allegedly derogatory term *mochi* (shoemaker) in *Aaja nachle* (2007), claiming that it demeaned the lower castes and hurt the feelings of Dalits; the film was banned for a period in both Utter Pradesh and Punjab. In the case of *Billu barber* (2009), the Salon and Beauty Parlour Association were up in arms about the use of the word *barber* in the title, claiming it to be demeaning. To appease them, the producer-actor Shah Rukh Khan dropped the name from the title. In pursuing this line of inquiry, one might consider the following questions: How and why have communities and political groups assumed such authority at this historical juncture? What impact does this rise in authority have on state censorship? Does the state-issued certificate no longer have any value, as many producers lament?

3. The film publicity sought to promote friendly relations between India and Pakistan by noting that the well-known Pakistani playback singers Shafqat Amanat Ali and Rahat Fateh Ali Khan were included on the soundtrack and that its cast boasted Sonya Jehan, the granddaughter of the famed playback singer and film star of yesteryear Noor Jehan.

4. Baradwaj Rangan makes this astute observation in his review of *My Name Is Khan*. See Rangan, "Review of *My Name Is Khan*," dir. Karan Johar, *Biological Conclusion*, http://baradwajrangan.wordpress.com/2010/02/13/review-my-name-is-khan/.

5. Parag Maniar, "Aamir Bashir Denied Visa," *Mumbai Mirror*, December 23, 2008, http://www.mumbaimirror.com/index.aspx?Page=article&sectname=Entertainment%20-%20Bollywood&sectid=30&contentid=20081223200812230220385533f1bbed4b (accessed June 4, 2010).

6. Subhash Jha, "KJo Denied Permission to Shoot in LA Mosque," *Mumbai News*, http://www.mid-day.com/news/2009/apr/250409-Mumbai-News-Karan-Johar-LA-mosque-Denied-Permission-Shahrukh-Khan-Kajol-My-Name-is-Khan.htm (accessed June 4, 2010).

7. Sarah Gordon, "Airport Denies Shah Rukh Khan's Body Scanner Image Was Printed for Autographs," *Daily Mail*, February 10, 2010, http://www.dailymail.co.uk/travel/article-1249929/Shah-Rukh-Khans-body-scanner-image-printed-says-Heathrow-Airport.html (accessed June 4, 2010).

8. Priyal Sanghavi, "My Name Is Khan and I Am an Indian," *Open Democracy*, February 11, 2010, http://www.opendemocracy.net/openindia/priyal-sanghavi/my-name-is-khan-and-i-am-indian (accessed June 4, 2010). Johar even wondered whether it would be best to delay the film's release; however, Fox thought otherwise.

9. "My Name Is Khan Rated a Social with a 'UA' Certificate," http://www.planet bollywood.com/displayArticle.php?id=n020910112013 (accessed June, 4, 2010).

10. In February, when *MNIK* released, I did not have access to the aural deletions demanded by the CBFC. Several months later, when I found that the CBFC web site had been relaunched, I did a search for *My Name Is Khan* and found the following, "[d]eleted the word 'Khol ke' (Replaced with approved word 'Salaa': Sound only)." This deletion is ripe for interpretation given that the seemingly innocuous *Khol ke* ("to open" or "after opening") has been replaced by the "approved word" *Salaa*, potentially an expletive. Clearly, context would be crucial for understanding the deletion. See the Central Board of Film Certification web site, <http://cbfc india.gov.in/html/uniquepage.aspx?va=my%20name%20is%20khan&Type=search> (accessed November 19, 2010).

11. Ironically, in a continued effort to avoid the imposition of state censorship, the BBFC mimics (and goes much beyond) a state bureaucratic precision. To view the classifications for *MNIK*, one can do a search for "My Name is Khan" on the British Board of Film Classification web site, *www.bbfc.co.uk (accessed June 11, 2010).*

12. Many of the positive reviews are collected on the *My Name Is Khan* web site and form a part of its ongoing publicity; see http://www.mynameiskhanthe film.com/. For more reviews and responses, see http://www.allbollywood.com/ab /movies/2010/1239/my_name_is_khan/, as well as the archives of satyamshot.word press.com, www.naachgaana.com, and www.indianauteur.com.

13. A film can see its shelf life reduced by piracy; audience comments on the Internet, in print, and on television; and film reviews. Johar stated that the film's serious topic stripped it of repeat value. The lack of repeat viewers decreased its box-office earnings.

14. For an innovative and well-written account of DVD censorship in the United States, see Caetlin Benson-Allot, "Sex versus the Small Screen: Home Video Censorship and Alfonso Cuarón's *Y tu mamá también*" *Jump Cut* 51 (2009), http://www .ejumpcut.org/archive/jc51.2009/tuMamaTambien/index.html (accessed June 22, 2010).

15. John Caldwell offers a useful taxonomy for understanding bonus features on DVDs; see John Caldwell, *Production Culture: Industrial Reflexivity and Critical Practice in Film and Television* (Durham, N.C.: Duke University Press, 2008), Appendix 2, 362–367.

16. "*My Name Is Khan*'s New Avatar to Open in U.S. Big Time," Rediff, May 5, 2010, http://movies.rediff.com/report/2010/may/05/fox-opens-my-name-is-khan-to-main stream-america.htm (accessed June 4, 2010). The "international director's cut" of *MNIK* premiered at the Indian Film Festival of Los Angeles on April 24, 2010.

17. This version was not successful and was removed from theaters within a couple of weeks.

18. A friend who was fortunate enough to view both versions told me that the Wilhelmina sequence had been cut entirely from this version.

19. "*My Name Is Khan*'s New Avatar." In his interviews, Johar suggested that Fox would be producing an "art-house" version of *My Name Is Khan*.

SELECTED BIBLIOGRAPHY

PUBLISHED SOURCES

Books and Articles

Abbas, K. A. *I Am Not an Island*. New Delhi: Vikas, 1977.

Ahmed, Rauf. "Raj Kapoor: Between Hope and Despair." *Super*, May 1978, 15.

Akoijam, Sunita. "Chopsticks in Manipur." *Himal South Asian*, September 2009. http://www.himalmag.com/himaledition=2009-09-01.

Alternative Law Forum. "Comments on Draft Cinematograph Act, 2010." http://www.altlawforum.org/law-and-media/campaigns/cinematograph-act-final%20 submission.doc/view. Accessed August 7, 2010.

Altman, Rick, ed. *Sound Theory and Sound Practice*. New York: Routledge, 1992.

Anderson, Benedict. *Imagined Communities*. New York: Verso, 1992.

Appignanesi, Lisa, and Sara Maitland, eds. *The Rushdie File*. Syracuse, N.Y.: Syracuse University Press, 1990.

Arendt, Hannah. *Eichmann in Jerusalem: A Report on the Banality of Evil*. New York: Viking, 1965.

Ariyal, Mallika. "Official Arbiters." *Himal South Asian*, September 2009. http://www.himalmag.com/himaledition=2009-09-01.

Arora, Poonam. "'Imperiling the Prestige of the White Woman': Colonial Anxiety and Film Censorship in British India." *Visual Anthropology Review* 11, no. 2 (Fall 1995): 36–50.

Awasthy, G. C. *Broadcasting in India*. Bombay: Allied, 1965.

Bacchetta, Paola. *Gender in the Hindu Nation: RSS Women as Ideologues*. New Delhi: Women Unlimited, 2004.

Banerjee, Shampa. *Profiles: Five Film-makers from India*. New Delhi: National Film Heritage, 1985.

Banerjee, Sumanta. *Family Planning Communication: A Critique of the Indian Programme*. New Delhi: Radiant, 1979.

"Banned, Banned and Banned Again!" *Queer India*, May 19, 2006. http://queer

india.blogspot.com/2006/05/banned-banned-and-banned-again.html. Accessed August 14, 2010.

Barnouw, Erik, and S. Krishnaswamy. *Indian Film*. 2d ed. New Delhi: Oxford University Press, 1980.

Barrier, N. Gerald. *Banned: Controversial Literature and Political Control in British India, 1907–1947*. Columbia: University of Missouri Press, 1974.

Benson-Allot, Caetlin. "Sex versus the Small Screen: Home Video Censorship and Alfonso Cuarón's Y tu mamá también." *Jump Cut* 51 (2009). http://www.ejump cut.org/archive/jc51.2009/tuMamaTambien/index.html. Accessed June 22, 2010.

Bhabha, Homi, ed. *Nation and Narration*. New York: Routledge, 1991.

Bharatan, Raju. *Lata Mangeshkar: A Biography*. New Delhi: UBSPD, 1995.

Bhaskaran, Theodore S., ed. *The Message Bearers: The Nationalist Politics and the Entertainment Media in South India, 1880–1945*. Chennai: Cre-A, 1981.

Bhatt, Mahesh. "Sex in Indian Cinema: Only Bad People Do It." In *Uncertain Liaisons: Sex, Strife and Togetherness in Urban India*, edited by Shobha De and Khuswant Singh, 109-126. New Delhi: Penguin, 1993.

Bhattacharya, Nilanjana, and Monika Mehta. "From Bombay to Bollywood: Tracking Cinematic and Musical Tours." In *Global Bollywood: Travels of Hindi Song and Dance*, edited by Sangita Gopal and Sujata Moorti, 105–131. Minneapolis: University of Minnesota Press, 2008.

Bhowmik, Someswar. *Cinema and Censorship: The Politics of Control in India*. New Delhi: Orient Longman, 2009.

Biswas, Shampa "Deconstructing the 'New Cold War': Religious Nationalisms, Orientalism and Postcoloniality". In *Power, Postcolonialism and International Relations: Reading Race, Gender and Class*, edited by Geeta Chowdhury and Sheila Nair, 184-208. New York: Routledge, 2002.

———. "W(h)ither the Nation State? National and State Identity in the Face of Fragmentation and Globalization." *Global Society* 16, no. 2 (Apr. 2002): 175-198.

Bose, Brinda, ed. *Gender and Censorship*. New Delhi: Women Unlimited, 2006.

Bose, Brinda, and Subhabrata Bhattacharyya, eds. *The Phobic and the Erotic: The Politics of Sexualities in Contemporary India*. London: Seagull, 2007.

Bose, Nandana. "Between the Godfather and the Mafia: Situating Right-Wing Interventions in the Bombay Film Industry (2002)." *Journal of South Asian Film and Media* 1, no. 1 (2009): 23–43.

———. "The Hindu Right and the Politics of Censorship: Three Case Studies Policing Hindi Cinema, 1992–2002." *Velvet Light Trap* 63 (Spring 2009): 22–33.

Boyd, Bruce Michael. "Film Censorship in India: A Reasonable Restriction on Freedom of Speech and Expression." *Journal of Indian Law Institute* 14, no. 4 (1972): 501-562.

Bradeanu, Adina, and Rosie Thomas. "Indian Summer, Romanian Winter: A 'Procession of Memories' in Post-Communist Romania." *South Asian Popular Culture* 4, no. 2 (Oct. 2006): 141–146.

Brass, Paul R. *Politics of India since Independence*. Cambridge: Cambridge University Press, 1994.

Brennan, Timothy. *Salman Rushdie and the Third World: Myths of a Nation*. London: Macmillan, 1989.

Brosius, Christiane, and Melissa Butcher, eds. *Image Journeys: Audio-Visual Media and Cultural Change in India*. New Delhi: Sage, 1999.

Butalia, Urvashi. "Community, State and Gender: On Women's Agency during Partition." *Economic and Political Weekly* 28, no. 17 (Apr. 24, 1993): WS 12–WS 24.

Butters, Gerald R., Jr. *Banned in Kansas: Motion Picture Censorship, 1915–1966*. Columbia: University of Missouri Press, 2007.

Caldwell, John. *Production Culture: Industrial Reflexivity and Critical Practice in Film and Television*. Durham, N.C.: Duke University Press, 2008.

Censored. Himal South Asian, September 2009. http://www.himalmag.com/himaledition=2009-09-01.

Chakravarty, Sumita. *National Identity in Indian Popular Cinema 1947–1987*. Austin: University of Texas Press, 1993.

Chandravarkar, Bhaskar. "Indian Film Song." In *Seventy Years of Indian Cinema (1913–1983)*, edited by T. M. Ramachandran, 244-251. Bombay: CINEMA India-International, 1983.

Chatterjee, Gayatri. *Awara*. New Delhi: Wiley Eastern, 1992.

Chatterjee, Partha. "The Nationalist Resolution of the Women's Question." In *Recasting Women: Essays in Indian Colonial History*, edited by Kumkum Sangari and Sudesh Vaid, 233–253. New Delhi: Kali for Women, 1989.

———. *Nationalist Thought and the Colonial World: A Derivative Discourse?* London: Zed, 1986.

———. *The Nation and Its Fragments: Colonial and Postcolonial Histories*. Princeton, N.J.: Princeton University Press, 1993.

———. "When Melody Ruled the Day." In "Frames of Mind: Reflections on Indian Cinema," edited by Aruna Vasudev. Special issue, *New Horizons* 44, no. 1 (1995): 51–68.

Chaubal, Devyani. "The RK Woman." *Star and Style*, August 16–29, 1985, 20–26.

Chaudhuri, Nupur, and Ruth Roach Pierson, eds. *Nation, Empire, and Colony: Historicizing Gender and Race*. Bloomington: Indiana University Press, 1998.

Chion, Michel. *Audio-Vision, Sound on Screen*. Translated by Claudia Gorbman. New York: Columbia University Press, 1993.

———. *The Voice in Cinema*. Edited and translated by Claudia Gorbman. New York: Columbia University Press, 1999.

Chopra, Anupama. *Dilwale Dulhania Le Jayenge*. London: British Film Institute, 2002.

———. *King of Bollywood: Shah Rukh Khan and the Seductive World of Indian Cinema*. New York: Warner, 2007.

———. *Sholay: The Making of a Classic*. New Delhi: Penguin, 2000.

Chowdhry, Prem. *Colonial India and the Making of Empire Cinema: Image, Ideology, and Identity*. Manchester, U.K.: Manchester University Press, 2000.

Clark, Randall. *At a Theater or Drive-in Near You: The History, Culture, and Politics of the American Exploitation Film*. New York: Garland, 1995.

Cronin, Theresa. "Media Effects and the Subjectification of Film Regulation." *Velvet Light Trap* 63 (Spring 2009): 3–21.

Das, Veena. "The Mythological Film and Its Framework of Meaning: An Analysis of *Jai Santoshi Ma*." *India International Centre Quarterly* 8, no. 1 (1981): 53–56.

Das Gupta, Chidananda. *The Painted Face: Studies in India's Popular Cinema*. New Delhi: Roli, 1991.

———. *Talking about Films*. New Delhi: Orient Longman, 1981.

Dass, Manishita. "The Crowd outside the Lettered City: Imagining the Mass Audience in 1920s India." *Cinema Journal* 48, no. 4 (Summer 2009): 77–98.

Del Rio, Elena. *Deleuze and the Cinemas of Performance: Powers of Affection*. Edinburgh: Edinburgh University Press, 2009.

Desai, Jigna. *Beyond Bollywood: The Cultural Politics of South Asian Diasporic Film*. New York: Routledge, 2004.

———. "Bollywood Abroad: South Asian Diasporic Cosmopolitanism and Indian Cinema." In *New Cosmopolitanisms: South Asians in the US*, edited by Gita Rajan and Shailja Sharma, 115–137. Stanford, Calif.: Stanford University Press, 2006.

———. "Planet Bollywood: Indian Cinema in Asian America." In *East Main Street: Asian American Popular Culture*, edited by Shilpa Daveé, LeiLani Nishime, and Tasha Oren, 55–71. New York: New York University Press, 2005.

Dharap, B. V. "Dadasaheb Phalke: Father of Indian Cinema." In *Seventy Years of Indian Cinema (1913–1983)*, edited by T. M. Ramachandran, 32–48. Bombay: CINEMA India-International, 1985.

———. "National Film Archive of India." In *Seventy Years of Indian Cinema (1913–1983)*, edited by T. M. Ramachandran, 528–536. Bombay: CINEMA India-International, 1985.

Dissanayake, Wimal, and Malti Sahai. *Raj Kapoor's Films: Harmony of Discourses*. New Delhi: Vikas, 1988.

Doane, Mary. "The Voice in the Cinema: The Articulation of Body and Space." In *Theory and Practice: Film and Sound*, edited by Elizabeth Weis and John Belton, 162–176. New York: Columbia University Press, 1985.

Doherty, Thomas. *Hollywood's Censor: Joseph I. Breen and the Production Code Administration*. New York: Columbia University Press, 2007.

Dubey, D. C. *Family Planning Communication Studies in India: A Review of Findings and Implications of Studies on Communications*. New Delhi: Central Family Planning Institute, 1969.

Dwyer, Rachel. *All You Want Is Money, All You Need Is Love: Sexuality and Romance in Modern India*. New York: Continuum, 2000.

———. *Yash Chopra*. London: British Film Institute, 2002.

Dwyer, Rachel, and Divia Patel. *Cinema India: The Visual Culture of Hindi Film*. New Brunswick, N.J.: Rutgers University Press, 2002.

Dwyer, Tessa, and Iona Uricaru. "Slashings and Subtitles: Romanian Media Piracy, Censorship, and Translation." *Velvet Light Trap* 63 (Spring 2009): 45-57.

Eberwein, Roger. *Sex Ed: Film, Video, and the Framework of Desire.* New Brunswick, N.J.: Rutgers University Press, 1999.

Eck, Diana L. *Darsan: Seeing the Divine Image in India.* 3d ed. New York: Columbia University Press, 1998.

Fanon, Frantz. *The Wretched of the Earth.* Translated by Constance Farrington. New York: Grove, 1963.

Foucault, Michel. *Aesthetics, Method, and Epistemology.* Vol. 2 of *The Essential Works of Foucault, 1945–1984.* Edited by James D. Faubion. New York: New Press, 1998.

———. "Afterword: Subject and Power." In *Michel Foucault: Beyond Structuralism and Hermeneutics,* edited by Hubert L. Dreyfus and Paul Rabinow, 208–226. Chicago: University of Chicago Press, 1983.

———. *Discipline and Punish: The Birth of the Prison.* Translated by Alan Sheridan. New York: Vintage, 1979.

———. *Ethics: Subjectivity and Truth.* Vol. 1 of *The Essential Works of Foucault, 1945–1984.* Edited by Paul Rabinow. New York: New Press, 1997.

———. *The Foucault Reader.* Edited by Paul Rabinow. New York: Pantheon, 1984.

———. *The History of Sexuality, Vol. 1: An Introduction.* Translated by Robert Hurley. New York: Vintage, 1980.

———. *The History of Sexuality, Vol. 2: The Use of Pleasure.* Translated by Robert Hurley. New York: Random House, 1985.

———. *The History of Sexuality, Vol. 3: The Care of the Self.* Translated by Robert Hurley. New York: Random House, 1986.

———. *Politics, Philosophy, Culture: Interviews and Other Writings, 1977–1984.* Edited by Lawrence Kritzman. Translated by Alan Sheridan. London: Routledge, 1990.

———. *Power.* Vol. 3 of *The Essential Works of Foucault, 1945–1984.* Edited by Colin Gordon. New York: New Press, 1999.

———. *Power/Knowledge: Selected Interviews and Other Writings, 1972–1977.* Edited by Colin Gordon. New York: Pantheon, 1980.

Freud, Sigmund. *Beyond the Pleasure Principle.* Translated by James Strachey. New York: Norton, 1961.

———. *Civilization and Its Discontents.* Translated by James Strachey. New York: Norton, 1961.

Gahlot, Deepa. "Out of Sync: What Went Wrong with Zeenat's Career." *Filmfare,* December 15, 1984.

Gandhi, Mahatma. *Cent per cent Swadeshi, or The Economics of Village Industries.* Ahmedabad, India: Navajivan, 1948.

Gandhy, Behroze, and Rosie Thomas. "Three Indian Film Stars." In *Stardom: Industry of Desire,* edited by Christine Gledhill, 107–131. New York: Routledge, 1991.

Gangoli, Geetanjali. *Indian Feminisms: Law, Patriarchies and Violence in India.* Hampshire, U.K.: Ashgate, 2007.

Gaur, Madan. *Other Side of the Coin.* Bombay: Trimurti Prakashan, 1973.

Ghosh, Shohini. "Censorship Myths and Imagined Harms." In *SARAI Reader: Crisis/Media*, edited by Shuddhabrata Sengupta et al., 447–454. New Delhi: SARAI, 2004.

———. "The Pleasures and Politics of Pornography." *Himal South Asian*, September 2009. http://www.himalmag.com/himaledition=2009-09-01.

———. "The Troubled Existence of Sex and Sexuality: Feminists Engage with Censorship." In *Image Journeys: Audio-Visual Media and Cultural Change in India*, edited by Christiane Brosius and Melissa Butcher, 233–260. New Delhi: Sage, 1999.

Ghosh, Shohini, and Ratna Kapur. "The Violence of Censoring." In *Gender and Censorship*, edited by Brinda Bose, 94–98. New Delhi: Women Unlimited, 2006.

Gianti, Tejaswini. "The Limits of Decency and the Decency of Limits: Censorship and the Bombay Film Industry." In *Censorship in South Asia: Cultural Regulation From Sedition to Seduction*, edited by Raminder Kaur and William Mazzarella, 87–121. Bloomington: Indiana University Press, 2009.

Gledhill, Christine. "Rethinking Genre." In *Reinventing Film Studies*, edited by Christine Gledhill and Linda Williams, 221–243. London: Arnold, 2000.

———, ed. *Stardom: Industry of Desire*. New York: Routledge, 1991.

Gopal, Sangita. "Sentimental Symptoms: The Films of Karan Johar and Bombay Cinema." In *Bollywood and Globalization: Indian Popular Cinema, Nation, and Diaspora*, edited by Rini Bhattacharya Mehta and Rajeshwari V. Pandharipande, 15–34. London: Anthem, 2010.

Gopal, Sangita, and Sujata Moorti. *Global Bollywood: Travels of Hindi Song and Dance*. Minneapolis: University of Minnesota Press, 2008.

Gopalan, Lalitha. *Bombay*. London: British Film Institute, 2005.

———. *Cinema of Interruptions: Action Genres in Contemporary Indian Cinema*. London: British Film Institute, 2002.

Gopinath, Gayatri. *Impossible Desires: Queer Diasporas and South Asian Public Cultures*. Durham, N.C.: Duke University Press, 2005.

Govil, Nitin. "Bollywood and the Frictions of Global Mobility." In *Media on the Move: Global Flow and Contra-flow*, edited by Daya Kishen Thussu, 84–98. London: Routledge, 2007.

Grant, Barry Keith, ed. *Film Genre Reader III*. Austin: University of Texas Press, 2003.

Grewal, Inderpal. *Home and Harem: Nation, Gender, Empire, and the Cultures of Travel*. Durham, N.C.: Duke University Press, 1996.

Gupta, Akhil. *Postcolonial Developments: Agriculture in the Making of Modern India*. Durham, N.C.: Duke University Press, 1998.

Das Gupta, Chidananda *Talking about Films*. New Delhi: Orient Longman, 1981.

Hamid, Mohsin. *Moth Smoke*. New York: Farrar, Strauss and Giroux, 2000.

Hasan, Zoya. *Forging Identities: Gender, Communities and the State*. Delhi: Kali for Women, 1994.

Hjort, Mette, and Scott Mackenzie, eds. *Cinema and Nation*. London: Routledge, 2000.

Hughes, Stephen. "Policing Silent Film Exhibition in Colonial South India." In *Making Meaning in Indian Cinema*, edited by Ravi S. Vasudevan, 39–64. New Delhi: Oxford University Press, 2000.

Jacobs, Lea. *The Wages of Sin: Censorship and the Fallen Woman, 1928–1942*. Berkeley: University of California Press, 1997.

Jaikumar, Priya. "An Act of Transition: Empire and the Making of a National British Film Industry, 1927." *Screen* 43, no. 2 (Summer 2002): 119–138.

———. *Cinema at the End of Empire: A Politics of Transition in Britain and India*. Durham, N.C.: Duke University Press, 2006.

———. "More Than Morality: The Indian Cinematograph Committee: Interviews." *Moving Image* 3, no. 1 (2003): 82–109.

Jain, Madhu. *The Kapoors: The First Family of Indian Cinema*. New Delhi: Viking, 2005.

Jaising, Indira, and Andrea Wolfe. "'The Ignoble Servility' of *Pati Parmeshwar* towards Equality of Women." In *Gender and Censorship*, edited by Brinda Bose, 127–137. New Delhi: Kali for Women, 2006.

Jayawardena, Kumari. *Feminism and Nationalism in the Third World*. London: Zed, 1986.

Jejeebhoy, Shireen, ed. *Looking Back Looking Forward: A Profile of Sexual and Reproductive Health in India*. New Delhi: Rawat, 2004.

John, Mary E. "Gender and Development in India, 1970–1990s: Some Reflections on the Constitutive Role of Contexts." In *Feminism in India*, edited by Maitreyee Chaudhuri, 246–258. New Delhi: Kali for Women/Women Unlimited, 2004.

———. "Globalisation, Sexuality and the Visual Field: Issues and Non-issues for Cultural Critique." In *A Question of Silence? The Sexual Economies of Modern India*, edited by Mary E. John and Janaki Nayar, 368–390. New Delhi: Kali for Women, 1998.

John, Mary E., and Janaki Nair. "A Question of Silence: An Introduction." In *A Question of Silence? The Sexual Economies of Modern India*, edited by Mary E. John and Janaki Nair, 1–51. New Delhi: Kali for Women, 1998.

John, Mary E., and Tejaswini Niranjana. "Mirror Politics: *Fire*, Hindutva and Indian Culture." *Economic and Political Weekly* 34, nos. 10-11 (Mar. 12, 1999): 581–585.

Joshi, Rama, and Joanna Liddle. *Daughters of Independence: Gender, Class and Caste in India*. London: Zed, 1986.

Kakar, Sudhir. *Intimate Relations: Exploring Indian Sexuality*. New Delhi: Oxford University Press, 1990.

Kaplan, Caren, Norma Alarcón, and Minoo Moallem, eds. *Between Woman and Nation: Nationalisms, Transnational Feminisms, and the State*. Durham, N.C.: Duke University Press, 1999.

Kapur, Ratna. "Cultural Politics of *Fire*." *Economic and Political Weekly* 34, no. 21 (May 28, 1999): 1297–1299.

———. "Too Hot to Handle." *Feminist Review* 64 (Spring 2000): 53–64.

———. "Who Draws the Line? Feminist Reflections on Speech and Censorship." *Economic and Political Weekly* 31, nos. 16–17 (Apr. 20, 1996): WS 15–WS 30.

Karlekar, Malavika. *Voices from Within: Early Personal Narratives of Bengali Women*. New Delhi: Oxford University Press, 1991.

Kaur, Raminder, and William Mazarella, eds. *Censorship in South Asia: Cultural Regulation from Sedition to Seduction*. Bloomington: Indiana University Press, 2009.

Kenna, Laura Cook. "Exemplary Consumer-Citizens and Protective State Stewards: How Reformers Shaped Censorship Outcomes Regarding *The Untouchables*." *Velvet Light Trap* 63 (Spring 2009): 34–44.

Khandpur, K. L. "Compulsory Screening of Documentaries in India." In *Seventy Years of Indian Cinema (1913–1983)*, edited by T. M. Ramachandran, 505–511. Bombay: CINEMA India-International, 1985.

Khubchandani, Lata. *Raj Kapoor: The Great Showman*. New Delhi: Rupa, 2003.

Kishwar, Madhu. "Gandhi on Women." *Economic and Political Weekly* 20, no. 40 (Oct. 5, 1985): 1691–1702.

———. "Gandhi on Women." *Economic and Political Weekly* 20, no. 41 (Oct. 12, 1985): 1753–1758.

"Kiss-Kiss, Smooch-Smooch, Bollywood Is No Longer Shy." *India Forums*, July 23, 2009. http://www.bollycurry.com/news/hot-n-happening/10172-kiss-kiss-smooch-smooch-bollywood-is-no-longer-shy.htm. Accessed August 12, 2010.

Koch, Gertrud. "The Body's Shadow Realm." In *Dirty Looks: Women, Pornography, Power*, edited by Pamela Church Gibson and Roma Gibson, 22–45. London: British Film Institute, 1993.

Krishnamurthy, J., ed. *Women in Colonial India*. New Delhi: Oxford University Press, 1989.

Kuhn, Annette. *Censorship, State and Sexuality 1909–1925*. New York: Routledge, 1988.

———. *The Power of Image: Essays on Representation and Sexuality*. London: Routledge and Kegan Paul, 1985.

Kumar, Amit. "The Lower Stall: The Sleaze-Sex Film Industry in India, an Introduction." *Spectator: The University of Southern California Journal of Film and Television* 26, no. 2 (Fall 2006): 27–41.

Kumar, Radha. *The History of Doing*. New Delhi: Kali for Women, 1993.

Kumar, Shanti. *Gandhi Meets Primetime: Globalization and Nationalism in Indian Television*. Urbana: University of Illinois Press, 2006.

Lahiri, Monojit. "The Commercial: The Dawn of a Golden Period?" In *Indian Cinema Superbazaar*, edited by Philippe Lenglet and Aruna Vasudev, 33–38. New Delhi: Vikas, 1983.

Lal, Vinay. "Travails of the Nation." *Third Text* 19, no. 2 (Mar. 2005): 177–187.

Lateef, Shahida. *Muslim Women in India: Political and Private Realities*. London: Zed, 1990.

Liang, Lawrence. "Watching Films Blindfolded." *Himal South Asian*, September 2009. http://www.himalmag.com/himaledition=2009-09-01.

Lutgendorf, Philip. "Hum Aapke Hain Koun." Iowa University. http://www.uiowa.edu/~incinema/humaapke.html.

———. "*Jai Santoshi Maa* Revisited: On Seeing a Hindu 'Mythological' Film." In *Representing Religion in World Cinema: Mythmaking, Culture Making, Filmmaking*, edited by S. Brent Plate, 19–42. New York: Palgrave/St. Martin's, 2003.

Majumdar, Neepa. "The Embodied Voice: Song Sequences and Stardom in Popular Hindi Cinema." In *Soundtrack Available: Essays on Film and Popular Music*, edited by Arthur Knight and Pamela Wojcik, 161–181. Durham, N.C.: Duke University Press, 2001.

———. *Wanted Cultured Ladies Only! Female Stardom and Cinema in India, 1930s-1950s*. Urbana: University of Illinois Press, 2009.

Majumdar, Rochona. "'Self-Sacrifice' versus 'Self-Interest': A Non-Historicist Reading of the History of Women's Rights in India." *Comparative Studies of South Asia, Africa and the Middle East* 33, nos. 1–2 (2002): 20–35.

Manderson, Lenore, and Margaret Jolly, eds. *Sites of Desire, Economies of Pleasure: Sexualities in Asia and the Pacific*. Chicago: University of Chicago Press, 1997.

Mankekar, Purnima. "Brides Who Travel: Gender, Transnationalism, and Nationalism in Hindi Film." *Positions* 7, no. 3 (1999): 731–762.

———. *Screening Culture, Viewing Politics*. Durham, N.C.: Duke University Press, 1999.

Manuel, Peter. *Cassette Culture: Popular Music and Technology in North India*. Chicago: University of Chicago Press, 1993.

Marsh, Julie, and Howard Brasted. "*Fire*, the BJP and Moral Society." In *Hindu Nationalism and Governance*, edited by John McGuire and Ian Copland, 283–302. New Delhi: Oxford University Press, 2007.

Mason, Edwina. "The *Water* Controversy and the Politics of Hindu Nationalism." In *Hindu Nationalism and Governance*, edited by John McGuire and Ian Copland, 303–315. New Delhi: Oxford University Press, 2007.

Mayer, Tamar, ed. *Gender Ironies of Nationalism: Sexing the Nation*. New York: Routledge, 2000.

Mazumdar, Sucheta. "Moving Away from a Secular Vision? Women, Nation, and the Cultural Construction of Hindu India." In *Identity Politics and Women: Cultural Reassertions and Feminisms in International Perspectives*, edited by Valentine Moghadam, 243–273. Boulder, Colo.: Westview, 1994.

———. "Women on the March: Right-Wing Mobilization in Contemporary India." *Feminist Review* 41, no. 1 (1995): 1–28.

Mazzarella, William. "Making Sense of the Cinema in Late Colonial India." In *Censorship in South Asia: Cultural Regulation from Sedition to Seduction*, edited by Raminder Kaur and William Mazzarella, 63–86. Bloomington: Indiana University Press, 2009.

———. "The Obscenity of Censorship: Rethinking a Middle-Class Technology." Department of Anthropology, University of Chicago. http://anthropology.uchicago.edu/pdfs/mazz_obscenity.pdf. Accessed August 12, 2010.

McClintock, Anne. *Imperial Leather*. New York: Routledge, 1995.

McClintock, Anne, Aamir Mufti, and Ella Shohat, eds. *Dangerous Liaisons: Gender, Nation, and Postcolonial Perspectives*. Minneapolis: University of Minnesota Press, 1997.

McGuire, John, and Ian Copland, eds. *Hindu Nationalism and Governance*. New Delhi: Oxford University Press, 2007.

Mehta, Monika. "Globalizing Bombay Cinema: Reproducing the Indian State and Family." *Cultural Dynamics* 17, no. 2 (2005): 135–154.

———. "Re-framing Censorship." *Velvet Light Trap* 63 (2009): 66–69.

Menon, Ritu, and Kamla Bhasin. "Recovery, Rupture, Resistance: Indian State and Abduction of Women during Partition." *Economic and Political Weekly* 28, no. 17 (Apr. 24, 1993): WS 2–WS 11.

Metz, Christian. "The Impersonal Enunciation, or the Site of Film." In *The Film Spectator: From Sign to Mind*, edited by Warren Buckland, 140–163. Amsterdam: Amsterdam University Press, 1995.

Mishra, Vijay. *Bollywood Cinema: Temples of Desire*. New York: Routledge, 2002.

———. "Towards a Theoretical Critique of Bombay Cinema." *Screen* 26, nos. 3–4 (1985): 133–146.

Mitchell, Timothy. "The Limits of the State: Beyond Statist Approaches and Their Critics." *American Political Science Review* 85, no. 1 (1991): 77–96.

———. "Society, Economy, and the State Effect." In *State/Culture: State Formation after the Cultural Turn*, edited by George Steinmetz, 76–97. Ithaca, N.Y.: Cornell University Press, 1999.

Mohanty, Chandra, Ann Russo, and Lourdes Torres, eds. *Third World Women and the Politics of Feminism*. Bloomington: Indiana University Press, 1991.

Mulvey, Laura. "Visual Pleasure and Narrative Cinema." In *Feminism and Film*, edited by E. Ann Kaplan, 34–47. London: Oxford University Press, 2000.

Naficy, Hamid. *An Accented Cinema: Exilic and Diasporic Filmmaking*. Princeton, N.J.: Princeton University Press, 2001.

Nanda, Ritu. *Raj Kapoor Speaks*. New Delhi: Viking, 2002.

Nanda, Shammi. "Censorship and Indian Cinema: The Case of *War and Peace*." *Bright Lights Film Journal* 38 (Nov. 2002). www.brightlightsfilm.com/38/india-censor.htm.

Nandy, Ashis. *The Intimate Enemy: Loss and Recovery of Self under Colonialism*. New Delhi: Oxford University Press, 1983.

Nandy, Ashis, and Vinay Lal, eds. *Fingerprinting Popular Culture: The Mythic and the Iconic in Indian Cinema*. New Delhi: Oxford University Press, 2006.

Narrain, Siddharth. "Exit, Anupam Kher." *Frontline* 21, no. 23 (Nov. 6–19, 2004). http://hinduonnet.com/fline/fl2123/stories/20041119008112600.htm. Accessed August 14, 2010.

Niranjana, Tejaswini. "Banning 'Bombayi': Nationalism, Communalism and Gender." *Economic and Political Weekly* 30, no. 22 (June 3, 1995): 1291–1292.

Oshima, Nagisa. *Cinema, Censorship and the State: The Writings of Nagisa Oshima, 1956–1978*. Translated by Annette Michelson. Cambridge, Mass.: MIT Press, 1992.

Pandey, Gyanendra. *The Construction of Communalism in Colonial North India*. New Delhi: Oxford University Press, 1990.

Pandey, Shruti, et al. *Coercion versus Empowerment: Perspectives from the People's Tribunal on Indian's Coercive Population Policies and Two-Child Norm.* New Delhi: Human Rights Law Network, 2006.

Pandian, M. S. S. *The Image Trap: M G Ramachandran in Film and Politics.* New Delhi: Sage, 1992.

Parker, Andrew, Mary Russo, Doris Sommer, and Patricia Yaeger, eds. *Nationalisms and Sexualities.* New York: Routledge, 1992.

Pendakur, Manjunath. "Censorship." In *Gender and Censorship*, edited by Brinda Bose, 19–30. New Delhi: Women Unlimited, 2006.

———. *Indian Popular Cinema: Industry, Ideology, and Consciousness.* Cresskill, N.J.: Hampton, 2003.

Pillai, Jitesh. "Shah Rukh Best Actor." *Filmfare* 43, no. 4 (Apr. 1996).

Prakash, Sanjeev. "Music, Dance and the Popular Film: Indian Fantasies, Indian Repressions." In *Indian Cinema Superbazaar*, edited by Philippe Lenglet and Aruna Vasudev, 114–118. New Delhi: Vikas, 1983.

Prasad, M. Madhava. "Cinema and the Desire for Modernity." *Journal of Arts and Ideas* 25–26 (1995): 71–86.

———. *Ideology of the Hindi Film: A Historical Construction.* New Delhi: Oxford University Press, 1998.

———. "The State of/in Cinema." In *Wages of Freedom: Fifty Years of the Indian Nation-State*, edited by Partha Chatterjee, 123–146. New Delhi: Oxford University Press, 1998.

Purhoit, Vinayak. *Arts of Transitional India 20th Century.* Vol. 2. Bombay: Popular Prakashan, 1988.

———. *Sociology of Indian Film.* Bombay: Indian Institute of Social Research, 1990.

Puri, Jyoti. *Woman, Body, Desire in Post-colonial India: Narratives of Gender and Sexuality.* New York: Routledge, 1999.

Radway, Janice. *Reading the Romance: Women, Patriarchy, and Popular Literature.* Chapel Hill: University of North Carolina Press, 1984.

Rai, Amit. *Untimely Bollywood: Globalization and India's New Media Assemblage.* Durham, N.C.: Duke University Press, 2009.

Rajadhyaskha, Ashish, and Paul Willemen. *Encyclopedia of Indian Cinema.* New Delhi: Oxford University Press, 1995.

Rajagopal, Arvind. *Politics after Television: Hindu Nationalism and the Reshaping of the Public in India.* Cambridge: Cambridge University Press, 2001.

Rajan, Rajeswari Sundar. *Real and Imagined Women: Gender, Culture and Postcolonialism.* London: Routledge, 1993.

Ramachandran, T. M., ed. *Seventy Years of Indian Cinema (1913–1983).* Bombay: CINEMA India-International, 1983.

Ray, R. M., ed. *Film Seminar Report.* New Delhi: Sangeet Natak Akademi, 1956.

Ray, Sangeeta. *En-gendering India: Woman and Nation in Colonial and Postcolonial Narratives.* Durham, N.C.: Duke University Press, 2000.

Razdan, C. K., ed. *Bare Breasts and Bare Bottoms.* Bombay: Jaico, 1975.

Reuben, Bunny. *Raj Kapoor: The Fabulous Showman.* New Delhi: Virgo, 1988.

———. "Satyam Shivam Sundaram." *Illustrated Weekly of India,* May 7, 1978.

Roy, Kum Kum. "Unravelling the *Kamasutra.*" In *A Question of Silence? The Sexual Economies of Modern India,* edited by Mary E. John and Janaki Nair, 52–76. New Delhi: Kali for Women, 1998.

Roy, Parama. *Indian Traffic: Identities in Question in Colonial and Postcolonial India.* Berkeley: University of California Press, 1998.

Rozario, Santi. *Purity and Communal Boundaries.* London: Zed, 1992.

Said, Edward. *Beginnings.* New York: Basic, 1975.

Sangari, Kumkum, and Sudesh Vaid, eds. *Recasting Women: Essays in Indian Colonial History.* New Delhi: Kali for Women, 1989.

Sanghvi, Vir. "Raj Kapoor's Biggest Gamble," *India Today,* November 1–15, 1977.

Sarkar, Bhaskar. *Mourning the Nation: Indian Cinema in the Wake of Partition.* Durham, N.C.: Duke University Press, 2009.

Sarkar, Kobita. *Indian Cinema Today.* New Delhi: Sterling, 1975.

———. *You Can't Please Everyone: Film Censorship, the Inside Story.* Bombay: India Book House, 1982.

Sarkar, Tanika. *Hindu Wife, Hindu Nation: Community, Religion, and Cultural Nationalism.* Bloomington: Indiana University Press, 2001.

———. "Politics and Women in Bengal—the Conditions and Meaning of Participation." In *Women in Colonial India,* edited by J. Krishnamurthy, 231–241. New Delhi: Oxford University Press, 1989.

Sassen, Saskia. *Globalization and Its Discontents.* New York: New Press, 1998.

Schaefer, Eric. *"Bold! Daring! Shocking! True!" A History of Exploitation Films, 1919–1959.* Durham, N.C.: Duke University Press, 1991.

Schwarz, Henry. "Aesthetic Imperialism: Literature and the Conquest of India." *Modern Language Quarterly* 61, no. 4 (Dec. 2000): 563–586.

Seshu, Geeta. "Pornography: Certification vs. Censorship." Boloji.com, August 11, 2002. http://www.boloji.com/wfs/wfs067.htm. Accessed August 14, 2010.

Sethi, Sunil, et al. "Who's Afraid of Film Censorship?" *India Today,* October 1–15, 1980, 61.

Shahani, Kumar. "Politics and Ideology: The Foundation of Bazaar Realism." In *Indian Cinema Superbazaar,* edited by Philippe Lenglet and Aruna Vasudev, 72–75. New Delhi: Vikas, 1983.

Sharma, Miriam. "Censoring India." *South Asia Research* 29, no. 1 (2009): 41–73.

Sharpe, Jenny. "Gender, Nation, and Globalization in *Monsoon Wedding* and *Dilwale Dulhania Le Jayenge.*" *Meridians: Feminism, Race, Transnationalism* 6, no. 1 (2005): 58–81.

Shohat, Ella, and Robert Stam. *Unthinking Eurocentrism: Multiculturalism and the Media.* New York: Routledge, 1994.

Silverman, Kaja. *The Acoustic Mirror: The Female Voice in Psychoanalysis and Cinema.* Bloomington: Indiana University Press, 1988.

Singh, Bikram. "The Commercial: Reality Disturbed." In *Indian Cinema*

Superbazaar, edited by Philippe Lenglet and Aruna Vasudev, 28–32. New Delhi: Vikas, 1983.

Spivak, Gayatri. *In Other Worlds: Essays in Cultural Politics*. New York: Methuen, 1987.

Srinivas, S. *Megastar Chiranjeevi and Telugu Cinema after N T Rama Rao*. New Delhi: Oxford University Press, 2009.

Srivastava, Sanjay. *Passionate Modernity: Sexuality, Class, and Consumption in India*. New Delhi: Routledge, 2007.

Steinmetz, George, ed. *State/Culture: State Formation after the Cultural Turn*. Ithaca, N.Y.: Cornell University Press, 1999.

Stewart, Ann. "Debating Gender Justice in India." *Social and Legal Studies* 4 (1995): 253–274.

Stoler, Ann. "Carnal Knowledge and Imperial Power: Matrimony, Race, and Morality in Colonial Asia." In *Gender at the Crossroads: Feminist Anthropology in the Postmodern Era*, edited by Micaela di Leonardo, 51–101. Berkeley: University of California Press, 1991.

———. "Educating Desire in Colonial Southeast Asia: Foucault, Freud, and Imperial Sexualities." In *Sites of Desire, Economies of Pleasure: Sexualities in Asia and the Pacific*, edited by Lenore Manderson and Margaret Jolly, 27–47. Chicago: University of Chicago Press, 1997.

———. *Race and the Education of Desire: Foucault's History of Sexuality and the Colonial Order of Things*. Durham, N.C.: Duke University Press, 1995.

Swart, Patricia. "Darson, Visuality and Indian Cinema." New School. http://www .newschool.edu/mediastudies/conference/visual_culture/patricia_swart.htm.

Tarlo, Emma. *Unsettling Memories: Narratives of the Emergency in Delhi*. Berkeley: University of California Press, 2003.

Tellis, Olga. "How Zeenat Won the Rat Race." *Sunday*, October 9, 1977.

Thapa, Devender Mohan. "The Evolution of Venerology in India." *Indian Journal of Dermatology, Venereology, Leprology*, 73, no. 3 (May–June 2006): 187–196.

Thapa, N. S. "The Documentary in India: Films Division at Work." In *Seventy Years of Indian Cinema (1913-1983)*, edited by T. M. Ramachandran, 512–519. Bombay: CINEMA: India-International, 1985.

Tharu, Susie, and Tejaswini Niranjana. "Problems for a Contemporary Theory of Gender." In *Writings in South Asian History and Society*, edited by Shahid Amin and Dipesh Chakrabarty, 232–260. New Delhi: Oxford University Press, 1996.

Thomas, Rosie. "Indian Cinema: Pleasures and Popularity." *Screen* 26, nos. 3–4 (1985): 116–131.

———. "Mythologies and Modern India." In *World Cinema since 1945*, edited by William Luhr, 301–329. New York: Ungar, 1987.

———. "Sanctity and Scandal: The Mythologization of Mother India." *Quarterly Review of Film and Video* 11, no. 3 (1989): 11–30.

Thorval, Yves. *The Cinemas of India*. New Delhi: Macmillan, 2000.

Uberoi, Patricia. "The Diaspora Comes Home: Disciplining Desire in *DDLJ*." *Contributions to Indian Sociology* 32, no. 2 (1998): 305–336.

Upadhya, Carol. "Set This House on Fire." *Economic and Political Weekly* 33, no. 50 (Dec. 12, 1998): 3176-3177.

Vasudev, Aruna, ed. *Frames of Mind: Reflections on Indian Cinema*. New Delhi: UBSPD, 1995.

———. *Liberty and Licence in the Indian Cinema*. New Delhi: Vikas, 1978.

———. "Women Beware Men." *Index on Censorship* 20, no. 3 (1991): 7-8.

Vasudev, Aruna, and Philippe Lenglet, eds. *Indian Cinema Superbazaar*. New Delhi: Vikas, 1983.

Vasudevan, Ravi. "Bombay and Its Public." *Journal of Arts and Ideas* 29 (1996): 45-65.

———. "The Melodramatic Mode and the Commercial Hindi Cinema: Notes on Film History, Narrative and Performance in the 1950s." *Screen* 30 (Summer 1989): 29-50.

———. "The Politics of Cultural Address in a 'Transitional' Cinema: A Case Study of Popular Indian Cinema." In *Reinventing Film Studies*, edited by Christine Gledhill and Linda Williams, 130-164. London: Arnold, 2000.

———. "Sexuality and the Film Apparatus: Continuity, Non-Continuity and Dis-Continuity in Bombay Cinema." In *A Question of Silence? The Sexual Economies of Modern India*, edited by Mary E. John and Janaki Nair, 192-215. New Delhi: Kali for Women, 1998.

———. "Shifting Codes, Dissolving Identities: The Hindi Social Film of the 1950s as Popular Culture." *Journal of Arts and Ideas* 20 (1993): 51-84.

———. "'You cannot live in society—and ignore it': Nationhood and Female Modernity in *Andaz*." In *Social Reform, Sexuality and the State*, edited by Patricia Uberoi, 83-108. New Delhi: Sage, 1996.

Vaughn, Stephen. *Freedom and Entertainment: Rating the Movies in an Age of New Media*. New York: Cambridge University Press, 2006.

Virdi, Jyotika. *The Cinematic ImagiNation*. New Brunswick, N.J.: Rutgers University Press, 2003.

Vitali, Valentina, and Paul Willemen, *Theorising National Cinema*. London: British Film Institute, 2006.

Weis, Elisabeth, and John Belton, eds. *Theory and Practice: Film Sound*. New York: Columbia University Press, 1985.

Wittern-Keller, Laura. *Freedom of the Screen: Legal Challenges to State Film Censorship, 1915-1981*. Lexington: University Press of Kentucky, 2008.

Yuval-Davis, Nira, and Davia Stasiulis, eds. *Unsettling Settler Societies: Articulations of Gender, Race, Ethnicity and Class*. London: Sage, 1995.

Case Law, Statutes, and Official Publications

Central Board of Film Certification. Government of India. *Annual Report 1996*. Mumbai: Central Board of Film Certification, n.d.

Enquiry Committee on Film Censorship. *Report of the Enquiry Committee on Film Censorship*. New Delhi: Government of India Press, 1969.

Film Enquiry Committee. *Report of the Film Enquiry Committee 1951.* New Delhi: Government of India Press, 1951.

Government of India. *The Cinematograph Act, 1952.* Delhi: Universal Law, 1997.

———. *The Cinematograph Act, 1952 (37 of 1952) and Censorship Guidelines.* New Delhi: Rakesh, 1992.

Indian Cinematograph Committee. *Report of the Indian Cinematograph Committee, 1927–1928 (as on 24-3-1992).* Madras: Government Press, 1928.

K. A. Abbas v. Union of India (1971) 2 SCR 446.

Ministry of Information and Broadcasting, Government of India. "Draft Cinematograph Bill, 2010." Acts and Rules [Films], Introduction (unnumbered first page). http://mib.nic.in/ShowContent.aspx?uid1=7&uid2=49&uid3=0&uid4=0&uid5=0&uid6=0&uid7=0.

———. *Film Censorship: What Everyone Should Know.* Delhi: Bengal Printing Press, 1992.

Mohite, Shri Subodh, M.P. "The Cinematograph (Amendment), 2005: A Bill to Further Amend the Cinematograph Act, 1952." As introduced in the Lok Sabha. http://mpa.nic.in/ar06-07/appendix.pdf. Accessed July 5, 2009.

Raj Kapoor and Others vs. State and Others, 1980 (1) SCR 1081.

Raj Kapoor v. Laxman, 1980 (2) SCR 512.

Ranjit D. Udeshi v. State of Maharashtra, AIR 1965 S.C. 881.

Ray, R. M., ed. *Film Seminar Report.* New Delhi: Sangeet Natak Akademi, 1955.

Section 292, Indian Penal Code (1860).

Subbarami Reddy, Dr. T., M.P. "The Cinematograph (Amendment), 2002: A Bill to Further Amend the Cinematograph Act, 1952." To be introduced in the Rajya Sabha. http://mpa.nic.in/ar03-04/append7.htm. Accessed July 5, 2009.

Working Group on National Film Policy. *Report of the Working Group on National Film Policy.* New Delhi: Government of India Press, 1980.

Archives

Film and Television Institute, Pune, India. Abbreviated FTI.

National Film Archive of India/NFAI, Pune, India. Abbreviated.

Central Board of Film Certification, Bombay/Mumbai office, Bombay/Mumbai. Abbreviated CBFCB.

Films

Dilwale dulhania le jayenge. DVD. Directed by Aditya Chopra, 1995. Mumbai: Yash Raj Films, 2002.

Gupt gyan. VCD. Directed by B. K. Adarsh, 1973. New Delhi: Bhola Plastic Industries, 2007.

Gupt gyan. VHS. Directed B. K. Adarsh, 1973. Sarathi Video (no other information provided).

Gupt gyan. VHS. Directed by B. K. Adarsh, 1973. New Delhi: Shanti Enterprises (no other information provided).

Khalnayak. DVD. Directed by Subhash Ghai, 1993. London: Eros Entertainment, 2003.

My Name Is Khan. DVD. Directed by Karan Johar, 2010. Bombay: Big Pictures, 2010.

Pati parmeshwar. VCD. Directed by Madan Joshi, 1989. Mumbai: Ultra Distributors, 2002.

Satyam shivam sundaram. DVD. Directed by Raj Kapoor, 1978. Mumbai: Yash Raj Films, 2004.

INDEX

Page numbers in italics refer to illustrations.

Munshi, Lilavati, 36
music, 90, 92–93, 111, 259n38; in films, 169–170, 268n25, 268–269n28. *See also* song-and-dance sequences
music industry, 159; and censorship, 169–170; growth of, 78. *See also* cassette tapes
music videos. *See* picturization
Muslims, 5, 138–139, 219; and the Emergency, 9
My Name Is Khan (2010), 24, 218–226; "arthouse cut," 225, 276n18; box office of, 222, 276n13; certification of, 221–222; deleted scenes, 221, 223–224, 276n10; distribution of, 225–226; and Hindu-Muslim relations, 219, 275n3; Hurricane Katrina depicted in, 220, 224; international director's cut, 224–225, 276nn16,17,18; and the media, 220; 9/11 depicted in, 219–220, 224; piracy, 225; plot, 219–220; and racial discrimination, 219, 220–221; ratings, international, 221; reviews of, 222; and Shiv Sena, 221; U.S. depicted in, 220; VCD and DVD releases, 222–224, 223, 226

Naaz, Farha, 139, 140
Nair, Mira: *Kama Sutra*, 56, 74–75; sexuality, representation of, 22, 242n59
Narayan, Jayaprakash, 8
Nargis, and relationship with Kapoor, 117, 258n3
Naseeb apna apna (Rao, 1986), 134; and women's servility, 139–140
"national cinema," 16, 241n40, 244n13
National Council of Women (Burma), 30–31
National Film Archive, 2, 48, 61, 73, 240n39
national identity: and censorship, 18, 21, 33; cinema and, 246n33; and diaspora,

191–192; and religion, 205; and women, 241n52. *See also* Hindustani identity
nationalism, 44–45, 138, 150–151, 155; and political parties, 265n60; and sexuality, 80–81; and women, 80
Nayyar, R. K., 133; and freedom of expression, 142–145; *Pati parmeshwar*, 133–134, 135–137, 142, 261n1; revising committee, appeal to, 137–142; and Sadhana Shivdasani, 261n2. See also *Pati parmeshwar*
Nehru, Jawaharlal, 35, 112, 253n14; and industrialization, 246n33
Nehru Memorial Library, 2, 240n39
Nehruvian State, 137, 146, 147
Network for the Promotion of Asian Cinema, 11
9/11, 219–220
nudity, 17, 43, 44; and Indian tradition, 46

Obama, Barack, and *My Name Is Khan*, depicted in, 220
obscenity, 51–52, 71, 128–130, 187, 248nn76-77

Pahili mangalagaur (Junnarkar), 248n69
Pakistan, 221, 275n3
Palekar, Amol, and *Daayara*, 249n90
Panicker, Prem, on Hindi film, 267n15
Parivar, Sangh, on Hindu nationalism, 265n60
parody, 165, 267–268n16
Partition, 273n20
Patil, S. K., 34
Pati parmeshwar (Nayyar, 1989), 3, 78, 132, 171, 172, 249n87; alternate reading of, 156–158; banning of, 134; and Bombay High Court, 149–151; Central Board of Film Certification, appeal by, 154–156; and certification, refusal of, 74, 135–137; and cuts, 14, 141–142,

264n30; as feminist film, 145; and Film
Certification Appellate Tribunal, 142–
145; modifications to, 151–153; plot,
131–133; production of, 133; reception
of, 158; revising committee, appeal
to, 137–142, 264n29; science and the
divine in, 145–149; and self-sacrificing
women, 13, 23–24, 201–203, 261n54;
social context of, 134–135; and spectacle, 163; and tradition, 144, 201–203
patriarchy, 190–194, 195–196, 197
PE certificate, 95, 97–99, 102, 257n48
Phalke, Dada, 60
picturization, 165, 185, 259n38. *See also*
song-and-dance sequences
piracy, 4, 54, 58, 59, 170, 225, 276n13; and
authenticity, 5
playback singing, 106, 110, 117, 120, 219;
Pakistani singers, 275n3
policing, 71–72
pornography, 32; and certification,
56–57; and profit, 57
Prasad, M. Madhava, 49, 83, 248n70
Pratap, S. C. (Justice), 149, 150, 151, 154,
157
publicity, 86, 106, 112–114, 120, 260n53
Purandare, B. N., 82, 98
purdah, 46–47

Qatl (Nayyar, 1986), 133
Q certificate, 53
Quota Act (1927), 29, 243n10

Radway, Janice, 183
Rai, Rajiv, 252n23
Rajasthan, 176–177, 179
Rajasthani. *See* tribal, female
*Raj Kapoor and Others vs. State and
Others*, 261nn59–60
Raj Kapoor v. Laxman, 261n61
Rajya Sabha, 35, 57, 249n95
Ramachandran, M. G., 247n63; in *Film-
fare*, 45–46

Ramayana, 138, 267n5
Rangachariar, T., 30–32, 244n13
Rangachariar committee. *See* Indian
Cinematograph Committee
Rangayan, Sridhar, and *Gulabi aaina*, 56
Rangoonwalla, Firoze, on sexuality,
representation of, 17
*Ranjit D. Udeshi vs. State of Maha-
rashtra*, 51–52, 71, 248n76
Rao, Dasari Narayana, 262n4
Rao, T. Rama, 134, 140; Hindi films, 134
rape, 55, 70; in Hindi film, 68, 255n31
Rashtriya Swayamsevak Sangh (RSS),
265n60
Ratnam, Mani, and *Bombay*, 218
Rawail, Rahul, 69. *See also Anjaam*
realism: and cinema, 41; vs. melodrama,
81, 88, 89–90
reception, 105–106, 159, 160n53; and cen-
sorship, 4; and spectatorship, 5, 16
Reddy, B. Nagi, 262n4
Reddy, T. Subarami, 57, 249n95
religion, 57, 88, 138, 152, 205, 273n20
Reuben, Bunny, 110, 112–113, 258–259n18
RK Studios, 108, 133
Roshan, Rakesh, 252n23

Sadma (Mahendra, 1983), 67
Saife, Nadeem, 72
Samanta, Shakti, 55, 85, 174, 254n20,
268n28
Samskara (1970), 11; certification of,
239–240n32
Sangh Parivar, 150
Sarkar, Kobita, and sexuality, representations of, 16–17, 19, 64
satellite television: and Indian culture, 2,
159, 213–214; regulation of, 54–55, 172
sati, 135, 142
Satyam shivam sundaram (Kapoor,
1978), 3, 14, 16, 78, *108*, *115*, 188, 216,
251n12, 253n14; certification of, 107–
112; court case against, 128–130, 171,

Lightning Source UK Ltd.
Milton Keynes UK
UKOW03f1235160414

230075UK00002B/161/P